COMBAT HISTORY OF
STURMPANZER-ABTEILUNG 217

TIMM HAASLER · SIMON VOSTERS

Published in 2020 by Panzerwrecks Limited

Design and maps by Simon Vosters
Artwork by Felipe Rodna
Printed by Finidr. s.r.o.

Website www.panzerwrecks.com

Panzerwrecks Limited
Great Priors
Church Street
Old Heathfield
Sussex TN21 9AJ
United Kingdom
lee@panzerwrecks.com

COMBAT HISTORY OF STURMPANZER-ABTEILUNG 217

TABLE OF CONTENTS

FOREWORD
AND ACKNOWLEDGEMENTS

Immediately after the beginning of the Second World War, the *Wehrmacht* began to develop a heavy weapon with high fragmentation effect and armored protection that could be used for direct fire against field fortifications and in urban combat. These efforts resulted in the Sturmpanzer I. A normal *schwere Infanteriegeschütz 33*, complete with wheels, was mounted on the turretless chassis of a Panzer I and protected on the front and sides by armor plates. A total of 38 Sturmpanzer I's were built, and distributed six vehicles each to *schweren Infanteriegeschützkompanien 701 - 706*. The vehicles were first used in the Western campaign of 1940, and proved the concept, but also revealed the limitations of the over-burdened Panzer I chassis. Nevertheless, the last Sturmpanzer I was decommissioned in Russia in 1943.

The Sturmpanzer II's design was based on a modified Panzer II chassis. Again, the *schwere Infanteriegeschütz 33* was used in a slightly modified form. Twelve vehicles were built and used in 1942 as part of *schweren Infanteriegeschützkompanien* 707 and 708 in North Africa. Once again, the effect of the weapon was impressive, unlike the Panzer II chassis. The vehicle was considered maintenance-intensive and technically unreliable. In 1942, the concept was developed further, and a total of 24 Sturm-Infanteriegeschütze 33 B were built on the chassis of Sturmgeschütze III. The main armament was a modified version of the *schwere Infanteriegeschütz 33*, designated 150mm s.IG 33 L/11. For the first time, there was complete armored protection for the gun and crew. The first 12 vehicles were sent to Stalingrad, where they were lost, and the remaining 12 tanks transferred to the 23. Panzer-Division.

It was only in 1943 that this development came to an end with the arrival of the Sturmpanzer IV. The concept with the newly developed 15cm StuH 43 L/12 was a convincing weapon, but the massive superstructure ultimately led to the same problems as the Sturmpanzer I and II.

A total of 299 vehicles (306 units according to some sources) were built in four different versions, but the top-heavy vehicle overtaxed the chassis and gearbox of the Panzer IV. The Sturmpanzers were distributed exclusively to Sturmpanzerabteilungen 216 - 219 between 1943 and 1945. Sturmpanzer-Abteilung 216, established in May 1943, was first employed at Kursk in 1943, then Ukraine and from 1944, Italy, where it ended the war. This book looks at the operational history of Sturmpanzer-Abteilung 217, which was created in May 1944 and fought only on the Western Front and was destroyed in the Ruhr in April 1945. By contrast, the other two Sturmpanzer-Abteilungen were used primarily on the Eastern front until the end of the war. Only 2. Kompanie of Sturmpanzer-Abteilung 218 z.b.V. was used in the West, and a separate chapter is devoted to it.

Research for this project began in 1998 but suffered from the problem that, for some periods, plenty of material was available, while for others, practically nothing could be found. The only common thread was the battalion's monthly reports to the General der Panzertruppen, but these too were incomplete. It must be assumed that the battalion's war diaries did not survive the war, and this is why the operational history had to be painstakingly reconstructed. It was only with the help of an extensive database that it was possible to find the operational locations, using additional sources to confirm this. Here, the countless American G-2 reports made a particularly valuable contribution. Nevertheless, after more than twenty years of intensive research, some of these operations are based on just one source, so the authors would be grateful for references to other sources. As with other joint projects, we have placed great emphasis on primary resources, leading to the well-known phenomenon that even primary sources can be extremely contradictory. In these cases, one inevitably comes to the point where one of the sources must be given greater credibility. Of course, this carries the risk of false statements and conclusions, so any errors are ours. A study of the battalion alone was impossible for the reasons outlined above, also against the background that we wanted to classify the respective assignments and subordination relationships in the historical context.

We hope that this book will be of interest to military history enthusiasts and model-makers, who, more than ever, want to tell a valid story with their models and to whom we hope to have provided enough photographic material.

This book would never have been written without the support of the many researchers, historians, veterans, collectors, archives and museums who shared their sources and photographs. We all owe them our gratitude, and we offer them our appreciation for their willingness to provide us with full and unlimited support.

For the full technical history of the Sturmpanzers, including accurate scale drawings, the authors and publisher recommend Panzer Tracts No. 8-1 by Thomas Jentz, Hilary Doyle and Lukas Friedli.

Sources and information were provided by: Martin Block, Fréderic Deprun, Roland Dusi, Wolfgang Grote, James Haley, Richard Hedrick, Oskar Klein, Markus Jaugitz, Oliver Lörscher, Doug Nash, Darren Neely, Danny S. Parker, Jeroen Appel, Tom Peters, Ralf Anton Schäfer, Bundesarchiv-Militärarchiv in Freiburg, the NARA in Washington and the Military Archive in Prague.

The following archives provided photographs: Archive of Modern Conflict, Bundesarchiv-Bildarchiv, ECPA, Library and Archives of Canada, NARA, Bildarchiv Preußischer Kulturbesitz, The Tank Museum in Bovington and the US Army.

The following people provided pictures from their private archives: Thomas Anderson, Lee Archer, William Auerbach †, Stefan De Meyer †, Hilary Doyle, Fréderic Deprun, Heiner Duske, Terry Keller, Oskar Klein, Markus Jaugitz, Roddy MacDougall †, Karlheinz Münch, Darren Neely, Alfred Schulte, Detlev Terlisten, James Haley, Chris Webber and Steve Zaloga.

A great deal of research was undertaken on the battlefields of Sturmpanzer-Abteilung 217. Here we were supported by: Martin Block, Fréderic Deprun, Wolfgang Grote, Alfred Schulte and Vincent Vandeberg.

Thanks to Mark Fowler for checking the manuscript.

To better understand the context of the photographs, we have added a QR code to a number of pages. Simply point your smartphone camera at the code to see the same scene today in Google Street View or Google Maps.

Last but not least, we thank Felipe Rodna for the extraordinary and stunning color profiles and, of course, our publisher, Lee Archer, who always believed in this project and supported and motivated us in every way.

Timm Haasler and Simon Vosters
December 2019

Field maintenance of a Sturmpanzer IV Ausf.I from Sturmpanzer-Abteilung 216 on the Eastern Front in 1943. The vehicle, tactical number '24', has its maintenance hatches opened, which suggests a damaged gearbox. Also, the tank is missing its right track. *Timm Haasler*

CHAPTER 01
ACTIVATION OF STURMPANZER-ABTEILUNG 217

Following the creation of Sturmpanzer-Abteilung 216 in April 1943, questions were asked in January 1944 as to whether to activate another Sturmpanzer-Abteilung.[1] On 6 February, the Organisationsabteilung im Generalstab des Heeres (Force Structure Directorate of the General Staff of the Army within the High Command of the Army) stated that the creation of such a unit was out of the question, as the production of the Sturmpanzer IV would be discontinued in March.[2] However, two months later, the same Organisationsabteilung approved the creation of Sturmpanzer-Abteilung 217 using Panzer-Kompanie 40 as the core, and the latter disbanded. The next day, orders were given to raise the unit with the following organization:

- *Stab (Headquarters): according to KStN 1107 dated 01.11.1943*
- *Stabskompanie (Headquarters Company): according to KStN 1156 dated 01.11.1943*
- *3 Sturmpanzer-Kompanie (Sturmpanzer Companies): according to KStN 1160 dated 01.11.1943*
- *Panzer-Werkstattkompanie (Tank Maintenance Company): according to KStN 1185 dated 01.06.1942*

The officer roster would be provided by the OKH/Personal Amt (Personnel Office of the High Command of the Army). Periodic status reports on the condition of the personnel and materiel had to be filed every 14 days, starting 1 May. These reports were to be forwarded to the Organisationsabteilung im Generalstab des Heeres and to the Generalinspekteur der Panzertruppen (Inspector General of the Armored Forces). Panzer-Ersatz-und-Ausbildungs-Abteilung 18 (Tank Replacement and Training Battalion 18) in Kamenz, south of Hoyerswerda, was assigned as the replacement pool.

1.1 Organization and Equipment

Stab (Headquarters)
The original issue of KstN or Kriegsstärkenachweisung (Wartime table of Organization and Equipment) 1107 dated 1 November 1943 allowed for an authorized strength of 8 officers, 4 NCOs and 12 privates, totalling 24 men. Headquarters were organized as follows:

- Gefechtsstab (Command Group):
  - 8 officers, 3 NCOs and 10 privates
  - 3x light and 3x medium passenger vehicles and 2x motorcycles 350cc
- Gepäcktross (Baggage Train):
  - 1 NCO, 2 privates
  - 1x 2-ton truck, open bed, off-road

Notwithstanding the original order, it was decided to raise the unit with just two Volkswagens instead of the planned six passenger vehicles.

Stabskompanie (Headquarters Company)
KstN 1156 dated 1 November 1943 provided the authorized personnel strength for the Headquarters Company of a Sturmpanzer-Abteilung: 5 officers, 1 civil servant, 36 NCOs and 154 privates, totaling 195 men plus 1 civilian. The company was organized as follows:

- Gruppe Führer (Commander's Group):
  - 2 officers, 1 NCO, 1 private
  - 1x medium passenger vehicle and 1x motorcycle 350cc

- Nachrichtenzug (Signals Platoon):
  - 1 officer, 14 NCOs, 9 privates
  - 1x 2-ton truck, open bed, off-road and 1x motorcycle 350cc
  - 3x Panzer III (5cm) as Panzerbefehlswagen
- Erkundungszug (Reconnaissance Platoon):
  - 1 officer, 4 NCOs, 21 privates
  - 7x light passenger vehicles and 6x motorcycles 350cc
- Pionierzug (Engineer Platoon):
  - 4 NCOs, 21 privates
  - 1x light passenger vehicle and 1x motorcycle 350cc
  - 2x 2-ton halftrack-trucks, open bed (Maultier)
  - 2x 4·5-ton trucks, open bed, off-road
- Kfz.Instandsetzungsgruppe (Motor Vehicle Repair and Maintenance Section):
  - 13 NCOs, 14 privates
  - 1x light passenger vehicle
  - 1x 2-ton truck, open bed, off-road or 1x Sd.Kfz.10
  - 2x 3-ton trucks, open bed, off-road
  - 1x 4·5-ton truck, open bed, off-road
- Gefechtstross (Combat Train):
  - 6 NCOs, 24 privates
  - 3x light passenger vehicles
  - 1x 2-ton truck, closed
  - 3x 3-ton trucks, open bed, off-road
  - 2x 4·5-ton trucks, open bed, off-road
  - 2x medium Krankenpanzerwagen (Sd.Kfz.251/8)
- Staffel für Verwaltung und Nachschub (Administration and Supply Train)
  - 1 officer, 1 civil servant, 7 NCOs, 54 privates
  - 2x light passenger vehicles and 2x motorcycles 350cc
  - 1x 2-ton truck, closed
  - 8x 3-ton trucks, open bed, off-road
  - 12x 4·5-ton trucks, open bed, off-road
- Abteilungs-Verpflegungstross (Battalion Ration Supply Train):
  - 1 NCO, 6 privates
  - 2x 3-ton trucks, open bed, off-road
- Gepäcktross (Baggage Train):
  - 1 NCO, 3 privates
  - 1x 3-ton truck, open bed, off-road

Sturmpanzer-Kompanie (Sturmpanzer Company)

KstN 1160 dated 1 November 1943 provided the authorized personnel strength for a Sturmpanzer Company: 3 officers, 55 NCOs and 68 privates, totaling 126 men.

With a complement of 14 Sturmpanzer IVs, 16 passenger vehicles, 8 halftrack-trucks and 3 motorcycles, its personnel was organized as follows:

- Gruppe Führer (Commander's Group):
  - 1x Sturmpanzer IV, Kompanieführerwagen with 1 officer, company commander and tank commander, 3 NCOs: tank driver, gunner, radio-operator (also loader)
  - 1x Sturmpanzer IV, Kompanietruppführerwagen with 1 NCO, company troop leader and tank commander, 2 NCOs: tank driver, gunner and 1 private: radio-operator (also loader)
  - 1x medium passenger vehicle (off-road) with 1 private: car driver
  - 3x light motorcycles 350cc with 3 privates: motorcyclists

- I. Zug (1st Platoon)
  - 1x Sturmpanzer IV, Zugführerwagen with 1 officer: platoon leader and tank commander and 3 NCOs: tank driver, gunner, radio-operator (also loader)
  - 3x Sturmpanzer IVs each tank: 3 NCOs: tank commander, driver and gunner, each tank: 1 private: radio-operator (also loader)
  - 2x 2-ton halftrack-trucks, open bed (Maultier) each Maultier 2 privates: truck driver, ammunition man

- II. Zug (2nd Platoon): as 1st Platoon
- III. Zug (3rd Platoon): as 1st Platoon, however:

  - 1x Sturmpanzer IV, Zugführerwagen with 1 NCO: platoon leader and tank commander and 3 NCOs: tank driver, gunner and radio-operator (also loader)

- Kfz. Instandsetzungsgruppe (Motor Vehicle Maintenance Troop)
  - 3 NCOs: armored maintenance men
  - 8 privates: armored maintenance men (2 also car drivers)
  - 2 privates: assistant armorer-artificers
  - 2 privates: armored communications maintenance men
  - 4 privates: car drivers
  - 1x light passenger vehicle, off-road
  - 1x 2-ton truck, open bed, off-road with equipment for Motor Vehicle Maintenance Troop
  - 1x 3-ton truck, open bed, off-road with equipment for Motor Vehicle Maintenance Troop
  - 1x 3-ton truck, open bed, off-road with spare parts
  - 2x leichte Zugkraftwagen 1-ton (Sd.Kfz.10) or 2-ton halftrack trucks (Maultier)

- Wechselbesatzung (Exchange crew):
  - 1 NCO: tank commander
  - 4 privates: gunner, loader, radio-operator, tank driver
  - 1 private: car driver
  - 1x 3-ton truck, open bed, off-road for transport of men and material

- Gefechtstross (Combat Train):
  - 7 NCOs, 17 privates
  - 1x light passenger vehicle
  - 2x light passenger vehicles, off-road (supply technician motor transport, medical NCO)
  - 1x 3-ton truck, open bed, off-road for large field kitchen
  - 3x 4·5-ton trucks, open bed, off-road, for fuel, fuel transport and ammunition

- Gepäcktross (Baggage Train):
  - 1 NCO, 3 privates
  - 1x 3-ton truck, open bed for baggage

Contrary to the original order, each company only received one Volkswagen. It is not clear from the KstN when the three Panzer IIIs were replaced by Sturmpanzer IVs. According to the August 1944 report, the battalion had an authorized strength of 45 Sturmpanzer IVs, but no Panzer IIIs.

Panzer-Werkstattkompanie (Tank Maintenance Company)

KstN 1185 dated 1 June 1942 planned an authorized personnel strength of 1 officer, 3 civil servants, 22 NCOs and 86 privates, totaling 109 men plus 3 civil servants. The company consisted of a commanders group, a workshop, a recovery troop, an armory and trains.

The activation order closed with the remark that deviations from the KStN would be handled separately. Regarding requests for additional vehicles, it was promised that organizational department III of the General staff of the Army would raise a separate demand, presumably in June/July 1944.[4]

1.2. Activation Period: April - June 1944

There is very little information available about the activation of the battalion. Apparently, there was no rush in equipping the unit. In April 1944, 195 men were assigned to the battalion, most probably arriving in May. The same month (no exact date was given), 19 men arrived for the battalion headquarters. On 12 May[5], the arrival of another 107 men was recorded. These men originated from

Panzer-Ersatz-und-Ausbildungs-Abteilung 11 and had been sent to the battalion in the form of a march unit. All were incorporated in the newly created Panzer-Werkstattkompanie. On 31 May, another 141 men arrived with the 1. Kompanie; 49 of which were former members of Panzer-Kompanie 40. There is no detailed information available for the other companies. Therefore it is not clear if the men from Panzer-Kompanie 40 all ended up in the 1. Kompanie, or whether they were dispersed across all three Sturmpanzer companies.[6]

On 16 May, the Organisationsabteilung im Generalstab des Heeres proposed to change the training grounds for the newly established Sturmpanzer-Abteilung 217. Instead of using the Oldebroek training facilities in the Netherlands, the unit should be raised at Grafenwöhr within the realms of the Befehlshaber des Ersatzheeres (Commander in Chief of the Replacement Army).[7] This proposal was approved and training continued at the Grafenwöhr training grounds.[8]

The command roster looked as follows:

Commander:	Major Eberhard Lemor
Adjutant:	Lt. Werner Pöttgen
CO Stabskompanie:	Olt. Eitel Maier
CO 1. Kompanie:	Olt. Hans Lucas
CO 2. Kompanie:	Lt. Gerhard J. Beduwé
CO 3. Kompanie	Olt. Hans-Jürgen Heigl
CO Werkstattkp.:	Lt. Hans Bruno Schulte[9]

The battalion commander, Major Lemor, reported that the formation and training of his unit didn't exactly run smoothly:

"In the first week of July, the battalion arrived from the Grafenwöhr training grounds on the Western front. It should be noted, that after the arrival of the first 18 Sturmpanzers (= 40% of the authorized strength), instruction and retraining of the crews (only 30% with combat experience) during the allotted time of approximately five weeks, specifically focused on the combat echelons. Due to the lack of Sturmpanzers, the late delivery of wheeled vehicles and equipment of all sorts, and the limited allocation of ammunition, training results are insufficient. An additional 14 days would have benefited the general training situation. Despite the awareness of their crucial task, tank, truck and car drivers, in relation to the constrained training conditions, could not do any driver training. The widely known technical difficulties with the Sturmpanzer and their effects on training conditions enforced certain restrictions. Intensive tactical training for commanders and others satisfied all requirements. The incomplete signals training program can be completed during combat, the same accounts for the radio-operators. Closed exercises, including a combat

school and battalion firing exercise, proved to be excellent".[10]

Major Lemor's reported shortages in the allocation of material will now be examined in detail.

On 27 April, the Organisationsabteilung im Generalstab des Heeres ordered the direct allocation of wheeled vehicles for the battalion. For this purpose, five Volkswagens and 10 trucks from I./ Panzer-Regiment 25 were made available. The allocation of these vehicles had to be arranged with the activation staff, and missing vehicles were to be reported immediately.[11]

The described delays in the allocation of the Sturmpanzer IVs, can be traced back indirectly in the official records:

- On 24 May, the battalion's first batch of 19 Sturmpanzer IVs left Sankt-Pölten on train number 7180412.[12] It is of interest that Major Lemor only mentioned 18 Sturmpanzer in his report.
- On 21 June another two Sturmpanzer IVs were allocated. They left Sankt-Pölten on 25 June.[13]
- On 22 June, seven additional Sturmpanzer IVs were earmarked for the battalion. They were only dispatched from Sankt-Pölten on 10 July.[14]

Officially, only 28 Sturmpanzer IVs were allocated to the battalion. This is contrary to a report from the Generalinspekteur der Panzertruppen dated 6 August, and the reports and data from Sturmpanzer-Abteilung 217 from 19 August. The Generalinspekteur der Panzertruppen mentioned in his report on 'Replenishment of armored vehicles for Ob.West' that Sturmpanzer-Abteilung 217, with 45 Sturmpanzer IVs, had been dispatched to Ob.West.[15] The battalion's own report of 19 August revealed that the unit had 31 Sturmpanzer IVs on hand (out of an authorized strength of 45). This figure probably only included those combat-ready and vehicles in short-term repair. In the same report, Major Lemor stated that his battalion arrived at the front with its full authorized strength of vehicles. Considering that the battalion had already suffered five total losses, it becomes clear that the files of the Generalinspekteur der Panzertruppen failed to record the allocation of at least 8 Sturmpanzer IVs. In the allocation reports of the Generalinspekteur der Panzertruppen for June 1944, there are two entries of interest: the allocation of the aforementioned 9 Sturmpanzer IVs for Sturmpanzer-Abteilung 217 and another 14 Sturmpanzer IVs as replacements for Ob.Südwest. This indicates that 23 Sturmpanzer IVs had been assigned. In the remarks field, there is a noteworthy entry, stating that *"36 Sturmpanzer IVs are awaiting despatch in Sankt-Pölten".*[16] Discounting the 23 officially allocated Sturmpanzer IVs, one wonders where the remaining 13 Sturmpanzer IVs ended up. It cannot be ruled out that these were actually assigned to Sturmpanzer-Abteilung 217. The

battalion had been earmarked for the Normandy fighting and urgently needed 17 Sturmpanzer IVs to reach its authorized strength. That the 36 Sturmpanzer IVs in Sankt-Pölten were readily available is reflected in the allocation of 14 vehicles to Ob Süd.West, although not directly to Sturmpanzer-Abteilung 216 but merely as a reserve. Interestingly, the files of the Generalinspekteur der Panzertruppen refer twice to the Sturmpanzers at Sankt-Pölten. It should be noted that 40 out the original 60 Sturmpanzer IVs allocated to Sturmpanzer-Abteilung 216 in early 1943, were returned to Sankt-Pölten for major refurbishment. The Sturmpanzer IVs in Sankt-Pölten therefore were not newly built vehicles, but reconditioned ones. This indicates that Sturmpanzer-Abteilung 217 was brought up to full strength prior to and during the Normandy campaign with reconditioned Sturmpanzer IVs originating from Sankt-Pölten. It remains unclear when the Sturmpanzer IVs, allocated in June 1944, arrived with Sturmpanzer-Abteilung 217. Nonetheless, there are signs that approximately 50% of the vehicles arrived during the transfer to the Western front. This would help to explain why the companies arrived at the Normandy front over two weeks.

On 25 July, the two missing *Krankenpanzerwagen* (Sd.Kfz.251/8) were assigned to the battalion. It is unclear when these vehicles arrived with the unit.[17] However, they are not mentioned in the battalion's authorized and actual strength report of 19 August.[18]

1.3 Establishing Combat Readiness

On 1 June 1944, the Organisationsabteilung im Generalstab des Heeres, still assumed that Sturmpanzer-Abteilung 217 would be ready for combat between 15 and 30 June.[19] Ten days later, they were still confident that the battalion would be ready between 20 and 24 June.[20] On 18 June, probably under pressure as a result of the Allied invasion, it was reported that the unit had to be ready for combat by 20 June. The deadline, however, was questioned.[21] On 20 June, it was decided to gather the battalion within the area of Ob.West[22] between 25 and 30 June, specifically in the area of Condé - Le Beny Bocage - Vire, close to the front of AOK 7.[23] In the briefing notes for the Führer by the General der Panzertruppen dated 26 June, it is however reported that Sturmpanzer-Abteilung 217 had been combat ready since 22 June.[24] It is not clear exactly when the battalion departed for the Normandy front as the unit was still in Grafenwöhr on 28 June.[25] By mid-July there were still several personnel transfers taking place within the battalion. On 18 and 26 June, additional personnel from Panzer-Ersatz-und-Ausbildungs-Abteilung 18 were transferred to Sturmpanzer-Abteilung 217, while on 15 May, 21 and 30 June, personnel were sent back to Panzer-Ersatz-und-Ausbildungs-Abteilung 18.[26]

When Sturmpanzer-Abteilung 216 was activated in 1943, it spent almost two months training in Amiens, France before being transferred to the Eastern Front for the Kursk offensive. A Panzer III of Panzer-Regiment 26 can be seen here, together with four Sturmpanzer IVs following in formation. *Timm Haasler*

A Sturmpanzer IV of Sturmpanzer-Abteilung 216 during an exercise with three Marder Is (7.5cm Pak auf GW Lorraine) from an unidentified tank destroyer unit in France, May 1943. *Timm Haasler*

A Sturmpanzer IV Ausf.I, during an exercise with infantry near Amiens in May 1943. A smoke grenade has been set off in the background, probably to conceal the Sturmpanzer in the open field. *Timm Haasler*

There is no information available as to whether Sturmpanzer-Abteilung 217 trained with other units during activation at Grafenwöhr before it moved to Normandy. In this image, a Sturmpanzer IV of Sturmpanzer-Abteilung 216 is accompanied by a Panzerbeobachtungswagen III of Panzer-Artillerie-Regiment 93, 26. Panzer-Division, in May 1943. *Timm Haasler*

At least three Sturmpanzer IVs are visible in another image from May 1943, taken during an exercise in the Amiens area. *Timm Haasler*

The Sturmpanzer IV from page 14 has now moved from the dirt track, on the right, and is climbing the embankment into the field. In the background, the infantry also advanced the protection of the embankment. The Sturmpanzer is painted in *Dunkelgelb* with just a white painted *Balkenkreuz* on the superstructure side. **Timm Haasler**

We have not found any photographs of Sturmpanzer-Abteilung 217 during their transfer to the Normandy front. The picture shows two Sturmpanzer IV Ausf.Is of Sturmpanzer-Abteilung 216 during their transfer from the Eastern Front to the Reich at the end of 1943. *Timm Haasler*

CHAPTER 02
STURMPANZER-ABTEILUNG 217 IN NORMANDY

According to Major Lemor's report, the transfer to Normandy took place in the first week of July 1944.[1/2] A message from Panzergruppe West, dated 7 July, seems to confirm this:

"After arrival, Stu.Pz.Abt.217 will bivouac in the wooded area to the West of Chicheboville (10 km southeast of Caen, sic.) and remain available at the disposal of Panzergruppe West."[3]

According to the transport records of Armee-Ober-Kommando 7 (AOK 7), three trains carrying the battalion arrived on the morning of 8 July at Houdan.[4] Houdan is located to the East of Dreux, approximately 150 kilometers southeast of Caen as the crow flies.

However, an organization chart of Panzergruppe West dated 17 July still showed the battalion in transit.[5] The following day, another report mentioned that the battalion had not yet arrived in Normandy.[6] In August, Major Lemor claimed that his battalion used the road network to advance the final 170 kilometers to the front and that many technical breakdowns occurred among the Sturmpanzers.[7]

There is no doubt that 2./ Sturmpanzer-Abteilung 217 arrived in Normandy at the end of July, i.e. as the first company of the battalion. The company was attached to the I.SS-Pz.Korps south of Caen and remained there until mid-August. During these engagements, the unit was attached to various divisions. Next to arrive was 1./ Sturmpanzer-Abteilung 217 just one day later and also attached to the I.SS-Pz. Korps south of Caen. At the end of the Allied 'Operation Totalize', the company was transferred to the LXXIV A.K. in the sector north of Condé-sur-Noireau. The 3./ Sturmpanzer-Abteilung 217 arrived in Normandy at the end of July and was attached to the II.SS-Pz.Korps or LXXIV A.K. depending on the developing military

situation. In mid-August, Sturmpanzer-Abteilung 217 disappeared from the radar.

Until now, no detailed combat experience reports have been found for the battalion. Major Lemor's report, however, gives an insight:

"The 170 km road march to the front compensated in this respect (driver's training, sic.) a lot; the technical breakdowns were considerable and unavoidable. The days in combat improved the general situation. They compensated for the lack of radio traffic training, the same was valid for the training of the radio-operators. The limited amount of ammunition that had been made available during training, resulted in a higher but necessary initial ammunition consumption during our first engagements. Gunnery training has improved through combat. Repair and maintenance groups completed their training on the Sturmpanzer IV owing to the many breakdowns during the march and following engagements. Coordination between the supply sections in the staff and combat companies improved each day. With regard to the well known technical vulnerability of the overloaded Panzer IV chassis, the allocation and availability of spare parts should be considered insufficient."[8]

2.1. Engagements of the 2. Kompanie in the Combat Zone of I.SS-Panzer-Korps

On 21 July, Panzergruppe West and LXXXVI A.K. both announced the arrival of a company of Sturmpanzer-Abteilung 217 in the area of 21.Pz.Div. While the LXXXVI A.K. immediately reported the attachment to the 21.Pz.Div., Panzergruppe West only announced two days later that 2./ Sturmpanzer-Abteilung 217 had been subordinated to 21.Panzer-Division southeast of Caen.[9] Up to 20 July, the 21.Pz.Div. had been fighting off the Allied 'Operation Goodwood' in a series of heavy defensive battles. The Sturmpanzer-Kompanie thus arrived in the Émiéville - Saint-Pair - Troarn area after the fighting had died down. No major engagements were recorded in the following days.[10] A situation report of the 2. Kompanie from 24 July listed 11 serviceable Sturmpanzer IVs and 2 Sturmpanzer IVs in short-term maintenance.[11] This indicates that the company was only short of one Sturmpanzer IV from its authorized strength of 14 vehicles. The missing Sturmpanzer IV probably broke down during the road march and so should be considered as being in long-term maintenance. On 27 July, the 21.Pz.Div. received orders to disengage and its positions taken over by elements of the 272.Inf.Div. over the next two days.[12] It is not clear why 14 men from 2./ Sturmpanzer-Abteilung 217 were transferred back to Panzer-Ersatz- und Ausbildungs-Abteilung 18 in Kamenz on 27 July.[13] On 29 July, the 272.Inf.Div. was attached to the I.SS-Pz.Korps. As a result, 2./ Sturmpanzer-Abteilung 217 was assigned to the 1.SS-Pz.Div. south of Caen. During the transfer to Tilly-la-Campagne, several Sturmpanzer IVs broke down. Only nine were serviceable and ready for action when the company reached the new deployment area. The 2nd Company reported two more vehicles in short-term repair.[14] Transfer of the company to the new area was confirmed by a report announcing the death of Oberschütze Horst Stötzner, killed in action at Saint-Aignan the same day.[15] The company strength report the following day showed no changes. On 31 July, the company announced 10 operational Sturmpanzer IVs, however, no vehicles were reported as being in short-term maintenance.[16]

At the beginning of August, the company was still attached to the 1.SS-Pz.Div. The number of combat-ready Sturmpanzer IVs increased from ten on 1 August to twelve on 3 and 4 August, due to the excellent work of the maintenance crews.[17] During this time, the 1.SS-Pz.Div. was engaged on both sides of the important Caen-Falaise highway in the area of May-sur-Orne and Tilly-la-Campagne. The Leibstandarte fought off attacks from Canadian forces who tried to advance along the N158 towards Falaise. On the night of 4/5 August, the 1.SS-Pz.Div. was relieved by elements of the 89.Inf.Div., as the unit had received a new assignment to stop the American breakthrough towards Avranches. Relief of the Leibstandarte's positions was essentially concluded during the night of 6 August and the 2./ Sturmpanzer-Abteilung 217 remained behind in this sector.[18] This is confirmed by two reports of the 89.Inf.Div. to I.SS-Pz.Korps on 6 and 7 August mentioning the presence of 13 operational Sturmpanzer IVs in its inventory.[19]

The **8 August** brought the start of 'Operation Totalize', with the aim of breaking through the German lines south of Caen, advancing south along the N158 highway into the direction of Falaise in order to occupy the high ground north and northwest of Potigny. The attack hit the frontline of the 89.Inf.Div. at full force. Despite putting up a fierce resistance, British and Canadian forces breached the lines around noon. I.SS-Pz.Korps tried to halt the advancing Canadians along the N158 near Cintheaux - Gaumesnil, by throwing in the corps' armored reserve.

This tactical reserve was formed from elements of II./SS-Pz.Rgt.12 and s.SS-Pz. Abt.101, whose Panzer IVs and Tiger Is advanced north on the east side of the N158. They soon clashed with Canadian armor advancing south. In a firefight northeast of Gaumesnil, the Germans lost a Panzer IV and four Tiger Is. Among the German casualties was Hstuf. Michael Wittmann, the most famous tank ace in the Waffen-SS. Other German sources mentioned the loss of yet another Panzer IV and Tiger I northwest of Gaumesnil.[20] At the same time, 2./ Sturmpanzer-Abteilung 217, supported by a number of anti-aircraft guns, were holding positions to the west of the N158 near Cintheaux. An investigation of the German tank losses on 8 August revealed the loss of one Sturmpanzer IV west of Gaumesnil, two others west of Cintheaux and a fourth Sturmpanzer IV southeast of Cintheaux.[21] The 2nd Company reported one seriously wounded officer, two enlisted men killed and one enlisted man missing in action in the village of Quilly.[22] One NCO and three privates are reported missing in action in Cintheaux.[23] According to information provided by the German War Graves Commission, the missing NCO lost his life in the village on 9 August. One of the three missing enlisted men was Schütze Rudolf Strache, who was captured by the Canadians. When interrogated he voluntarily provided some interesting information on the order of battle and strength of his unit. He claimed that Major Lemor was his battalion commander, Oberleutnant Lucas the commander of the 1st Company, and Oberleutnant von Manteuffel the commander of the 2nd Company. He also mentioned that von Manteuffel was hospitalized at present due to an illness.[24] He confirmed that the battalion had been formed in Grafenwöhr in May 1944. Regarding the order of battle, he claimed that the battalion's staff was equipped with two Sturmpanzer IVs, while the other three companies were equipped with 14 Sturmpanzer IVs each. The order of battle per company was a commander's group with 2 Sturmpanzer IVs and three platoons with 4 Sturmpanzer IVs each. The personnel strength per company was 2 officers, 80 NCOs and privates. Besides the 14 Sturmpanzer IVs, the 2nd Company had 3 trucks, 1 Schwimmwagen, 1 Volkswagen and 2 motorcycles.[25] On 9 August, the I.SS-Pz.Korps reported that only one Sturmpanzer IV was combat ready in the 89. Inf.Div. area.[26] Although the Allies continued 'Operation Totalize' until 11 August, they failed to achieve an operational breakthrough of the German lines. The clash at Gaumesnil and Cintheaux in the evening of 8 August had taken the steam out of the Allied offensive right from the start.

On **12 August**, orders were issued by I. SS-Pz.Korps to place the 12.SS-Pz.Div. in reserve and assemble the unit northeast of Falaise. This force was further strengthened by attaching a Sturmpanzer-Kompanie, the remnants of s.SS-Pz. Abt.101, s.SS-Pz.Abt.102 (minus one company), a remote controlled tank company and two self-propelled rocket launcher companies.[27/28] This decision basically merged all available armor under command of the 12.SS-Pz.Div. The attached Sturmpanzer-Kompanie must have been the 2./ Sturmpanzer-Abteilung 217 (see chapter 2.2). No further information has been found on the whereabouts of the

2nd Company in the Normandy fighting after this date.

2.2. Engagements of the 1st Company in the Combat Zone of I.SS-Panzer-Korps and LXXIV Armee-Korps

The 1./ Sturmpanzer-Abteilung 217 was attached to I./SS-Pz.Rgt.12 (by this time part of *Kampfgruppe Wünsche*) on 22 July and received orders to transfer to the Vimont area. The company was committed the very same day and fired 250-270 rounds at enemy positions in Frénouville northwest of Vimont.[29] On 30 July, Stubaf. Prinz, commanding officer of II./SS-Pz.Rgt.12, took over the positions of *Kampfgruppe Wünsche* by exchanging I./SS-Pz.Rgt.12 with II./SS-Pz.Rgt.12. The newly formed *Kampfgruppe Prinz* was formed around the following units:

• Staff II./SS-Panzer-Regiment 12
• II./SS-Panzer-Regiment 12
• III./SS-Panzer-Grenadier-Regiment 26
• 1./ Sturmpanzer-Abteilung 217
• Security Company

While the staff of II./SS-Pz.Rgt.12 occupied the *Kampfgruppe Wünsche* command post, the change in command had no effect on 1./ Sturmpanzer-Abteilung 217 and III.(gp.)/ SS-Pz.Gren.Rgt.26, who remained in their positions.[30] During the next two days, *Kampfgruppe Prinz* reorganized some of its forces but these changes had no effect on the 1st Company in the Vimont - Moult area.[31] The first elements of 272.Inf.Div. arrived to relieve 12.SS-Pz.Div. starting 2 August.[32] On the night of 2/3 August, enemy artillery fire hit the bivouac of 1./ Sturmpanzer-Abteilung 217, seriously wounding a soldier of the 1st Company, who later died from his wounds at the clearing station near Vieux-Fumé.[33] The following night, 3/4 August, the 272. Inf.Div. (LXXXVI. Armee-Korps) took control of the combat zone of *Kampfgruppe Meyer* of 12.SS-Pz.Div., which became reserve of the I.SS-Pz.Korps. II./SS-Pz.Rgt.12, with attached 1./ Sturmpanzer-Abteilung 217, transferred to a new assembly area near Condé-sur-Ifs (village excluded) - Maizières (included) - Ernes (included).[34] Both units remained in there until 6 August, carrying out technical maintenance on the vehicles and weapons as well as conducting a medical muster.[35]

On the night of 6/7 August, the British army launched an offensive near the River Orne between Saint-Martin-de-Fontenay and 2 kilometers north of Thury-Harcourt. The 271.Inf.Div., who were occupying this sector, could not stop the British from establishing two bridgeheads over the Orne near the village of Grimbosq. In the early hours, Füs.Btl.271 launched an unsuccessful counterattack, which was repelled with heavy losses.[36]

In anticipation of these events, I.SS-Pz.Korps issued orders for II./SS-Pz.Rgt.12 with

attached 1./ Sturmpanzer-Abteilung 217, to relocate to a new assembly area east of Thury-Harcourt. The armor reached the new area by morning without any major problems. The command post of the II./SS-Pz.Rgt.12 was set up east of Acqueville in the village of Puant, while 1./ Sturmpanzer-Abteilung 217 established its company command post at Fontaine-Halbout.[37] At 01:45 on 7 August, the I.SS-Pz. Korps alerted the Panther battalion of the Hitlerjugend division, I./SS-Pz.Rgt.12, to move to a new assembly area 8 kilometers south of Grimbosq. The battalion arrived by 04:30. Half an hour later, the 3rd Company with a strength of 10 Panthers under command of Ustuf. Alban[38], continued its advance. The company received orders to report at the battalion command post of an infantry unit (most likely an infantry unit of the 271.Inf.Div.) at Château les Moutiers. In close cooperation with the infantry, Alban's Panthers had to destroy the enemy bridgehead near Grimbosq, situated on the east bank of the Orne. Elements of III.(gp.)/ SS-Pz.Gren. Rgt.26 were attached to SS-Pz.Rgt.12 and received orders at 10:30 to redeploy to Les Moutiers, secure the area and prepare for an imminent counterattack.[39] During the course of the day, elements of the 12.SS-Pz.Div. advanced closer to Grimbosq. The platoon of Oscha. Mende with its three Panthers and the Panther of Ustuf. Alban were engaged north of Grimbosq, while the other two platoons of 3./SS-Pz.Rgt.12, commanded by Ustuf. Bogensperger and Mathis fought south of the village. Only one enemy tank was engaged, but despite scoring a direct hit, the tank managed to pull back.[40] The heavy fighting for Grimbosq continued until 9 August. The 12.SS-Pz.Div. suffered 24 soldiers killed, 91 wounded and 7 missing in action by 8 August. SS-Pz.Rgt.12 lost a total of nine Panthers,[41] at least four from the 3rd Company, which also reported three damaged tanks due to combat and mechanical failure. All of the company's platoon leaders were killed during these engagements.[42]

Although never mentioned, 1./ Sturmpanzer-Abteilung 217 must have been engaged in the Grimbosq area since 7 August as part of I./SS-Pz.Rgt.12. Even II./SS-Pz.Rgt.12, which was engaged in the area of Cintheaux on 8 August during the Allied Operation 'Totalize' (see chapter 2.1), did not report the previously attached Sturmpanzer-Kompanie any more. There are several indications in favor of this assumption. First, there are a couple of reported personnel losses for the 1st Company on 7 August in the Grimbosq area. Oberleutnant Hans Lucas, the company commander, and four enlisted men[43] of his company were reported missing in action that day[44], while platoon leader Leutnant Felix Haslinger was seriously wounded near the village the same day.[45] Another soldier from the company died from his wounds, obviously suffered in the days before, at the clearing station of the 277.Inf.Div. in Cui on 9 August.[46] A report of the 1st Company dated 7 August confirmed that Leutnant Björn-Dieter Olowson took command of the company after Oberleutnant Lucas had vanished.[47] Although the 12.SS-Pz. Div. no longer mentioned the presence of 1./ Sturmpanzer-Abteilung 217 after 7 August, the I.SS-Pz.Korps reported ten combat ready Sturmpanzer IVs attached to

This Sturmpanzer IV Ausf.III, was destroyed near Ondefontaine in early August 1944. Like all known tanks of the Stu.Pz.Abt.217 in Normandy, it is missing the *Balkenkreuz* on the superstructure sides. Instead, seven spare track links have been bracketed to the superstructure, a typical Stu.Pz.Abt.217 feature only seen in Normandy.
The Tank Museum

RODNA

The tank possibly received a direct artillery hit which blew up the engine compartment. The image clearly shows the rail attached to the superstructure to hold the spare tracks links. Looking through the open rear hatch it becomes clear, that at least a part of the roof was blown away by an internal explosion. *The Tank Museum*

The crew of this Sturmpanzer IV Ausf. IV, abandoned their vehicle between Cintheaux and Bretteville. It is likely that this was the first late version of the Sturmpanzer IV captured by the Allies as it was photographed a number of times.
Library and Archives of Canada

This image shows another difference between the Ausf.III and IV in Sturmpanzer-Abteilung 217 - a second, shorter, bracket for spare track added to the forward section of the superstructure side. Although the mount for the *Schürzen* is still in place, all the plates have been lost. As these plates were simply hung on the mount they were probably lost when the tank moved through close-country. *Library and Archives of Canada*

Zimmerit had been applied to almost every part of the tank. From September 1944, *Zimmerit* was no longer applied during production. The tank has eight steel roadwheels, an identifying feature of Sturmpanzers built by Deutsche Eisenwerke in Duisburg between May and August 1944. Starting in September, only the first four roadwheels were steel, the other four were substituted for rubber-tyred examples. The steel wheels were introduced to reduce wear while moving and firing.

Library and Archives of Canada

This view through the rear hatch offers some details of the fighting compartment. To the right, the breechblock of the 15cm howitzer with closed breech. The sight mount and the traversing handle are fixed to the left of the gun mount. In the foreground, one can see an ammunition bin with brass cartridges filled with propellant charges. In the left upper corner, the ball mount for the machine gun is just visible above the driver's seat.
Library and Archives of Canada

the division on 9 August.[48] For the next two days the I.SS-Pz.Korps reported five combat ready Sturmpanzer IVs attached to the 12.SS-Pz.Div.[49]

On 11 August, Panzer-Armee-Oberkommando 5 reported that 1./ Sturmpanzer-Abteilung 217 would be attached to the 271.Inf.Div. in the area of LXXIV A.K.[50] However, two days later the company was actually engaged in the 276.Inf.Div area.

Elements of 1./ Sturmpanzer-Abteilung 217 supported by two Jagdpanthers of s.H.Pz.Jg.Abt.654 and two Tigers of s.Pz.Abt.503 were merged into *Kompanie Olowson* and went into position at the La Vendie crossroads, southeast of Proussy in support of Gren.Rgt.989. Although Gren.Rgt.989 was an organic element of the 277.Inf.Div., it was obviously attached to the 276.Inf.Div. that day together with elements of Gren.Rgt.752 of the 326.Inf.Div., an indication of the crucial situation developing in the area south of Caen during the second week of August 1944.[51]

During the night of 13/14 August, an enemy attack against Hill 261 (2 kilometers north-east of Proussy) destroyed the two Tigers from s.Pz.Abt.503. The tanks of s.H.Pz.Jg.Abt.654 were unable to reach the hill, hampered by the dense smoke screen laid down by the attackers. In the morning, the two Jagdpanthers fell back to La Vendie. Around noon, enemy forces advancing south from Proussy into the direction of Condé-sur-Noireau threatened the flank of the 276.Inf.Div. near Saint-Denis-de-Méré. To counter this threat, the division commander ordered the three combat-ready Sturmpanzer IVs of 1./ Sturmpanzer-Abteilung 217 and the two Jagdpanthers to occupy a defensive position along the road from La Vendie to Condé-sur-Noireau at Hill 196, located northeast of Saint-Denis-de-Méré. When *Kompanie Olowson* reached the appointed hill, they were attached to *Kompanie Bongert* with the mission of launching a counterattack through Saint-Denis-de-Méré. However, the attack ran head-on into an Allied attack. Both Jagdpanthers were damaged and had to withdraw. The fate of the three Sturmpanzer IVs remains unclear.[52] On 15 August, Leutnant Olowson and an enlisted man of his company met their fate near Notre Dame des Courson.[53] It remains unclear how Leutnant Olowson managed to cover a distance of more than 50 kilometers between Saint-Denis-de-Méré and Notre Dame des Courson in a single day. One has to consider that the Falaise pocket was almost closed and the ever-present Allied fighter bombers were not only dominating the skies but also all road movements. While Saint-Denis-de-Méré was located within the expanding pocket, Notre Dame des Courson is situated outside the gap on the road between Livarot and Orbec. In view of the 11 soldiers of 1./ Sturmpanzer-Abteilung 217 missing in the Falaise area on 20 August, the death of Leutnant Olowson five days earlier and outside the pocket has raised many questions. Until the arrival of Oberleutnant Josef Gauglitz on 21 September, Leutnant Wolfgang Kiefer would take command of the 1st Company.[54]

2.3 Engagements of 3rd Company in the Combat Zone of II. SS-Panzer-Korps and LXXIV Armee-Korps

Before its arrival at the Normandy front, 3./ Sturmpanzer-Abteilung 217 handed over 29 soldiers on 18 July. The reason for this decision remains unknown as well as to which unit these soldiers were transferred. Furthermore, hardly any personnel losses are recorded for the engagements of the 3rd Company in July and August.[55] The company was first reported on 30 July in the area of II.SS-Pz.Korps. However, a few days before, an enlisted man had died on 25 July.[56] There must have been engagements prior to 1 August, because I. SS-Panzer-Korps awarded Leutnant Egon Schmitz the Iron Cross 2 on 1 August.[57] On the morning of 30 July, the enemy launched an attack along the entire front of LXXIV Armee-Korps, breaching the frontline of the 326.Inf.Div. On the orders of Panzergruppe West, the II. SS-Panzer-Korps had to detach 3./ Sturmpanzer-Abteilung 217 and Werfer-Lehr-Regiment 1 (less the I. Abteilung) to LXXIV A.K. Further reinforcements for the corps included the remnants of the 21.Pz.Div. and a heavy anti-aircraft-artillery battalion with three batteries. The 3rd Company received instructions to move to Longvillers, south of Villers-Bocage.[58] The next day, four enlisted men of the company were killed in combat, but no location was provided.[59] During the engagements in this sector at least two Sturmpanzer IVs were destroyed. One Sturmpanzer IV was blown up by its own crew on 8 August near Roucamps, the other vehicle was destroyed three kilometers west of Roucamps at Ondefontaine. The attachment to LXXIV Armee-Korps most likely lasted until 5 August. The following day, Panzergruppe West (officially renamed on 5 August into Panzer-Armee-Ober-Kommando 5) reported that 2./ Sturmpanzer-Abteilung 217 was attached to II. SS-Panzer-Korps with three combat ready Sturmpanzer IVs. On 7 August, this information was repeated in the daily notes of the Army.[60] The information, however, is probably inaccurate as the 2nd Company was still attached to the I.SS-Pz.Korps on both days. This makes us finally understand that the report actually referred to 3./ Sturmpanzer-Abteilung 217.

The information provided by Panzer-Armee-Ober-Kommando 5 on 6 August is not only imprecise in respect of the unit's identification. Shortly before midnight, LXXIV A.K. received a message that s.Pz.Abt.503 and a Sturmpanzer-Kompanie would be detached from II.SS-Pz.Korps.[61] The step taken by Pz.AOK. 5 was obviously a preventive measure, as the Germans were already expecting a large scale enemy attack in the sector of LXXIV A.K. The commander-in-chief warned not to deploy the heavy tank battalion piecemeal. He further suggested to place the Sturmpanzer IVs and the heavy tank destroyers (s.H.Pz.Jg.Abt.654, sic.) behind the frontline of the 277.Inf.Div., because he expected the enemy's main effort in this direction.[62] Aside from the two independent general headquarters tank units and the Sturmpanzer-Kompanie, II. SS-Panzer-Korps also received instructions to transfer the 21.Pz.Div. to LXXIV Armee-Korps on 7 August.[63] This is the last trace of the 3rd Company in the official Normandy records. We only know that 3./ Sturmpanzer-Abteilung 217 reported two soldiers killed on 7 and 8 August, but no location was given.[64] Three more soldiers from the company are recorded as missing in action in August 1944. Their places of death give an indication of the route taken by the company during the retreat from Normandy towards the Reich. One enlisted man is reported missing at Bosrobert, 15 kilometers west of Elbeuf, and another enlisted man went missing in the Rouen area. In both cases no date was given. One officer is reported missing near Montdidier on 28 August. We guess that he was captured by the Allies.[65]

2.4 Status Report from 15 August 1944

On 19 August, Sturmpanzer-Abteilung 217 issued its first status report since the activation of the battalion in May. The report is dated 15 August and covered the personnel and material situation during the period of 1-15 August. The battalion was still assigned to Pz. AOK. 5 when the report was issued. Considering the seriousness of the previous fighting in Normandy, losses were relatively small. The figures given for the actual strength and the recorded personnel losses are coherent, which allows for the conclusion that the battalion only lost two officers and five enlisted men in July.

Based on the authorized strength of 772 soldiers and 2 clerks, the battalion was short of 5 officers and 64 enlisted men on 15 August. Out of these 69 soldiers, 10 were killed in action (1 officer and 9 enlisted men), 33 were wounded (2 officers and 31 enlisted men), 12 were missing in action (1 officer and 11 enlisted men),

8 were ill (8 enlisted men), and 6 fell out due to other reasons (1 officer and 5 enlisted men).

In contrast to KStN 1156 and 1160, the authorized strength of the Sturmpanzer IVs was based on 45 Sturmpanzer IVs instead of 42 vehicles. The report is lacking information on the number of tanks in long-term maintenance. Therefore, it is difficult to figure out the overall number of lost Sturmpanzer IVs. We assume that a maximum of 14 Sturmpanzer IVs were lost up to 15 August.[66]

Status Report 15 August 1944				
Material	Authorized strength	Actual strength	Combat-ready	Short-term maintenance
Sturmpanzer IV	45	31	17	14
Motorcycle/sidecars	4	0	0	0
Motorcycles	22	17	16	1
CC passenger cars	34	41	36	5
CO passenger cars	7	5	4	1
Maultiere	27	25	25	0
CC trucks	57	81	78	3
CO trucks	28	16	15	1
Halftracks	5	5	3	2
Machine guns	71	57	57	0

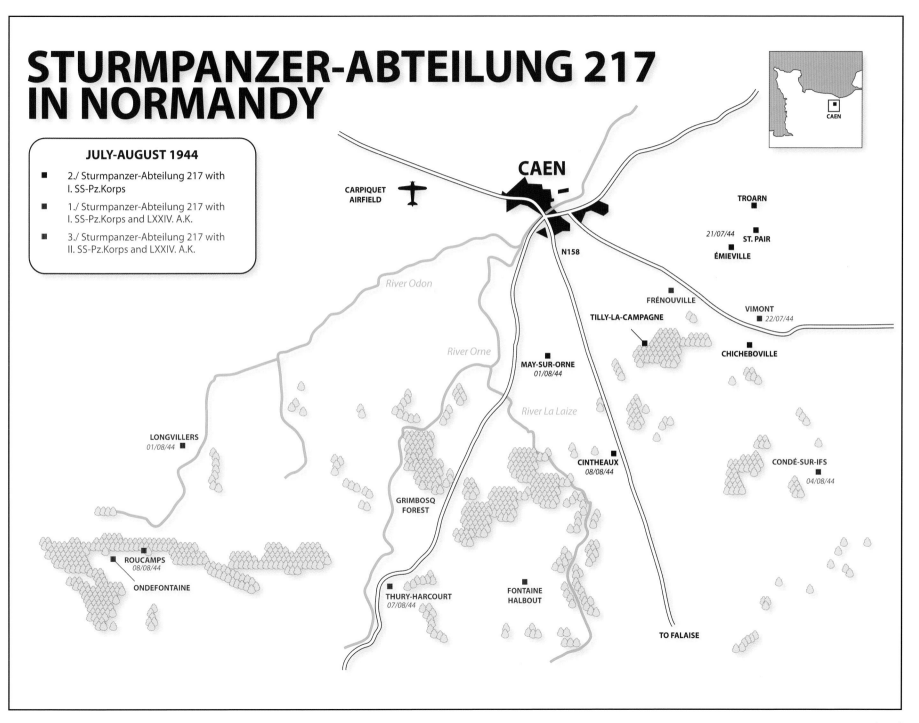

STURMPANZER-ABTEILUNG 217 IN NORMANDY

CAEN

JULY-AUGUST 1944

- 2./ Sturmpanzer-Abteilung 217 with I. SS-Pz.Korps
- 1./ Sturmpanzer-Abteilung 217 with I. SS-Pz.Korps and LXXIV. A.K.
- 3./ Sturmpanzer-Abteilung 217 with II. SS-Pz.Korps and LXXIV. A.K.

CARPIQUET AIRFIELD

CAEN

TROARN

21/07/44
ST. PAIR

ÉMIEVILLE

N158

River Odon

FRÉNOUVILLE

VIMONT
22/07/44

TILLY-LA-CAMPAGNE

CHICHEBOVILLE

River Orne

MAY-SUR-ORNE
01/08/44

River La Laize

LONGVILLERS
01/08/44

CINTHEAUX
08/08/44

CONDÉ-SUR-IFS

04/08/44

GRIMBOSQ FOREST

ROUCAMPS
08/08/44

ONDEFONTAINE

THURY-HARCOURT
07/08/44

FONTAINE HALBOUT

TO FALAISE

CHAPTER 03

WITHDRAWAL FROM NORMANDY AND ENGAGEMENTS IN THE AACHEN AREA

The battalion perished in the Falaise pocket, like so many other German units. The series of images on the next few pages show a destroyed Sturmpanzer IV of the 3rd Company in the Falaise gap with the tactical number '36'.[1]

Another Sturmpanzer IV, Ausführung IV was blown up by its crew on **20 August** near Saint-Lambert-sur-Dives. The bridge across the river Dives, nicknamed 'Quantité', was under the control of Canadian troops, thus eliminating the crew's final chance to save their tank.[2]

On 20 August, the 331.Inf.Div., at the time engaged in the Broglie - Gacé area southwest of Evreux, reported to LXXXI A.K. that four Sturmpanzer IVs were en route to the division. Unfortunately, there are no further details as to the engagements of Sturmpanzer-Abteilung 217 in this area.[3] The repair and maintenance crews of the battalion managed to bring 12 damaged Sturmpanzer IVs back to the Rouen area and subsequently repair them. Meanwhile, plans were forged to send these Sturmpanzer IVs back into combat in the form of Kompanie Mentzel, clearly named after Oberleutnant Max Mentzel, a platoon leader in the 3rd Company. However, the Sturmpanzers ran out of fuel en route. The vehicles had to be blown up in face of the Allied advance as no fuel could be secured and allocated by Pz.AOK. 5.[4] Oberleutnant Mentzel and Obergefreiter Johann Wallerstorfer[5] went missing in action near Montdidier, northeast of Beauvais, around 28 August. It is highly likely that both soldiers were captured by the advancing British forces.[6] Another was killed in action on 29 August in the village of Vaumoise, 24 kilometers southeast of Compiègne, on the road from Meaux to Soissons. On 5 September two soldiers of Sturmpanzer-Abteilung 217 were captured in the vicinity of Landrecies east of

Cambrai by members of 22nd Inf Rgt, 4th Inf Div.[7] Around 5 September, a number of soldiers from Gren.Rgt.983 (275.Inf.Div.) were captured in the area of the VII Corps. They claimed that elements of Sturmpanzer-Abteilung 217 were attached to their regiment, but that they had lost all their Sturmpanzer IVs. The soldiers who had not been captured or killed in the Falaise pocket, retreated through northern France and Belgium, and eventually reached the battalion's assembly area near Venlo in early September 1944.[8]

On **2 September** 1944, Oberbefehlshaber West (Commander-in-Chief in the West) issued an order dictating the refitting area for 2.Pz.Div., 116.Pz.Div., Sturmpanzer-Abteilung 217 and s.H.Pz.Jg.Abt.654 in the vicinity of Werbomont - Spa - Liège - Huy. As a logical consequence of the rapidly changing situation in the West, the Generalinspekteur der Panzertruppen, requested all armored formations be moved back across the Rhine so as to preserve the integrity of the force.[9]

On **3 September**, Heeresgruppe B (Army Group B) issued an order for refitting the armored forces and independent armored battalions under the command of Ob.West:

"Ob.West has made the following arrangements:

The following units will remain at the front with their combat-ready elements: 2.Pz.Div., 116.Pz.Div., 9.SS-Pz.Div., 10.SS-Pz.Div. and Sturmpanzer-Abteilung 217."

A Sturmpanzer IV Ausf.III was discovered by the US 1st Army Ordnance Technical Intelligence Unit E in the Falaise pocket. Note the *Balkenkreuz* on the fender. This feature is unique as no other picture shows this marking in the same position. The Americans measured the thickness of the superstructure front as 104mm at an angle of 38°, the front oblique was 60mm at 23° and the front of the chassis was 80mm. ***NARA via Lee Archer***

The thickness of the side armor was 52mm at 18°. Both pistol port plugs are still in situ, unlike the photo opposite. Only one *Schürzen* bracket remains; below the leg of the American soldier investigating the hole where the howitzer used to be. ***NARA via Lee Archer***

The right of the Sturmpanzer clearly shows the damage to the engine compartment. The chassis is typical of the Panzer IV Ausf.H. *Zimmerit* was applied to all upright surfaces. Note the missing pistol port plugs. ***NARA via Lee Archer***

The rear of the tank, showing that one of the rear doors is missing as well as the large hatch in the roof above the loader's position. Both spare roadwheels on the left of the rear wall are in situ, unlike those on the right that disappeared with the explosion. The exhaust muffler has come away from its bracket but the rack above is still in position. *NARA via Lee Archer*

A view of the superstructure roof, looking towards the front, shows the commander's hatch with just one of the hatch covers remaining; behind this is the sliding cover for the gunsight. To the right of this is the armoured cover for the roof ventilator. The roof armor was 20mm thick and the rear wall of the fighting compartment was 30mm. *NARA via Lee Archer*

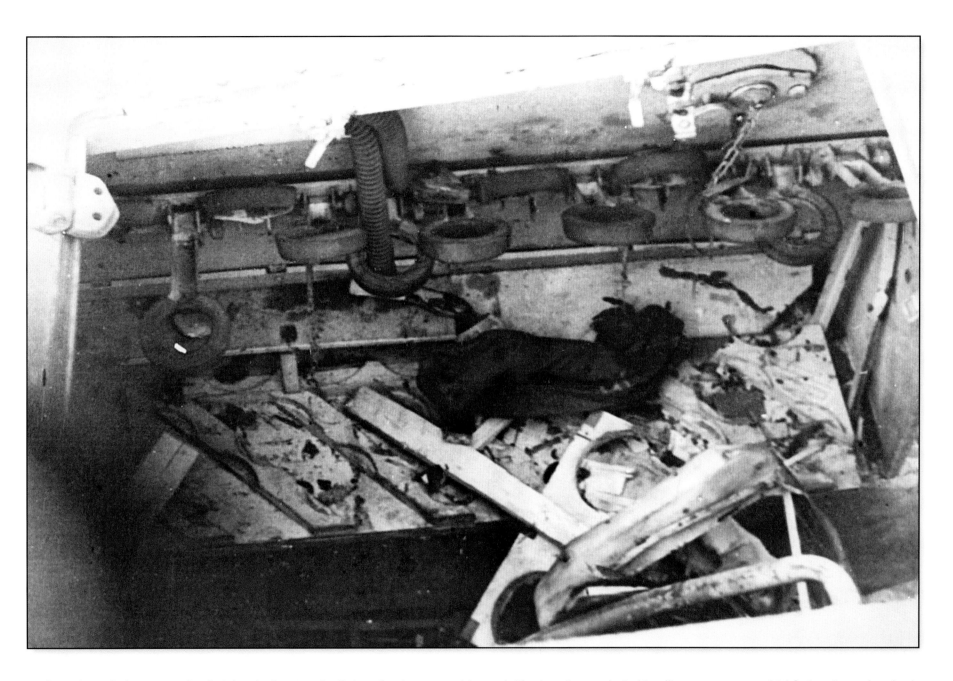

Looking through the missing loader's hatch showing the fittings for the ammunition rack. The American technical intelligence team noted 26 fittings in total on both sides of the fighting compartment. Note the method of retaining the pistol port plug. *NARA via Lee Archer*

This section of Sturmpanzer IV Ausf.IV roof was recovered at Saint-Lambert-Sur-Dives in 2013 and is now today part of the Wheatcroft Collection. *Collection Le Triangle Normand - Frédéric Deprun*

Another Sturmpanzer IV Ausf.III was found by the Americans in Elbeuf. This vehicle was also destroyed by an internal explosion, like so many other Sturmpanzers in Normandy. It is clear that the crew tried everything to avoid their tank from falling into enemy hands when they had to abandon their vehicle. The roof of this Sturmpanzer has been blown away and the superstructure shifted forward, leaving the howitzer in its original initial position. Note the name '*Gudrun*' painted onto the gun barrel jacket. *Lee Archer*

A German photographer pictured this Sturmpanzer IV in mid of August outside the Falaise pocket at Orbec, 20 kilometers northeast of Vimoutiers. The vehicle is heavily camouflaged which makes it almost impossible to identify the correct version of the Sturmpanzer. The earlier driver's vision port (*Fahrerlucke 80*) implies this Sturmpanzer is an early version   Ausf.II. *ECPAD*

Non-committed elements are to be transferred to the area of Venlo - Arnhem - 's-Hertogenbosch by Pz.AOK 5, for refitting purposes. Each division must merge their units into battlegroups, and will keep them available at the tactical disposal of Pz.AOK 5. An advance message center should be set up in Eindhoven. Questions relating to the refitting and allocation of forces from the homeland area are the responsibility of the General der Panzertruppen (West) with the Befehlshaber des Ersatzheeres."[10]

Apparently the Oberbefehlshaber West knew that ten Sturmpanzer IVs were in transit to Sturmpanzer-Abteilung 217, otherwise these orders would have not made sense, especially because the unit had lost all of its Sturmpanzer IVs in Normandy and the subsequent retreat to the German border. On **5 September**, ten Sturmpanzer IVs finally arrived by rail. Although the vehicles had been allocated on 8 August, they had only shipped to the battalion on 24 August.[11] That it took almost twelve days to ship these vehicles, reflects the chaotic situation in the West at the end of August and beginning of September 1944.

In addition to the aforementioned directives of the Oberbefehlshaber West, the General der Panzertruppen West ordered that it was of utmost importance that personnel, especially stragglers, earmarked for refitting the armored divisions and independent armored units, were to be assembled and led back to their units. Personnel at the Panzerstützpunkten Nord and Mitte (Armor Support Centers North and Center) could only remain at these installations, when they were absolutely necessary for conducting the maintenance and repair or the shipment of vehicles. All other personnel, as long as they were crew members without tanks, had to be transferred back to the message centers of their respective units. This particular order planned a message center for Sturmpanzer-Abteilung 217 in Eindhoven.[12] On 5 September, II. SS-Pz.Korps became responsible for the reconstitution of the armored units still in combat. For this purpose, II. SS-Pz.Korps was detached from Pz.AOK 5 and was directly subordinated to *Heeresgruppe B*. The corps had to relocate to Eindhoven for refitting and collaborate closely with the General der Panzertruppen West to reconstitute the 2.Pz.Div., 116.Pz.Div, 9.SS-Pz. Div. and Sturmpanzer-Abteilung 217.[13]

On **6 September**, another order was issued for Panzerstützpunkt Nord to continue with taking care of 2.Pz.Div., 116.Pz.Div., 9.SS-Pz.Div., 10.SS-Pz.Div. and Sturmpanzer-Abteilung 217. Fetching parties of these units had to remain in their current billeting areas each with:

- 15 Sturmgeschütz crews
- 15 Panzer crews
- 10 Sturmpanzer IV crews

A person to receive the orders for the fetching parties had to be available at the Riemann barracks at Panzerstützpunkt Nord.[14]

After this short reconstitution period, the battalion would be committed to an uninterrupted series of engagements within the combat zone of LXXXI A.K. Sturmpanzer-Abteilung 217 would be in continuous defensive combat in the center of gravity. While being attached to Pz.Brig.105, Sturmpanzer-Abteilung 217 would be deployed in the area of Limbourg - Eynatten and Stolberg against 3rd Armd Div. Subsequently, fighting took place with the 49.Inf.Div. against elements of the 30th Inf Div during the battles for the Westwall north of Aachen. The battalion would see even more combat with the 183.Volks-Gren.Div. against the 30th Inf Div supporting elements of the 2nd Armd Div in the Übach - Palenberg area. After the Americans completed the encirclement of Aachen, the battalion was sent into the pocket to reinforce the 246.Volks-Gren.Div. Another reconstitution period then ended the deployment with LXXXI A.K.

3.1 Engagements between Liège and the Westwall

When the Allied advance reached the Meuse river near Hasselt and Liège on **7 September**, the situation for the Germans became critical as there was almost no time left to properly occupy the Westwall due to speed of the advance. Every available unit was thrown into battle to block the Allied advance: Normandy survivors, newly raised units without combat experience, and others that were practically decimated. Around noon, the 'Ia' of the Oberbefehlshaber West informed Heeresgruppe B that Sturmpanzer-Abteilung 217 had been in transit from the Venlo area since the evening of 6 September and was now near Hasselt. However, according to the AOK 7's evening report of 7 September, one company of Sturmpanzer-Abteilung 217 with 10 Sturmpanzer IVs was still in transit to the Hasselt area.[15] This makes it clear that the battalion had raised a combat company on 6 September out of the 10 Sturmpanzer IVs it received the day before. Oberleutnant Hans-Jürgen Heigl, a former Stalingrad veteran and commander of 3./ Sturmpanzer-Abteilung 217 took command of the improvised company.[16] During the evening of 7 September, the Oberbefehlshaber West made an assessment of the precarious situation on the Western front:

"I beg the Führer to give him on 7 September 1944 the following assessment of the situation, based on a personal discussion with Generalfeldmarschall Model and the last available reports:

I. Appreciation of the enemy's capabilities:
...
II. On the other hand we can conclude that:
All our own forces are engaged, heavily battered and partly burned-out. They

lack artillery support and anti-tank weapons. There are no substantial reserves on hand. Enemy armor clearly outnumbers our own. At this time there are approximately 100 tanks operational within Heeresgruppe B. The enemy's airforce dominates the combat zone deep into our rear area. Enemy pressure towards Liège, with a clear point of attack to Aachen in the direction of the industrial area of North Rhine-Westphalia, has developed into a dangerous situation. The repeatedly requested allocation of strong forces, at least five, preferably 10 divisions with Sturmgeschützabteilungen and sufficient anti-tank weapons and a number of armored divisions, is absolutely crucial for me. All my available forces; weak elements of the 9.Pz.Div., 1 weak Sturm-Pz. Abt. [Sturmpanzer-Abteilung 217, sic], two Sturmgeschütz-Brigaden [StuG. Brig.394 and 902, sic] with their Sturmgeschütze still in transit, have been sent to the Aachen area. The 12.Volks-Gren.Div. has also not yet arrived. In concurrence with Generalfeldmarschall Model, I detect an acute threat, which also endangers the rear of the southern adjoining Westwall."[17]

Fresh orders must have been issued for the battalion during 7 September. On **8 September**, the LXXXI A.K. war diary recorded that the Kampfkommandant of Lüttich (Local Area Commander for Lüttich) executed an early morning attack with the Sturmpanzer IVs of Sturmpanzer-Abteilung 217 available to him, against the advancing Americans and elements of the 'White Army', the local resistance movement known as the 'Armee Blanche', in the southeast of Liège.[18] Until noon, the situation inside the city developed as follows: German stragglers were still holding out in the western parts of the city, while in the east of the city elements of Sich.Btl.1030, Sturmpanzer-Abteilung 217 and Panzer-Kompanie (Fkl) 319 were fighting off the American advance.[19]

During the evening, the Chef des Generalstabes (Chief-of-Staff) of Heeresgruppe B informed the Chef des Generalstabes of AOK 7 on the planned allocations. Aside from the ten Sturmpanzer IVs which were already in combat, another ten vehicles, and at some point later, a further seventeen Sturmpanzer IVs, were to be expected.[20] Ten of these Sturmpanzer IVs would arrive on 17 September. Out of the seventeen other Sturmpanzer IVs on the table, only four vehicles arrived in September.[21]

After the heavy fighting of the previous day, it remained unclear what had happened to the Kampfkommandant. To this end, the 49.Inf.Div., who were engaged north of the city, sent a liaison officer to Thimister to clarify whether the Kampfkommandant was there and, if so, in what strength. In fact, only Panzer-Kompanie (Fkl) 319, 1./Sich. Btl.1030 and the combat company of Sturmpanzer-Abteilung 217 succeeded in breaking out of the city. The badly battered Funklenkkompanie was subsequently attached to 116.Pz.Div., the Sicherungskompanie was subordinated to the 49.Inf. Div. and the Sturmpanzer-Kompanie was transferred and attached to Pz.Brig.105.[22]

The latter's main force was halted in the area of Battice - Verviers due to a lack of fuel. During the night of **9/10 September**, Pz.Brig.105 set up new defensive positions in a line running from Villers - Bilstain - Dolhain to Goé.[23] East of Goé, near Béthane, five halftracks of Pz.Gren.Btl.2105 (of which three were Sd.Kfz.251/21s) were knocked out when they ran into an American ambush near Béthane railroad station.[24] On the morning of 10 September, elements of Pz.Brig.105 moved to the area around Limbourg. Around 07:12, the first German columns moving north out of Limbourg were observed by elements of the 83rd Armd Rcn Bn of the 3rd Armd Div. Around 09:30, another concentration of German armor was reported in the vicinity of Bilstain - Villers. Shortly before noon, the 3rd Armd Div attacked from Hèvremont towards Goé. The latter became the scene of bitter fighting between elements of Pz.Brig.105 and the 3rd Armd Div. In the afternoon, the Americans employed additional fighter-bombers against the German positions south of Limbourg, but were unable to advance further. The situation around Limbourg remained serious, with additional American attacks coming in from the north. Despite all this, the brigade continued holding its positions.[25] According to a report from Oberleutnant Heigl, the brigade managed to repel these attacks with relatively modest means, as there were only 8 Panthers and 6 Sturmpanzer IVs on hand, supported by an unknown number of Panzergrenadiere and Panzerpioniere. These elements of Pz.Brig.105 were led by Hauptmann Nohse, commander of Pz. Gren.Btl.2105. His Grenadiere, supported by two Panthers and two Sturmpanzer IV, defended a position south of the road leading from Limbourg to Eupen. On the north side of the road, another six Panthers and four Sturmpanzer IVs reinforced his defenses. There are no details about the Sturmpanzer IVs that saw action south of the road. Two Sturmpanzer IVs took up new positions at the southern exit of Honthem, south of the road leading to Dolhain, with their guns pointing in the direction of Dolhain and Kapellenberg. The other two Sturmpanzer IVs changed position during the night of 10/11 September and moved to the Köttgen brothers' farm not far from Houyoux castle.[26]

On the night of **10/11 September**, the first elements of the 9.Pz.Div. arrived in the Eupen area. Its *Bataillon Schemm* was immediately subordinated to Pz. Brig.105. At 02:30, Hauptmann Schemm moved forward to the command post of Pz.Brig.105 located in the village of Heggen. Upon arrival, a meeting took place with the commander of Pz.Brig.105; Major Volker. An assessment of the situation revealed that Goé was occupied by the Americans who were attacking with strong armored forces. Operating on the right flank of Pz.Brig.105 was a battlegroup of the 116.Pz.Div. *Kampfgruppe Schemm* was tasked with holding a defensive position running from Château de la Verne across the area 900 meters southwest of Villers to the southwestern corner of Grünholz to Hockelbach. This sector was 3.5 kilometers wide. Two Panthers and two Sturmpanzer IVs reinforced the defenses in the sector between the Grünholz woods and Hockelbach, while two more Panthers moved into position at the southwestern corner of the same

This Sturmpanzer IV Ausf.IV, was abandoned by its crew south of Houyoux, on the road from Dolhain to Honthem. The road was littered with many other vehicles from Panzer-Brigade 105 that fought with the Combat Company of Sturmpanzer-Abteilung 217 west of Eupen on 11 September. A closer look reveals that the vehicle also had a name painted onto the gun barrel jacket and a tactical number '15' is visible on the side. It is notable that the spare track brackets seen on vehicles in Normandy were not seen on the battalion's vehicles from September 1944. *Stefan De Meyer*

RODNA

A second Sturmpanzer IV Ausf.IV was destroyed on 11 September on the Chemin de la Grappe, south of Houyoux. The tank was in a partly covered position next to the Murders' house. The howitzer was facing west in the direction of the Villers crossroads, defended by *Kampfgruppe Schemm*. **Chris Webber**

Ten Sturmpanzer IV Ausf.IV were allocated to the Combat Company of Sturmpanzer-Abteilung 217 only a few days before their engagement in Eastern Belgium. These tanks came from the first batch of Sturmpanzers assembled at Deutsche Eisenwerke in Duisburg between May and September 1944. This photo was taken by an American soldier from the 460th Anti-Aircraft-Artillery Battalion. *Timm Haasler*

The Honthem and the Houyoux Sturmpanzers both had *Zimmerit* applied. We have to assume that the Houyoux tank also had 16 steel roadwheels. Both tanks do not appear to have *Balkenkreuze* applied, although it is remarkable that the crew still found time to paint a name onto the gun barrel jacket. *Lee Archer*

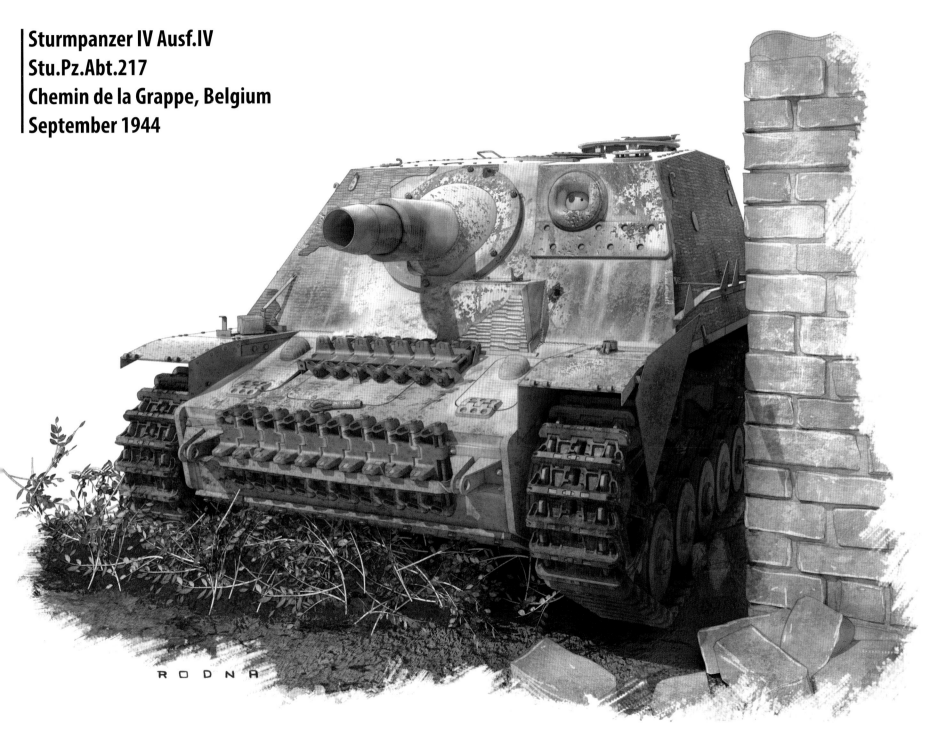

Sturmpanzer IV Ausf.IV
Stu.Pz.Abt.217
Chemin de la Grappe, Belgium
September 1944

T5 M. George Webber from 'B' Company, 75th Medical Battalion, 5th US Armored Division, took this photograph (and the one on page 44) in the autumn of 1944 which clearly shows the destruction of the Murders' house next to the Sturmpanzer. *Chris Webber*

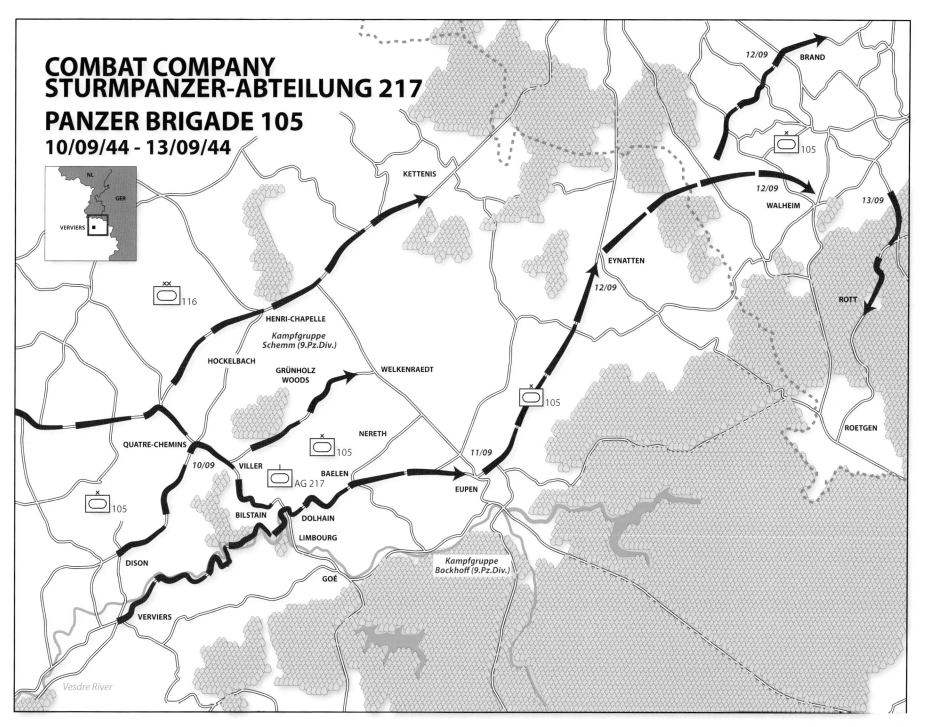

COMBAT COMPANY
STURMPANZER-ABTEILUNG 217
PANZER BRIGADE 105
10/09/44 - 13/09/44

NL

GER

VERVIERS

BRAND

12/09

105

12/09

KETTENIS

WALHEIM

13/09

EYNATTEN

12/09

ROTT

116

HENRI-CHAPELLE

*Kampfgruppe
Schemm (9.Pz.Div.)*

HOCKELBACH

GRÜNHOLZ
WOODS

WELKENRAEDT

105

ROETGEN

NERETH

105

QUATRE-CHEMINS

11/09

10/09

VILLER

BAELEN

AG 217

EUPEN

105

BILSTAIN

DOLHAIN

LIMBOURG

DISON

GOÉ

*Kampfgruppe
Bockhoff (9.Pz.Div.)*

VERVIERS

Vesdre River

woods. The elements of the 3./Pz.Gren.Btl.2105 that had been in Limbourg pulled back to the ridge line northeast of the town. As far as can be ascertained, the main body of the company, which was reinforced by two Panthers and two Sturmpanzer IVs, was positioned on a hill north of the Verviers - Eupen road. Combat engineers from the brigade defended the city itself. Elements of Pz.Gren. Btl.2105 were employed south of the road, also reinforced by two Panthers and two Sturmpanzer IVs. The employment of tanks in pairs along the entire length of the front has been confirmed by several sources, as well as vehemently criticized. While Hauptmann Hanemann held the 9.Pz.Div. responsible for this questionable technique, Oberleutnant Heigl from Sturmpanzer-Abteilung 217 stated that the order came from the commander of Pz.Gren.Btl.2105 himself. At 06:00, the 9.Pz. Div. assumed command of the brigade's sector.

The German forces around Limbourg and Eupen were merged into *Kampfgruppe Müller*, commanded by the divisional commander of the 9.Pz.Div., Generalmajor Müller.[27]

The main objective for the 3rd Armd Div that day was to attack the area of Lichtenbusch - Kettenis. To do this, the division intended to send its Combat Command A (CCA) from the area north of Dison, move through Lohierville - Welkenraedt - Lontzen and advance as far as Lichtenbusch. The start time for the attack was set for 09:30. It was intended for CCB to take Eupen from the south with Task Force 1; its attack was to start at 08:00 by swinging to the south and advancing through Jalhay and Baraque Michel. The day's objective for Task Force 1 was the area northeast of Eupen as far as Kettenis. Task Force 2, on the other hand, was to advance directly on Eupen via Limbourg.

Decisions were made that led to *Kampfgruppe Müller*, with attached Pz.Brig.105 and combat company of Sturmpanzer-Abteilung 217, being attacked on each flank by a task force of the 3rd Armd Div as well as being attacked from the front by another task force. At 09:55, eight enemy tanks were observed on the Kapellenberg, 1500 meters southwest of Limbourg; they were attacking in the direction of the city. At almost the same time, the attack was supported by fighter-bombers. German artillery attempted to hold up the attack on the Hèvremont - Limbourg road but it was unable to prevent Task Force 2 from penetrating into Limbourg at 10:30 after elements of the brigade had withdrawn from the city at 10:20. In the meantime, the Americans started to clear Limbourg. Sporadic resistance from machine-gun fire and hand grenades slowed the advance, as did the mine barriers that had been emplaced by the Germans. Task Force 2 then held in Limbourg and secured the objective. For the time being, an effort to roll up the German front was not undertaken. It should be mentioned, however, that elements of the 83rd Armd Rcn Bn felt their way forward along the Limbourg - Eupen road. At 11:45, the brigade attempted to take the initiative in Limbourg again. Although 30 enemy

tanks and infantry had been observed right outside of Limbourg castle, the brigade employed only two groups against them. No information can be found concerning the outcome of this immediate German counterattack, but Limbourg and Dolhain were not finally liberated by the Americans until 20:00, according to a Belgian observer.[28]

A platoon leader in the 3./Pz.Gren.Btl.2105 provided an account of the situation near Dolhain. In the morning he received orders from his company commander to reconnoiter the situation in Dolhain with his driver. The men approached the hilltop on which two Sturmpanzer IVs had occupied reverse slope positions. Crouched over, the two men went at least another 50 meters and reached a point from which they could observe Dolhain and the bridge. American tanks were spotted moving across the bridge and heading in the direction of Eupen. At the same time, several fighter-bombers flew over their heads and attacked the armored vehicles behind them and the hilltop. Both men immediately ran back to the other side of the hill to their SPW, which had been damaged on the weapons mount by the fighter-bomber attack. The other two soldiers from the SPW were lying on the ground behind it, and were at the end of their tether as a result of the low-level attack. The platoon leader sent his driver back to the maintenance facility with the vehicle, while he remained with the rest of the crew. An order was circulated throughout the company to camouflage their vehicles just like the Americans, since American aerial observers were constantly circling over the German positions. Red and white curtains and tablecloths were taken from the surrounding houses and placed over the rear decks of the vehicles. When one squad leader thought that the company was about to be encircled by the Americans, he decided that he would break out to the east in his SPW after siphoning fuel from other SPWs. His company commander forbade this, instead the officer wanted to break out with his company on foot.[29]

As early as 08:30, elements of *Kampfgruppe Schemm* tracked a motorized column with mounted infantry that was approaching Château de la Verne from the west; this was probably elements of Task Force X. At 09:35, heavy artillery fire opened up for exactly one hour on the positions and command post of *Kampfgruppe Schemm*. The task force started to receive mortar and tank main-gun fire in the area around Lohierville after it started its attack at 09:30. German infantry was observed by the task force pulling back into the woods to the southwest (Grünholz Woods) when the attack started. At this point, the task force started to deploy. A Panther was discovered, which was quickly eliminated. A few fighter-bombers supported the advance in the direction of Hockelbach and reported an additional six German tanks in this area, which probably belonged to 116.Panzer-Division.

The Allied fighter-bombers attacked everything that moved on the ground for 45 minutes. According to Belgian eyewitnesses, the main effort of the German defense was in the area around the crossroads of Les Quatre Chemins and the crossroads 500 meters southwest of Villers. A German tank was knocked out at the crossroads southwest of Villers (it was possibly the Panther already mentioned), as well as both Sturmpanzer IVs in this area. Both vehicles had spent the night in the cesspool of Köttgen farm. In the morning, after ordering the inhabitants to take shelter in their cellars, both vehicles drove off for a new combat assignment. One of them was later knocked out near the Murders' House at the Chemin de La Grappe at Houyoux. The other Sturmpanzer IV was destroyed south of the Saint-Rochus chapel. Apparently, both vehicles were used as mobile artillery behind the forward German lines. In addition, at least 150 German soldiers were taken prisoner in the area of Les Quatre Chemins - Villers. After breaking the German resistance around Les Quatre Chemins, Task Force X continued its advance in the direction of Welkenraedt, threatening the left flank of the 116.Pz.Div.[30] Six German tanks were sent in by 116.Pz.Div. to counter the 1st Inf Div's northern advance from Villers, but could not prevent them from reaching Henri-Chapelle in the afternoon.[31]

In the meantime, Task Force 1 of the 3rd Armd Div had launched its southern flank attack towards Eupen and reached the south of the city with very little German resistance. In less than two hours, the Task Force had liberated the city completely. Sporadic, but disorganized counterattacks by elements of the 9.Pz.Div. and Pz. Brig.105 were easily repelled.[32]

After Eupen and Hockelbach were taken at almost the same time by Task Force 1 and Task Force X, *Kampfgruppe Müller* was threatened with encirclement in the Limbourg - Bilstain area. Although the danger of encirclement was readily identified by the Germans, it proved to be practically impossible to disengage from the enemy as the *Kampfgruppe* was in a direct firefight with Task Force 2. The task force started heading east towards Eupen, northeast towards Welkenraedt and north towards Bilstain. In addition to engaging the task force, American fighter-bombers forestalled every movement on the ground. By 13:00, American tanks and infantry were already in front of the command post of *Kampfgruppe Schemm*. As a result, Schemm moved his command post some 200 meters to the north. At about the same time, four tanks and a company of infantry entered Bilstain. Hauptmann Schemm realized that his companies had pulled back far beyond his command post, so he pulled back through the woods with his battalion headquarters at 13:35. He assembled the rest of his *Kampfgruppe* at Herbesthal.

A motorized column advanced to the south of Membach; this put it in the rear of Panzer-Brigade 105. These elements were from the 83rd Armored Reconnaissance Battalion, which had crossed the bridge across the River Vesdre in Béthane around noon and moved into Membach via the Les Fusillés road. Dismounted soldiers then moved into the northern part of the village and engaged in a short firefight with two German soldiers, one of whom was wounded. An American tank, which had reached the church, engaged the Panther that was in the south of the village. Both tanks missed each another; only the cemetery wall was destroyed. The Panther pulled back and looked for a better firing position. Once there, it engaged and knocked out an M8 armored car, killing two of the crew.[33] The column of smoke from the exploding armored car drew 16 American fighter-bombers, which then attacked the German forces for 10 minutes. Following this, the Germans pulled back from the village, with the Panther and an Sd.Kfz.7/1 breaking trail as they went, crashing through hedges and fences. While pulling back, the quad Flak fired at the attacking fighter-bombers. The American tank next to the church moved forward. It knocked out the Panther with its fourth round, hitting the vehicle between the tracks sending it up in flames. At this point, the crew of the Sd.Kfz.7/1 jumped from their vehicle and ran away. The American tank then hit the halftrack with its next round, and the vehicle seemingly exploded into a thousand pieces. The American fighter-bombers turned away following this and the fighting for Membach was over.[34]

At around 14:00, the remaining elements of Panzer-Brigade 105 attempted to pull back to the east on secondary roads on both sides of the Limbourg - Eupen road. Task Force 2 advanced east along this road as well as along the Dolhain - Honthem and Goé - Eupen roads. The task force left the job of destroying the two German columns to the fighter-bombers, which were able to continuously engage with 40-60 aircraft, especially since the Germans had no more air-defense weapons.

For reasons that have not been clarified, most of the brigade's mechanized infantry had to pull back on foot, as their SPWs had been sent back behind the Westwall that morning. It was in this situation that an ad hoc German group was formed north of Dolhain. It consisted of elements of the 1. and 3./Panzergrenadier-Bataillon 2105, Panzer-Pionier-Kompanie 2105, two Sturmpanzers from Sturmpanzer-Abteilung 217, an unknown number of Panthers and other vehicles. It attempted to move on secondary roads from Dolhain to Eupen. An armored vehicle was knocked out by an antitank round in the vicinity of the Nols Building in Heggen. The driver of the vehicle, a soldier who had been decorated numerous times on the Eastern Front, lost his life and the rest of the crew was wounded. Other German soldiers evacuated the wounded and fled with them through Gemehret and to the east. Also, it is claimed that another four German soldiers were killed at Heggen. The armored vehicle had not been knocked out by tanks of Task Force 2. Instead, it had been hit by tanks of Task Force X, which was advancing on Welkenraedt after having taken Villers.

An American aerial observer spotted a German column moving parallel to the Americans on the Honthem - Heggen road. The columns were so close to one another that the observer was unable to call for fire; instead, he submitted a report.

South of Lanzenberg, a few Shermans turned south on the Heggenbrück road, which led to Heggen. The tanks went into position behind a hedge in the vicinity of the St. Maur Chapel and opened fire on the German column. During this engagement, the Americans succeeded in knocking out several other German vehicles in addition to the aforementioned armor.[35]

The Germans tried to pull back south via Baelen. In Baelen, an out-of-fuel Panther was abandoned in front of the Ahn Building; it blocked the avenue of advance being used by the Americans. The Germans set the vehicle on fire and fled to the east. The inhabitants of Baelen extinguished the burning tank with an old fire hose, preventing the fire from spreading to the Ahn Building.[36]

A member of the 3./Panzergrenadier-Bataillon 2105 provided the following first-hand account concerning the breakout attempt:

"There was a stoppage up ahead. A Yank reconnaissance aircraft appeared; a small one, not unlike our Fieseler Storch. We sought to conceal ourselves in the buildings. One building was burning brightly; the Belgians were attempting to extinguish the flames by simple means. We heard a lot of vehicles outside. Then: "Camouflage the vehicles like the enemy!"

We tore red and white curtains from the windows and placed them on the rear of the vehicles. We immediately mounted the first vehicle; it was equipped with a short main gun. I think it was an infantry gun [Author: A Sturmpanzer IV of Sturmpanzer-Abteilung 217]

When we were up on the hill [Author: Heggen], we were already anticipated. The antitank rounds whizzed past us to the left and the right. The road we were on was like a narrow path; to the left and right were fenced-in cattle pastures. The armored vehicle was unable to move out of the way without the fences pulling us off the vehicle.

Suddenly, there was a turning to the right. We moved in there quickly. The armored vehicle behind us flew in the air. The path led downhill and into a village [Author: Baelen]. We had barely covered 30 meters when there was a crash. The armored vehicle tipped forward and we were flying more than we were jumping. We had never dismounted so quickly.

We were barely on the ground when the vehicle commander, a lieutenant, yelled out: "Prepare for destruction!" We ran down the path; the machine-gun salvos hissed above our heads. We heard a voice somewhere: "Assemble in the village!" There was an explosion behind us; the [Sturmpanzer] was flying through the air. I looked around as I was running; a large hunk of steel was

flying past us. Fortunately, no one was injured.

My noncommissioned officer, Martin Hundt, was sitting in the [Sturmpanzer] when we were hit. He later stated that the vehicle had been hit in the front plate. The driver had been wounded in the left arm. Martin had a hole in his left breast pocket. When I asked him about it, he looked with amazement at it. He pulled his fat note book out of his pocket; there was a piece of shrapnel in there as big as a hazelnut.

Fighter-bombers were circling the skies above; we looked for concealed positions under the hedges in the meadows. There were still 9 men from our platoon there as well as 20 others whom we did not know. Below, in the village, we saw a group of vehicles that were assembling for a breakout attempt. We all felt that would not work. I later discovered that for a fact from a friend who was captured while trying to get out. The rest of us split up into three groups. When it turned dark, we felt our way forward to the axis of advance of the Yanks. The supply vehicles rolled from Limbourg towards Eupen with hardly any gaps."[37]

A Belgian eyewitness has confirmed that a destroyed German armored vehicle was on the road to Heggen, in addition to a number of German SPWs.[38]

Additional elements of the 3./Panzergrenadier-Bataillon 2105 attempted to break out in the direction of Aachen by going through Heggen. One of the platoon leaders at the time, Erwin Lies, recalled that they had refueled the remaining SPWs in pasture land shortly before the planned breakout attempt. They headed east together with another company - the 1./Panzergrenadier-Bataillon 2105 - and Sturmpanzer. He stated that they were unable to proceed beyond the next village (Heggen?), at which time several of the SPWs were blown up. Since neither of the two company commanders could agree on which way to head, two march groups were formed.

According to Lies, one of the groups wanted to head east. The other group, under the command of Oberleutnant Thöring, CO of the 3./Pz.Gren.Btl.2105, decided to break out to the south. During the course of the afternoon, Oberleutnant Thöring ordered the company be further broken down and for smaller groups to break out to the southeast.[39]

Although a few soldiers of the 1./ and 3./Pz.Gren.Btl.2105 managed to fight their way back to the German lines, elements of Pz.Brig.105 and Sturmpanzer-Abteilung 217 were captured in the Baelen pocket. There were 69 soldiers reported as missing in action just from the 3./ Panzergrenadier-Bataillon 2105 on this day. The headquarters company of Pz.Gren.Btl.2105, which had also been in this sector, reported 24 missing soldiers in the Heggen - Baelen area, of which two later turned out to have been killed in Heggen. The company commander of Panzer-Pionier-Kompanie 2105 was reported as missing in action at Baelen.[40] The wrecks of at least one Panther, two Sturmpanzer IVs, eight SPWs (including four Sd.Kfz.251/21s and one Sd.Kfz.251/16) and two other vehicles littered the road between Honthem and Baelen.

After the fighting south of Hockelbach, Task Force X followed up briskly. Some of its elements had advanced to Welkenraedt after swinging north of the Grünholz Woods. The advance in the direction of Herbesthal was continued after a short firefight with two Panthers from Pz.Brig.105. Herbesthal was taken by the Americans at 16:25. The column continued in the direction of Walhorn where they bivouacked for the night.[41]

To the south, Task Force 1 advanced from Eupen in the direction of Kettenis during the afternoon. Disorganized German opposition was quickly overcome. Kettenis was taken at 16:20, and Task Force 1 continued in the direction of the Libermé castle, where the advance was to be halted for the day. While moving in that direction, along Aachen Straße, the advancing Americans discovered German armored cars[42] on the high road to the north and fired on them. After half an hour, they were eliminated and most of the crew killed. These vehicles probably belonged to the 5./Pz.Gren.Btl.2105, which reported 32 missing soldiers between Herbesthal and the Walhorn Heath.[43]

In the afternoon, the remaining elements of *Kampfgruppe 9.Pz.Div.* started moving in the direction of Eynatten. Around 18:00, remnants of Pz.Brig.105 reached Eynatten with 2-3 Panthers and 30-40 men. The rest of the brigade had been scattered by low-level air attacks; some of it had been destroyed. As ordered, the Kampfgruppe of the 9. Panzer-Division established its new defensive positions along the line Eynatten - Raeren - Roetgen.[44] It remains an open question where the remnants of Sturmpanzer-Abteilung 217 were located.

The exact German losses in the area around Limbourg are not known and they only allow themselves to be reconstructed in part: in total 8 or 9 Panthers and 3 Sturmpanzer IVs. The personnel losses of Pz.Gren.Btl.2105, in contrast, were shocking. The Headquarters Company reported 3 dead and 22 missing. Although the 1./Pz.Gren.Btl.2105 reported no losses for 11 September, it was also employed in the Heggen - Baelen area like its sister company, the 3./Pz.Gren.Btl.2105. Therefore, the 37 soldiers reported as missing on 12 September were most likely missing on 11 September. The 3./Pz.Gren.Btl.2105 reported 2 dead, 69 missing and 4 wounded. The 4./Pz.Gren.Btl.2105 gave no solid data concerning its losses, other than heavy losses were incurred around Herbesthal. Finally, the 5./Pz.Gren. Btl.2105 reported 38 missing. In all, there were 5 dead, 166 missing and 4 wounded reported; a total of 175 men.

The losses sustained by *Kampfgruppe Schemm* were just as bad. At the start of the day, it had a morning report strength of 10 officers, 86 noncommissioned officers and 548 enlisted personnel for a total of 644 men. That evening, it could only report 3 officers, 8 noncommissioned officers and 72 enlisted personnel for a total of 83 men. It should be noted that this was only a snapshot in time, inasmuch as elements that had been scattered may have been able to fight their way back to the German lines, thus raising the overall end strength of the *Kampfgruppe*. Sturmpanzer-Abteilung 217 reported three men of 2. Kompanie missing in action. This indicates that the combat company consists of members of all companies. The reported losses, however, are not complete.[45]

Ten Sturmpanzer IVs for Sturmpanzer-Abteilung 217 had already been requested by the General der Panzertruppen West on 10 September. The following day, the direct allocation was approved by the Wehrmachtsführungsstab im OKW and the General der Panzertruppen West reported to Panzerstützpunkt Nord that the vehicles had departed Bielefeld by rail transport 1232. Later reports, however, prove that the transport actually departed on 16 September and reached Düren the next day.[46]

On **12 September**, *Kampfgruppe 9.Pz.Div.* failed to slow the American advance towards the Westwall. It is not clear if and where the two operational Sturmpanzer IVs, mentioned in the activity report of the General der Panzertruppen West, were brought into action.[47] According to Oberleutnant Heigl, the remaining crews of the combat company at Eynatten were employed as infantry.[48] An interesting file in the records of the LXXXI A.K. revealed that the supply trains of Sturmpanzer-Abteilung 217 had relocated to the area of Dürwiss, north of Eschweiler. The document, a permit pass, said:

> "LXXXI A.K., - Ia -:
> Permit pass for Uffz Langer[49], Stu.Pz.Abt.217, to drive 1 VW, 4 Büssing Lkw, 3 Maultiere and 2 Opel to the trains of his battalion, load new ammunition and await further orders. He is allowed to search for the trains in the area of Dürwiss."[50]

3.2 The first Battle for Aachen

Although Sturmpanzer-Abteilung 217 was still subordinated to Pz.Brig.105, respectively 9.Pz.Div., there is no trace in their combat records until 16 September implying a commitment of the battalion. The upcoming engagements, however, which would mainly take place in an urban area, would bring new opportunities. On **14 September**, the General der Panzertruppen West assigned the 9.Pz.Div., Pz. Brig.105 and Sturmpanzer-Abteilung 217 to Panzerstützpunkt Nord in Bergisch-Gladbach. He further ordered that the previously appointed refitting area in the

Netherlands had to be moved back across the Rhine.[51] Based upon the minutes of a visit of the General der Panzertruppen West at Panzerstützpunkt Nord on 17 September, we can conclude that the transfer of the battalion from Goor-Rijssen (near Arnhem) to the Düren area had not been completed by 17 September.[52]

On **15 September**, the 9.Pz.Div. reported two operational Sturmpanzer IVs.[53] The following day, this figure had not changed, but a remark was added that both vehicles were operating with Pz.Brig.105. At the time, the brigade as part of *Kampfgruppe Sperling*, was engaged between Stolberg and Gressenich against elements of Task Force 1 of the 3rd Armd Div.[54]

Whereas the situation for LXXXI A.K. remained critical in the Stolberg area, the situation on its right flank, northwest of Aachen, was also developing into a major threat. A breach in the German frontline between the 49. and 275.Inf.Div. forced the corps to deploy and attach *Regiment Munninger* to the 49.Inf.Div.[55] As it was impossible to transport the regiment to the front, the 49.Inf.Div. was unable to hold the line and prevent the American armor from reaching the heights south of Ubachsberg by 15:00, and the area of Banenheide and Bocholtzerheide to the south. The 49.Inf.Div. counterattacked with SS-Pz.Jg.Abt.10 and a group of Grenadiers against an enemy concentration near Bocholtzerheide and Simpelveld. The Americans entered Simpelveld by 19:00. The continuous artillery fire and fighter-bomber attacks resulted in heavy losses for the Germans. Just an hour later, American forces liberated Ubachsberg and planned to continue their advance in the direction of Welten and Huls. By evening, a two kilometer wide gap had been punched through the German frontline between Ubachsberg and Ransdaal.[56]

Shortly after midnight on **17 September**, LXXXI A.K. made it very clear that it would no longer accept any further retreat by the 49.Inf.Div.; the division had to hold the line, with the center of gravity on its left flank.[57]

In the morning, *Regiment Munninger* was subordinated to the 49.Inf.Div. in order to close the gap between the 49. and 275.Inf.Div.[58] Both its battalions were still deployed in the Westwall and would be transferred into their assembly zones near Bardenberg-Nord (for Bataillon 302) and around Herbach and Geilenkirchen (for Bataillon 305). At least one company remained behind in the Westwall, as they were apparently engaged with enemy forces.[59]

In the meantime, the Americans continued their attacks at 10:00 from the area of Ubachsberg and Simpelveld and managed to slowly push the positions of the 49.Inf.Div. back. On foot and by truck, Bataillon 302 and 305 reached the combat zone of the 49.Inf.Div. by 11:00. Bataillon 302 took up defensive positions in the gap near Eygelshoven. The German command was concerned about the quality of both battalions, which were poorly rated. In the morning, SS-Pz.Jg.Abt.10 launched a counterattack against Klimmen via Heerlen, supported by an infantry company from Bataillon 305. At the same time, SS-Pz.Jg.Abt.10 was subordinated to the 275.Inf.Div. The hard-pressed division had withdrawn its left flank, further expanding the gap between it and the 49.Inf.Div.[60]

Around noon, the Americans reached the outskirts of Kerkrade, forcing the Germans to alter their original attack orders for SS-Pz.Jg.Abt.10. The new directive demanded a joint-counterattack by SS-Pz.Jg.Abt.10 and the whole of Bataillon 305 in the area of Kerkrade to prevent the Americans from reaching the undefended Westwall.[61]. Around 13:00, enemy armor was observed north and south of Bocholtz, threatening the northern flank of the 116.Pz.Div between Herzogenrath and Schneeberg. This forced the 116.Pz.Div. to extend its frontline to Schneeberg via Horbach. For this purpose, elements of the Fallschirm-Jagdkommandos, who occupied the Westwall, near Orsbach and a company of Bataillon 302 near Vetschau, were subordinated to the division. Elements of Sturmpanzer-Abteilung 217, with ten recently arrived Sturmpanzer IVs in Düren[62], were brought forward. These Sturmpanzer IVs supposedly left the Heereszeugamt in Magdeburg[63] on 9 September, however, it is more likely that these vehicles were actually transported by rail (train 1232) from Bielefeld to Düren on 11 September.[64] The 49.Inf.Div. received orders to establish a connection with 116.Pz.Div. at the Westwall near Horbach. Festungs-Maschinengewehr-Bataillon 47, which was already in transit, was sent to the Herzogenrath area and attached to the division.[65] Around 15:00, the corps tasked the 116.Pz.Div. with the defense of the Westwall to Horbach. As a result, only the Fallschirm-Jagdkommando was subordinated to the division. Further to the north, the 49.Inf.Div. became responsible for the defense of the Westwall and was reinforced by the single company of Bataillon 302 at Vetschau. The ten Sturmpanzer IVs of Sturmpanzer-Abteilung 217 were to oversee the sector behind the 116.Pz.Div. up to the connection point at Horbach. Around 16:00, the situation calmed down. American forces started to dig in at the eastern exit of Bocholtz after their attack was repulsed.[66] During the course of the evening, the 49.Inf.Div. became responsible for the defense of the sector south of Heerlen, to Horbach. Between Heerlen and Nuth, the 275.Inf.Div. desperately struggled to hold off the American advance.[67] Late in the afternoon, the first elements of the newly raised 183.Volks-Gren.Div. arrived in the Geilenkirchen area.[68]

The division was ordered to take over the defense of the Westwall between Geilenkirchen and Herzogenrath. Gren.Rgt.330, which was the first to arrive on the scene, would be attached to the retreating 49.Inf.Div. and 275.Inf.Div. Due to the quick arrival of the 183.Volks-Gren.Div., Luftwaffen-Festungs-Bataillon XIII was subordinated to the 116.Pz.Div. The battalion would be directly committed at the Westwall as Horbach was reportedly already occupied by the enemy. Sturmpanzer-Abteilung 217 remained in the assigned sector, but could only be committed with the corps' approval.[69] At 22:00, the 116.Pz.Div. reported that Horbach was free of enemy. At the same time the combat company of Sturmpanzer-Abteilung 217 departed for Broichweiden.[70]

Proof of the despair in the German command can be deduced from the messages of the LXXXI A.K. during the day. At 11:30, a message on the arrival in Düren of 10 Sturmpanzer IVs for Sturmpanzer-Abteilung 217.[71] At 12:50, another report, stating that the 10 Sturmpanzer IVs and their crews in Düren were ready to move out.[72] At 14:00 instructions to subordinate these vehicles to the 116.Pz.Div. Takeover, getting ready for combat, and instructions for the new assignment in just 2.5 hours!

The armor and anti-tank weapons situation report of the LXXXI A.K. from 22:00, revealed that beside the ten freshly arrived Sturmpanzer IVs, another combat-ready Sturmpanzer IV was with Pz.Brig.105. The newly formed *Kampfgruppe Bockhoff* with attached *Kampfgruppe Pz.Brig.105* was engaged in the area of Donnerberg - Gressenich against elements of Task Force 1 of the 3rd Armd Div.[73] Another, clearly unserviceable Sturmpanzer IV, was located at the Panzerstützpunkt Nord. During a meeting at this location, which included the General der Panzertruppen West, and Oberleutnant Heigl of Sturmpanzer-Abteilung 217, it was noted that the battalion was lacking an *Entfernungsmesser auf 90cm Basis* (a 90cm range finder). Oberleutnant Heigl further mentioned that the men of the battalion were astonished that their commander was not with his troops. Heigl gave a detailed briefing on the actions of the combat company within Pz.Brig.105 during the engagements in Eastern Belgium. His report must have made an impression on the General der Panzertruppen West as he recommended Heigl for the Iron Cross First Class.[74]

As a result of the Allied air landings near Arnhem, orders were given by the General der Panzertruppen West at 19:00, to promptly reestablish the combat readiness of Sturmpanzer-Abteilung 217's combat company. In case of a possible transfer, sufficient supplies, in particular fuel and ammunition, had to be made available to the maintenance crews. A train of empty wagons for short-term railway transport had to be prepared. Command of the combat company was again given to Oberleutnant Heigl.[75]

A transfer to the area of Arnhem, however, never materialized. The battalion commander arrived in the Aachen area the next day and took command. It is not known when the battalion was reunited in the Aachen area. A telex from Heeresgruppe B to AOK 7 dated 2 October, reported that one company of Sturmpanzer-Abteilung 217 was engaged with AOK 7, while the bulk of the battalion was still being reconstituted with II. SS-Pz.Korps. The battalion, however, would now be completely subordinated to AOK 7.[76]

The proposal of the 116.Pz.Div. to transfer the attached Sturmpanzer-Abteilung 217 to Richterich was rejected on the morning of **18 September**. Instead, the battalion would be placed behind the left wing of the 49.Inf.Div. near Broichweiden. During the morning, fighting broke out on the boundary between the 49. and 275.Inf. Div. and in the areas of Eygelshoven and Molenberg.[77] Around 13:00, significant armored forces were observed moving into position in the area of Terwinselen and Spekholzerheide. A heavy artillery barrage was coming down in the area north of Terwinselen and near Kerkrade. An enemy attack was to be expected in a northeasterly direction.[78] Shortly after, American forces attacked the division's right flank and advanced to Strijthagen. *Kampfgruppe Schrader* reacted by setting up a blocking line on both sides of Hopel. At the same time, the battalion commander of Sturmpanzer-Abteilung 217 arrived at the 49.Inf.Div. command post.[79] Around 14:00, the Americans crossed the Heerlen - Kerkrade road and continued their push towards Eygelshoven.[80] By the end of the day, the 49.Inf.Div. held a 15 kilometer long line running from Niewenhagen - Eygelshoven - Kerkrade to the Westwall.[81] At 23:00 American armor and infantry entered Groenstraat, north of Eygelshoven and continued their easterly attack around midnight.[82] Sturmpanzer-Abteilung 217, which was now attached to the 49.Inf.Div., reported ten combat-ready Sturmpanzer IVs that evening. At least one other Sturmpanzer IV was still with Pz.Brig.105.[83] The battalion's command post was transferred to Merkstein.[84] The General der Panzertruppen West ordered the battalion's maintenance units, who were still held up in Auffrischungsraum Nord (reconstitution area North), to relocate to Panzerstützpunkt Nord in Bergisch-Gladbach.[85]

Since 14:00 on **19 September**, the 49.Inf.Div. had been engaged against American armor and infantry advancing to the Westwall from the direction of Eygelshoven.[86] At about 18:00, the Americans launched another attack from Spekholzerheide and occupied Gracht and Frohrath. Around 19:00, a report came in from the army stating that SS-Pz.Jg.Abt.10 would remain attached to the 49.Inf.Div.[87] Gren.Rgt.148 was engaged on the division's right-hand side, while the left flank was covered by the attached Sich.Rgt.16. The bridgehead at Kerkrade was the responsibility of both units.[88] Sturmpanzer-Abteilung 217 initially reported ten operational Sturmpanzer IVs, later reducing this figure to nine and then finally eleven Sturmpanzer IVs. Apparently, the Sturmpanzer IV with Pz.Brig.105, had returned to the battalion, as for the last time, separate information on the battalion was entered in the corps' armor and anti-tank weapons strength returns.[89]

September 20 was uneventful in the 49.Inf.Div. sector. Both sides sent out reconnaissance patrols. American artillery put down interdicting and harassing fire in the area of Merkstein and Alsdorf at irregular intervals.[90] Sturmpanzer-Abteilung 217 initially reported nine combat-ready Sturmpanzer IVs[91], which was later corrected to eleven in the corps' armor and anti-tank weapons strength return of 22:00.[92] According to the corps' instructions, 49.Inf.Div. had to deploy

Sturmpanzer-Abteilung 217 in such a way that it might intervene in both the sector of 49.Inf.Div. and 183.Volks-Gren.Div.[93.]

September 21 also passed without any notable incidents. The number of eleven operational Sturmpanzer IVs remained unchanged.[94]

The 49.Inf.Div. sector remained quiet throughout **22 September**. American scouting raids, partly supported by armor, were observed. The main combat line and rear area were under harassing fire. German artillery successfully fired a number of counter-battery missions at Eygelshoven and Groenstraat.[95] The battalion reported eight combat-ready Sturmpanzer IVs at its disposal.[96]

On **23 September**, 49.Inf.Div. experienced a quiet day. The still attached Sturmpanzer-Abteilung 217 reported eight operational Sturmpanzer IVs. Two members of the 1. Kompanie died after an air attack on the town of Neuss.[97]

September 24 was again uneventful. American artillery fire harassed the main combat line and rear area.[98] A report came at 13:30 that enemy columns had been observed for several hours on the road leading from Heerlen to Nieuwenhagen. These columns were then attacked by German artillery.[99] In the sector neighboring 183.Volks-Gren.Div., Sturmpanzer-Abteilung 217's combat company successfully engaged seven Shermans and four reconnaissance cars that were advancing in the direction of Bauchem.[100] Sturmpanzer-Abteilung 217 remained subordinated to the 49.Inf.Div. and reported eight combat-ready Sturmpanzer IVs.[101] However, an organizational chart of the 116.Pz.Div., showed Sturmpanzer-Abteilung 217 and its combat company as being in corps' reserve.[102]

September 25 remained quiet until the evening when enemy artillery and machine gun fire hit the main combat line and rear area around 22:00.[103] Sturmpanzer-Abteilung 217 reported eight serviceable Sturmpanzer IVs.[104]

At 01:00 on **26 September**, an enemy reconnaissance patrol and armored vehicle were repulsed at the boundary with the left neighbor.[105] Apart from that, no other incidents were reported. During the morning, LXXXI A.K. issued a series of orders on the reorganization and incorporation of units, training issues and the construction of defenses by subordinated divisions. The 49.Inf.Div., who had become a melting pot of marching, straggler, fortress and security battalions, was given the opportunity to incorporate these units and reorganize the division's original structure. The incorporation of the attached Sturmpanzer-Abteilung 217 was explicitly prohibited.[106] During the evening, the battalion was pulled out of the line and kept at the disposal of LXXXI A.K.[107] Only eight Sturmpanzer IVs were ready for combat, while four replacement vehicles were to be shipped directly from the manufacturer.[108]

On **27 and 28 September**, Sturmpanzer-Abteilung 217 was billeted in the area of Baesweiler as corps reserve. On the evening of 27 September, LXXXI A.K. announced the arrival of four Sturmpanzer IVs for the battalion.[109] Exactly when these vehicles arrived is not known, as no strength returns prior to 30 September survived the war. These replacement vehicles most likely arrived on 28 September, as they came directly from the manufacturer, Deutsche Eisenwerke in Duisburg.

On **29 September**, the battalion was again subordinated to the 49.Inf.Div. It remains an open question as to the motivation behind this decision, as the 49.Inf. Div. reported no major events in its sector. Sturmpanzer-Abteilung 217 reported eight combat-ready Sturmpanzer IVs.[110]

When the Americans attacked Kerkrade on **30 September** and entered the city from the north in the afternoon, Sturmpanzer-Abteilung 217 was no longer attached to the 49.Inf.Div., but together with Stu.Gesch.Brig.394 and Panzer-Kompanie (Fkl) 319 subordinated to the 183.Volks-Gren.Div. The battalion command post was located in Baesweiler.[111]

On **1 October**, Sturmpanzer-Abteilung 217 filed two reports for the period 1-30 September, which differ slightly in terms of personnel losses. Why two different reports were compiled is unclear. The first report contained an assessment from the battalion commander and illustrated the subordination of the battalion to AOK 7. The other report, however, contained an assessment by General der Infanterie Köchling, the commanding General of LXXXI A.K. and depicted the subordination of the battalion to the LXXXI A.K.

The battalion had an authorized personnel strength of 772 men and 2 civil servants. The actual personnel strength at the date of the first filed inventory was 600 men, but in the report filed later, was only 592 men, indicating a shortage of 172 or 180 men respectively. Personnel losses during September are reported to be as high as 180, respectively 193 men. On the other hand, 11 replacements arrived at the battalion during this period.

Status Report 1 October 1944[112]			
Materiel	Authorized strength	Actual strength	Combat-ready
Sturmpanzer IV	45	19	14
Motorcycle & sidecars	4	0	
Motorcycles	22	12	10
CC passenger cars	34	25	22
CO passenger cars	7	4	4
Maultiere	27	17	7
CC trucks	57	62	57
CO trucks	28	16	15
Halftracks	5	5	3
Machine guns	71	70	70

In his report, Major Lemor, also referred to the state of the equipment and noted:

"In the month of September: two batches of 10 Sturmpanzer IVs and one batch of four Sturmpanzer IV were allocated to the battalion. Five vehicles were lost in combat with Pz.Brig.105. There were 19 Sturmpanzer IVs in the battalion's inventory at the end of the month, of which 14 were actually combat-ready. The battalion should be reconstituted. It still possessed 50% of the authorized wheeled vehicles and halftrack trucks, and 25% of its prime movers = 1 vehicle. The wheeled vehicles have been serviced and are fully operational."

This confirms once more that the battalion was unable to bring back its Sturmpanzer IVs from Normandy and therefore had to be rebuilt from scratch. It remains an open question as to when and where the other two Sturmpanzer IVs were lost during their time with Pz.Brig.105. It is likely that these vehicles had already been lost in Eastern Belgium, particularly because since reaching the Westwall on 13 September, there were never more than two Sturmpanzer IVs reported in the Pz.Brig.105 area. Oberleutnant Heigl's report mentioned six Sturmpanzer IVs during the engagements in the Limbourg area, which indicates that already four Sturmpanzer IVs had dropped out with technical breakdowns or were total write-offs. Based on the latest research, reports on self-propelled 15cm guns in the area of Pepinster and Elsenborn, should be seen in connection with the 347.Inf.Div. who had a number of these vehicles in its inventory.[113]

The training and the health of the battalion's men were described as follows:

"The level of training is satisfactory. After the fighting in France and Belgium, the Sturmpanzer IV crews are experienced and familiar with modern attrition warfare. If technical failures appeared to be unusually high, this is solely due to the technical susceptibility of the vehicle and can only be imposed on the drivers in exceptional cases. Their health is very good, however colds have begun to appear. The morale of the troops is good and enthusiastic, despite the weaknesses of their vehicle."

The commanding General of the LXXXI A.K. added in his report that the combat value of the battalion was limited to defense. The allocation of additional Sturmpanzer IVs would make the battalion suitable for offensive missions.[114]

None of these reports can hide the fact that the battalion could only arm little more than a combat company with its available Sturmpanzer IVs. This is confirmed in a message from Heeresgruppe B to AOK 7 dated 2 October 1944, mentioning the commitment of one company with AOK 7 and the bulk of the battalion being reconstituted with II.SS-Pz.Korps. The complete battalion was subordinated to AOK 7, but remained in the area of Grevenbroich. Depending on the arrival of new Sturmpanzer IVs, the combat company had to be reinforced. By the end of September, orders were issued by the general staff of the High Command of the Army to reorganize Sturmpanzer-Abteilung 217 on a *freie Gliederung* (variable structure). Reorganization had to be carried out after agreement between AOK 7 and the General der Panzertruppen West. It is not clear why it took Heeresgruppe B ten days to forward this reorganization order to AOK 7.[115] The following KstN were ordered:

- Stab and Stabskompanie Stu.Pz.Abt.(f.G.) 1107 d (f.G.) dated 01.09.1944
- Sturm-Panzer-Kompanie (f.G.) 1160 (f.G.) dated 01.09.1944
- Versorgungskompanie Stu.Pz.Abt.(f.G.) 1151 d (F.G.) dated 01.09.1944
- Panzer-Werkstatt-Zug 1105 (Ausf. A) dated 01.06.1944

The corresponding KstN would be forwarded by the Chef Heeresrüstung und Befehlshaber des Ersatzheeres (Chief of Army Armament and Supreme Commander of the Replacement Army). Excess personnel were to be sent back to the relevant replacement pool. Redundant vehicles would be kept at the disposal of armored and anti-tank units under the command of Oberbefehlshaber West. The General der Panzertruppen West was responsible for a final report after completing the reorganization.[116] However, the second battle for Aachen, which began the same day, would prevent the implementation of this order.

A pair of brand-new Sturmpanzer IV Ausf.IV sent by Heereszeugamt (Army Depot) Bielefeld to Sturmpanzer-Abteilung 217 in September 1944. These tanks show the typical features of the first batch manufactured by Deutsche Eisenwerke. *Zimmerit* was applied to almost every surface of the tank, except for the *Schürzen* - one of which has a large '8' chalked on. The fourth and fifth roadwheels of the left Sturmpanzer are steel-tyred wheels, indicating that all wheels were steel-tyred. *Markus Jaugitz*

The crew's souvenir photograph. Note the reduced number of spare roadwheels on the back of the vehicle, which we have already seen on Sturmpanzer IV Ausf.IVs in Normandy. In the foreground is an interesting detail of the method of mounting the *Schürzen* on their rails: a small metal bracket welded to the back of the *Schürze* which fits over a triangular fixing. ***Markus Jaugitz***

Right: A close-up of the left Sturmpanzer permits a good view of the *Schürzen* rail and metal toolbox fitted to the left of the Sturmpanzer IV Ausf.IV. The plug for the second pistol port has been pushed outside. ***Markus Jaugitz***

3.3 The second Battle for Aachen

On **2 October,** the second battle for Aachen kicked off. The Americans planned a pincer movement that would cut the city off from its rear communications, while the city itself would be captured from the East. The northern pincer movement was executed by the XIX Corps' 30th Inf Div with the objective of establishing a bridgehead across the River Wurm near Palenberg and advancing in a southeasterly direction to Würselen. The southern pincer comprised the VII Corps' 1st Inf Div. At a later stage, they would advance from the area of Eilendorf to Verlautenheide and continue in a northwesterly direction. Both forces were to meet south of Würselen in the Ravelsberg area and close the Aachen pocket. The 1st Inf Div was tasked with the destruction of the encircled German forces. The American attack completely surprised the LXXXI A.K. In a complete misunderstanding of the imminent danger, the Germans even considered a series of counterattacks to improve their own positions. The 183.Volks-Gren.Div. planned to recapture the lost ground west of Geilenkirchen. The divisional staff were convinced that they had sufficient strength to carry out this mission, given that enough artillery ammunition was available together with an artillery observation battalion and the Sturmpanzer IVs of Sturmpanzer-Abteilung 217. It remains unclear why the division completely misjudged the situation, especially as large American concentrations had already been observed in the area of Rimburg - Scherpenseel on the night of 1-2 October.[117] In the morning, the Germans reported the usual American artillery fire. After the morning fog had lifted, the attack of the 30th Inf Div started at 11:00 between Rimburg and Marienberg, supported by an enormous artillery barrage and fighter-bombers. The attack hit the boundary between 183.Volks-Gren.Div. and 49.Inf. Div., specifically the two battalions of Gren.Rgt.330, who occupied a defensive position along the Westwall between Rimburg and Geilenkirchen. The III./Gren. Rgt.148 occupied the Westwall bunkers south of Rimburg along the River Wurm. The Germans were still able to hold off the American attack during the morning. In the afternoon, however, a breakthrough occurred northeast of Rimburg, and American forces succeeded in occupying a series of bunkers at the southwestern exit of Palenberg. Finally, the 183.Volks-Gren.Div. understood the American's point of main effort and attached the divisional reserve to its Gren.Rgt.330. With concern, however, they observed how the Americans steadily increased their forces from the direction of Scherpenseel. After sending in additional forces, the 30th Inf Div continued its attacks at 16:30 from the area east of Marienberg and the eastern district of Rimburg. During the evening, the Americans reported the capture of Palenberg, with sporadic street fighting in the town. Other elements of the 30th Inf Div entered Rimburg and reached the railroad 1 kilometer south of the town. To restore the situation, the 183.Volks-Gren.Div. proposed a counterattack with the reinforced II./Gren.Rgt.330 during the night of 2/3 October. The LXXXI A.K. in turn attached Sturmpanzer-Abteilung 217 and additional artillery to the 183.Volks-Gren.Div. The heavy American artillery fire delayed the commitment of the divisional reserve until the early hours of 3 October. During the evening, Sturmpanzer-Abteilung 217 reported fourteen combat-ready Sturmpanzer IVs and five others in short-term maintenance.[118]

Shortly after midnight, the reinforced II./Gren.Rgt.330 counterattacked north along the Merkstein Straße from the vicinity of Bunkers 23 and 25, and the area east towards Palenberg. Heavy American fire halted the German attack around 04:00 near the crossroads 118,0 and the chapel south of Palenberg. In the Rimburg area, the 30th Inf Div continued their nightly attack against the positions of the III./Gren.Rgt.148 and by 02:30 had captured Bunker 45 at the edge of Rimburg castle. During the night, the main combat line and the rear were shelled by American artillery and mortar fire. In the meantime, the 183.Volks-Gren.Div. had concentrated additional forces. Sturmpanzer-Abteilung 217, which had been subordinated to the division the previous evening, arrived in the Beggendorf area by 04:00. Sturmgeschütz-Abteilung 1219 was brought forward to the Loverich sector. Pionier-Bataillon 219 assembled in Prümmern at the disposal of the division. In addition, the corps' artillery was gathered opposite the point of penetration.

Although the morning attack of the 30th Inf Div managed to make some progress, it failed to seize the high ground north of Palenberg. Besides, the attack on Übach was halted at the west of town. The German defenders, however, could not prevent the Americans from sending additional forces to the bridgehead. In the Palenberg area, the 117th Inf Rgt (30th Inf Div) supported by the armor from Task Force Heintz of the 2nd Armd Div, advanced to the northeast in order to cover the rear and flanks of the 30th Inf Div for the upcoming attack towards Aachen. Due to Allied air superiority, the LXXXI A.K.'s actions were limited to blocking the American advance (3 October) and launching a coordinated counterattack (4 October). For this counterattack, the 183.Volks-Gren.Div. was reinforced with additional units. The attacking force had to assemble in the area north of Alsdorf – Merkstein and consisted of following units:

- II./ Grenadier-Regiment 148 (49.Inf.Div.)
- II./ Grenadier-Regiment 149 (49.Inf.Div.)
- Sturmgeschütz-Brigade 341
- Sturmgeschütz-Brigade 902
- Sturmgeschütz-Abteilung 1219
- Sturmpanzer-Abteilung 217

Meanwhile, the Americans continued their attacks and reached the western and southwestern districts of Übach by 13:00. The staff of the 183.Volks-Gren.Div. now feared that the enemy would turn to the southeast. The entire Sturmgeschütz-Abteilung 1219 was attached to Gren.Rgt.330 as was Sturmpanzer-Abteilung 217. Pionier-Bataillon 219 was transferred from Prümmern to the Waurichen area

The photo on the left probably shows the temporary company commander of 1./ Sturmpanzer-Abteilung 217 in the autumn of 1944. We know that the company commander, Oberleutnant Lucas, had been missing in action since 7 August 1944. Leutnant Olowson then took command, but was killed on 15 August. For the next five weeks, Leutnant Kiefer became the temporary commander, until Oberleutnant Gauglitz finally took over on 21 September. Therefore, it is highly likely that we see Leutnant Kiefer in the photo. Kiefer was in charge of the combat company sent to Aachen before the gap was closed in mid-October. He was seriously wounded during the final battles for the city, and became a prisoner of war on 18 October. On the right the *Spieß* (company sergeant major). **Markus Jaugitz**

and remained at the disposal of the division. In the afternoon, several American attacks with armored support were halted by the Jagdpanzers of Sturmgeschütz-Abteilung 1219 and a combination of artillery and anti-aircraft fire. By evening, the Americans had captured Übach completely. Early in the afternoon, the 183.Volks-Gren.Div. was obliged to commit part of its attacking force, after the Americans, supported by armor, managed to breach the right flank of the 49. Inf.Div. and advanced towards Merkstein - Herbach. This forced the LXXXI A.K. to extract additional infantry, armor and artillery units from the other sectors of the front. During the evening, Sturmpanzer-Abteilung 217 reported 14 combat-ready Sturmpanzer IVs and five vehicles in short-term repair.

The German counterattack against the Übach - Palenberg sector was planned to start at 01:30, but actually started with the attack of Pionier-Bataillon 219 at 02:15. The attacking force, under the command of 183.Volks-Gren.Div. was composed of the following units:

- Southern attacking force - Hptm. Schrader
  - II./ Grenadier-Regiment 148 (49.Inf.Div.)
  - II./ Grenadier-Regiment 149 (49.Inf.Div.)
  - I./ Grenadier-Regiment 352 (246.V.G.Div.)
  - Sturmgeschütz-Abteilung 1219 (183.V.G.Div.)
  - Sturmgeschütz-Brigade 341
  - Sturmgeschütz-Brigade 902,
  - Sturmpanzer-Abteilung 217
- Northern attacking force:
  - Pionier-Bataillon 219 (183.V.G.Div.)[119]

In the early hours of **4 October**, bloody close combat broke out in the streets of Übach - Palenberg. In reality, the German attackers had been unable to reach their attacking positions in time, i.e. they had already been attacked, annihilated or at least delayed in their assembly areas by American artillery. The Americans reported the first German counterattack taking place at 04:00 from an easterly direction and hitting northeast Übach. German infantry and armor managed to break into the town and started to sweep the streets with machine guns, forcing the American defenders to hole up in the cellars. The accompanying infantry would then search and clear each individual house. In turn, the American defenders engaged the German armor with rifle-grenades, forcing the German forces to pull out of town. According to German sources, the attacks on Übach - Palenberg took place from the north or the south. Therefore it remains unclear which German forces were actually involved in this initial counterattack. It cannot be ruled out that elements of II./Gren.Rgt.148 were temporarily reinforced with Sturmpanzer IVs of Sturmpanzer-Abteilung 217, although the latter was ordered to cooperate with Gren.Rgt.330. According to PWs of Gren.Rgt.330, I./Gren.Rgt.330 in the area of Beggendorf had been relieved during the night by II./Gren.Rgt.148. Although no mention of the employment of Sturmpanzer-Abteilung 217 has been made, it is clear that it must have been engaged in the area northeast of Übach. At noon, in the context of the fighting east of Übach, the battalion reported only three combat-ready Sturmpanzer IVs. In the evening the battalion announced the loss of three Sturmpanzer IVs as total write offs[120] and sixteen vehicles on hand of which twelve were operational.

From the American perspective, another German counterattack developed from the area around the Übach barracks, located southeast of the town. This attack involved I./Gren.Rgt.352 supported by elements of Pz.Jg.Abt.1219. The Germans tried all day to enter the town but only local successes could be recorded. In the afternoon, American forces managed to push the Germans out of town. At the end of the day I./Gren.Rgt.352 ceased to exist.

The northern attack by Pionier-Bataillon 219 was halted at the buildings of the Carolus Magnus coal mine and could not be continued. A forward observer with the battalion reported the arrival of fresh American forces, including 80 tanks of the 2nd Armd Div, preparing themselves for a new attack in a northern and northeastern direction. In the morning, the Americans continued their attack between the pithead stocks of Palenberg and the north of Übach, slowly pushing Pionier-Bataillon 219 back. The American armor continued north via Hoverhof. At 17:00, the Germans launched a failed counterattack from the area north of Übach. The Americans continued their attacks and reached Stegh, Muthagen, Drinhausen and the north of Blaustein with their armored spearheads. Meanwhile, other elements of the 2nd Armd Div overran the positions of Gren.Rgt.330 along the River Wurm and continued their advance to Zweibrücken and Frelenberg.

The German counterattacks south of Rimburg were more successful, pushing the 30th Inf Div back into the wooded valley of the River Wurm. But here too, the German attack stalled during the morning.[121] Despite these setbacks, the German command was still convinced that they would be able to seal off the penetration in the Palenberg area with the forces available to the LXXXI A.K. Specifically:

1. The 183.V.G.Div. leads the fight in cleaning up the enemy incursion near Palenberg
2. Will remain attached:
Regimental group Schrader with:

- I./ Grenadier-Regiment 352
- II./ Grenadier-Regiment 148
- II./ Grenadier-Regiment 149
- Sturmpanzer-Abteilung 217
- Sturmgeschütz-Brigade 902
- Sturmgeschütz-Brigade 341

3. Will be transferred with direct approval:
- Bataillon 771 B of the 12.Inf.Div.
- 1 Pak-Batterie of the 246.V.G.Div.
- Sturmgeschütz-Brigade 394 from corps' reserve of the 12.Inf.Div. and all committed elements of the 49.Inf.Div. in the new sector[122]

By 20:40 the directive was a shambles and a new order was released:

"The 183.Volks-Gren.Div. and 49.Inf.Div. will narrow the enemy penetration near Palenberg with the objective of complete elimination. For this purpose:

1. Boundary as in the morning of 4 October
2. a. Will be attached and transferred to the 183.Volks-Gren.Div. with motor transport of the army corps:
- *Brigade Raeseler with Officer Candidate School Düren and Officer Candidate School Jülich to Süggerath in order to relieve Gren.Rgt.343*
- *Grenadier-Regiment 404 by the 246.V.G.Div. to Immendorf*
Will remain subordinated:
- *Sturmgeschütz-Brigade 394*
- *Sturmgeschütz-Abteilung 1219*
- *Sturmpanzer-Abteilung 217*
- *Panzer-Kompanie 319 (Fkl)*
- *Landesschützen-Bataillon 771 B*
- *Granatwerfer-Kompanie*

2. b. 49.Inf.Div. will take command of regimental group Schrader including:
- *I./ Grenadier-Regiment 352*
- *Sturmgeschütz-Brigade 902*
- *Sturmgeschütz-Brigade 341*
- *Pak-Batterie 246*

The divisions will immediately work through the necessary details."[123]

After the destruction of most of Gren.Rgt.330, Pio.Btl.219 and I./Gren.Rgt.352 the day before, the 49.Inf.Div. sector between the Westwall south of Rimburg and Boscheln was now defended only by the remnants of five infantry battalions and two Sturmgeschütz-Brigades with only 17 combat-ready Sturmgeschützen and Sturmhaubitzen. The area between Boscheln - Holthausen and Beggendorf was defended by the remnants of I./Gren.Rgt.352 and II./Gren.Rgt.148, most likely supported by Sturmgeschütz-Abteilung 1219 and Sturmpanzer-Abteilung 217. To the south of Geilenkirchen, Sturmgeschütz-Brigade 394 and the remnants of Gren. Rgt.330 and Pio.Btl.219 were tasked with the impossible mission of containing the northern advance of the 2nd Armd Div. The promised reinforcements arrived slowly in the area of the 183.Volks-Gren.Div. The Sturmgeschütz-Brigade 394 had been transferred to the sector south of Geilenkirchen the previous evening. On the morning of **5 October** it became clear that it was impossible to set up a blocking line as the required infantry forces were not available. At 09:00, the Americans continued their attack along the road from Übach to Geilenkirchen. The Sturmgeschütze and Jagdpanzers deployed to the east managed to destroy 10 enemy tanks. Around noon, the Americans forced a break through at Muthagen and continued their advance to the north and northeast.

The forward elements of Gren.Rgt.404, which had just arrived in their assembly area, were ordered to counterattack in the direction of Breil and Muthagen, and restore the situation. Sturmgeschütz-Abteilung 1219 and Sturmpanzer-Abteilung 217 were in support. At 17:00, the Gren.Rgt.404 attack successfully blocked the American advance at the southern edges of Breil and Waurichen; even Muthagen manor was recaptured at 21:00. In the evening, 183.Volks-Gren. Div. reported its positions as follows: sector Walderath - Geilenkirchen as before, from here onwards north to Frelenberg, south of Breil, Muthagen to the southern edge of Beggendorf. While the German infantry again suffered terrible losses, Sturmgeschütz-Brigade 394 reported the loss of one Sturmgeschütz with another 13 combat-ready. Sturmgeschütz-Abteilung 1219 had several Jagdpanzer 38(t)s operational and Sturmpanzer-Abteilung 217 only two combat-ready Sturmpanzer IVs. On 6 October, the 183.Volks-Gren.Div. was organized as follows:

- Grenadier-Regiment 351 in the area of Waldenrath.
- Grenadier-Regiment 343 in the area of Geilenkirchen.
  - with attached Army Officer Candidate Schools Düren and Jülich
- Grenadier-Regiment 404 in the area of Muthagen.
  - Dependent on cooperation with Sturmpanzer-Abteilung 217 and Sturmgeschütz-Abteilung 1219
- Remnants of Grenadier-Regiment 330 in the area of Beggendorf and Frelenberg.
  - with attached Landesschützen-Bataillon 771
  - Dependent on cooperation with Sturmgeschütz-Brigade 394 and Panzer-Kompanie 319 (Fkl)[124]

During the day, the 30th Inf Div continued its attacks in a south and southeasterly direction. The 49.Inf.Div. had to retreat almost everywhere. In the evening they occupied a defensive line running from the southern edge of Beggendorf - northwest corner of Boscheln - north of the Adolf mine - Herbach - Hofstadt to Wurm.[125]

Elements of the 2nd Armd Div continued their advance in the direction of Geilenkirchen in the morning of **6 October**, supported by artillery and fighter-bombers. The first American tanks reached the area southeast of Hommerschen by 10:30, while at the same time, American armor and infantry in unknown strength were observed in the Übach sector advancing east. Eight Jagdpanzers from Sturmgeschütz-Abteilung 1219 and five Sturmpanzer IVs from Sturmpanzer-Abteilung 217 attempted to delay the American advance near Hommerschen. Combined fire from both units destroyed seven enemy tanks at Jacobshäuschen and halted the Americans along the line Hommerschen's sports area - Jacobshäuschen. The Americans then launched a secondary thrust along the R221 through Muthagen and Breil, whereupon five Jagpanzers and five Sturmpanzer IVs were relocated to Immendorf in another effort to block the enemy's advance. Only 3 Jagdpanzers remained in Hommerschen and they continued to engage the enemy armor. During the afternoon, concentrated fire from the artillery regiment and anti-aircraft battlegroup destroyed another five enemy tanks south of Jacobshäuschen. South of Waurichen, eight enemy tanks advanced towards Floverich. This put the localities of Floverich and Loverich under pressure and American armor managed to enter the German artillery firing positions. The village of Waurichen was attacked by infantry supported by 20 tanks in the afternoon. The attack extended to Muthagen Manor west of Waurichen and Breil castle to the northwest. Four Sturmhaubitzen and one Sturmpanzer IV were engaged in the sector of 4./Gren.Rgt.404. By evening, both towns were lost. Sturmpanzer-Abteilung 217 reported six combat-ready Sturmpanzer IVs and ten other vehicles in maintenance.

On the left flank of 183.Volks-Gren.Div., armor and infantry attacked from the Übach area via Blaustein towards Beggendorf, which was defended by 12 assault guns of Sturmgeschütz-Brigade 394. Throughout the day, the battle raged back and forth. Around 21:00, the Americans finally entered Beggendorf and pushed the Germans back to its eastern outskirts. In the 49.Inf.Div. sector, elements of the 30th Inf Div managed to overcome the stronghold near Boscheln and continued their advance to Altmerberen against weakening German opposition. To the west, the 49.Inf.Div. tried to regain the initiative and recapture the bunkers lost the previous day in Merkstein - Herbach. The attack, supported by several Sturmgeschütze, obviously surprised the Americans as six bunkers were abandoned in quick succession. Resistance then stiffened, and the Americans attacked, driving the Germans back to their positions near Hofstadt and Herbach that afternoon. The LXXXI A.K., realizing the potential break-up of 49.Inf.Div.'s front, transferred a battalion from 12.Inf.Div. and freshly arrived elements of the Sturmgeschütz-Kompanie of Pz.

Jg.Abt.12 to the Alsdorf area.[126]

On the morning of **7 October**, in the sector south of Geilenkirchen, the 2nd Armd Div attacked and occupied the village of Breil with armor and infantry. Further progress towards Immendorf was stopped by flanking fire originating east of Jacobshäuschen. The 183.Volks-Gren.Div. had concentrated its armored forces: Sturmgeschütz-Brigade 394, Sturmgeschütz-Abteilung 1219 and Sturmpanzer-Abteilung 217 in Apweiler with 4 Sturmgeschütze and 1 Sturmpanzer IV, and a further 4 Sturmgeschütze and 5 Sturmpanzer IVs in Floverich. During the morning, several American armor concentrations were observed and harassed by concentrated fire from German artillery. The Americans repeatedly tried to advance in the direction of Geilenkirchen and Immendorf throughout the day but were repelled by the combined fire of German armor, anti-tank weapons and artillery. In the evening, the Americans were reported to be digging in. On the extreme left flank of the 183.Volks-Gren.Div., the situation was quiet. The 2nd Armd Div went on the defensive in the line south of Geilenkirchen - east of Beggendorf - west of Oidtweiler to protect the 30th Inf Div flank. During the evening, Sturmpanzer-Abteilung 217 reported eight operational Sturmpanzer IVs and eight vehicles in short-term repair.

In the 49.Inf.Div. sector, the Americans harried the German formations decimated in the preceding days, and during the morning, elements of the 117th Inf Rgt entered Baesweiler and Alsdorf. The recently arrived II./Gren.Rgt.48, which had taken up defensive positions between both villages, was bypassed and then annihilated. In the course of the day, the Americans captured Baesweiler, Neuweiler and Alsdorf, making the situation for the German defenders precarious. An American breakthrough in the direction of Mariadorf and subsequent loss of the R57 near Alsdorf meant that another vital supply route into Aachen had gone. Therefore, the Germans decided to counterattack with fresh forces and close the gap at Alsdorf on 8 October. The situation west of Alsdorf had now become critical. The Americans captured Merkstein and advanced south along a broad front towards Herzogenrath.[127]

Local American attacks in the 183.Volks-Gren.Div. sector defined **8 October**. Sturmpanzer-Abteilung 217 received orders in the morning to redirect to the 49. Inf.Div. The battalion commander was to report to the divisional headquarters at Hoengen immediately, ending the battalion's six-day deployment with 183. Volks-Gren.Div. The war diary of the LXXXI A.K., however, recorded a change in command and placed the Sturmpanzer-Abteilung 217 under the command of 12. Inf.Div. It can be assumed that the corps initially intended to use the division as part of the counterattack in the Alsdorf area, but then, due to developments in the Aachen area, the battalion was transferred south to 12.Inf.Div. The corps' order on 9 October stated: *"In addition, the enemy breach at Haaren should be destroyed.*

Füs.Btl.246 and Sturmpanzer-Abteilung 217 will be attached to the 12.Inf.Div." The battalion's strength return of 8 October reflected the situation the previous day, i.e. sixteen Sturmpanzer IVs on hand of which eight were combat-ready and eight others in short-term maintenance.

In the 49.Inf.Div. sector, the 117th Inf Rgt intended, as feared by the Germans, to continue its advance from Alsdorf to Mariadorf and thus cut the supply route between Aldenhoven and Aachen. German forces in the Mariadorf sector, however, were set on recapturing Alsdorf. The German leadership placed a great hope in the newly arrived *Schnelle Regiment von Fritschen.* Sturmgeschütz-Brigaden 341 and 902 and Sturmgeschütz-Abteilung 1012 with a total of 22 Sturmgeschützen were assigned to support the regiment. Initially, the Americans dictated events and their leading elements entered Mariadorf. By 09:00 on **9 October**, the German counterattack made itself felt, forcing the Americans to abandon Mariadorf. A battalion of *Schnelle Regiment von Fritschen* advanced through Schaufenberg and dug in at Alsdorf. American counterattacks were repelled throughout the day. In the afternoon, however, the Germans were forced to abandon Alsdorf once again. Even an attack by the newly arrived Pz.Brig.108 failed. The 30th Inf Div also recognized that with the available forces, further attacks in the direction of Mariadorf would have little success. The 117th Inf Rgt went over to defense. To the west, in the 246.Volks-Gren.Div. sector; Herzogenrath, Niederbardenberg, Reifeld and Duffesheide were lost. In the Aachen sector, the 1st Inf Div was thrown into battle and attacked north from Eilendorf, the leading elements reaching Verlautenheide and Haarener Steinkreuz by evening. After the successful defense of Mariadorf, a link-up between the 1st and 30th Inf Divs in the Würselen sector now threatened the German front. The German leadership planned to push the Americans back in a series of separate actions the next day.[128]

While the fighting between Geilenkirchen and Alsdorf almost came to a standstill on 9 October, events moved to the left and right flanks of 246.Volks-Gren.Div. During the morning, the 119th and 120th Inf Rgt advanced to the Schleibach - Birk - Bardenberg - Pley line. Elements of the 119th Inf Rgt were already moving toward Morsbach when a counterattack by Pz.Brig.108 started at midday. Birk was recaptured despite significant American opposition. That evening, lead elements of Pz.Brig.108 entered Bardenberg and cut off the 119th's advance in Morsbach from their rear communications. This ended the fighting in the area.

The American attacks towards Haaren, from Verlautenheide, forced elements of 246.Volks-Gren.Div. to retreat northeast, and during the day, these forces were placed under the command of 12.Inf.Div. The division had intended to recapture Verlautenheide early in the morning but with insufficient forces and armored support, this resulted in heavy German losses. Sturmpanzer-Abteilung 217 did not reach the new combat area in time; this is confirmed by the corps' armor strength return which again reflected the situation on the evening of 7 October. It is noteworthy, however, that for unexplained reasons, personnel from the 3rd Company were transferred to the Stabskompanie on 8/9 October. The same goes for personnel of the Panzerwerkstattkompanie who were transferred back to Pz. Ers.u.Ausb.Abt.18 at Kamenz.

After resisting German counterattacks, the 1st Inf Div continued its advance. On the night of 9/10 October, they captured Ravelsberg and its bunkers by surprise. Other elements passed through Forst in the direction of Aachen, intending to clear the eastern suburbs and reach the Aachen - Cologne railroad.[129]

Elements of 30th Inf Div recaptured Birk on **10 October**, and in turn, cut off Pz. Brig.108, who had advanced to Bardenberg. German attempts to reopen the supply road failed because of combined fire from the defending Americans and the relief troops being exhausted. The German main combat line was consolidated at the northern edge of Würselen and along the Würselen - Euchen - Mariadorf road. Without fresh reserves, the German troops at Bardenberg could not be relieved. Meanwhile, the 1st Inf Div handed a 24-hour ultimatum to the combat commander of Aachen with the request to surrender the city. Other than that, the division consolidated its positions, in particular, the northeastern defense front between Ravelsberg - Haarener Steinkreuz -Verlautenheide and Eilendorf, against the expected German counterattacks. In fact, the Germans did attack again that day. The progress of the newly arrived Pionier-Sturm-Regiment 1 to the area of Haarener Steinkreuz was checked, as had been the case with Pio.Btl.12 in the Verlautenheide sector. Once again, no armor was available to the attackers.

The corps' actual counterattack against the enemy penetration at Verlautenheide - Haaren - Kalkofen was scheduled for the next day. The 12.Inf.Div. together with the remnants of II./Gren.Rgt.352, a Kampfgruppe from the 2.Pz.Div. (*Bataillon Bucher*), Pionier-Sturm-Regiment 1 and Sturmgeschütz-Brigade 394 reinforced by Sturmpanzer-Abteilung 217, was tasked with recapturing the old positions in the 2nd Westwall line. *Kampfgruppe Bucher*, however, still had to arrive from the Eifel before the attack order could be implemented and Sturmgeschütz-Brigade 394, which had been deployed in the area of the 183.Volks-Gren.Div., only received its marching orders at 22:15. The Germans clearly did not realize that II./Gren. Rgt.352 had been annihilated in the preceding days. Conversely, Sturmpanzer-Abteilung 217 arrived with four Sturmpanzer IVs in the 12.Inf.Div. sector at 00:20 on 11 October. Why did it take two and a half days to transfer the battalion from Geilenkirchen to the Weiden sector? Even if the American advance blocked the shortest route, the battalion should still have arrived in the 12.Inf.Div.'s area by 9 October. It is possible that the battalion was redirected at short notice and engaged in the Würselen area.

According to the somewhat inaccurate post war report of Oberst Wilck, divisional commander of the 246.Volks-Gren.Div., Sturmpanzer-Abteilung 217 and I./Gren. Rgt.352 defended the Bardenberg area on 10 October. The infantry battalion was supposedly withdrawn in order to lead a counterattack with an SS regiment. It is correct that I./Gren.Rgt.352 had been decimated in previous engagements. The SS regiment, however, which was probably *Bataillon Rink* of *Kampfgruppe Diefenthal*, did not arrive in the Würselen area until 11 October which suggests that Wilck's memory failed him. His recollections more likely refer to *Bataillon Bucher's* attack on Haaren the following day. The commitment of Sturmpanzer-Abteilung 217, however, cannot be excluded. According to the corps' armor strength return, the battalion was attached to the 12.Inf.Div; this was later corrected by hand to 246. Volks-Gren.Div. Sturmpanzer-Abteilung 217 reported five combat-ready and 11 vehicles in repair on the evening of 10 October.[130]

The arrival of the first elements of 116.Pz.Div. on **11 October** raised hopes within the German command, who not only intended to stabilize the current situation through a series of counterattacks but also hoped to recapture some lost ground. For these counterattacks, only one armored Kampfgruppe from 116.Pz.Div. and *Kampfgruppe Diefenthal* with two weak infantry battalions were available. The German command did not concentrate these forces but instead formed two attacking groups with different objectives. The northern force consisted of *Kampfgruppe Bayer* of 116.Pz.Div., remnants of Pz.Brig.108 with attached s.Pz. Abt.506, a battalion of *Kampfgruppe Diefenthal* and Sturmgeschütz-Brigade 902. They were tasked with restoring the situation in the Würselen area and the relief of the rest of Pz.Brig.108 encircled in Bardenberg. Although the group recaptured Würselen that afternoon, accomplishing the second part of the order proved to be impossible. Instead, they went over to the defense. At the end of the day, the German defenders in Bardenberg capitulated.

The southern attacking force was formed around II./Gren.Rgt.352, the other battalion from *Kampfgruppe Diefenthal*, Pionier-Sturm-Regiment 1, Sturmgeschütz-Brigade 394 and Sturmpanzer-Abteilung 217. It had considerable problems in becoming operational. *Kampfgruppe Diefenthal's Bataillon Bucher* had still not arrived by morning, II./Gren.Rgt.352 had been decimated in previous days, and Pionier-Sturm-Regiment 1 suffered severe losses the day before and was forced onto the defensive.

The 12.Inf.Div. canceled the scheduled counter-attack in the morning and reported at 05:00 to the LXXXI A.K:

"The division must point out the difficult position on its right flank, where the newly attached Gren.Rgt.352 with one battalion [author: II./Gren.Rgt.352] was pushed back on a 3 kilometer wide front, holding its current positions in the form of strongpoints without any connection to its left neighbor. One kilometer northeast of the battalion's left flank, elements of the not combat-ready Pionier Bataillon [author: Pionier-Sturm-Regiment 1] were holding a switch position with connection to both sides. It is expected that the enemy will attack our weak defensive line with strong armored forces and make the final assault into the city. The division has not been able to communicate with the commander of Kampfgruppe Diefenthal. This means that it will be impossible to bring the battalion [author: Kampfgruppe Bucher] forward by morning, in time for the planned flanking attack against enemy forces advancing towards Aachen. With the exception of weak alarm units and stragglers, additional forces are not available to reinforce the battalion on the division's extreme right flank. The division will endeavor to prevent the enemy from advancing westward with heavy weapons, particularly artillery and Sturmgeschütze and Sturmpanzers that arrived last night, and delay his advance westward at the blocking position southeast of Haarener Steinkreuz." [131]

Only with the arrival of *Bataillon Bucher*, did the Germans realize that the 1st Inf Div had taken the Ravelsberg and its bunkers during the night. The battalion, therefore, had to recapture these positions, and the counterattack was scheduled for 15:00. Due to the unclear situation, both companies would execute a pincer movement from their positions south of Würselen against the bunker line on the Ravelsberg. Developing enemy resistance would be destroyed by the assault guns of Sturmgeschütz-Brigade 394. The four Sturmpanzer IVs of Sturmpanzer-Abteilung 217 were tasked with supporting the brigade. American artillery and mortar fire rained down on the Grenadier companies as they reached their starting positions. The battalion finally attacked at 17:00. The left company made good progress until pinned down in front of the woods by heavy flanking machine gunfire. With the support of the Sturmgeschütze, they managed to enter the woods but the Sturmgeschütze were unable to follow in the dense woods. A sudden American counterattack supported by two Shermans succeeded in pushing the weakened company back out of the woods. The redeployment of the Sturmgeschütze triggered the retreat of the Grenadiers, who fell back to their starting positions. The already weak company lost 26 men. The company on the right flank initially managed to capture several bunkers on the western part of the Ravelsberg, but were pinned down by enemy fire and could only recapture a few bunkers during the night. The company lacked the necessary men to occupy all recaptured bunkers. In its evening report, Sturmpanzer-Abteilung 217 recorded four combat-ready Sturmpanzer IVs and twelve vehicles in short-term maintenance. After the American ultimatum to surrender Aachen remained unanswered, approximately 300 bombers attacked the city. In the evening, the 1st Inf Div infiltrated German positions near Rothe Erde (Red Earth) railway station, which could only be repelled after the combat commander of Aachen had released its reserves.[132]

This Sturmpanzer IV Ausf.IV was pictured by a German photographer in the Löffelstraße in Baesweiler on 3 October 1944, moving in the direction of Übach-Palenberg. Although the American attack to encircle Aachen started the day before, no camouflage materials are visible on the Sturmpanzer. The crew appears to be quite relaxed considering the front was less than four kilometers away. The tank must have been from the second production batch manufactured by Deutsche Eisenwerke, because it shows no sign of *Zimmerit*. The vehicle has a three-tone camouflage pattern, and a *Balkenkreuz* on the left side of the superstructure. *Timm Haasler*

On the night of **11/12 October**, I.SS-Pz.Korps took command of the right flank of LXXXI A.K. The 183.Volks-Gren.Div., 49.Inf.Div., 116.Pz.Div. and the remnants of a number of units were placed under the corps' command in the sector stretching from Geilenkirchen - Siersdorf - Mariadorf - Euchen - Würselen to Kohlscheid. The reinforced 116.Pz.Div. received orders once again to recapture Bardenberg to restore the situation between Euchen and Kohlscheid. The division assembled two attacking forces. The first group would attack between Euchen and Würselen, reach Birk and then advance west to Bardenberg. Under combined fire from American infantry, artillery and fighter-bombers, the attack barely gained any ground. The second group advanced through Würselen in the direction of the Gouley coal mine. Here, too, the Germans met heavy fire and were forced to halt the attack during the morning. An American infantry attack on the division's left flank against Würselen, forced *Kampfgruppe Diefenthal* to go over to defense. During the night of 12/13 October, the German leadership chose to continue these attacks with the same objectives.

The LXXXI A.K. was not only tasked with holding Aachen and the line between Verlautenheide - Stolberg - Gressenich with the remnants of 246.Volks-Gren. Div. and 12.Inf.Div., they also had to contain the American incursion between Ravelsberg - Haaren and Verlautenheide. The corps' efforts centered on Ravelsberg, as the American positions threatened Reichstraße 57, i.e. the last remaining supply route into Aachen. *Kampfgruppe Bucher*, with II./Gren.Rgt.352, Sturmgeschütz-Brigade 394 and Sturmpanzer-Abteilung 217, was ordered to repeat the attack on the Ravelsberg heights and thus finally close the gap on the northern edge of Aachen. Although the attack was scheduled for the morning, *Kampfgruppe Bucher* did not move out till 10:00. The development of the situation remained unclear for the German leadership; it was only in the afternoon that it became clear that the Americans had recaptured a large number of bunkers lost the previous day. *Kampfgruppe Bucher's* losses were so high that the remaining men could no longer occupy the recaptured bunkers. There are no detailed records regarding Sturmpanzer-Abteilung 217 on this day. During the evening, the battalion reported seven combat-ready Sturmpanzer IVs and nine vehicles in short-term repair. The Americans continued air attacks on Aachen. The 1st Inf Div continued their attack and reached the industrial area between Aachen and Haaren by evening, threatening the Nordbahnhof area. The combat commander had no reserves left to contain the attack. All future efforts would depend on reinforcements.[133]

The 116.Pz.Div.'s continuation of the counterattack on **13 October** was canceled. Instead, the division was ordered to release the attached elements of *Kampfgruppe Rink* and transfer them to the combat commander of Aachen. The relief attempt failed when the attacking Americans decimated the division's relief force (Pionier-Bataillon); *Kampfgruppe Diefenthal* was forced back to its old positions.

The situation in Aachen became more critical by the hour. Instead of the promised reinforcements, only Gren.Rgt.404 arrived. A week after the division had to give up the regiment to 183.Volks-Gren.Div., it had a strength of fewer than 300 men. Unaware of the presence and location of American positions, elements of the regiment were annihilated when they moved to their assigned positions. The 1st Inf Div advanced east to west and pushed the German defenders back behind the Jülicher Straße. The 26th Inf Rgt reached a line stretching along the Viktoriastraße - Ostfriedhof and Jülicher Straße. In the current situation, the corps ordered Sturmpanzer-Abteilung 217[134], Sturmgeschütz-Brigade 341 and 2./Art.Rgt.246, with fuel and ammunition, to Aachen. Supposedly, Soers and Kohlscheid (Klein) had not been occupied by the Americans by 16:30. This meant that there was still an open road from Wolfsfurt to Kohlscheid (Klein) and Soers to Aachen. The first breakthrough attempt failed due to the intense Americans artillery and anti-tank fire in the area of Ravelsberg. Also, *Kampfgruppe Bucher* was forced to go on the defense.

At 21:10, orders were issued for Sturmgeschütz-Brigade 341 and Sturmpanzer-Abteilung 217 to prepare themselves behind the front line of Landes-Schützen-Bataillon II/6 along the River Wurm, southwest of Würselen. They were tasked with advancing to Wilck's headquarters when the situation improved. As with the previous day, Sturmpanzer-Abteilung 217 reported seven combat-ready Sturmpanzer IVs and nine vehicles in short-term repair. During the night, AOK 7 inserted the 3.Pz.Gren.Div. into the line near Verlautenheide, in the vicinity of 12. Inf.Div. The next day's attack was intended to breach the American front line near Verlautenheide and move through Haaren to Aachen. The German command promised a clear relief of the combat commander and restoration of the German positions in the east and northeast of the city.[135]

On the morning of **14 October**, American units attacking the positions of the 116. Pz.Div. in the Würselen area were resisted. Generally, the opposing forces between Euchen and Würselen were neutralized. The American command instructed the 30th Inf Div to establish a connection with the 1st Inf Div near the Ravelsberg, and thereby close the Aachen pocket. That night, *Kampfgruppe Rink* was released from the defense of Würselen and moved to Aachen. The decimated *Kampfgruppe Bucher* in the Ravelsberg sector was reinforced with a company from *Kampfgruppe Rink*. In the meantime, the Germans had given up trying to recapture the strategic heights. Attacks against Würselen by the 30th Inf Div forced *Kampfgruppe Bucher* to deploy its reserves in a rearward blocking line so as not to be surprised by an attack from the rear. In Aachen, the combat commander reported intense attacks coming from the east against his headquarters at Quellenhof and repeatedly called for the immediate allocation of reinforcements. After the failure to reach Aachen the previous day, LXXXI A.K. ordered at 00:00 that Sturmgeschütz-Brigade 341 and Sturmpanzer-Abteilung 217 were to reach Aachen, if necessary without infantry protection! At 05:00 both armored units and 2./Art.Rgt.246 advanced along the Krefelder-Straße, but were soon subjected to American fire, forcing them to turn back. Meanwhile, the 26th Inf Rgt continued advancing on a line to the west in the morning. The 3rd Battalion reached Paßstraße and entered the city park. The advance was halted when the 2nd Battalion, advancing on its southern flank, was held up.

It would take until the next morning before the 2nd and 3rd Battalions could link up. Therefore the battalion's actions were limited to improving their forward lines. The tower of the meteorological observatory located in the city park and the Hansemannplatz were the points of gravity during the fighting. The remnants of Gren.Rgt.404 succeeded in halting the American advance.

At 11:30, the commanding general of LXXXI A.K. again requested the reckless commitment of Sturmgeschütz-Brigade 341 and Sturmpanzer-Abteilung 217. Both armored units and the Pak-Artilleriebatterie were to force a breakthrough towards Quellenhof. At 12:38, LXXXI A.K. again pointed out to 246.Volks-Gren.Div. that the road through Soers and Teuterhof was still open. The Sturmgeschützbrigade, Sturmpanzerabteilung and Pakbatterie were to advance by that route. An American incursion in Würselen, however, prevented an immediate start. At 16:30, 1./Sturmgeschütz-Brigade 341 with seven Sturmhaubitzen, the combat company of Sturmpanzer-Abteilung 217 with six Sturmpanzer IVs and 2./Art. Rgt.246 with four 7.5cm Pak under the command of Hptm. Fink (commander of the Pz.Jg.Abt.246), started their attack. At 20:00, the combat commander reported that six Sturmgeschütze and two Sturmhaubitzen had arrived in Quellenhof. This report is confirmed by the statement of three enlisted men of the 1st Company who were captured on 17 October near Weiden. Later reports proved that a total of seven assault guns, three assault tanks, and four anti-tank guns had managed to push into Aachen. Three Sturmpanzer IVs suffered damage to their running gear and had to be destroyed. The armor did not encounter enemy resistance during their drive from Wolsfurth - Soers to Quellenhof. The combat company of Sturmpanzer-Abteilung 217 was essentially a platoon of the 1st Company under the command of Leutnant Wolfgang Kiefer. Although Kiefer was captured on 18 October, he was still awarded the *Ehrenblattspange des Heeres* (The Honor Roll Clasp of the Army) on 5 December.

The Württemberger Zeitung, stated on 8 January 1945:

> **"Fought fiercely despite heavy injury**
> *Twenty year old Leutnant Wolfgang Kiefer from Stuttgart-Feuerbach has performed with excellence during the fighting on the Western front in the month of October (on 14.10.1944), and was awarded the Honor Roll Clasp of the Army. As a platoon leader in a Sturmpanzer-Abteilung, Kiefer received an*

> *order to reach the combat commander of Aachen with his battlegroup. He was severely injured in his neck and the back of his head by cut tram wires, but this did not prevent him from carrying out the mission and finding a route unoccupied by the enemy. Even though he was wounded again in the next few days by grenade splinters on the thigh and back, as well as a head wound, he continued to fight at the front of his Sturmpanzers, until he collapsed as a result of the injuries."* [136]

The value of these armored vehicles must be regarded as dubious. The Sturmhaubitze and Sturmpanzer IV are not suited for direct tank combat and are only useful in urban fighting when they are used as mobile artillery pieces capable of shelling the opponent's positions. The vehicles require fuel, which is already scarce, and special ammunition. Regarding the 15cm ammunition for the Sturmpanzer IV, Colonel Wilck later reported that this had already been exhausted by 15 October and that the remaining Sturmpanzer IVs had broken down before further combat. On the evening of 14 October, the combat commander Aachen had seven 10.5cm Sturmhaubitzen, three 15cm Sturmpanzer, four 7.5cm Pak/Artillery guns, thirteen 10.5cm light field howitzers, and a number of Pak guns that were not quantifiable. Obviously, the corps planned to transfer additional armored elements to Aachen.

In a report to the army group at 23:10:

> *"Reinforcement by Sturmpanzer-Abteilung and Sturmgeschützbrigade of which the first has arrived and the second will follow with infantry and anti-tank guns".* [137]

This was the only message that has been found. There is no question that both Sturmpanzer-Abteilung 217 and Sturmgeschütz-Brigade 341 had serviceable elements outside the pocket. In the evening, Sturmpanzer-Abteilung 217 reported an actual strength of thirteen Sturmpanzer IVs, of which five were ready for combat and eight were in short-term repair. By nightfall on 14 October, the 3.Pz.Gren.Div. attacked American positions near Verlautenheide. Although the German deployment was initially not spotted by the Americans, they reacted quickly and with intensity. American artillery effectively sealed-off the combat area and prevented the Germans from sending in further reinforcements, which could have assisted the attackers at Verlautenheide. [138]

In Aachen on **15 October**, Sturmgeschütz-Brigade 341 reported five combat-ready Sturmhaubitzen, and Sturmpanzer-Abteilung 217, two operational Sturmpanzer IVs. By morning, the long-awaited *Kampfgruppe Rink* finally arrived at the combat commander's headquarters. The Kampfgruppe was not the anticipated reinforcement because it numbered only 128 men. Oberst Wilck intended to use the Kampfgruppe to recapture the area around the meteorological observatory, which endangered the position of his headquarters. Ostuf. Rink brought his mortars into position near the tower of the Quellenhof. Following a ten-minute mortar barrage, the Kampfgruppe attacked in the early morning with the remnants of Gren.Rgt.404 and the combat-ready Sturmgeschütze and Sturmpanzer IVs.

The attack reached the heights of the meteorological observatory and the spa gardens. Both sides suffered terrible losses. Elements of the Kampfgruppe executed a flanking maneuver along the Pippinstraße - Chlodwigstraße, captured a series of houses and then went over to defense. The 3rd Battalion of the 26th Inf Rgt managed to recapture the meteorological observatory. Several tanks were knocked out by a Sturmgeschütz from Sturmgeschütz-Brigade 341. In the course of the evening, *Kampfgruppe Rink* was forced to defend the Quellenhof. To the south, the 2nd Battalion of the 26th Inf Rgt secured the open left flank of the 3rd Bn. While the Americans maintained pressure on German positions in the east of the city, the situation in the south and west of the city remained calm. This allowed the combat commander to withdraw some forces from these areas which was critical, as more and more units were showing signs of disintegration and turning themselves into to the Americans. Another attempt to push reinforcements in the city on the night of 16 October was only partially successful. Of the 130 Schutzpolizisten who started on the Krefeld road, only 47 'policemen' reached the combat commander's command post.

Outside the city, attack and counterattack in the Würselen area alternated, with neither side making any real progress. In the Ravelsberg - Haaren sector, local attacks took place despite the omnipresent American artillery.

The situation at Verlautenheide, where 3.Pz.Gren.Div. was ordered to restart counterattacks, remained confusing. The division sent in reinforcements, which should only have been used once they broke through American lines near Verlautenheide and Knapp. The breakthrough had to be consolidated but failed due to uninterrupted fire from American artillery, infantry, and armored units. Allied fighter-bombers dropped their bombs close to friendly positions. After dark, 3.Pz.Gren.Div. reorganized its depleted units and tried once more to force a breakthrough before midnight. After finally breaking the American lines, artillery fire set in preventing any further movement. During the night, the German command decided to no longer reinforce the combat commander as no more reinforcements were available. That evening, Sturmpanzer-Abteilung 217 reported five combat-ready Sturmpanzer IVs and eight in short-term maintenance.[139]

On **16 October**, the 30th Inf Div intended to reestablish a connection with 1st Inf Div in the Ravelsberg area, thereby closing the Aachen pocket. For the first time in days, the division executed a spoiling attack between Würselen and Mariadorf to draw away important German forces from the Würselen sector. West of Würselen, other divisional elements worked their way south on both sides of the River Wurm, bypassing German defensive positions. The attack made good progress and reached a point south of Teuterhof, where German resistance increased and halted the advance. It was only after preparations for the assault between Würselen and Mariadorf were made, that the focus of the German artillery was shifted to this area, enabling the American forces west of Würselen to continue their advance and establish a connection with the 1st Inf Div. East and northeast of Verlautenheide, 3.Pz.Gren.Div. were preparing for combat. While the division's armored group was held up by a minefield at the northeastern edge of town, other parts of the division entered the village from the east and drove a significant wedge into the American defenses. German infantry supported by armor also infiltrated in the area between Quinx and Knapp. By the end of the day, all attacks had been stopped. The division's heavy losses prompted the army to cancel the attack in the afternoon of 16 October.

In Aachen, the Americans continued their systematic approach during the morning. Supported by armor and self-propelled artillery, infantry forces advanced and overwhelmed the German strong points with direct fire from heavy weapons. The 3rd Bn of 26th Inf Rgt tried to hold the line and reorganized its troops. In the morning, the Germans attacked south of Quellenhof with two infantry companies supported by several Sturmgeschützen. The canon platoon of the 3rd Bn destroyed one Sturmgeschütz south of Quellenhof, in the Monheimsallee. This action set the German retreat into motion. The 2nd Bn of the 26th Inf Rgt reached the Kaiserplatz in the afternoon, but the fighting turned into a stalemate. To the south, other elements of the battalion advanced to Wilhelmstraße. Around 17:00, American artillery harassed a concentration of German infantry and armor near Theaterstraße - Bahnhofstraße. Shortly after, a German counterattack with infantry and two Sturmgeschütze developed along the Theaterstraße. The Sturmgeschütze fired a few shots and then pulled back. The Americans repeatedly reported the presence of German Sturmgeschütze throughout the day, but no Sturmpanzer IVs. It is possible that the remaining Sturmpanzer IVs were not operational, or that they were not identified as such by the Americans. Around noon, an officer from the 246.Volks-Gren.Div. managed to escape the pocket. He reported to the divisional combat post and delivered the strength return to the combat commander, shown on the next page.[140]

The interesting point about this report is that it does not mention Sturmhaubitzen or Sturmpanzers. The reported personnel, however, are the equivalent of ten Sturmhaubitze 42 crews and four Sturmpanzer IVs crews. On 14 October, only seven Sturmhaubitzen and three Sturmpanzer IVs managed to return to the city. Therefore, it cannot be ruled out that the reported total actually contains administrative or maintenance personnel. That evening, the combat commander's headquarters moved to a bunker on the corner of Rütscherstraße and Försterstraße, at the foot of the Lousberg. The strength return of Sturmpanzer-Abteilung 217 reported only three combat-ready Sturmpanzer IVs. The other ten vehicles were all in short-term maintenance.[141]

After their failed attempts to keep the Aachen pocket open, AOK 7 used **17 October** to reorganize its units. Meanwhile, the 30th Inf Div continued to clear the terrain east of the River Wurm and advanced towards the west of Würselen. Some German defenders, supported by Sturmgeschütze managed to resist local attacks, but the fighting ability of the majority was broken. Only the allocation of a

Elements of 246.Volks-Gren.Div.:

• Stab des Kampfkommandanten	20
• Remains of Stabskompanie Gren.Rgt.689	20
• I./ Grenadier-Regiment 404	90
• Feld-Ersatz-Bataillon 246	422 (11:144:297; HQ & 3 Cos)
• Elements Art.Rgt.246	95 (3 Batteries.)

Attached Units:

• Festungs-Infanterie-Bataillon 1421	419 (10:78:406; HQ & 4 Cos.)
• Fallschirmjäger-Jagd-Kommando	436 (8:64:366, HQ & 2 Cos.)
• I./ Grenadier-Regiment 149	458 (9:49:400, HQ & 4 Cos.)
• 6./ Grenadier-Regiment 984	50
• Kampfgruppe Rink	124 (4:20:100, HQ & 2 Cos.)
• Sturmgeschütz-Brigade 341	42
• Sturmpanzer-Abteilung 217	20

Weapons:

• Panzerjäger (anti-tank)	20 Pak & 1 Kpfw. kanone
• Flak (anti-aircraft)	5x 2cm Flak
• schwere Infanterie-Waffen	2 le.Inf.Ges. + 4x 8cm Gr.W.

Together:

- Infantry, HQs, Heavy weapons: 2,039 | Artillery and Sturmhaubitzen: 57
- Battle strength of the combat commander: 2,196 | Medical personnel: 11 doctors and 34 medics.

battalion of stragglers prevented the collapse of the front between Ravelsberg, the stop point at Kaiseruh and the west of Würselen. Otherwise, the day outside the pocket was relatively quiet. In Aachen, American forces attacked simultaneously from the east and south, broke through the German positions and systematically cleared all the houses. The remaining forces could do no more than hold out. The 3rd Bn of the 26th Inf Rgt not only defended its positions in the area of Quellenhof, but also tried to outflank the position by advancing against the Lousberg. At 16:00, a German self-propelled vehicle fired a few shots at the meteorological observatory and destroyed its tower which the Americans were using as an artillery observation post.[142] To the south, the 2nd Bn, 26th Inf Rgt turned to defense between Jülicher Straße and Aldalbertsteinweg. German anti-tank guns covered the likely axis of approach. Other elements of the battalion tried in vain to cross the nearby Wilhelmstraße. Despite German resistance, the battalion pushed its own line further to the west.

During the day, the positions of the combat commander came under pressure from the north. The 30th Inf Div, who had worked their way down the River Wurm to Kohlscheid, succeeded in throwing back the Germans to a blocking position north of Richterich. To make matters worse, the men inside the pocket were deprived of supplies. Multiple attempts to supply the city through an airlift had not produced any results. Sturmgeschütz-Brigade 341 reported only one combat-ready Sturmhaubitze, Sturmpanzer-Abteilung 217 did report the number Sturmpanzer IVs within the pocket but reported a fighting strength of 20 men. The battalion itself reported a strength of four combat-ready Sturmpanzer IVs and nine in short-term maintenance. It remains unclear if this number includes the vehicles both inside and outside the Aachen pocket.

Three enlisted men of 1./ Sturmpanzer-Abteilung 217 were captured near Weiden after trying to escape the pocket. They confirmed that they tried to break through to Aachen on 14 October with six Sturmpanzer IVs, but only two were still available on 16 October. They claimed that the unit was almost destroyed in Normandy and therefore the actual order of battle was three companies, each with 120 men and ten Sturmpanzer IVs. However, as the 1st Company was the only company that had so far received tank replacements, it was chosen to go to Aachen while the 2nd and 3rd Company remained in the Grevenbroich area. Both companies had received orders before 14 October to build and improve defenses on a line 500 meters west of Grevenbroich, although the area was flat and swampy. All companies had received personnel replacements in September from the replacement unit in Kamenz. Despite the lack of tanks, both companies outside the pocket were said to have had a personnel strength of two-thirds of their original.[143]

On **18 October**, a counterattack was scheduled for 116.Pz.Div. and 3.Pz.Gren. Div. to reopen the Aachen pocket. However, the battlegroups failed to attack

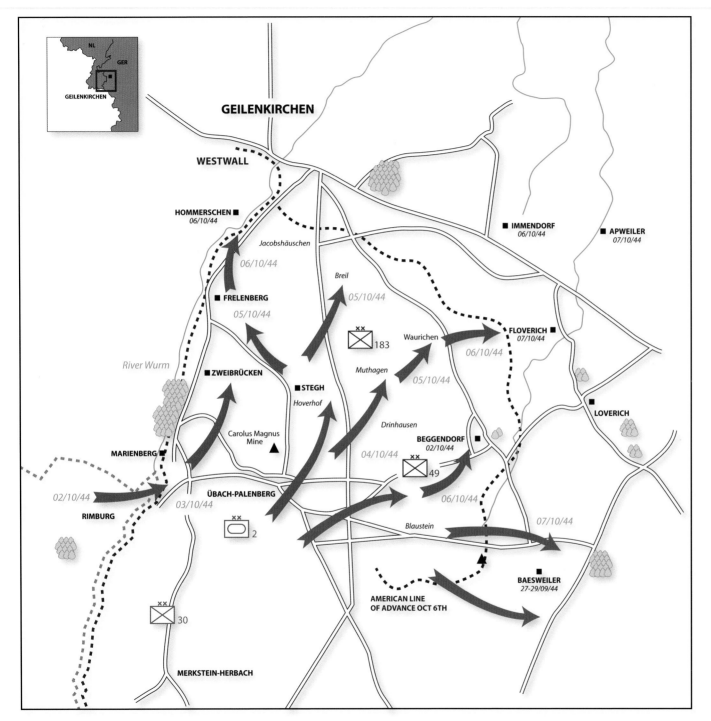

This page: An overview of the recorded combat areas of Sturmpanzer-Abteilung 217 northeast of Übach-Palenberg and the American 2nd Armored Division direction of attack between 2 and 9 October 1944.

Right: An excerpt from Sheet 59 'Aachen' 1:50.000 from the GSGS series Belgium and Northeastern France showing Aachen and the surrounding area.

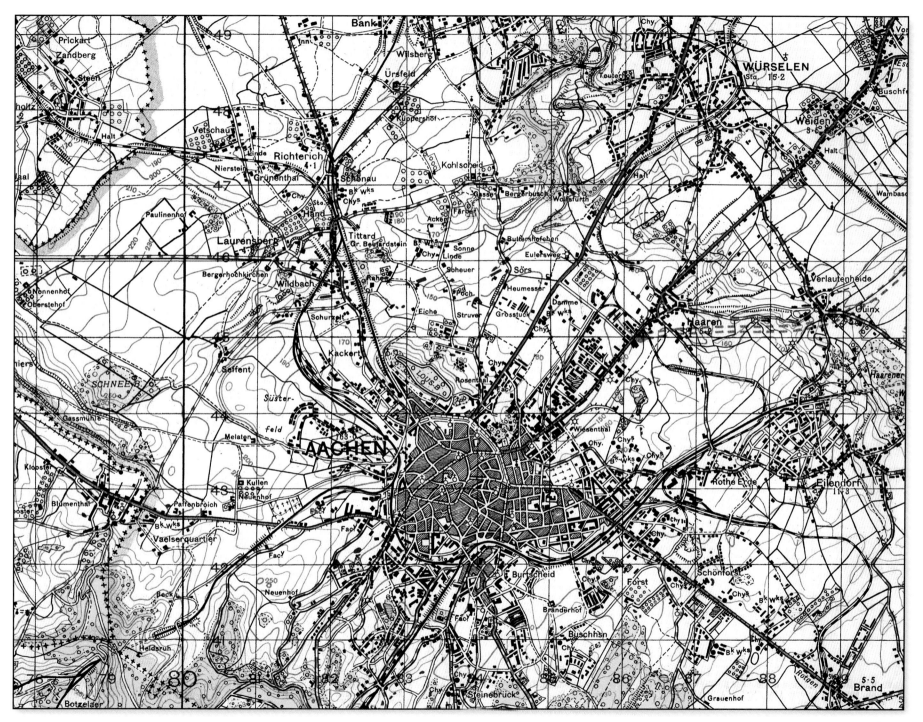

simultaneously. While a reinforced regiment of 3.Pz.Gren.Div., supported by Sturmgeschütze, managed to attack under cover of darkness and recaptured a number of bunkers on the Ravelsberg, elements of 116.Pz.Div.'s *Kampfgruppe Musculus* only started at 14:00. By this time, the 3.Pz.Gren.Div. attack had already been halted. *Kampfgruppe Musculus'* advance was stopped in its tracks after the recapture of several bunkers at stop point Kaiseruh, the accompanying infantry reporting losses of 50%. The 3.Pz.Gren.Div. tried to bring additional forces into the Ravelsberg sector, but American artillery prevented all but a few groups reaching the strategic bunkers. During the night, the Americans counterattacked, and the Germans were pushed back to their starting positions by the morning of 19 October.

After a relatively quiet night, the Americans continued their concentric attacks on the urban area of Aachen on 18 October. In the northwest, Vetschau, Laurensberg and Richterich were captured, and almost all the Germans captured. In the west, Vaalserquartier was given up for new positions at Königshügel. In the southern district, American engineers had sporadic contact with German forces. At 06:30, the 3rd Bn of the 26th Inf Rgt attacked against the sanatorium and Quellenhof. Elements of *Kampfgruppe Rink's Kompanie Zaag* were cut off and captured. The remnants of I./Gren.Rgt.404 and *Kampfgruppe Rink* were being pushed backwards, and close-quarters fighting broke out at the Quellenhof. In the evening, the Germans redeployed to a new line between Salvatorberg and Kupferstraße. Prisoners from Sturmgeschütz-Brigade 341 later confirmed the presence of the unit in this area. To the south, elements of 2nd Bn, 26th Inf Rgt advanced on Hindenburgstraße. In the area around the theater, German infantry and armor had established a blocking position towards the 'Aachener Dom' (Aachen Cathedral). The Americans used direct fire from their self-propelled artillery against the German strongpoints. The theater was turned to rubble, while a German self-propelled vehicle was knocked out by falling debris from a nearby building. The American report, mentions a bunker-like vehicle, probably a Sturmpanzer IV.[144] The 2nd Bn claimed the destruction of yet another tank in this area. Oberst Wilck saw no other option than to shorten his frontline and free troops for other duties. The final defense was now centered around the Lousberg. Oberst Wilck reported unflatteringly:

> *"Collapse of resistance in Aachen is expected on 19 October as a result of enemy superiority".*[145]

As on previous days, there is no mention of Sturmpanzer-Abteilung 217 in German reports. In the evening, the battalion reported seven Sturmpanzer IVs as combat-ready with another five in short-term maintenance. Three enlisted men were captured in the 30th Inf Div sector, and told their interrogators that they tried to break out and only two of their vehicles remained in the city.[146]

On **19 October**, the I.SS-Pz.Korps made a final attempt to breach the encirclement of the Aachen pocket from the outside. Once again, the battlegroups of the 116. Pz.Div. and 3.Pz.Gren.Div. failed to attack simultaneously. Except for a minor gain near Würselen, there was not much success. German losses were extremely high and American artillery dominated the battlefield. In the evening, the corps ordered its units to turn over to defense, which finally sealed Aachen's fate. The headquarters of the I.SS-Pz.Korps was relieved in the night of 19/20 October, with responsibility being transferred to the LXXXI A.K. The main combat line in Aachen stretched from St-Raphael (excl.) - Haussen - Rahe Castle (excl.) - railroad line - Königshügel - Westpark (excl.) - Veltmanplatz to the Lousberg. The 3rd Bn, 26th Inf Rgt reorganized its forces during the night and restarted its attack against German positions in the area of Salvatorberg. Once again a 155mm self-propelled gun supported the infantry, which must have been an M12 Gun Motor Carriage. The battalion made good progress against very light resistance. *Kampfgruppe Rink* could not hold its position at the Salvatorberg and pulled back to the Kupferstraße. In the course of the day, the Americans forced *Kampfgruppe Rink* to redeploy at the foot of the Lousberg. Elements of the 1st Bn were inserted between the 2nd and 3rd Bn and advanced against the Lousberg. To the south, the 2nd Bn had reached the Cathedral and the southern district. Oberst Wilck reported at 18:30 that two attacks had been repelled and five armored vehicles destroyed. Apparently, the Germans succeeded in fending off the American attack on the east of the Lousberg.

The combat commander only had two combat-ready Sturmhaubitzen and two Sturmpanzer IVs at his disposal as heavy weapons. The 246.Volks-Gren.Div. presented a report on the attached units outside the pocket. It is of note that the division reported that the previously attached Sturmpanzer-Abteilung 217 had been relieved and was now being reconditioned. The report, however, is not entirely accurate. Sturmpanzer-Abteilung 217 only received this maintenance order on 22 October and had to leave a combat platoon with three Sturmpanzer IVs with the division (see chapter 4). On the evening of 19 October, the battalion possessed four combat-ready Sturmpanzer IVs and 8 in short-term repair.[147]

At 00:00 on **20 October**, the LXXXI A.K. relieved the I.SS-Pz.Korps and took control of 116.Pz.Div, 3.Pz.Gren.Div. and 49.Inf.Div. To the west and southwest of Würselen, the 30th Inf Div pushed the 116.Pz.Div. further back. In particular *Kampfgruppe Musculus* had to regain its positions in the area of 'stop point' Kaisersruh to avoid being cut off. Conversely, the 3.Pz.Gren.Div. sector remained largely calm, as can be seen from the intense artillery fire on both sides. The situation was similar in the 12. Inf.Div. combat zone. Meanwhile, the final battle for Aachen entered its penultimate phase. At 01:55, the main combat line was reported as running from St-Raphael (excl.) - Haussen (excl.) - Rahe Castle (excl.) - Veltmanplatz to Lousberg. During the day the Americans proceeded with their concentric attacks against the German positions. Heavy fighting took place at the Guter Hirte convent in Königshügel, the technical high school and at the Lousberg. The Americans advanced against very little resistance. The 2n Bn, 26th Inf Rgt encountered its first opposition near the technical high school. The German defenders had turned the building into a strongpoint with anti-tank guns and machine guns. As with the day before, a 155mm self-propelled gun was used to fire directly at these positions. In general there was no coordinated German defense and one tank which came under fire in the Lousberg area was forced to withdraw. German artillery fire almost came to a complete standstill in the city area. The same day, the last two Sturmpanzer IVs inside the pocket were lost or broke down. Sturmpanzer-Abteilung 217 reported three combat-ready Sturmpanzer IVs and seven in short-term maintenance that evening. According to corps directive nr. 325 from 20 October, Sturmpanzer-Abteilung 217 would remain attached to the 246.Volks-Gren.Div. In the corps armor strength return, however, the battalion is listed as a corps troop.[148]

While the first German city in the Second World War fell with the surrender of Aachen on **21 October**, the LXXXI A.K. had already returned to its agenda, and strove to reorganize and refit its badly mixed up units. The corps feared that the Americans would immediately launch a new offensive towards the Rhine after the fall of Aachen. The focus was set upon immediately merging the 246.Volks-Gren. Div. with the 49.Inf.Div. as well as the release of the 116.Pz.Div., to create a mobile intervention reserve. In Aachen, negotiations to surrender the city started at 10:00. Resistance was almost nonexistent and the majority of defenders were holding out in cellars and bunkers waiting for their capture. There were more than 500 German soldiers at the combat commander's command post in the bunker in Rütscherstraße. At 12:00, Oberst Wilck signed the surrender order at the 3rd Bn of the 26th Inf Rgt combat post, and asked them to rephrase *"unconditional surrender"* to a different wording.

At 14:15, the last German soldiers, who had not previously learned of the capitulation, lay down their weapons. On 21 October, more than 1,600 German soldiers surrendered to the Americans. The 26th Inf Rgt, which was primarily charged with the liberation of the city, had captured nearly 3,500 German soldiers in the last ten days of fighting. These figures also include nine members of the Sturmpanzer-Abteilung 217, who were imprisoned on 18 and 21 October. Obviously, they were not subjected to a detailed interrogation, as no further information is available on the battalion in the American G-2 reports. On the evening of 21 October, the battalion had three combat-ready Sturmpanzer IVs, which were deployed in the area of the 246.Volks-Gren.Div. The remaining seven Sturmpanzer IVs were all in short-term repair, and located in the rear corps area.[149] Officially, the deployment of Sturmpanzer-Abteilung 217 in the second Aachen battle ended with the return of the combat platoon with its three Sturmpanzer IVs on 7 November. During this period, the platoon together with the remains of the Sturmgeschütz-Brigade 341 was attached to the newly established 246.

Volks-Gren.Div. There is no information available as to the whereabouts of the combat platoon. The three-week mission in the Übach-Planeberg, Würselen and Aachen area cost the battalion 176 soldiers, with 22 dead, 68 wounded and 86 missing in action. A total of nine Sturmpanzer IVs were lost as total write-offs:

- 04/10/1944: 3 Sturmpanzers at Übach-Palenberg
- 14/10/1944: 3 Sturmpanzers between Würselen and Aachen
- 18/10/1944: 1 Sturmpanzer in Aachen
- 20/10/1944: 2 Sturmpanzers in Aachen[150]

1. Demoralized German soldiers surrendering after the bombardment of Aachen on 17 October 1944. **2.** German soldiers are sent to the rear after the German surrender on 21 October. **3.** Three German soldiers, one carrying a white flag, surrender in Aachen on 19 October 1944. **4.** German civilians, who held out in the ruins of Aachen until the surrender, are evacuated in the direction of Brand. *NARA*

Aachen in ruins after the German surrender on 21 October 1944. *Timm Haasler*

The Schießschule der Panzertruppen (Shooting School of the Armored Forces) in Putlos also had a Sturmpanzer IV, with the tactical number '540'. *Timm Haasler*

CHAPTER 04
REST AND REFITTING

On 20 October 1944, several officers of the General der Panzertruppen West visited Sturmpanzer-Abteilung 217 to get a clearer picture of the battalion's condition. On their way to the unit they ran into four Sturmpanzer IVs which had just been collected from Deutsche Eisenwerke in Duisburg. The battalion was in a sorry state according to a report that was later issued by the General der Panzertruppen:

- 3 Sturmpanzers were trapped in Aachen[1]
- 3 Sturmpanzers were attached to the 246.Volks-Gren.Div. outside the pocket
- 5 Sturmpanzers were in short-term maintenance, with the goal of having three out of these five tanks combat-ready again by 22 October

With the four tanks in transfer, the battalion had only fifteen Sturmpanzer IVs at its disposal, equal to the strength of just one company. The unit was in need of a 22-ton flatbed truck for the recovery platoon, as well as four trucks and three light passenger cars according to the report.

The figures relating to the Sturmpanzer IVs were in contrast to a report issued by LXXXI A.K. at 22:00 on 20 October. According to this report, the battalion had ten Sturmpanzer IVs outside Aachen, of which three were combat-ready and seven in short-term maintenance. Together with the two Sturmpanzer IVs trapped in Aachen, which were destroyed that day, the battalion still had twelve Sturmpanzer IVs on hand. The four Sturmpanzer IVs in transfer were not part of this report. This means there was a discrepancy of one Sturmpanzer between the two reports.[2] This discrepancy should be kept in mind for future reference.

During a meeting at the battalion's command post in Ralshoven, the topic of a rest and refitting period was once more discussed. The idea was to withdraw the battalion to an area near to Deutsche Eisenwerke in Duisburg, and to bring the battalion back to a total strength of two companies. After the meeting, the team of inspectors drove in the direction of Aachen in order to join the combat company for another situational briefing.[3]

The following day, the representatives from the General der Panzertruppen drove to Duisburg-Hochfeld and paid a visit to the steel plant of Deutsche Eisenwerke. The actual production situation was as follows:

- 5 Sturmpanzers on hand, ready for dispatch
- 3 Sturmpanzers on the production line, ready for dispatch by 25 October

These five combat-ready tanks were immediately allocated to Sturmpanzer-Abteilung 217, and the battalion was given orders to pick them up at once. The battalion was very fortunate that the plant at Duisburg-Hochfeld was less than 50 kilometers away from its operational area. The same day, Heeresgruppe B issued secret order Ia, No. 8898/44 which arranged the 'preferred maintenance' of Sturmpanzer-Abteilung 217. An additional order, issued on 22 October, instructed the battalion to transfer immediately to Grevenbroich for refitting. The three combat-ready Sturmpanzer IVs with the 246.Volks-Gren.Div., were to be left behind. Grevenbroich was chosen as the advance message center as Panzerstützpunkt Nord was located there.[4]

On 27 October, the General der Panzertruppen West issued another secret order, No. 1668/44, which contained further details on the 'preferred maintenance' of Sturmpanzer-Abteilung 217:

The ordered reorganization to freie Gliederung (variable structure) has to take place at the same time. Final organization of the battalion:

Staff and staff company
2 Sturmpanzer companies
Supply company
Maintenance platoon

1. Implementation instructions:
Personnel instructions
1. Redundant personnel are to be sent back to the replacement unit to form a cadre for a new company, as the material situation did not allow the formation of a third company.
2. Sturmpanzer-Abteilung 217 is in charge of the officers' roster. Redundant officers have to be reported to the General der Panzertruppen West and sent back to the replacement unit, while requests should be issued for missing officers.
3. Missing personnel for the available tanks, weapons and maintenance services have to be requested via the General der Panzertruppen West, broken down into non-commissioned officers and privates.

Material instructions
4. Twelve Sturmpanzer 43 will be allocated from production.
5. No motorcars will be allocated.
6. Any missing weapons and material have to be reported to the General der Panzertruppen West immediately.
7. Necessary maintenance of weapons and vehicles is to be preferentially executed by Panzerstützpunkt Nord. Spare parts for tanks have to be ordered at the Bergisch-Gladbach spare parts depot.

2. Final instructions:
On the order of OB West, "Ia No. 8013/44 secret", dated 30.09.1944, all units assigned to preferred maintenance will be placed under the control of the General der Panzertruppen West until the end of the activity. An alert group is to be formed from the combat ready elements, which is only to be engaged on exclusive orders of OB West. Sturmpanzer-Abteilung 217 will report:
8. The progress of the preferred maintenance and reorganization to freie Gliederung every fifth day, starting 1 November 1944
9. Strength and composition of the alert group (twofold copy) every fifth day, starting 1 November 1944.
10. The departure date of the cadre company, including the strength of the company.
11. The end of the preferred maintenance and reorganization to freie

Gliederung.

After completion of the preferred maintenance by General der Panzertruppen West, Sturmpanzer-Abteilung 217 will be reassigned for future engagement upon the orders of OB West. It is vital that combat readiness of the battalion be achieved by 5 November 1944.[5]

It is interesting to note that the order for *freie Gliederung* reorganization had already been issued on 21 September by Heeresgruppe D [= OB West] (order I/10792, dated 21/09/44).[6] The decision for the preferred maintenance put an end to the battalion's continuous engagement since the start of September. The battalion's losses[7] can be understood from the table on the next page.

The battalion received a total of thirty-six Sturmpanzer IVs during September and October 1944. Out of these thirty-six tanks, five Sturmpanzer IVs were lost when the battalion was attached to Pz.Brig.105 in Eastern Belgium. Three Sturmpanzer IVs were lost north of Aachen while the battalion was attached to 183.Volks-Gren. Div. Another six Sturmpanzer IVs were lost in the Aachen pocket while the unit was attached to the 246.Volks-Gren.Div. Consequently, the battalion had lost more than one third of its combat strength.

On 1 November, Sturmpanzer-Abteilung 217 issued its monthly report to the General der Panzertruppen. The report had the same reporting date. The section with personnel strength revealed that the unit was short of one officer and 156 men compared to the authorized strength of 772 Officers, NCOs and privates. Another report showed a total strength of 577 soldiers on 8 November 1944, or a decrease of 38 men. The difference was likely caused by the transfer of the 3. Kompanie to Kamenz. The strength of this company should have been 77 men according to the wartime table of organization, but it must be considered that the 3. Kompanie was under strength and had probably transferred some of its personnel to the other companies. In corroboration of this theory is the fact that the company commander of the 3. Kompanie, Oberleutnant Heigl, was officially

Replacements and Convalescents			
		Replacements	Convalescents
Officers	September	2	0
	October	7	0
NCO/Privates	September	9	0
	October	85	11
Total		103	11

Losses Since September 1944		Dead	Wounded	Missing	Ill	Others
Officers	September	1	2	2	0	0
	October	2	3	2	0	1
NCO/ Privates	September	15	53	73	21	26
	October	20	65	84	25	58
Total		38	123	161	46	85

Status Report 1 November 1944			
Materiel	Authorized strength	Actual Strength	Combat Ready
Sturmpanzer IV	45	22	18
Motorcycle/sidecars	4	0	0
Motorcycles	22	10	10
CC passenger cars	34	28	24
CO passenger cars	7	7	5
Maultiere	27	8	8
CC trucks	57	44	42
CO trucks	28	34	31
Halftracks	5	3	3
Machine guns	113	72	72

transferred to Panzer-Ersatz- und Ausbildungs-Abteilung 18 in Kamenz on 5 November. A soldier from the 1. Kompanie later reported that the 3. Kompanie was transferred from Grevenbroich to Kamenz on 6 November, after handing over all its remaining vehicles to the 1. and 2. Kompanies.[8]

According to the monthly report, twenty-two Sturmpanzer IVs were on hand, of which eighteen were actually combat-ready. Starting 20 October, Deutsche Eisenwerke in Duisburg began to deliver the first batch of four Sturmpanzer IVs, followed by a second batch of five tanks and a final batch of three tanks. A total of twelve Sturmpanzer IVs were delivered by the end of October, but the files of the General der Panzertruppen show a total of thirteen delivered to Sturmpanzer-Abteilung 217 between 15 and 31 October. It remains questionable whether Deutsche Eisenwerke allocated another Sturmpanzer by 1 November.

An order from the General der Panzertruppen, dated 27 October, also mentioned only twelve Sturmpanzers that had been allocated during the rest and refitting period.[9] Considering the various strength reports, the Sturmpanzers in question should have raised the actual strength to twenty-three. If there had been an additional tank, then there must have been a further total loss, but there are no reports confirming this.

The actual material strength situation on 1 November 1944 is shown in the table top right.[10]

The report was summarized by the value judgment of the commanding officer, Oberleutnant Gauglitz:

"1. Training status:
Good, partly excellent

2. Material status:
Out of 22 Sturmpanzers, 18 are in use. The condition of the tanks is considered good despite the poor spare parts supply situation. Out of 142 wheeled vehicles, 69 are in immediate use. The overall status and the preservation of the vehicles should be considered good.

3. Health and moral:
The health status is excellent, signs of slight colds are starting to become apparent due to the engagement in the Eifel region and the predominant climatic conditions. Spirit of the troops: highest anticipation for action and the best of attitudes."[11]

It is interesting to note that a 9th Army interrogation report, issued at the end of October 1944, included the statement of a prisoner, who claimed that the battalion had undergone a reorganization, and now consisted of three companies each with ten Sturmpanzers.[12]

On 2 November, it was reported that the battalion had carried out the reorganization and changed over to the *freie Gliederung* with two Sturmpanzer companies.[13]

Oberleutnant Gauglitz mentioned an engagement in the Eifel. It remains an open question if he was referring to the preceding engagements in the Aachen area, or if the battalion was forced into combat during the rest and refitting period. It is doubtful that there was another engagement as the battalion was earmarked as corps reserve of LXXXI A.K. on 6 November with an actual strength of twenty-one Sturmpanzers.[14] On the other hand, there must be some truth in Gauglitz's statement, because on 7 November, LXXXI A.K. reported that the task force had returned to the battalion and became Army Group reserve the same day.[15] This task force could have been the Sturmpanzer platoon attached to the 246.Volks-Gren.Div. with three Sturmpanzers. According to the daily armor and anti-tank gun strength return of the LXXXI A.K., the platoon reported the following strength:

- 30-31/10/44: attached to 246.V.G.Div.
  3 Sturmpanzers, all combat-ready
- 01/11/44: attached to 246.V.G.Div.
  3 Sturmpanzers: 2 combat-ready, 1 in short-term maintenance
- 02-06/11/44: attached to 246.V.G.Div.
  3 Sturmpanzers: 2 combat-ready, 1 in long-term maintenance

It is notable that the strength returns ended the same day the platoon officially returned to the battalion. On 6 November, at 10:30, Oberleutnant Tetzner reported to the command post of the LXXXI A.K. and introduced himself as the commanding officer of Sturmpanzer-Abteilung 217.[16] He continued to report that the battalion had finished rest and refitting, and on orders from Generalfeldmarschall Model, was now assigned as corps reserve with twenty-one Sturmpanzers. The corps intended to attach the battalion to s.Pz.Abt.506. For this, the battalion was ordered to move to the area of Koslar-Barmen during the nights of 6-7 and 7-8 November. Furthermore, the battalion was ordered to reconnoiter operational areas in conjunction with s.Pz.Abt.506, 246.Volks-Gren.Div., and 3.Pz.Gren.Div. By 21:00, these plans were ready for the bin. The corps informed the 246.Volks-Gren. Div. and 3.Pz.Gren.Div. that the plan to move Sturmpanzer-Abteilung 217 to the Koslar-Barmen area had been canceled. The battalion was to remain in its previous billeting area as Army Group reserve. The next day, the task force returned to its mother unit. This finally ended the Sturmpanzer-Abteilung 217 attachment to LXXXI A.K. that had lasted for more than two months in the Aachen area.[17]

The battalion issued another strength report dated 8 November 1944, shown on the right.[18]

On 8 November, another three Sturmpanzer were allocated and sent to the battalion. There is no information as to when these tanks finally arrived with the battalion, but the new strength was twenty-five Sturmpanzers.[19]

Status Report 8 November 1944		
Materiel	1 November	8 November
Sturmpanzer IV	22	22
Medium APC	not reported	2
Medium motorcycles	10	14
CC passenger cars	28	27
CO passenger cars	7	8
Maultiere	8	8
CC trucks	44	43
CO trucks	34	34
Halftracks	3	3
Machine guns	72	63
Rifles	not reported	288
Pistols	not reported	169
Machine pistols	not reported	43
Omnibus	not reported	1
Trailer	not reported	1

A Sturmpanzer IV of Panzer-Ersatz- und Ausbildungs-Abteilung 18 in Königsbrück market place during a ceremony in 1944. A Panzer IV from the same unit is just visible behind the Sturmpanzer. *Timm Haasler*

The following series of photos were probably taken during a live-firing exercise by Panzer-Ersatz- und Ausbildungs-Abteilung 18 in the Kamenz area in late 1943 or early 1944. *Timm Haasler*

Here, the Commanding Officer, Spieß and several decorated NCOs standing together during the exercise with a Sturmpanzer IV in the background. *Timm Haasler*

Two early Sturmpanzer IVs in a forest clearing, while the conscripts wait for the exercise to start. *Timm Haasler*

A Sturmpanzer IV Ausf.II, fires from its position in a forest clearing. Immediately after the round left the gun, the commander checks the effect on the target. *Timm Haasler*

The replacement unit for all four Sturmpanzer-Abteilungen was Panzer-Ersatz- und Ausbildungs-Abteilung 18 in Kamenz. The unit had several Sturmpanzer IVs which were used for training. *Karlheinz Münch*

A Sturmpanzer IV Ausf.II photographed at the Kamenz barracks. The vehicle is in remarkably good condition, which could indicate that it is factory fresh. With the exception of the *Schürzen*, the entire vehicle is covered in *Zimmerit* and has a *Balkenkreuz* painted on each side. The cylindrical object on the engine deck is one of the *Filzbalg* air pre-cleaners. **Karlheinz Münch**

A front three-quarter view of the vehicle on page 89. Being fresh from the factory, the tracks have barely any wear and ice sprags show as being bright metal. For travelling, a tarpaulin could be fitted to the top of the fighting compartment and around the gun mount, as seen here. *Karlheinz Münch*

At least one other Sturmpanzer IV was available at the Schießschule der Panzertruppen (Shooting School of the Armored Forces) in Putlos, Schleswig-Holstein. The Sturmpanzer, an Ausf.I, had the tactical number '540'. Note the small *Balkenkreuz* and the rectangular symbol on the front fender. ***Karlheinz Münch***

The Schießschule der Panzertruppen in Putlos was located on the Baltic coast. Here, an Allied soldier in swimming trunks has interrupted his sunbathing on the beach for a photograph with the Sturmpanzer IV. The roadwheels have no tires left, unlike the return rollers. *AMC S39074*

A British soldier photographed in the Sturmpanzer IV in 1945. Some moving parts have already been removed, the engine access cover is open, and the left track has been split. *The Tank Museum*

A Sturmpanzer IV Ausf.IV, knocked out in the Hürtgen Forest in December 1944 and photographed by Robert H. Adams of the US 62nd Armored Field Artillery Battalion in March 1945. The vehicle has a disc camouflage pattern and a tactical number '4' painted below the *Balkenkreuz*. The left drive sprocket was removed and lies behind the vehicle. A barely visible name has been painted on the gun barrel jacket. *Timm Haasler*

CHAPTER 05
BETWEEN AACHEN AND THE ARDENNES

5.1 The Hürtgen-Forest

The fighting in the Hürtgen Forest primarily took place in the area of the LXXIV A.K., which was in charge of the section between Zweifall and Losheim. On **2 November 1944**, the Americans continued their attacks in the Hürtgen Forest with much more conviction than the previous month. The target of the 28th Inf Div was the village of Vossenack and the high ground around Schmidt. On the first day of the offensive, Vossenack fell into American hands. The next morning the Americans continued their attack via Kommerscheidt in the direction of Schmidt. At 14:30 on **3 November**, the forward elements of 112th Inf Rgt captured Schmidt. The Germans reacted very quickly and elements of 116.Pz.Div. together with other Army reserves were attached to LXXIV A.K. The combat group of 116. Pz.Div. counterattacked the next morning and pushed the Americans out of Schmidt. On **5 November**, Kommerscheidt was back in German hands and the combat group headed for Vossenack. The next day, the combat group managed to enter Vossenack, but was unable to hold the village against fierce American resistance. On **7 November**, the village was completely back in American hands. Both sides went over to the defense during the next few days. The combat group of 116.Pz.Div. was finally withdrawn from the battlefield until 16 November, while 272.VG.Div., 89. and 275.Inf.Div. held defensive positions in the Hürtgen Forest.[1] It cannot be clarified whether Sturmpanzer-Abteilung 217 was used during the fighting in early November in the Hürtgen forest. A single source mentions the deployment of the battalion with *Kampfgruppe Bayer* (reinforced Pz.Rgt.24 of 116. Pz.Div.) during the fighting for Kommerscheidt on 5/6 November. On the other hand, the excellent chronicle of the 116.Pz.Div. did not mention this assignment at all and the few official German sources that survived the war do not mention Sturmpanzer-Abteilung 217 in this area.[2] Nevertheless, a report by Sturmpanzer-

Abteilung 217 issued on 15 November clearly showed that the battalion had suffered losses during the first week of the month:[3]

Killed in action	0
Wounded in action	5
Missing in action	13
Newly ill	13
Still ill	10
Wounded, not evacuated	1
Returned fit for duty	17

This does not mean that these losses necessarily occurred in the Hürtgen Forest, instead they could also have occurred during the engagement of the platoon-sized task force that was still attached to 246.VG.Div. on the Aachen front.[4]

From **11 November**, Sturmpanzer-Abteilung 217 was subordinated to LXXIV A.K. and assembled in the area of Obermaubach. At this time, the village was still in the rear corps area, but within range of the American artillery. On 15 November, OLt. Gero von der Schulenburg, CO of the Versorgungskompanie Sturmpanzer-Abteilung 217, was seriously wounded in Obermaubach when shrapnel hit his left leg resulting in a broken upper and lower leg. Von der Schulenburg was transferred to the military hospital in Düren.[5] On 17 November, Gefreiter Gerhard Fröhlich, 2./ Sturmpanzer-Abteilung 217 was wounded in Obermaubach by a piece of shrapnel which hit his upper left leg. He was evacuated to the reserve hospital in Bad Rothenfelde.[6] On the same day, Walter Lorenz, St./ Sturmpanzer-Abteilung 217, was killed in action at Obermaubach.[7]

After the previously mentioned assignment of three more Sturmpanzers on 8

November, the battalion must have reached the new combat area with 25 assault tanks, indicating a shortage of six Sturmpanzers despite the reduction to only two companies. This shortage was compensated for on 16 November when the battalion was assigned another six Sturmpanzers from the Heereszeugamt Bielefeld. However, these were only transported on 27 November (five Sturmpanzers)[8] and 29 November (one Sturmpanzer). This equipment would have resulted in an organization with three assault tanks with the battalion staff and fourteen assault tanks per company.

When the US V and VII Corps launched their next large offensive (Operation Queen) on **16 November 1944**, the 4th and 8th Inf Div opposed two burned out German divisions composed of replacement units and stragglers with dubious combat value. After the departure of the 116.Pz.Div., the LXXIV A.K. only had two armored units left, i.e. StuG.Brig.394 and Sturmpanzer-Abteilung 217, with StuG. Brig.394 being in reserve since 11 November in the area of Hürtgen-Kleinhau.[9] The new deployment of Sturmpanzer-Abteilung 217 in the Hürtgen forest would last until 16 December, when the battalion was pulled out and transferred to the Ardennes for further combat within the I. SS-Pz.Korps. It was extremely difficult to research the combat history of Sturmpanzer-Abteilung 217 during this period, as few German sources have survived and American sources are not always clear or were contradictory. This difficulty begins with the daily reports of German armored vehicle numbers, which made it almost impossible to identify and link these to their units. The reports mentioned tanks, assault tanks, self-propelled guns, Panzer IVs, Panzer Vs, Panzer VIs or 'Tiger' tanks. With the benefit of hindsight regarding the equipment of the two armored units mentioned above, there were only Sturmgeschütze III, Sturmhaubitzen III and Sturmpanzer IV in action. This would not change in December, when another Sturmgeschütz unit, Stu.Art.Brig.667, was sent to the Gey area, as this brigade was also equipped with Sturmgeschütze III and Sturmhaubitzen III. In early December, Jagdpanzer IVs (Pz IV/70 (V)) and Jagdpanzer 38t ('Hetzer') would see action in the Bergstein area, but these could clearly be differentiated in their combat areas from the other tank units. Unless otherwise stated, the authors have used the American designations.

The American attacks, which started on 16 November, appeared to the Germans to be local attacks in the sector of the 275.Inf.Div., as very little progress was made until 19 November. Nevertheless, the ragged 275.Inf.Div. came under pressure and the German leadership moved the 91.Inf.Div. (formerly 91.LL.Div.) from the Eifel to the 275.Inf.Div. sector. Grenadier regiments 1057 and 1058 were composed of mostly stragglers and replacements units, and therefore of questionable combat value. The Germans continued their defense on **20 November** from well prepared positions, which were further secured by minefields. For the first time, however, there was a decline in resistance in the woods west of Gey - Großhau - Hürtgen. Despite the use of tanks and self-propelled guns (most likely elements of StuG.

Brig.394), eastward of Vossenack between 11:00 and 13:00 and massive artillery support, Gren.Rgt.984 (275.Inf.Div.) and Gren.Rgt.1058 (91.Inf.Div.) had to pull back 3 kilometers west and northwest of Großhau. The II./Gren.Rgt.1055 (89.Inf. Div.) was able to hold its positions in the area west of Hürtgen. On **21 November**, the American attack stalled again. In the vicinity of Hof Roßbroich in Kleinhau the Americans observed one or two German tanks, which they subjected to artillery fire. Due to the bad weather situation, it was impossible to see the outcome and effects of this barrage.[10]

In the 4th Inf Div sector, the Germans defended persistently on **22 November** from well fortified and upgraded positions and bunkers east of the 'Valley of the White Woe' (Weißen Wehe). In the zone of Combat Team 22 (CT 22), 4th Inf Div, northwest of Großhau, the Germans were driven back to rear positions, which at least offered protection against artillery fire. A few smaller German counterattacks were repulsed by CT 22.

During the day, the Germans committed four to six Panzer IVs in groups of two tanks west of Großhau. They laid a smoke screen on the American spearheads before they fell back. Most likely these were Sturmpanzer of Sturmpanzer-Abteilung 217, which supported the Grenadiere in the densely wooded area. In the forest west of Kleinhau - Großhau and Gey, elements of the 275.Inf.Div. and I./ and III./ Gren.Rgt.1058 (91.Inf.Div.) were in action and, west of this position, elements of Gren.Rgt.1055 (89.Inf.Div.). Compared to previous days, the Americans noticed an increase in medium caliber artillery fire. Prisoners from the 91.Inf.Div. mentioned heavy casualties due to friendly artillery fire which fell short onto their own lines. Another prisoner stated that he saw four 'Tiger' tanks about 400 meters south of Forsthaus Kleinhau, which were allegedly subordinated to Pz.A.O.K. 5.[11]

On **23 November**, two minor German attacks were repelled by CT 22, 4th Inf Div. CT 22 itself advanced to the forest's edge west of Großhau. On the western outskirts of Großhau, a dug in German gun defended the position. It is possible that this was a tank. On the right wing of CT 22, along the course of the forest track which led from Forsthaus Kleinhau to the northwest, they came upon three other German tanks, which were also entrenched. Dug in German Panzers would cause the Americans problems in the coming days when they tried to cross the open spaces on both sides of Großhau and Kleinhau. In the sector of CT 12, 4th Inf Div, there were signs which made it clear that the Germans were ready to fall back to prepared positions. Prisoners in this zone stated that engineers were responsible for the expansion of these rear positions. Combat Teams 22 and 12 made contact with elements of I./Gren.Rgt.1057 and III./Gren.Rgt.1058 (both 91. Inf.Div.) and remnants from the 275.Inf.Div. In the Hürtgen area, the Germans also had to give up some ground. In this sector, elements of Gren.Rgt.1055 and 1056 (89.Inf.Div.), I./Gren.Rgt.1058 (91.Inf.Div.) and stragglers from the 275.Inf.Div. were

M5A1 Stuarts of the 709th Tk Bn in Kleinhau.
NARA via Darren Neely

A view of the battered town of Gey after liberation.
NARA via Darren Neely

identified. However, it was primarily German mines, artillery and mortar fire which slowed the American advance. Prisoners from the 275.Inf.Div. reported that the headquarters of the division had been pulled out and transferred to Denmark. The remainder of the division had been incorporated into the 91.Inf.Div. This was entirely in line with reality and given the large number of units involved in this area, this measure was an essential prerequisite for guiding the units in a uniform and coordinated manner.[12]

24 November saw a continuation of the fighting by the Germans in the same style as the previous day. During the morning, the 4th Inf Div reported a German light artillery concentration coming from four directions in the forest area west of Großhau. At 10:00, the Germans fired smoke rounds so that movements in the villages of Hürtgen, Kleinhau, Großhau and at the Forsthaus Kleinhau were obscured. In addition, there was light and medium German artillery fire on the main road junctions. From North (forest area west of Gey) to South (forest area west of Kleinhau), the 4th Inf Div was in contact with I./Gren.Rgt.1057, II./Gren.Rgt.1058, III./Gren.Rgt.1058 and I./Gren.Rgt.1058 (all 91.Inf.Div.). Mixed with these units were again remnants of the 275.Inf.Div.

West of Kleinhau, in the sector of the I./Gren.Rgt.1058, the Germans had to give up further ground but reorganized again in a hastily prepared rear position, which was immediately expanded. Reinforcements had been delivered the previous night. These new additions included the III./Gren.Rgt.1056 (89.Inf.Div.), which was previously in position in the Brandenberg area in a less threatened section and was now west of Kleinhau, adjacent to the I./Gren.Rgt.1058 in order to close the increasingly long flank north of Hürtgen. The Hürtgen area was defended by a combination of German units, which illustrates the confused situation. From the 89.Inf.Div., II./Gren.Rgt.1055 and parts of the Gren.Rgt.1056 were identified, from the former 275.Inf.Div. came elements of II./Gren.Rgt.985 and the Lw.Fest.Btl. XVIII, whilst from the 91.Inf.Div. came the staff company of Gren.Rgt.1058. Several German tanks were reported during the day. A forward observer in the area of CT 22, 4th Inf Div, reported tanks west of Großhau. Another tank was reported at Forsthaus Kleinhau. However, this tank retreated into the forest after the Americans fired at it. Another tank and a halftrack vehicle were observed at 12:15, as they moved from Hürtgen along the road to Kleinhau. The German leadership observed the development of the situation in the area Hürtgen - Kleinhau - Großhau with increasing concern and transferred the I./Gren.Rgt.980 (272.VG.Div.) to the Bergstein area to support the right wing of the 7.Armee, and thus free further forces of the 89.Inf.Div. for the fight in the Hürtgen area. The positions of the I./Gren.Rgt.980 were now occupied by the II./Gren.Rgt.989 (277.VG.Div.), which was transferred to the Schmidt area.[13]

In the forested area north of Hürtgen, the Germans were slowly pushed back on

25 November. However, with the aid of mortar fire and through the use of self-propelled guns and assault guns which had been set up in the woods northeast of Großhau, they were able to prevent the CT22 from exiting the forested area west of Großhau and Kleinhau and crossing the open ground around the two villages. To restore the situation in the area of Großhau, the I./Gren.Rgt.1057 (91.Inf.Div.) was to counterattack on the edge of the forest west of the village. However, this attack ran directly into the American attack of CT 22 aimed at encircling Großhau from the north with the 3rd Bn. The 2nd Bn had to reach the forest's edge west of Großhau, in order to put direct fire into Großhau and Kleinhau. Not only did the 3./Gren.Rgt.1057 suffer heavy losses, but other companies of the battalion recorded very high personnel losses. The 2. Kompanie attacked with 70 men, but was badly hit by its own artillery fire in the area of Großhau and as a result lost 50 men. At the end of the day the company only had a strength of 5 men. Also the 4. Kompanie suffered heavy losses, and the remaining 18 men were divided among the other companies. By evening, the battalion would have a total strength of only 37 men. A PW officer of the I./Gren.Rgt.1057 stated that the 91.Inf.Div. had been renamed as the 344.Inf.Div.[14] The reason for this was unknown to him. In fact, the division had merely been renamed, but without renaming the former Grenadier regiments of the 91.Inf.Div.

Meanwhile, the 2nd Bn, 22nd Inf Rgt, had been able to reach its objective by 10:30 and had a clear view of Großhau. The 3rd Bn launched its attack on Großhau from the north at 11:45, but came under heavy fire from self-propelled guns, mortars and artillery. Four accompanying tanks and two tank destroyers were destroyed by the Germans and the battalion had to stop its attack at 15:00 and return to the defense after suffering further personnel losses.[15]

In the CT 12 sector, 4th Inf Div, the Germans north of Hürtgen were surprised and thrown out of their positions. The 2nd Bn, 12th Inf Rgt, settled on the northern edge of Hürtgen and supported the attack by CCR 5th Arm Div. A German rear position was overrun before the Germans could regroup. In the process, a battalion command post was raided, completely surprising the Germans. Some German units could not retreat in time and were encircled by the Americans. The 2nd Bn, 12th Inf Rgt, began to consolidate the position achieved and by evening had made contact on its left with the 3rd Bn of the same regiment and on the right with the 121st Inf Rgt of the 8th Inf Div. A German barrage of 30 shells was fired on the area northwest of the Forsthaus (forest hut) Kleinhau at 18:30. Overall, there was a general decline in German artillery activity during the day.

Otherwise, apart from a combat group in the Hürtgen area, no more new German units were identified during the day. The unit in the Hürtgen area was *Kampfgruppe Schmitz*, consisting of the remains of I./Gren.Rgt.985, the 14./Gren.Rgt.985, Füs. Btl.275 and *Kampfgruppe Weinen* (all former 275.Inf.Div.). The fighting power and

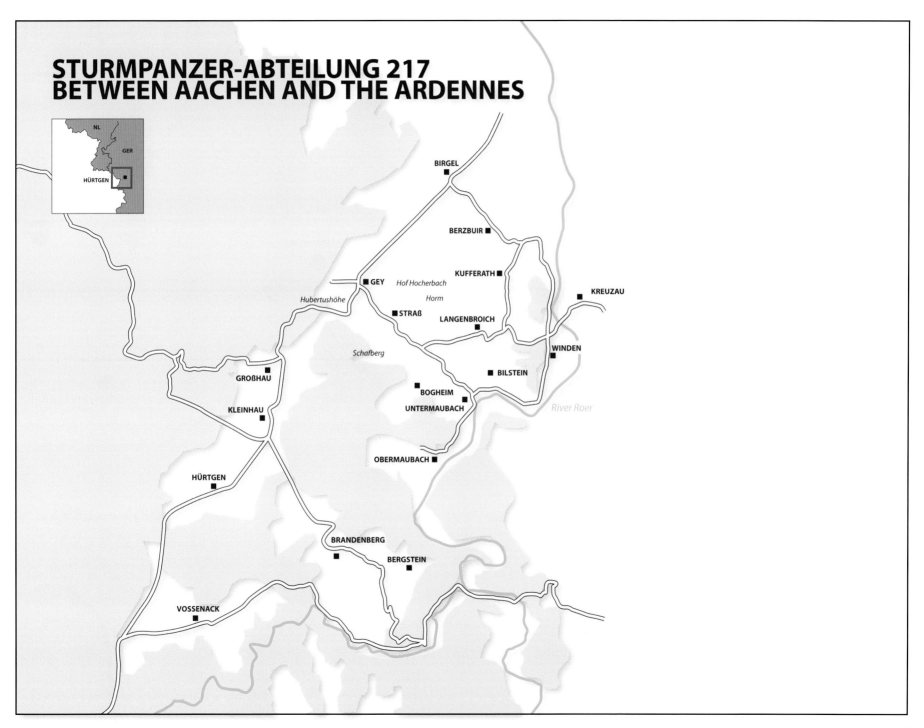

STURMPANZER-ABTEILUNG 217
BETWEEN AACHEN AND THE ARDENNES

NL

GER

HÜRTGEN

BIRGEL

BERZBUIR

KUFFERATH

GEY   *Hof Hocherbach*

KREUZAU

Hubertushöhe   *Horm*

STRAß   LANGENBROICH

WINDEN

Schafberg

BILSTEIN

GROßHAU

BOGHEIM

KLEINHAU   UNTERMAUBACH

River Roer

OBERMAUBACH

HÜRTGEN

BRANDENBERG

BERGSTEIN

VOSSENACK

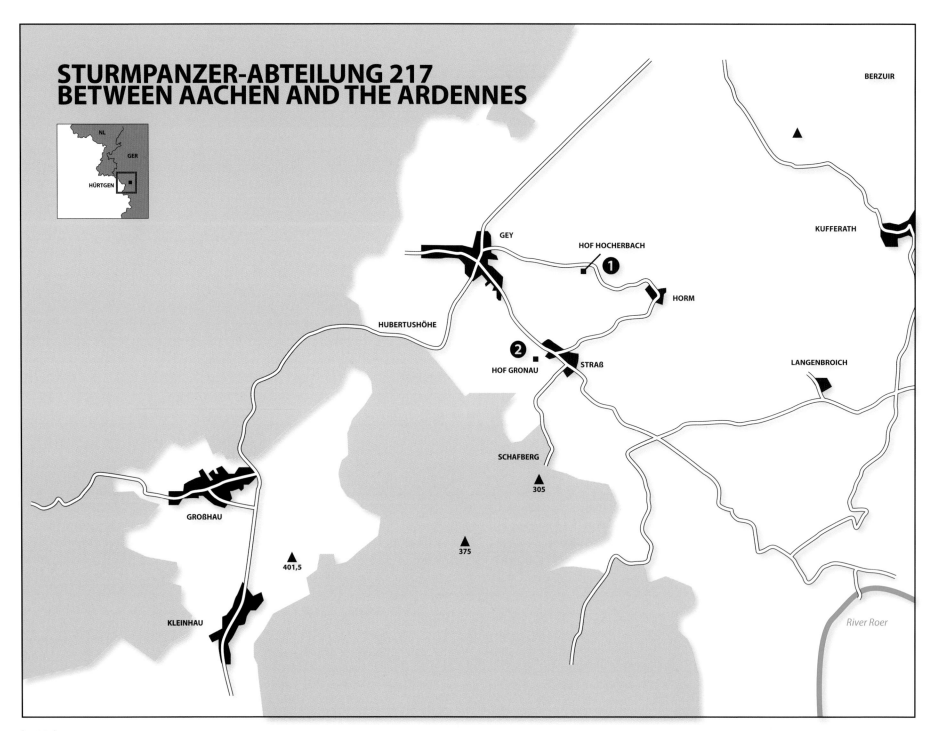

STURMPANZER-ABTEILUNG 217
BETWEEN AACHEN AND THE ARDENNES

NL

GER

HÜRTGEN

BERZUIR

KUFFERATH

GEY

HOF HOCHERBACH

1

HORM

HUBERTUSHÖHE

2

HOF GRONAU

STRAß

LANGENBROICH

SCHAFBERG

▲
305

GROßHAU

▲
375

▲
401,5

KLEINHAU

River Roer

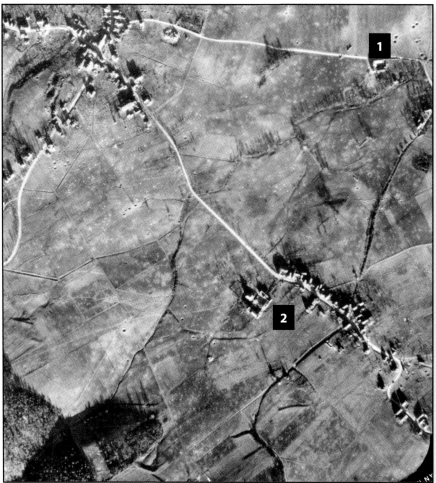

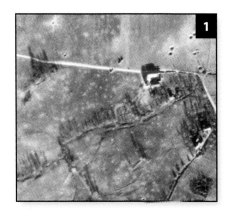

morale of the German units decreased significantly in this period. The recently arrived III./Gren.Rgt.1056 (89.Inf.Div.) had only about 30 soldiers in its 10. and 11. Kompanie. These soldiers had received no food for days. The II./Gren.Rgt.1055 (89. Inf.Div.) was forced to combine the remains of the 3 rifle companies, which had a total strength of only 50 men.[16]

During the day, several German tanks were spotted and partially attacked. A German tank was observed at 11:45 at the intersection west of Hürtgen. Two more tanks were detected northeast at 11:50. The tanks were immediately fired on and forced to retreat. The Americans later reported the destruction of a German tank by artillery fire southeast of Point 385.8. All the tanks must have been assault guns of StuG.Brig.394. The CT 22 reported 2 German tanks in the Kleinhau area and some German assault guns, which had fired in the direction of Großhau. Since the same source differentiates between tanks and assault guns, it is plausible that both Sturmpanzer-Abteilung 217 and StuG.Brig.394 saw combat. Another German tank is said to have been destroyed by a fighter-bomber attack near the intersection south of Kleinhau.[17]

In its status report of 25 November, Sturmpanzer-Abteilung 217 reported their current strength to the General der Panzertruppen West as twenty-four Sturmpanzers, of which twenty-one were combat ready and three in maintenance. If we consider that the battalion started its deployment in the Hürtgen forest with twenty-five Sturmpanzer, it looks as though the unit had lost one Sturmpanzer IV by 25 November. On the other hand, as already described, six further Sturmpanzer IV were assigned on 16 November, in order for the unit to attain the nominal strength of 31 tanks. If the battalion had actually suffered a total loss before 25 November, the report would have had to be 30 Sturmpanzer on 8 December, but the battalion reported 31 tanks on that date. The discrepancy is likely to be clarified by the statement of a deserter from the battalion, who said in his interrogation by the Americans, that at the beginning of December his unit was given seven instead of six Sturmpanzer. This additional tank was most likely the last Sturmpanzer IV of the 2./Stu.Pz.Abt.218 z.b.V. (see chapter 5.2.). This would confirm that the Abteilung had actually lost an assault tank before 25 November.[18]

In the sector of CT 22, 4th Inf Div, the Germans maintained their positions on **26 November**. Strong resistance was provided from well camouflaged positions and by dug in tanks and self-propelled guns. German wire obstacles and extensive minefields were encountered almost everywhere. The American front line was under constant German fire from small arms, artillery and mortars. The greatest concentration of fire took place around 11:00, when 30 shells were fired at the area north of the Forsthaus Kleinhau. Overall, however, there was a decline in German artillery activity in the area of 4th Inf Div.[19]

In the area of Großhau, the Germans allowed an American patrol of company strength to cross the open area to the west and enter the village early in the morning. Only then did the Germans react and, after a preparatory heavy artillery and mortar barrage, launched a counterattack at dawn. Approximately 70-100 infantrymen and four assault guns attacked and drove the Americans back into the forest. The German counterattack was then halted by American fire. Attempts to infiltrate American positions 1.6 kilometers west of Kleinhau were repelled by the Americans. Prisoners of the 275.Inf.Div. stated that the Pz.Jg.Kp.275 had made the village of Kleinhau their center of gravity and placed its eight 7.5cm Pak in and around the village.[20] In the area of CT 12, 4th Inf Div, resistance was initially provided by small German groups with handguns. Gradually, these resistance nests were destroyed and at the end of the day, the Americans had reached the edge of the forest southwest of Kleinhau. In the afternoon, elements of the 8th Inf Div tried to penetrate into the village of Hürtgen at six different points, but were repulsed each time. Around 20:00, the American advance on Hürtgen from the south was stopped on the outskirts. Hürtgen and the area to the edge of the forest south of the village was defended by *Kampfgruppe Schmitz* (formerly 275.Inf.Div.). While a German prisoner reported five German self-propelled guns in Hürtgen, American reconnaissance forces reported only three German self-propelled guns in this area.[21]

The tense situation in the Hürtgen area forced the 272.VG.Div., on 26 November, to extend their right flank north to the southern edge of Germeter - northeast edge Vossenack - Giesenheck - Zweifallshammer, so that the 89.Inf.Div. could release more forces. However, this was not the only measure of the German leadership to master the increasingly critical situation in the Hürtgenwald. According to a captured German order, the Gren.Rgt.1057 (344.Inf.Div.) would be replaced during the night of 25/26 November by Gren.Rgt.942 (353.Inf.Div.). Thus, the Americans knew that more German reinforcements had arrived in the Hürtgenwald. It is of note however, that the transfer of the 353.Inf.Div. in the Prüm area had first started on 24 November with the relieving troops still marching, and that upon arrival, Gren.Rgt.942 would be positioned much further north, on the right wing of the division.[22]

On **27 November** German resistance in the area Großhau - Kleinhau increased considerably, which the Americans falsely interpreted as the arrival of Gren. Rgt.942 (353.Inf.Div.). In Großhau, the Grenadiers were supported by tanks, assault guns and self-propelled guns from well-prepared positions, which stopped the attack of CT 22, 4th Inf Div that had started at 09:00. The Germans again laid smoke over the area Großhau - Kleinhau. At 12:30, elements of the 1st and 2nd Bn, 22nd Inf Rgt, attacked again and reached the western edge of the village by 14:40. This position was then fortified with heavy weapons, as a German counterattack was expected. Self-propelled guns, assault guns, numerous minefields and wire

An aerial view of the area between Großhau and Kleinhau taken in December 1944. Großhau is visible at the top. The main road runs south to Kleinhau, located in the bottom right. A secondary road is visible going from Kleinhau to the east in the direction of Schafberg/Straß. Although the area is blanketed with snow, we can clearly see hundreds of large shell-holes and several German trenches, particularly north of Kleinhau. Southwest of Großhau some black spots are visible, which could be vehicles or tanks.

An aerial view of Gey and Straß taken on 26 December 1944. In the bottom left, the road center of Gey is clearly visible. The road to the left leads from Rölsdorf via Gey to Großhau. The center road began in Gey and led to Horm and from there to Kreuzau on the River Roer, while the road to the right connects Gey with Straß, visible in the center right. The area is littered with shell-holes, a testament to the ferocity of the fighting here in December 1944.

The Langenbroich - Bergheim area on 26 December 1944. **1.** Langenbroich **2.** Bergheim.

Aerial showing the Kufferath - Bergheim area on 26 December 1944. **1.** Langenbroich **2.** Bergheim **3.** Kufferath.

This Sturmpanzer IV Ausf.IV was captured by the Americans in the Hürtgen Forest. The vehicle lost its right track and was abandoned by its crew. A soldier of the 987th Field Artillery Battalion took this picture somewhere between Straß and Kufferath. Note the name painted on the gun barrel jacket and the *Balkenkreuz* below the driver's periscope, a feature of almost all the tanks of Sturmpanzer-Abteilung 217 since late autumn 1944. *Terry Keller*

obstacles had again seriously impeded the American advance. In the evening, the Americans observed vehicle traffic on the road between Kleinhau-Großhau, including numerous German tanks, which moved north and south of Großhau along the course of this road. For the first time parts of the II./Gren.Rgt.1056 (89. Inf.Div.) were identified. This suggests that the shift of the right wing of the 272. VG.Div. had made another battalion of the 89.Inf.Div. available for use in the Hürtgen - Großhau area. CT 12, 4th Inf Div, reorganized later that day and shifted forces to the southwest of Großhau, which had previously been relieved north of Hürtgen by parts of the 8th Inf Div.[23]

In the Hürtgen area, the Americans reported continuing stubborn German resistance, aided by fierce German artillery and mortar fire. The 8th Inf Div attacked from the southwest and finally reached the northern edge of the village. The Germans were still able to keep the road to the northeast under their control. In the village house to house fighting developed, which continued during the night of 28 November. In the forests south of Hürtgen, the Americans were able to capture some ground. In the morning, American air reconnaissance reported eight German tanks in Hürtgen, two of which could allegedly be destroyed by fighter-bombers. In the afternoon there were still three active German tanks or self-propelled vehicles in the village. V Corps reported that StuG.Brig.394 with eighteen Sturmgeschütze 7.5cm and twelve Sturmgeschütze 10.5cm would be deployed east of Hürtgen.[24] On 27 November, Panzerschütze Tkaczyk of 2./ Sturmpanzer-Abteilung 217 succumbed to his wounds on the HVP in Kelz. When and where Tkaczyk was wounded is unclear.[25]

In the wooded area to the west of Großhau and Kleinhau, the Germans showed no signs of diminishing their resistance on **28 November**. They also continued their highly efficient form of defense with dug in tanks and self-propelled guns. Once again, parts of CT 22, 4th Inf Div, were able to infiltrate Großhau, but intensive German defensive fire made it impossible to hold the village. In addition, there were signs that parts of the 353.Inf.Div. had arrived. In fact, the I./Gren.Rgt.941 had unloaded at Vettweis and marched through Kreuzau and Strass to Gey. The II./Gren. Rgt.941, however, was unloaded further east in Dürscheven near Euskirchen and marched along a route from Zülpich - Drove - Kreuzau - Langenbroich to Gey. In the evening, the first parts of the regiment had reached Gey. The 4th Inf Div had planned the final capture of Großhau for the next day. The attack was to be coordinated with the attack of the CCR, 5th Arm Div on Kleinhau.[26] In the Hürtgen area, the American troops crossed the intersection north of the village at 07:00 and continued in the direction of Brandenberg. Those troops who wanted to pass through Hürtgen from the south, had to continue to fight their way through the village until the last German resistance there finally silenced at 18:00. At 15:30 the Germans had attacked from the Kleinhau area and harassed the American forces in the direction of Brandenberg at the edge of the forest, south of the intersection.

The German counterattack was carried out by Grenadiers in company strength, who were supported by a self-propelled gun. The German counterattack would be fought off with heavy losses for the attackers.[27]

Several prisoners also gave information on German armored vehicles; for the first time there was a clear reference to Sturmpanzer-Abteilung 217. A few days previously, these prisoners had observed five 15cm Sturmgeschütze, which during the day occupied firing positions at the edge of the forest east of Großhau, and from there fired directly at the American positions. During the night, these Sturmgeschütze retreated about 700 meters to the east into the forest, where they moved into a reverse-slope position and from there were used as artillery. These guns are said to have fired for the last time at 19:30 on 28 November from the latter position. A map of the 89.Inf.Div. shows the staff of the battalion on this day to have been in Obermaubach.[28] Lt. Pörschmann of 1./ Sturmpanzer-Abteilung 217 was reported wounded by the battalion on this date.[29]

Other prisoners reported two Sturmgeschütze 7.5cm in a barn in Gey. Further prisoners had seen fifteen tanks and self-propelled guns in the forest southwest of Gürzenich a few days previously, probably belonging to StuG.Brig.902 or the Stu.Art.Brig.667. On 28 November, Stu.Art.Brig.667 was in position southwest of Etzweiler, and had four Sturmgeschütze in Merken.[30]

On **29 November**, the Germans again managed to prevent the CT 22, 4th Inf Div, from penetrating the town of Großhau or flanking the town. The German Grenadiers were in their defense supported by Sturmgeschütze of StuG.Brig.394 positioned behind the houses in the village or in elevated positions east of the village and which fought the attacking Americans with direct fire. In addition, there were single 7.5cm Pak guns of the Fest.Pak-Abt.501 in the area of Großhau. At 11:00, the 3rd Bn, 22nd Inf Rgt, began its flanking attack north of Großhau with the aim of taking the heights northeast of Großhau. This only succeeded by nightfall at 18:30 against heavy German resistance. The 1st Bn, 22nd Inf Rgt, followed the 3rd Bn and took over its initial starting positions. Thus, the danger of new German forces being introduced or a counterattack from the Gey area was clearly minimized.

The 2nd Bn, 22nd Inf Rgt, on the other hand, had the mission to attack the village head-on from the west. The battalion's attack began at 12:50. Companies E and F were accompanied by tanks and tank destroyers. Company F attacking on the right was threatened by a German counterattack in the flank shortly after the attack had started at 13:30. Grenadiers in company strength and some self-propelled guns attacked from the east. However, the self-propelled guns retreated into the forest east of the village after firing a few rounds at the American positions. This caused the Grenadiers to lose their support and Company F was able to fend off the German counterattack.

The attack developed very slowly, and by 16:35 had progressed no more than 100 meters. There was heavy fighting in the village, with the remnants of II./Gren. Rgt.1056 (89.Inf.Div.) and I./Gren.Rgt.1057 (344.Inf.Div.) being unable to provide much opposition. At 18:45, the Germans had only three houses in their hands and at 19:15 the Americans reported the capture of Großhau. Thus the Americans finally cut the road between Gey-Großhau-Kleinhau. The German self-propelled guns referred to were probably elements of Sturmpanzer-Abteilung 217, which according to a report of Heeresgruppe B on that day, were in position with one company each east of Großhau and north of Brandenberg. Analysis of aerial photos also showed a significant increase of track traces in this section of the VII Corps area, especially in the area around Hürtgen and Großhau. At least twelve different tanks could be identified. On this day, Unteroffizier Herbert Schimanski[31] from the staff of Sturmpanzer-Abteilung 217 was wounded in action. Unfortunately, there is no information as to where this took place.[32]

V Corps reported heavy German resistance against the American forces that attacked north through Kleinhau that day. The German defenders included elements of II./Gren.Rgt.1056 (89.Inf.Div.), remnants of Fest.MG.Btl.31 and Gren. Rgt.985 (both 275.Inf.Div.), and single 7.5cm Pak guns of the 2./Fest.Pak-Abt.501 who did not depend upon cooperation with the infantry. Despite the report from Heeresgruppe B, according to which StuG.Brig.394 was in reserve on 29 November east of Kleinhau, parts of the brigade were actually used in the area around Kleinhau. Unteroffizier Benno Kiefer, an assault gun commander in 3./StuG. Brig.394, destroyed an American tank at Kleinhau. Further north and northeast, the American spearheads took Height 401.5 northeast of the village by the evening, against the newly arrived 7./Gren.Rgt.941 (353.Inf.Div.). In Kleinhau, smaller German groups initially held out in the cellars and defended to the last man. German resistance in the village ended at around 16:00. Shortly thereafter, the German artillery fire in the area around Hürtgen-Kleinhau increased significantly.

The significance of the loss of Kleinhau for the Germans was also demonstrated by the fact that forward observers of the III./ and IV./VAK 403 and the 1./H.Art.Abt.992 were captured in the village. Meanwhile, other troops of V Corps pushed into the woods south of Hürtgen. Prisoners reported the arrival of further reinforcements. On 26 November, two paratroop battalions from the Düren area were said to have arrived in Gey. The paratroopers allegedly had the task of defending the Großhau-Kleinhau road to the last man.[33] Due to the developing situation in the zone of the LXXIV A.K., Generalfeldmarschall Model ordered Stu.Art.Brig.667, which was located behind the left flank of LXXXI A.K., to be transferred to the 'Jagdhaus' area, east of Hürtgen, (probably the 'Forsthaus Kleinhau'). The brigade had fourteen combat ready Sturmgeschütze, but in the evening only eleven Sturmgeschütze

were on their way to Gey. The brigade was now attached to the LXXIV A.K.[34]

More and more German units were identified by the Americans. The majority, however, were combat groups formed from stragglers, or by combing out the rear elements. As a rule, these combat groups were of company strength and led by an officer who was also the namesake of the unit. The combat value of these units was low and they usually dissolved during their first enemy contact or simply retreated. As an example, *Kampfgruppe Pirschmann* (40 prisoners), *Kampfgruppe Braun* (41 prisoners) and *Kampfgruppe Schmitz* (31 prisoners) were identified on 29 November.[35]

The CT 12, 4th Inf Div, had been relocated north of the division's right wing with the bulk of its units the previous day, to close the emerging gap between CT 8 and CT 22. On **30 November**, the 1st and 2nd Bn, 12th Inf Rgt, attacked in an easterly direction with the aim of reaching the edge of the forest east of Gey. The advance was slowed down less by German Grenadiers and artillery than by mines and hidden explosive charges. By the end of the day, the regiment had reached its objective and captured the high ground west of Gey. After the capture of Großhau, the 3rd Bn, 22nd Inf Rgt, also passed through the forest area northeast of the village towards Gey. The main battle line in this area was manned by I./Gren.Rgt.941 (353.Inf.Div.), which had just arrived in the Hürtgenwald the previous day. The I./Gren.Rgt.941 had occupied the front line with its 1. and 2. Kompanie and kept the 3. Kompanie in reserve. However, the two companies could not oppose the American attack with anything more than small arms. Even the usually heavy German artillery and mortar fire had significantly diminished after the loss of Großhau. The I./Gren.Rgt.941 had to give in, so that parts of the CT 22 reached a position only 1000 meters from Gey. There was a breakthrough at the eastern edge of the Hürtgenwald. In the area of the Forsthaus (forest hut) Hubertushöhe, CT 22 stopped attacking to the great surprise of the Germans. Despite considerable losses, the I./Gren.Rgt.941 reorganized and occupied a thin line, which was not attacked by the Americans until 5 December. German prisoners stated that Gey was the central point of retreat for all German soldiers in the area of CT 22. Meanwhile, the 2nd Bn, 22nd Inf Rgt, had made little headway to the east. Despite the addition of four tanks and two tank destroyers, the battalion had to stop the attack at 16:30, just 300 meters from its starting point. South of it, the subordinated 46th Armd Inf Bn, 5th Armd Div, also attacked to the east, but had problems reaching its starting position, as it received flanking fire from the area of Height 401.5, which allegedly had been taken the previous day by the CCR, 5th Armd Div. After heavy fighting in the open field, where more than 40 Germans surrendered, the battalion reached its initial starting point by noon. Shortly after 15:00, the battalion halted its advance at the edge of the forest about 500 meters east of Height 401.5 and dug in for the night.

During the day, the last German resistance nests in and to the west of Großhau were destroyed. In the area of Hürtgen-Kleinhau, the Germans laid down few artillery concentrations and only a little German reconnaissance activity was registered. The Germans once again used self-propelled guns and Sturmgeschütze and a considerable number of mortars and artillery in the CT 22 zone. As on previous days when Sturmgeschütze were reported they were used as artillery. At 15:45, four tanks and six Sturmgeschütze were reported east of Großhau. At 13:30 four German tanks and seven self-propelled guns[36] were reported east of Height 401.5, which fired directly into Kleinhau. The Americans came under fire from these tanks, claiming the destruction of one tank and allegedly knocking out three others. At 17:00, once again eight tanks were sighted on the dirt road east of Großhau. The American infantry continued to encounter minefields and hidden charges throughout the zone of attack. The Germans had mined their abandoned trenches and controlled the open area by weapons in excellent firing position.[37]

German prisoners of war reported five Sturmgeschütze in the little forest north of Gronau farm on the western outskirts of Straß on the evening of 30 November. Another report spoke of four to five 'Tiger' tanks in the center of Straß.[38]

Further south, the Germans defended themselves from a closed defensive line at the edge of the forest east of Hürtgen between the dirt road to Brandenberg and the Kleinhau-Brandenberg road and slowed the only thrust of the 8th Inf Div through the forest area in a southeasterly direction. From a position behind this line, a German self-propelled gun fired at the American positions in Hürtgen.[39]

The **1 December** brought a continuation of German fighting west of Gey and Straß. The Grenadiers continued to defend themselves from prepared positions. Dug in self-propelled guns, mortars and artillery supported the infantry defense. At night and at dawn, reinforcements had apparently been fed. For the first time, German attempts to infiltrate the American positions became apparent. In the forested area northwest of Gey, the Germans, apparently the Füs.Btl.353 (353. Inf.Div.), retreated after having placed numerous minefields, which significantly slowed the advance of the Americans. At noon, the Americans in the area of Gey discovered a column of about 150 German soldiers marching in the direction of the front. The Americans shelled this column with artillery fire and dispersed it, allegedly causing the Germans considerable losses. Parts of CT 22, 4th Inf Div, with the subordinated 46th Armd Inf Bn, 5th Armd Div, had been attempting since morning to advance from Großhau to the east and at the same time from Kleinhau to the northeast, to destroy the German positions northeast of Großhau. CT 22, however, got stuck in front of the German defense line, which was defended with small arms, machine guns and mortars. In the area around the intersection, 1 kilometer northeast of Großhau, three German tanks and two or three halftrack vehicles participated in the fighting and gave the Grenadiers some relief. In the

area between Großhau and Gey, Schanz-Kompanie Drove was surprised and shattered by the Americans. The Schanz-Kompanie (entrenchment company) had been set up in Drove on 26 November 1944, and consisted of stragglers and men from the supply trains of the Füs.Kp.344, F.Ers.Btl.344, Fest.MG.Btl.31 and other stragglers from the 89., 91. and 275.Inf.Div. The company had a strength of 90 men when it was transferred to Gey at the end of November to dig positions. Fourteen soldiers were captured that day. During the course of the day German artillery activity increased again, with the bulk of the fire coming from positions in the towns of Gey and Straß. At about 15:00, German troops attacked the 3rd Bn, 22nd Inf Rgt, southwest of Gey. The attack, by about two companies, seemed well prepared, but was to be repelled by the 3rd Bn. The attacking Grenadiers suffered heavy casualties, despite being accompanied by three tanks and a few halftrack vehicles (presumably the same armored vehicles previously reported northeast of Großhau). Shortly after, the German attackers retreated to the outskirts of Gey and Straß. A later interrogation of German prisoners revealed that both the German march column in the morning and the assault group in the afternoon were part of F.Ers.Btl.344 of the 344.Inf.Div. This battalion had been set up in the Winden area in the fall of 1944 and had seven companies to form the basis for a new Grenadier regiment. The companies each had a strength of 60-90 men. It was planned to completely incorporate the Feldersatzbataillon within Gren.Rgt.1057. However, due to the developing situation, the battalion was committed in the Gey area and the totally inexperienced Grenadiers were completely wiped out that day. At 16:00, a company of Grenadiers headed north over the open area west of Gey in the zone of Company C, 12th Inf Rgt. Several Germans were killed, 2 officers and 15 men were captured and only about 20 Germans escaped. These were parts of Kampfgruppe Braun (remnants of Gren.Rgt.1057, Gren.Rgt.1058 and F.Ers.Btl.191 all from 91.Inf.Div.) and the Armee Waffenschule AOK 7, which was re-identified by the capture of 91 prisoners, including one officer. In the area north of Großhau, Kampfgruppe Pirschmann (remnants of II./Gren.Rgt.1056 (89. Inf.Div.)) was identified, which allegedly still had a strength of 40 men, of which 34 Grenadiers and one officer fell into captivity. Southwest of Gey, 25 soldiers of the Gren.Rgt.941 (353.Inf.Div.) went into American captivity. It seems likely that Gren.Rgt.941 and 943 were subordinated to the 344.Inf.Div. after their arrival in the Hürtgen forest.[40]

On 1 December, 2./ Sturmpanzer-Abteilung 217 was deployed in the area of Schafberg with five Sturmpanzers, with orders to support Gren.Rgt.941. Prisoners of Gren.Rgt.941 reported that they had previously relieved the Gren.Rgt.1058 (344. Inf.Div.). If one follows later prisoner statements, the 2./ Sturmpanzer-Abteilung 217 was cooperating with the 89.Inf.Div. in the area of Hürtgen-Brandenberg, while the 1./ Sturmpanzer-Abteilung 217 was working together with the 91.Inf. Div./344.Inf.Div. At the beginning of December, 2./ Sturmpanzer-Abteilung 217 was transferred from the area of Brandenberg to Schafberg. The 1./ Sturmpanzer-

Abteilung 217 was transferred from the Schafberg to the Gey area.

On 1 December, Unteroffizier August Korte[41] was killed as a member of *Kampfgruppe Böhme* (Sturmpanzer-Abteilung 217) in Kufferath. In the village were the rear elements of Sturmpanzer-Abteilung 217, but at the time it was behind the front line, which is why it has to be assumed that Korte was a victim of Allied artillery or fighter-bombers. Even with little information about *Kampfgruppe Böhme,* this unit must have been connected to 2./ Sturmpanzer-Abteilung 217. To the south, the Germans continued to resist stubbornly in the area southeast of Hürtgen. The Americans made only limited gains. Only when it was possible to bypass the German positions southeast of Kleinhau did the Germans retreat rapidly by several hundred meters over a 1 kilometer front, without putting up significant resistance. Over 100 German soldiers surrendered in this area. In the area south and southeast of Kleinhau remnants of the 89.Inf.Div. (Gren.Rgt.1055, Gren.Rgt.1056, Pi.Btl.89) together with the remainder of the Gren.Rgt.983 were committed. At 16:30, approximately 100 Germans were observed moving from Brandenberg to the southeast, in the direction of Bergstein and later from Bergstein to the south. More Germans retreated east towards Obermaubach.[42]

At the beginning of December 1944, Operation Queen began to have a significant impact on the planned German Ardennes offensive. Up to the end of November, units had been supplied primarily to the Hürtgenwald, which were not intended for the Battle of the Bulge and also had a dubious combat value. The situation at the beginning of December not only forced the German leadership to deploy units intended for use in the Ardennes, but also to keep units in operation which urgently needed refitting, even though they were also intended for the Ardennes offensive. The battle also consumed vast quantities of ammunition, fuel, and other supplies that had been gathered with such care for the coming offensive.

In the Gey area, the remains of Gren.Rgt.1057 (344.Inf.Div.) retreated from the forest edge west of the village back to the village during the morning of **2 December 1944**, apparently to regroup.

CT 12, 4th Inf Div, observed German activity from the forest edge west of the village, suggesting that the Germans intended to keep the town as long as possible. The CT 22, 4th Inf Div, with subordinated 46th Armd Inf Bn, 5th Armd Div, came under attack just before 07:00 by I./Gren.Rgt.943 (353.Inf.Div., but subordinated to the 344.Inf.Div.) under the leadership of Hptm. Garten with approximately 250 men. The objective of the counterattack, which had been planned the previous day, was the high ground north of Heidbüchel to the east of Großhau. The battalion used only three Grenadier companies, and declined the use of the heavy company according to prisoner statements. At the start of the attack the 1. Kompanie had a strength of approximately 80 soldiers, the 2. Kompanie had about 65 men with 8

MGs and the 3. Kompanie had a strength of 96 men with 7 MGs. The attack started without artillery or armor support. A small cluster of German tanks, which had probably been deployed to support the German counterattack west of Straß, had recently been targeted by the American Air Force. The attack reached a line about 800 meters west of Gey, when a Kampfgruppe from Gren.Rgt.1057 with about 40 soldiers also attacked at 08:30, apparently the same group that had retired in the morning. From the outset, this attack was smashed by the Americans, with the Gren.Rgt.1057 unable to gain any ground. The I./Gren.Rgt.943 attempted to get the attack rolling again during the day, and plenty of artillery and mortar fire was laid down on the American positions. The attack was finally stopped at about 15:00, and the Grenadiers fell back to their original positions, while the American line was able to be restored. The 1./Gren.Rgt.943 lost 70 men during the fighting and reported a strength of only 30 men afterwards. The 46th Armd Inf Bn reported 75 enemy dead in its section, belonging to one of the three companies of I./Gren. Rgt.943.[43] In the area of Combat Teams 12 and 22, numerous German soldiers had again surrendered. 20 soldiers were members of the 344.Inf.Div., 59 men of 353. Inf.Div., 14 men of 275.Inf.Div. and a single member of *Kampfgruppe Hilt*. This was the former 2./Pi.Btl.33, an alarm unit that had been used since the Fall of 1944 in the Prüm area on the Westwall. On 24 November, the unit was transferred to the Gey-Großhau area, where it was used as infantry with a strength of 50 men with six light MGs and two light mortars. When the company took up its position on 2 December, they were attacked and routed by the Americans. The light mortars could not be used because there were no trained personnel for them.[44] Transferring from Luxembourg, the 330th Inf Rgt, 83rd Inf Div was subordinated to the 4th Inf Div when it arrived in the Schevenhütte area on 2 December, initiating the forthcoming replacement of the 4th Inf Div.[45]

The German leadership intended to construct a solid defensive front southwest of Gey in the gap between the 353.Inf.Div. and the 344.Inf.Div., and planned to insert the Gren.Rgt.981 (272.VG.Div.). At the same time, elements of Gren.Rgt.941 and 943, as well as the remaining splinter groups of Gren.Rgt.1057 and 1058 would be pulled out and refitted. Another regiment of the 272.VG.Div. would be detached and become Army reserve. The I./Gren.Rgt.981 started its march in the Untermaubach area during the evening. After the first parts had arrived in the village around 17:00, an order was received at 21:40 to transfer the regimental staff, the I. Bataillon and the regimental units to Horm, east of Gey. The regimental commander and the 1st Ordonnanzoffizier immediately had to report at the command post of the 344.Inf.Div. At the divisional headquarters, the regimental commander received the following order:

"During the night of 3 December 1944, Gren.Rgt.981 will relieve Gren.Rgt.1057 in its previous position with the II. Bataillon on the right (by this time the II./Gren. Rgt.981 was already in use in the switch position at Beythal northeast of Gey)

and I. Battalion on the left. The regiment deliberately occupies a broad front, so that a continuous main battle line can be constructed with the right and left neighbors. When encountering weak enemy resistance, the main battle line is to be pushed to the Merode-Gey position."

Awaiting the return of the regimental commander, the I. Bataillon moved to Horm and the 13. and 14. Kompanie moved to Kufferath. The previous march was not without problems. As a result of exhaustion and artillery fire, some horses had died and so the transport of heavy weapons was significantly delayed.[46] Meanwhile, parts of the 8th Inf Div moved east from the Kleinhau area, but were only able to move forward a few hundred meters before encountering strong German resistance. In this section, elements of Füs.Btl.89 were identified. Again, the Americans reported the use of German self-propelled guns as artillery. At 10:40, three German tanks were reported west of Schafberg.[47]

South of Kleinhau, elements of the 8th Inf Div and CCR, 5th Arm Div, had been moving towards Brandenberg since 08:00. Here, remnants of the 89.Inf.Div. put up desperate resistance, especially in the forest area west of the Kleinhau-Brandenberg road, which was very heavily mined. Small arms and extensive anti-tank fire prevented clearance of the mines. Nevertheless, the Grenadiers could not stop the American advance. As the Americans advanced through the forest east of the road and flanked the barrier, the Germans had to leave the edge of the forest and retreat 100 meters to the west. The following units were identified: III./Gren.Rgt.1055, parts of I./Gren.Rgt.1056, Pz.Jg.Kp.189, Pi.Btl.189 and St./I./Art. Rgt.189. Further interrogation of German prisoners revealed that less than 10% of the prisoners had been members of the division for more than 6 weeks. The Americans reported 70 prisoners from the Gren.Rgt.1055 and 71 men from the Gren.Rgt.1056.[48]

At 01:00 on **3 December**, the regimental commander of Gren.Rgt.981 returned to his command post, which was situated in Gut Hocherbach, west of Horm. He immediately gave verbal orders to the two battalion commanders and the leaders of the regimental units:

"Assignments:

- *I. Battalion moves forward to the ordered line in the left part of the regimental sector, and looks for connection to the right and left. Because the forest south of Hubertushöhe is occupied, the 2. Kompanie executes a feint attack from Straß, while the 1. and 3. Kompanie flank the enemy from the north.*
- *II. Battalion moves forward to the ordered line in the right part of the regimental sector, and looks for connection to the right*

- *13. Kompanie supports the attack with all heavy weapons.*
- *14. Kompanie transfers one platoon of tank destroyers to each of both battalions*
- *The regimental bicycle and engineer platoons remain with the regimental headquarters as reserve."*

Shortly after the orders were given, the two battalions moved out. Artillery fire made contact between the two battalions difficult, so the regiment relied on radio and messengers. At 08:20, the regiment reported to the 344.Inf.Div. that it had taken over the sector. Due to the lack of contact with the front, officers were sent out as reconnaissance parties to the I. and II. Battalion to collect the first detailed messages. At 09:10, I./Gren.Rgt.981 reported over the radio, that it had reached the Hubertushöhe around 05:50 and that it had occupied the 'Forsthaus'. At 12:10 the Ordonnanzoffizier returned to the command post with detailed messages from I. and II. Bataillon. He reported that the II. Bataillon had pushed the enemy out of the forest edge west of Gey. The battalion was now stopped in confusing terrain in front of a strong opponent. The enemy had used tanks, whereas support by their own Sturmgeschütze was not possible. The attack was also minus the support of its own artillery. The battalion had to dig in. There was no connection to the right and left, but the opponent was sitting on the right flank at the edge of the forest. The battalion has suffered severe personnel losses. Meanwhile, Gey was under sustained fire from heavy weapons. The supply of ammunition by day was almost impossible in this situation. The battalion commander requested artillery fire on the identified enemy positions. The I. Battalion had reached Hubertushöhe at 04:30, and relieved the Gren.Rgt.1057 sector by 06:00. At 06:30, the 3. Kompanie encountered strong enemy forces south of a small fish pond. A concentric attack by the 1. and 3. Kompanie, which started at 08:00 southeast of the forester's lodge, was cut off by the Americans. A renewed attack finally brought success and ten American soldiers were captured but at 09:00 the Americans counterattacked with artillery support. As a result, the 3. Kompanie was for the most part annihilated. The previously won ground was lost again and the 1. Kompanie had to extend its own position to the south, so as not to lose the connection to the 3. Kompanie. The Americans continued their pressure on the I. Bataillon, forcing the 1. and 3. Kompanie to take up new positions around the Hubertushöhe forester's lodge. The 2. Kompanie in Straß was to be used as a reinforcement.[49] Since morning, the replacement of the 22nd Inf Rgt by the 330th Inf Rgt southwest of Gey had started and lasted throughout the day. During the relief there was strong German artillery and mortar fire on the American positions. The necessary freedom of movement during the replacement was hampered by the numerous German minefields. A company each of 629th TD Bn and 774th Tk Bn relied on cooperation with the 330th Inf Rgt. The attack by Gren.Rgt.981 hit the positions of CT 22, according to American messages, between 07:00 and 08:00 and the positions of CT 12 west of Gey at 09:00.

The attack took place without armored support. On the other hand, the presence of numerous German tanks had been reported in the Gey area during the day, suggesting that the Gren.Rgt.981 had attacked with insufficient coordination with StuG.Brig.394 and Sturmpanzer-Abteilung 217 who were in the area. German prisoners spoke of two 'Panther' tanks hiding in destroyed houses in the north of Gey, and two or three tanks hiding in a hollow between Gey and Hubertushöhe during the day and emerging from their cover only in the dark to go into firing positions. Other prisoners reported two or three assault guns in northern Gey, and four tanks in the same area in the evening. VII Corps also reported that they had destroyed seven German tanks being readied by artillery fire and fighter-bombers in the Gey area.[50]

According to American reports, parts of CT 12, 4th Inf Div, were able to repel the attacks in their area. The bulk of the fighting was carried out by Cos B and C, 12th Inf Rgt. Prisoners were identified from 5., 6. and 8./Gren.Rgt.981. They reported that II./Gren.Rgt.981 had started in the dark from the area northeast of Gey and had initially proceeded along the road to Gey before attacking the edge of the forest northwest of the village. According to reports from CT 22, 4th Inf Div, the German attack on the Hubertushöhe area began at 08:45 in company strength and was also beaten back. Prisoners of the 3./Gren.Rgt.981 were identified.[51] Contrary to the original plan, at 12:50 the commander of Gren.Rgt.981 ordered that the 2. Kompanie should continue to occupy the southwestern border of Straß and prevent the enemy from escaping from the forest from the direction of Point 314.4. After a briefing by the commander of 344.Inf.Div., the regiment received orders at 13:20 to make contact with Füsilier-Bataillon 353, which was supposedly located in the 'Forsthaus Gey' area. An order was issued to I./Gren.Rgt.981 at 14:25, to establish a continuous line and make contact with its neighbors to the left and right. For this purpose, the 2. Kompanie had to be withdrawn from Straß to make the connection with the left-hand neighbor, which was allegedly located on the stream south of Point 314.4.[52] Attempts to contact the I./Gren.Rgt.943 on the right had failed.[53]

In the evening, the 4th Inf Div reported that the Germans had reached the forest's edge in the area of CT 12. CT 12 had captured 10 soldiers of II./Gren.Rgt.981, while in the area of CT 22, the relief of the regiment by CT 330, 83rd Inf Div, was also completed. The CT 330 initially remained under the 4th Inf Div and established a connection to the south with the 121st Inf Rgt, 8th Inf Div, just before midnight. The 4th Inf Div reported more prisoners in the Gey-Schafberg area, belonging to the 353.Inf.Div. (62 soldiers) and the 344.Inf.Div. (31 soldiers). Soldiers, who were previously engaged west of Schafberg, reported that the remains of the III./Gren.Rgt.1058 were combined into one company, which had to defend a 100 meter wide stretch in the forest.

Meanwhile, CCR, 5th Armd Div, and elements of 8th Inf Div attacked Brandenberg. North of the village, German resistance from 89.Inf.Div. was encountered, who tried to stop the American advance unsuccessfully. Brandenberg fell after a brief battle. The commander of the III./Gren.Rgt.1055 with the majority of his staff and 11 members of Pi.Btl.189 went into American captivity. The Americans destroyed two Pak guns from Pz.Jg.Abt.189 in the village. In total, the Americans captured 200 German prisoners in the Brandenberg area. In contrast, other parts of the 89. Inf.Div. put up a fierce resistance in the forest west of Brandenberg. However, these forces were able to be pushed aside following the capture of Brandenberg and were further squeezed during the day. The head of CCR reached the outskirts of Bergstein in the evening. After the rapid loss of Brandenberg, the 89.Inf.Div. tried to reorganize in Bergstein. Gren.Rgt.1055 was tasked with the defense, which was further strengthened by Gren.Rgt.980 (272 V.G.Div.). In the evening, the Americans reported three to four German tanks in the Bergstein area.[54]

During the night of **4 December**, the I./Gren.Rgt.981 managed to restore contact to the left (I./Gren.Rgt.941) south of Point 314.4. Also there was contact with the II./Gren.Rgt.981 to the right, about 700 meters west of Gey. On the other hand, the II. Bataillon continued to report no connection to its right (Füs.Btl.353). During the night, the Americans were remarkably calm, which was almost certainly due to the ongoing relief of the 4th Inf Div. At 03:00, the regimental commander, Major Kleinkorres, ordered the II. Bataillon to make contact again to its right. In the twilight, the I. Bataillon intended to eliminate the remaining enemy position at the Forsthaus Hubertushöhe with a pincer attack; the 2. Kompanie on the left and 3. Kompanie on the right. However, the 3. Kompanie only had a strength of 21 soldiers. In addition, the battalion commander demanded that an advanced artillery observer be drafted in, not only to support the 2. Kompanie's attack, but primarily to keep watch on the thinly occupied main line in case of enemy counterattacks. He also asked that the Sturmgeschützen be given the order to move with a few vehicles to the Hubertushöhe to strengthen the defense there. It should be noted that the war diary of Gren.Rgt.981 on that day did not mention StuG.Brig.394, but referred to two combat groups from Sturmpanzer-Abteilung 217. The commander of I./Gren.Rgt.981 urgently demanded a supply of ammunition, since the 1. Kompanie and the 3. Kompanie had almost run out.[55]

At 08:40 the divisional commander of the 344.Inf.Div. arrived at the Gren.Rgt.981 command post in Hof Hocherbach. After the regimental commander described the situation, the divisional commander confirmed that the regiment was in a very difficult situation, due to the terrain, the strong enemy artillery fire and its own high losses. However, due to the generally precarious situation, the army had ordered that this position must be maintained in order to prevent the enemy from escaping onto the Düren plain. At 13:30, the divisional commander ordered that the command post of Gren.Rgt.981 be moved to Horm. The engineer platoon of

Gren.Rgt. 943 (353.Inf.Div.) was assigned to Gren.Rgt.981 for this move.[56]

At 14:00, the regiment received word that a patrol from Gren.Rgt.941 had observed that the Americans had reached the stream 250 meters southeast of Point 314.4. This severed the connection between 2./Gren.Rgt.941 and 2./Gren.Rgt.981. The 2./Gren.Rgt.941 was then tasked to make contact with the north independently. The I./Gren.Rgt.981, however, reported at 15:25 that a continuous HKL (main combat line) was available in the battalion sector, but then admitted that the connection to I./Gren.Rgt.941 was last confirmed at dawn. Only now did the I. Bataillon report that the attack of the 2. Kompanie had failed during the night, as the enemy was too strong in the forest south of Hubertushöhe. The company suffered heavy losses and therefore could not continue the attack. At 16:25, the Adjutant of the Gren.Rgt.941 advised Gren.Rgt.981 that there was still no contact with the 2./Gren.Rgt.981. Instead, they received infantry fire from the forest edge east of Point 314.4. At 16:30, a message came in that the 2./Gren.Rgt.981 was in a position 200 meters east of the forest edge and was being pushed back to their previous position at the edge of the forest. Immediately German artillery fired on the edge of the forest to prevent the Americans from coming out of the woods. To restore the situation, the Gren.Rgt.981 initially planned a counterattack with the regimental Pionierzug, but this plan was later rejected. At 17:30 the I. Bataillon reported heavy losses due to artillery and mortar fire. From the forest in front of their own HKL, tank noises and machine gun fire were heard, so an American attack was to be expected.[57]

The German reports are surprising in relation to the I./Gren.Rgt.981 sector. The 330th Inf Rgt, according to its own report, acted passively following the takeover of the 22nd Inf Rgt sector, and was primarily occupied with the expansion of its own positions. No German activity was reported during the day, which makes the alleged attack of the 2./Gren.Rgt.981 in the morning questionable. The 330th Inf Rgt even reported that it had no physical contact with the Germans throughout the day. Only German smoke grenades were reported, which were fired at American positions southwest of Straß. Co B, 629th TD Bn relieved elements of the 803rd TD Bn and Co C, 774th Tk Bn replaced elements of the 70th Tk Bn. Prisoners from I./Gren.Rgt.981 later testified that the battalion had a combat strength of 284 men at the beginning of the attack on 3 December, of which only 80 men remained on 4 December. 92 soldiers were killed or missing and 112 men were wounded.[58]

Around 15:00, Gren.Rgt.981's right neighbor reported through the 'Ia' (first general staff officer) of 353.Inf.Div., that the Americans had attacked the division's right flank (Füs.Btl.353)[59] with tanks and infantry. CT 12 made a limited attack in the sector of II./Gren.Rgt.981, primarily to recapture ground lost the previous day.[60]

At 18:00 Gren.Rgt.981 issued an order to comb the battalions for personnel who would be used in case of an emergency. At 21:30 an order was given to the regimental Pionierzug to obtain any supplies required as quickly as possible, and then move towards the I. Bataillon command post. The Pionierzug would be subordinated to the decimated 3. Kompanie. At 21:50, I./Gren.Rgt.981 reported that it intended to attack the forest edge southeast of Hubertushöhe with two companies on the morning of 5 December. The area of the attack would be limited on the right by the fish pond and on the left by the creek south of Point 314.4. The plan of attack provided that the 3. Kompanie would attack on the right. For this purpose parts of the Fahrradzug and Pionierzug were subordinated.

On the left, the 2. Kompanie was to attack with the two remaining platoons and the attached Ofenrohre of the 14. Kompanie. The dividing line between the 2. and 3. Kompanie was the path northwest of Straß to the northern part of Point 314.4. Sturmgeschütze were to monitor the attack from the southeastern area of Gey. The assault gun commanders were ordered to the battalion headquarters for instructions. Major Thürmer, commander of I./Gren.Rgt.981 complained that their own artillery and infantry guns repeatedly shot too short. One shell had landed in the 1. Kompanie headquarters, killing one man and wounding three others. As a consequence, he demanded that the fire be moved forward by 300 meters. Also, 7./Gren.Rgt.981 reported multiple losses due to friendly fire from artillery, tanks and anti-tank guns.[61]

During the day, elements of the 8th Inf Div advanced further into the forest southeast of the Großhau-Brandenberg road and pushed the Germans further back. The Americans reported intense German artillery fire, but no offensive action. Southwest of Brandenberg, however, the Americans met slight German resistance. According to an entry on the map of Heeresgruppe B for 4 December, Sturmpanzer-Abteilung 217, StuG.Brig.394 and Stu.Art.Brig.667 were subordinated to the LXXIV A.K.[62]

Contrary to the order the previous day, the command post of Gren.Rgt.981 was still located in Hof Hocherbach on **5 December 1944**. The situation on II. Bataillon's right flank developed as follows. During the night, the battalion tried in vain to restore the connection with Füs.Btl.353 on the left flank. At 07:05 the battalion was attacked on its left flank, and 20 minutes later they called for an artillery barrage in front of the battalion's left section. Shortly after 09:00, after the battalion had defended against two attacks, the Americans shelled the German positions with artillery. As a result, just over 30% of the personnel were out of action. Nevertheless, the order was renewed to establish contact with the right neighbor at all costs. Only in the course of the afternoon, did a patrol from Füs.Btl.353 succeed in making contact with the 6./Gren.Rgt.981. Meanwhile, Füs.Btl.353 was able to drive the enemy back behind the main combat line. The Americans went over to the defense and started to dig in.[63] In the left regimental sector, the attack of the I.

Bataillon to restore the main battle line, began at 06:00. It quickly became clear that the attacked sector was heavily occupied. From the American point of view, the 2. and 3./Gren.Rgt.981 attacked the positions of the 330th Inf Rgt southwest of Gey at 06:45 and 07:00 respectively, and preceded by German artillery and mortar fire. The German attack had essentially hit the positions of Co B, 330th Inf Rgt, at the northeast corner of the forest west of Straß. The American infantrymen allowed the Grenadiers to approach and opened fire only at the shortest distance. At 07:27, the 1./ Sturmartillerie-Brigade 667 arrived in Gey to support I./Gren.Rgt.981 with seven Sturmgeschütze. Shortly after, a forward observer reported that the enemy was resisting south of Hubertushöhe. The regiment therefore ordered the 13. Kompanie to concentrate the fire of all its heavy weapons on the area south of Hubertushöhe. By 07:45, the I. Bataillon with 2. and 3. Kompanie reached the edge of the forest on a broad front. Later reports said that the Americans continued to hold their positions about 10 meters from the edge of the forest. Wounded soldiers of the I. Bataillon were being tended to by the Americans and then sent back to their own lines. The I. Bataillon could not make any further progress and remained in their present positions. Even the combined fire of the regimental heavy weapons could not change the outcome of the situation. The 330th Inf Rgt reported 15-20 Germans killed and 20 prisoners, all members of I./Gren.Rgt.981. Most of them had been captured southeast of the Hubertushöhe. Afterwards, the Americans observed how the Germans dug in west of Straß. The remainder of the day was calm despite continuing German artillery fire. In the morning, news of the failed attack of I./Gren.Rgt.981 was confirmed. The 2. Kompanie had been almost completely wiped out and had to withdraw from the forest. The situation south of the Hubertushöhe, however, initially remained unclear.[64]

At 08:33, OLt. Tetzner[65], the company commander of 1./ Sturmpanzer-Abteilung 217 reported to the regimental command post in Hof Hocherbach that his battle group would be replaced the following night by seven other Sturmpanzers from the battalion. This message suggests that the Sturmpanzers had already been in use in the area of Gey for several days. Whether this replacement has to be seen in connection with the development of the situation in the Bergstein area, can no longer be confirmed. At 16:15, the divisional commander of the 344.Inf. Div. informed Gren.Rgt.981 that the enemy had entered Bergstein, which is why Stu.Art.Brig.667 was immediately to be relocated to Nideggen. A German prisoner later testified that on 5 December he had seen 20 light, medium and heavy tanks in Drove, most likely assault guns and assault howitzers of the Stu. Art.Brig.667 on the way to the Bergstein area. On the other hand, the situation in the Schafberg area, remained calm. Fourteen prisoners were captured by the Americans and identified as belonging to several different units: Gren.Rgt.1057, Gren.Rgt.1058, F.Ers.Btl.344, Gren.Rgt.941, Gren.Rgt.943.[66] At 21:40, Lt. Böhme[67] of 2./ Sturmpanzer-Abteilung 217 reported to the command post of Gren. Rgt.981. Instead of the seven Sturmpanzers stated by OLt. Tetzner, Lt. Böhme had

brought only four Sturmpanzers with him. In the loss reports of Sturmpanzer-Abteilung 217 there is a reference to a *Kampfgruppe Böhme* in the Hürtgenwald. However, during interrogation, prisoners stated that Lt. Schmidt was the CO of the 2. Kompanie. The assumption is that Lt. Böhme was actually a platoon leader in the 2. Kompanie or acted as the leader of a mixed battle group, including all operational Sturmpanzer IVs which were not in use with the 1. and 2. Kompanie. In the evening, the 4th Inf Div reported that it had eliminated all remaining enemy strongpoints in its sector. Combat Teams 8 and 330 reported that they had had no direct contact with German forces. However, they still recorded heavy German artillery and mortar fire on their own positions. An attempt by the 3rd Bn, 330th Inf Rgt, to send patrols towards the southern outskirts of Gey at about 23:30 was rebuffed with well placed fire.[68]

Further to the south, CCR, 5th Armd Div, started to attack from Brandenberg to the southeast at about 14:15 with heavy artillery support, smoke and fighter-bomber attacks. At 15:30, they entered Bergstein with twenty to thirty tanks. Another fifty tanks, halftracks and trucks were observed on the road from Kleinhau to Brandenberg. The American advance could be temporarily stopped at the south and southeast edges of town; some of the American tanks then turned to the northeast. According to German reports five or seven enemy tanks were knocked out. At 16:30, however, the CCR reported that it had taken over the village completely and secured it.

The Americans reported 25 prisoners from Gren.Rgt.1055 and 13 prisoners from Gren.Rgt.1056. This increased the number of prisoners in the last three days from I./Gren.Rgt.1056 to more than 200 men. It was not until the loss of the village that heavy German artillery fire fell on the American positions. The Burgberg could still be held by the II./Gren.Rgt.980 (272.VG.Div.). The Pz.Jg.Abt.1272 and its twelve tank destroyers[69] were to cooperate with the II. Bataillon. On the other hand, the Americans reported only five German tank destroyers in the Bergstein area. Due to the great importance of Bergstein, the German leadership transferred Pz. Jg.Abt.1277[70] (277.VG.Div.) from Harscheidt to Zerkall and the Stu.Art.Brig.667[71] from Straß to Nideggen. Elements of the 12.VG.Div. in the Urfttalsperre area were also alerted. The commander-in-chief of Heeresgruppe B also alerted a battle group of the 3.Pz.Gren.Div., consisting of tanks, heavy anti-tank weapons, a grenadier battalion and an artillery battalion, and ordered them to be prepared for future combat.[72]

At 02:00 on **6 December**, Gren.Rgt.943 (subordinated to the 344.Inf.Div.) tried to close the gap between the creek and the path northeast of Point 314.4. *Alarm-Kompanie Krämer* managed to cross the stream. However, on the other side, they ran into concentrated defensive fire and were annihilated. The company commander was wounded and the remains of the company were absorbed by

I./Gren.Rgt.981. According to a report by I. Bataillon, the 2. Kompanie had nine soldiers left and the Pionierzug just eighteen men. Together they took over the defense of Straß. Since the forest edge had been lost as the first line of defense, it was intended to control the edge of the forest with fire. The entire area of the 330th Inf Rgt there received significant German artillery and mortar fire. Meanwhile, the Gren.Rgt.981 tried to strengthen its II. Bataillon sector west of Gey. Otherwise, the day was quiet in this sector. The 4th Inf Div reorganized and prepared for their relief by the 83rd Inf Div.[73]

In the area of Bergstein, the first German counterattack started around 07:00. I./Gren.Rgt.980 and elements of II./Gren.Rgt.980 attacked with 500 men and about 10 armored vehicles against the positions of CCR, 5th Armd Div. The energetic attack managed to reach the first houses in the south of the town, but was halted by 09:30. CCR reported the destruction of six tanks and five anti-tank guns. At 11:30, an attack in company strength, supported by one tank was quickly repelled. Another attack at 15:45, this time without armor support, was stopped. During these attacks 42 soldiers from Gren.Rgt.980 were captured. Meanwhile, Heeresgruppe B planned the relief of 2/3 of the 272.VG.Div. by the 85.Inf.Div. The other 1/3 of the division would be relieved by 353.Inf.Div. This shift of forces should be seen in relation to the upcoming Ardennes offensive.[74]

On **7 December**, the command post of Gren.Rgt.981 was finally transferred to Horm. In the morning, connection was made with Füs.Btl.353 on the right. The I./Gren.Rgt.981 received orders to use their firearms primarily against the frontal gap towards the positions of the Gren.Rgt.941 on the left. The 2. Kompanie, which had reached a strength of 60 men by taking men from the supply trains, remained responsible for the defense of Straß. At 12:30, a forward artillery observer reported heavy engine noises from the direction of Großhau towards Gey and in front of the left regimental sector. At 16:00, the divisional commander of the 344.Inf.Div. at the command post of Gren.Rgt.981 phoned Major Kleinkorres and ordered him to arrange the connection with the Sturmpanzers of Sturmpanzer-Abteilung 217. The regiment laid down interdiction fire on the edge of the forest south of Gey and in the area of Point 257.73. At 17:00, engine noises in front of the left sector were heard again. The enemy, however, remained calm except for the artillery and mortar fire on the German main combat line and rear areas.[75]

At 16:00, the 330th Inf Rgt was released from the 4th Inf Div, after the staff of 83rd Inf Div arrived at Hürtgenwald and took the lead from the Ivy Division. The 330th Inf Rgt sent two patrols in the direction of Schafberg and Height 375. Some 600 meters southwest of Schafberg, one patrol ran into German opposition and returned to its start position. The other patrol reported reaching the height without opposition. It was only at 23:00 that they realized they had not occupied Height 375, but a point much farther west! In the course of the day, the 1st and

2nd Bn, 331st Inf Rgt, relieved the 1st and 2nd Bn, 12th Inf Rgt west of Gey. On their left, 14 soldiers of Füs.Btl.353 went into captivity. Connection to the right, toward 330th Inf Rgt, was reestablished.[76]

After taking over the 4th Inf Div positions, the 83rd Inf Div reported the following German units in their sector. The strength is based on estimates by the G-2 department:

- I./Fs.Jg.Rgt.5   Approx. 500 men
- I./Gren.Rgt.942   Approx. 250 men
- II./Gren.Rgt.942   Approx. 250 men
- Füs.Btl.353   Approx. 170 men
- II./Gren.Rgt.981   Approx. 400 men
- Rest Gren.Rgt.1057 & 1058   Approx. 400 men
- I./Gren.Rgt.981   Approx. 400 men
- F.Ers.Btl.191   Approx. 400 men
- Gren.Rgt.943   Approx. 500 men
- Gren.Rgt.941   Approx. 600 men[77]

The 2nd Ranger Bn arrived in Bergstein during the night of 6/7 December, with the order to capture the Burgberg. The II./Gren.Rgt.980 under Hptm. Thomae and elements of I./Gren.Rgt.980 fought desperately. Nonetheless, the 2nd Ranger Bn with support of the 893rd TD Bn and elements of CCR, 5th Armd Div was able to occupy the Burgberg. Two German counterattacks jumped off around 18:00, of which one was carried out by a temporarily assigned battalion of the 3.Pz.Gren. Div. Both attacks were carried out from the depression southeast of the Burgberg. The attacking groups were each 150 Grenadiers strong, but the attacks were repelled by the Americans.[78]

On **8 December**, the Germans remained on the defense against the 83rd Inf Div, and German mortar fire fell on the American positions all day. The 331st Inf Rgt further extended its positions west of Gey and sent patrols towards Gey and into the woods north of the village, but did not encounter any German troops. Due south, in the area west of Schafberg, the 1st Bn, 330th Inf Rgt, had recognized its mistake regarding Height 375. During the night of 7/8 December, Cos A and B, 330th Inf Rgt attacked the height and captured the position by 06:25. On the height they surprised a German outpost, which should have warned their own troops in case of an attack. 2 officers and 15 men[79] were surprised and captured in their sleep. The American outpost was reinforced by midday by a platoon of light tanks from Co A, 759th Lt Tk Bn. Meanwhile, Co I , 330th Inf Rgt was inserted between Cos A and C for flank protection. Initially the Germans responded to the loss of Height 375 with artillery fire onto the height and the access roads.[80]

From American interrogation reports, the German outpost on Height 375 consisted of elements of 7./Gren.Rgt.943 and a squad of forward observers from 8./Art. Rgt.191. The prisoners of 7./Gren.Rgt.943 reported that their company had only 50-60 men. The entire battalion consisted of only 3 companies and had been in this area for a week. It had suffered heavy casualties (80%), primarily from its own artillery, which was constantly shooting too short. The remnants of the battalion were therefore grouped into *Kampfgruppe Zorn* (Hptm. Zorn, commander II./Gren. Rgt.943). Both forward observers stated that their battery had three horse-drawn 105mm field howitzers, and were instructed to collaborate with the 7./Gren. Rgt.943. Other soldiers captured in the area later that day belonged to the neighboring Gren.Rgt.941. They testified that the remains of I./Gren.Rgt.941 had been combined into one company, and had the task of relieving the remnants of II./Gren.Rgt.941.[81] On 8 December, Sturmpanzer-Abteilung 217 reported an inventory of 31 Sturmpanzers, which confirms that the 6 Sturmpanzers allocated to the battalion in November, and the Sturmpanzer from 2./ Stu.Pz.Abt.218 z.b.V. (see chapter 5.2) had finally arrived with the battalion.

For the first time since its formation, the staff and the two companies had their full complement of Sturmpanzers.[82] The battalion also reported a soldier killed in the Schafberg-Straß area; this was Obergefreiter Paul Wolff of the 1. Kompanie.[83]

In the Bergstein area, the Germans started two new attacks at 07:40 and 09:00. Both were launched with heavy artillery and mortar fire, but were again repelled with the attackers suffering heavy losses. Prisoners were identified from 3./Pz.Gren. Rgt.29 (3.Pz.Gren.Div.) and Pz.Jg.Abt.1277 (277.VG.Div.). German troops north of Bergstein were forced to retreat east by the Americans. The Gren.Rgt.980 attacked the Burgberg again from the southeast at 17:00, and reached the observation tower, before the attack had to be called off. A total of 43 soldiers were captured. The Americans reported five German self-propelled guns southeast of Bergstein, of which two were knocked out.[84] Meanwhile, the arrival of the 85.Inf.Div. was delayed. On the German side, it was expected that the relief of the 272.VG.Div. in the Bergstein and Vossenack area would start on the night of 10/11 December at the earliest. This in turn would mean that only 2/3 of the division would arrive on 14 December in its new combat area for the Ardennes Offensive.[85]

The Germans remained largely passive in the sector of the 83rd Inf Div on **9 December**, but continued to shell the leading US positions with artillery and mortar fire. In the area west of Gey, the 331st Inf Rgt reported numerous concentrations of mortar fire on the regimental section at night and during the morning. In the evening, German movements were spotted in Gey and targeted by American artillery. During the night of 10 December German artillery fire subsided.

On the night of 8/9 December, positions of the 330th Inf Rgt in the area of Height 375 came under attack from the east by German infantry supported by a tank or assault gun. American light tanks tried to attack the German tank, but could not maneuver into a favorable firing position. Ultimately, the German attack was stopped. Another German attack with infantry and tanks against the positions of Co I would also be turned back during the day. Two members of the Gren.Rgt.943 were captured in this sector, essentially confirming the information received the previous day about the structure and strength of II./Gren.Rgt.943. Meanwhile, the 83rd Inf Div completed its preparations for the attack on Gey and Straß on 10 December.[86]

In the meantime, fighting continued in the Bergstein area. Six men of 89.Inf.Div. went into American captivity. A soldier of the Gren.Rgt.1055 stated that after his regiment had been almost completely wiped out in the previous fighting, it currently consisted of only two companies with a total of 100 poorly trained air force soldiers. The state of Gren.Rgt.1056 was similar. The 89.Inf.Div. supposedly had all its reserves in use.[87]

The 2nd Bn, 331st Inf Rgt (83rd Inf Div) started its attack on Gey at 06:30 on **10 December**. The battalion initially encountered only sporadic defensive fire and very little artillery and mortar fire. Throughout the day, the intensity of the artillery and mortar fire increased. Due to bad road conditions and mines, the American tanks were unable to follow the infantry. A platoon of the accompanying tanks tried to detour through the sector of the 330th Inf Rgt but got stuck. All attempts by the engineers at clearing the mines were hindered by the German artillery. At 15:20, the 2nd Bn with two platoons from Co B, 774th Tk Bn and the tank battalion's mortar platoon, entered Gey. In the town the Germans resisted, and house to house fighting broke out. At dawn, Cos E and F announced that they had reached the center of Gey. The accompanying tanks of Co B, 774th Tk Bn reported the destruction of three German anti-tank guns, four Panzer IVs, two reconnaissance cars and three MGs as well as thirty-five Germans killed. The 2nd Bn reported the capture of thirty-six German soldiers. Among the prisoners were eighteen men from Gren.Rgt.981, of which many belonged to the Stabskompanie or the regimental units. The fact that the mass of prisoners belonged to these companies was proof that the regiment had combed through all the companies in order to keep the infantry strength high. Prisoners from Gren.Rgt.981 reported that it was planned to relieve the regiment with II./Fs.Jg.Rgt.6 during the night of 10/11 December 1944. This did not occur, because II./Fs.Jg.Rgt.6 under Hauptmann Mager had been in use since the night of 9/10 December 1944 in the area of Bogheim and could not be redeployed due to the American attack on Schafberg.[88]

Meanwhile, 1st and 3rd Bn, 331st Inf Rgt, held their positions outside the village. Throughout the day, there were no German counterattacks in the Gey area. German tanks were only detected in the Horm area. American observers identified

A Sturmpanzer IV Ausf.IV from 2./ Sturmpanzer-Abteilung 217 in a field west of Straß, probably destroyed on 10 December 1944. While the disc camouflage pattern is still clearly visible on the side armored plates, it is not obvious on the front, indicating that it may have burned out after being hit. Note the post for the Fla.MG on a 360° rotating mount on the cupola. *NARA via Darren Neely*

RODNA

five tanks in this sector. At night the German artillery and mortar fire increased.[89]

In the area east of Großhau and around Height 375, the 330th Inf Rgt (83rd Inf Div) had taken up positions during the night for a future attack. The area south of Gey to Schafberg was occupied by elements of Gren.Rgt.943 on the right and Gren.Rgt.941 on the left (both subordinated to the 344.Inf.Div.). There was obviously a gap between the two regiments around the Kleinhau-Schafberg road, through which the 3rd Bn, 330th Inf Rgt could infiltrate. The 3rd Bn had crossed the line of departure at about 06:00 and intended to proceed via Schafberg to the village of Straß. Unlike three days before, they encountered no German resistance and by 06:30 had passed Schafberg under cover of darkness. Only then did they encounter sporadic resistance; massive artillery and mortar fire was brought down on the German frontline positions. The first prisoners were brought in. At 07:26, the 3rd Bn reported that it had pushed into Straß and started to clean up the village. German Grenadiers in the village defended from houses, cellars and prepared positions and were supported by the Sturmpanzers from 2./Sturmpanzer-Abteilung 217.[90] The American infantry managed to knock out three of these tanks with bazookas. The 3rd Bn, 330th Inf Rgt, nevertheless requested the immediate support of Co C, 774th Tk Bn. At about 10:00, the Americans reported that the last Germans had withdrawn from the village of Schafberg. At 11:00, two platoons from Co C, 774th Tk Bn arrived in Straß. Shortly before, one of their tanks had hit a mine between Schafberg and Straß, and was later destroyed by German fire. In general, the freedom of movement of American tanks was considerably limited by numerous German minefields and concealed Pak guns. In addition, there was intense German artillery and cannon fire on Straß. During the morning, a platoon of Co B, 629th TD Bn was also sent to Straß. Again, a tank destroyer was lost on the way to the village through enemy action. The last Germans left Straß by noon. American artillery attacked German tanks and infantry which tried to reenter the village. Co C, 774th Tk Bn claimed the destruction of an anti-tank gun and a MG position. Only later in the day did the Germans react with organized resistance by placing guns on the ridge southeast of Straß, which dominated the Schafberg - Straß road. In addition, the road was no longer passable where the Co B tank destroyer had been knocked out. Cos L and K, which were in Straß, were practically cut off from their rear connections. Co G, 330th Inf Rgt in action north of Schafberg, bumped into German positions 400 meters northwest of Schafberg at 15:30 and made no further progress. Early in the afternoon, about 100 Germans infiltrated into Schafberg. From here they threatened the supply route to Straß, which was only defended by a platoon of Co C, 774th Tk Bn. During the night of 11 December, numerous attempts failed to supply the two cut-off companies in the village.

Meanwhile, the 1st Bn, 330th Inf Rgt, had attacked at 06:30 in southerly and southeasterly directions in order to occupy the forward slope of Height 375 and prevent potential German counterattacks. However, the battalion advanced no more than 300 meters before they met German positions and came under artillery and mortar fire. A German tank, supporting the Grenadiers, was knocked out by the Americans, while three American light tanks were also destroyed.[91] During the American advance in the morning several German soldiers in Schafberg had been surprised and taken prisoner. Among them were men of II./Gren.Rgt.941, who later informed their captors that their battalion command post was located south of Schafberg near Height 305. A forward observation squad from 3./Art.Rgt.344, working in cooperation with II./Gren.Rgt.941 was also captured. They told their American interrogators that their battery was in position south of Bergheim with three 105mm field howitzers. The ammunition supply had been very good thus far, so that they fired between 350-400 rounds per day, with the ammunition resupplied every night.[92]

For the first time, members of Sturmpanzer-Abteilung 217 were also captured. Two soldiers of the 2./ Sturmpanzer-Abteilung 217 who were captured in the Straß area on 10 December, readily testified during their interrogation on 11 or 12 December by the 1st Army, although they were not happy to have been taken prisoner. Their battalion had been almost completely destroyed during the retreat from France. With its arrival in Holland, the battalion had been rebuilt and equipped with new 15cm Sturmpanzers. The battalion was organized into two companies each with five Sturmpanzers and 120 men. The maintenance platoon had a strength of 117 men and had two tank recovery vehicles. The battalion CO was Major Lemor[93], with CO of the 1. Kompanie OLt. Magner, CO of the 2. Kompanie OLt. Schmitz and CO of the maintenance platoon OLt. Schulz.[94] The 2. Kompanie had been in position at Schafberg near Straß since 1 December, and tasked with supporting the infantry: Gren.Rgt.941 or Gren.Rgt.981, the prisoners were not sure about this. On 10 December, the 2. Kompanie was surprised when American forces suddenly appeared in the rear. All Sturmpanzers were lost. The prisoners did not know anything about the whereabouts of the 1. Kompanie.[95] Another soldier of the 2./ Sturmpanzer-Abteilung 217, who was captured in the Schafberg area on 10 December, told his interrogators that his battalion was organized in two companies each with eight Sturmpanzers. On 10 December, the 2. Kompanie only had three Sturmpanzers at its disposal, as four others had been sent to Lövenich for repairs shortly beforehand. Contrary to his comrades, he stated that the Kompanie was supporting Gren.Rgt.1055 (89.Inf.Div.). He suspected the 1./ Sturmpanzer-Abteilung 217 to be in the same area. The battalion command post was in Kreuzau, and the supply train in Kelz. The prisoner went on to mention the following officers: battalion CO OLt. Lemor, CO 1. Kompanie Lt. Schulenberg[96] and CO 2. Kompanie Lt. Schmidt.[97] Probably on 10 or 11 December another prisoner was taken in Schafberg or southwest of the village. VII Corps reported on 12 December about another soldier of the 2./ Sturmpanzer-Abteilung 217, whose statement basically coincided with the testimony of the other prisoners captured in the Schafberg area. However, this soldier named OLt. Gauglitz[98] as battalion CO and Lt. Schmitz as CO of 2./ Sturmpanzer-Abteilung 217. In total, the 1st Army reported five prisoners from Sturmpanzer-Abteilung 217 up to 13 December. The G-2 of the 5th Armd Div, based on a report from the 83rd Inf Div, identified 'Sturm-Geschütz-Btl.277' in Straß, which was subordinated to 89.Inf.Div., while it was organic to the 277.VG.Div. Before its retreat, this battalion had resisted stubbornly during the battle for Straß. Undoubtedly, this unit was also the Sturmpanzer-Abteilung 217.[99]

Interestingly, Sturmpanzer-Abteilung 217 reported its strength on this day. Unlike two days earlier, however, the battalion now only had a strength of 28 tanks. The loss of three assault tanks would fit with the American reports of 10 December, although it is questionable as to whether the battalion would have an overview of the losses that day. On the other hand, the two previous days had been relatively uneventful. The Americans claimed no German tanks destroyed between 8 and 9 December.[100]

Dug-in German infantry, anti-tank fire and mines delayed the advance of the American tanks in the 83rd Inf Div sector on **11 December**. Cos E and F, 331st Inf Rgt continued their attack on Gey at 06:30 with the support of Co B, 774th Tk Bn. The entire village was heavily mined, many of these being wooden mines, which were difficult to find. Therefore, the two infantry companies made slow progress, and some Germans continued their fierce resistance, and only one surrendered to the Americans. Meanwhile, Co G attacked the village from the south along the Großhau-Gey road. At 11:45, Co A, 331st Inf Rgt also entered the fighting. The company tried to penetrate south of the 2nd Bn in the southern part of Gey but, at the end of the day, its whereabouts was unknown. After its heavy losses, II./Gren. Rgt.981 combined all available forces into two companies; *Kompanie Pieper* and the 6. Kompanie.[101] Southeast of Straß, II./Gren.Rgt.941 managed to hold its positions between the two forests. Behind their positions, I./Fs.Jg.Rgt.6 occupied a rear position between Bogheim and Untermaubach. II./Fs.Jg.Rgt.6 held positions south of Schafberg up to the wooded area west of Bogheim. These were followed by the positions of the III./Fs.Jg.Rgt.6, which ran in a southwesterly direction for 1.5 kilometers east of Brandenberg. According to prisoners' statements, Fs.Jg.Rgt.6 had been subordinated to the newly arrived 85.Inf.Div. After the Germans had evacuated Straß the day before, several German tanks of an unknown type were spotted moving towards Straß at 08:10 in the forest east of the village. Shortly after, Cos L and K, 330th Inf Rgt were attacked by these tanks and infantry. The American tanks and tank destroyers opened fire and reported the destruction of three armored vehicles. This half-hearted German attack collapsed shortly after. During the day, the American infantry in the village fought off individual German grenadiers, who continued to infiltrate. The day was rather quiet despite the German artillery and mortars firing all day. The 3rd Bn reported the loss of

four officers. Co C, 774th Tk Bn, lost one tank after it was hit by mortar fire, and two tanks which had hit mines. Around 19:30, about 90 Grenadiers and some self-propelled guns attacked the village from the south-east. At about 22:00, the Germans broke off the attack without having gained any ground at all. The Americans had paid a high price for their defensive success; all the tank destroyers had broken down or had been destroyed and Co C, 774th Tk Bn, reported only seven combat ready tanks. About 60 American wounded were stuck in Straß and could not be evacuated. Only a small patrol managed to enter the village and bring food, ammunition and medicines. A platoon of Co A, 774th Tk Bn, which was previously held in reserve, received the order to break through with five tanks and reach Straß. On the way, two tanks hit mines and only two reached Straß. Later, the crews of these two tank crews claimed the destruction of two Panzer IVs and a self-propelled gun. It quite is possible that in the dark, they had actually hit tanks which were knocked out the previous day.[102] However, the decisive factor for the critical situation in Straß remained that German troops continued to attack the American positions near Schafberg and continued to shell the only supply route available to the Americans. Two German tanks, possibly Sturmpanzers, were knocked out by the Americans during the day southwest of Schafberg. In the Straß-Schafberg area, the Americans reported the capture of numerous soldiers from II./Gren.Rgt.941 and II./Fs.Jg.Rgt.6. These prisoners reported that it had been planned to extract both units at 17:00, and take them back behind the Roer. The 1st Bn, 330th Inf Rgt, meanwhile, had been able to maintain its position in the area of Height 375 despite the heavy artillery and mortar fire. Since that morning, parts of CCB, 5th Armd Div, had been deployed in the area of the 1st Bn, 330th Inf Rgt, to attack eastwards. A soldier of the 2./ Sturmpanzer-Abteilung 217 succumbed to his wounds at the dressing station in Kelz which he may have suffered the day before.[103]

During the night of 11/12 December, Cos E, F, G and A, 331st Inf Rgt, continued their efforts to clear Gey of Germans. By 01:45, Co A was able to cut the southbound route out of Gey. Between 03:30 and 07:00, the 3rd Bn, 331st Inf Rgt, replaced the 2nd Bn in Gey. Shortly after, the 3rd Bn together with a platoon from Co B, 774th Tk Bn, attacked German MG positions. The tanks managed to destroy several positions which had halted the infantry's advance, but their movement was seriously hindered by German mines. Co I took over the south of the village, while Co L secured the north. In this area, however, there were still some pockets of German resistance. Co K initially remained in reserve on the western outskirts. Apparently, a German counterattack in the Gey area was beaten back. However, it was not possible to find any further information on the German strength and from which direction the attack may have come. During the whole time there was still heavy German mortar and artillery fire on Gey. Co B, 774th Tk Bn, lost a tank with damage to its tracks, and while attempting its recovery on the night of 13 December, they were surprised by German artillery fire and three crew were killed.

During the day, Co I made contact with CCA, 5th Armd Div south of Gey and made arrangements for the further advance. It has to be appreciated that all roads from the village to the east were heavily mined. The 331st Inf Rgt reported the capture of 61 German soldiers and the deployment of a German tank[104] in the Gey - Straß area.[105] The 3rd Bn, 330th Inf Rgt, which was cut off in Straß, was air-dropped medicines during the day. Throughout this period, the Germans made no further attempts to recapture the village. In Straß, Co C, 774th Tk Bn with two platoons and a subordinated platoon of Co A, 774th Tk Bn were relying on cooperation with the 3rd Bn, 330th Inf Rgt. While Co C spent the day anticipating a German attack, Co B, 629th TD Bn (also supporting 3rd Bn, 330th Inf Rgt) reported heavy German attacks on Straß and the alleged destruction of two German 'Tiger' tanks. The assumption is that the 629th TD Bn's December After Action Report confused the events of 12 December with those of the previous day. It can also be ruled out that German 'Tiger' tanks were in the Straß - Gey area.

Meanwhile, Cos E and G, 330th Inf Rgt continued their attacks against German infantry and self-propelled guns in the area of Schafberg. While Co G tried to tie down the German forces, Cos E and F flanked the German positions from the south. This made it possible to disrupt the German resistance nests from behind, so that the Co G was free and could proceed towards Straß. The 2nd Bn, 330th Inf Rgt, reported more than 100 German prisoners taken in the Schafberg area at the end of the day. Co G, 330th Inf Rgt, made contact with the 3rd Bn in Straß at 17:55. In the evening, Cos E and F also followed to Straß, while the 1st Bn, 330th Inf Rgt, took over positions in the Schafberg area around 22:00. For the first time in days, the Americans were able to bring sufficient supplies to Straß on the night of 13 December. German prisoners captured to the south and southeast of Straß primarily belonged to Gren.Rgt.941 (156 men), Gren.Rgt.943 and the II./Fs.Jg.Rgt.6.[106]

At 09:25 on **13 December**, the 1st Bn, 331st Inf Rgt started their final attack against Gey supported by tanks of the 774th Tk Bn. At 11:00, Co B reached the center and by 12:25 1st Bn reported that it had occupied the town. 122 prisoners were taken. Co A, 774th Tk Bn lost two tanks in the fighting to *Panzerschreck* fire and to an 8.8cm Pak from 3./H.Pz.Jg.Abt.682 which had three 8.8cm Pak in Gey. That morning, *Kompanie Pieper* of I./Gren.Rgt.981 reportedly had a strength of 32 men with three light and two heavy MGs and several *Panzerfausts*. Prisoners stated that most of the losses occurred as a result of American artillery and mortar fire. For three days, the Germans had stubbornly resisted in the rubble of Gey and denied the 83rd Inf Div a quick breakthrough to the Roer. For the time being, only German artillery prevented an immediate advance by the Americans to the east, by firing several heavy artillery barrages on Gey. This slowed down the advance of Co C, 331st Inf Rgt to the east until 15:45. Thereafter, the Co C attack could only be carried forward 300 meters to the northeast. The actual goal of the company, the slope

1200 meters east of Gey, initially remained a long way off. VII Corps also reported strong German resistance north of Gey in the area of Mariaweiler. As the German fire from north and east increased in intensity, Co C retreated. Although German self-propelled guns were reported throughout the day in the Gey - Bogheim area, the Americans considered that the general absence of German tanks were a sign that they had withdrawn to the east bank of the Roer.[107]

After the liberation of Straß the day before, the 1st Bn, 330th Inf Rgt, remained responsible for the Schafberg area, and the 3rd Bn, 330th Inf Rgt defended its positions in the Straß area.

Elsewhere, 2nd Bn, 330th Inf Rgt, was preparing for a deployment as part of CCB, 5th Armd Div. For this purpose, the battalion was subordinated to the CCB. Meanwhile, engineers had cleared the mines along the road from Gey to Straß making contact with the 331st Inf Rgt possible. A prisoner from Fs.Jg.Rgt.6 told his interrogators that his regiment was collaborating with the 85.Inf.Div., and thereby confirmed statements from previous days. Co C, 774th Tk Bn reported that during the last three days they had destroyed one Panzer V, three self-propelled guns, two tanks of an unknown type, two anti-tank guns, two MGs, one bunker and a *Panzerfaust* team. Their own losses were ten tanks and 29 soldiers. An attempt to bring supplies along with the tanks to Straß allegedly led to a sudden encounter with a German Panzer IV, which had been knocked out and left burning. This is surprising, as no other sources reported a German tank near Straß. Perhaps the German tank was a Sturmpanzer IV, destroyed on 10 December in the field west of the village? Although Straß had been controlled by the Americans for two days, German artillery and a few cannons continued to dominate the road from Schafberg to Straß and hampered all attempts to resupply the village. In addition, many roads in this area were still littered with mines.[108]

The Germans continued to defend their positions in the 330th and 331st Inf Rgt sector on **14 December**. The Americans continued to encounter large numbers of mines almost everywhere, but for the first time they discovered piles of mines on the roadsides, which could not be relocated in time by the Germans. German light artillery, still positioned west of the Roer, quickly shifted their fire wherever the Americans showed themselves. The focus of the German artillery was at Straß, Gey, Birgel and Gürzenich. A reduction in German artillery fire during the day suggested a change of position of the heavy artillery to the east, behind the Roer. The terrain on the approach to the river allowed the Germans to funnel the American advance and dominate the undulating, uncovered terrain with cannon fire. As far as the Americans could see, the Germans had not yet demolished the bridges over the Roer. The Americans feared that the Germans might blow up the Roer dams near Schmidt and thereby flood the Roer valley. That morning, the 1st Bn, 331st Inf Rgt, resumed its attack from the previous day, supported by a platoon of Co B, 774th

Tk Bn, setting off 1200 meters northeast of Gey. At 08:30, the battalion reached its objective, but was immediately fired on by German heavy weapons; however, no German counterattack took place. The 2nd Bn, 331st Inf Rgt, passed the 1st Bn on the right towards the height southwest of Berzbuir. The battalion took its objective and secured its positions for the night. The regiment reported taking 32 prisoners, of which some belonged to the 2./Fest.Pak.Abt.501, which had taken up positions northeast of Gey. The 3rd Bn remained in at Gey. Engineers from the 83rd Inf Div continued to clear the road of mines from Gey to Straß of mines. After the loss of Gürzenich and Birgel, the Germans started a series of counterattacks. The first attack began at 15:30 and was composed of infantry with six tanks in support. In combination with the artillery, American infantry managed to repel this attack. However, the German tanks had managed to push into Birgel. The second German attack was repelled at 17:00 in the Gürzenich area. The final counterattack started around 19:00 against Gürzenich. Infantry and three or four tanks attacked the village, but were quickly repelled. The Americans claimed the destruction of four German tanks in the area.[109]

Most of the prisoners taken in Gey and Gürzenich were from 353.Inf.Div. The Gren.Rgt.942 was particularly badly hit (284 prisoners), but Gren.Rgt.943 east of Gey (172 prisoners) and Gren.Rgt.941 (12 prisoners) east of Straß, suffered heavy losses. A messenger from 1./Gren.Rgt.943 told his captors that his battalion was refitted in Kreuzau on 11 December. The I. Bataillon had been given the mission to relieve the Gren.Rgt.981 (272.VG.Div.). In fact, the remains of Gren.Rgt.981 were relieved that day and moved to Kreuzau.[110]

The 2nd Bn, 330th Inf Rgt with CCB, 5th Armd Div, advanced from Straß to Langenbroich. Halfway there, the battalion took small arms fire. Two German self-propelled guns or tanks supported the Grenadiers, but were knocked out with bazookas. The further advance of the 2nd Bn was stopped by fire from field positions on the left flank. In order to secure the supply route from Schafberg to Straß, 3rd Bn, 330th would attack from Straß to the northeast in the direction of the Hocherbach height. The remaining tanks of Co C, 774th Tk Bn were attached to Co I, 330th Inf Rgt. The attack was slowed by artillery and self-propelled gun fire. An American tank was knocked out by cannon fire and burnt out; another was disabled after being hit. Then the 2nd Bn deployed Co L as a flanking force, which was able to take the objective by 10:45. After an American air attack, thirty to forty burning German vehicles were counted in the fields around Obermaubach.[111]

Sturmpanzer-Abteilung 217 reported the loss of three officers. Hptm. Gauglitz,[112] the battalion CO was evacuated to hospital on 14 December. OLt. Tetzner[113], CO of the 1. Kompanie was also transferred to a hospital after being wounded. Lt. Beduwé[114] was killed. He had briefly commanded the 2. and 3. Kompanie.

While the 1st Bn, 330th Inf Rgt further secured the Schafberg area on **15 December**; the 3rd Bn held Straß with Cos I and K and Hof Hocherbach with Co L. Only the 2nd Bn, 330th Inf Rgt, together with CCB, 5th Armd Div, attacked on a broad front eastwards from 08:00. German resistance was initially much lighter than the day before and by 10:15 the attack had reached 1 kilometer east of Straß. At about 11:00, lead elements took Langenbroich. In the meantime, a second assault group to the south moved from positions east of Schafberg into the forest west of Bergheim, reaching a point north of Untermaubach. The Germans tried to stop the attack with artillery and mortar fire. By 11:30 the Americans had cleared the forest west of Bergheim; 2nd Bn, 330th Inf Rgt started to occupy the village. The small German garrison in Bergheim was easily routed. Resistance was light and one German anti-tank gun knocked out. The 2nd Bn held their positions until 20:00 after which they retreated from the village leaving one company behind. The rest of the battalion moved to a wooded area near Langenbroich. Co A, 774th Tk Bn, which was attached to the 330th Inf Rgt reported eight combat ready tanks, the loss of two tanks and seven in short-term maintenance. In the evening, the 1st and 3rd Bn, 330th Inf Rgt were relieved and transferred to Großhau as reserve. The 4th Cav Grp set up a backup line to the south by evening to cover the flank of the CCB. German artillery and mortar fire in this sector remained heavy. CCB reported: 127 Germans killed, 100 German prisoners, and the destruction of a tank, five self-propelled guns, three 8.8cm Pak, four Pak of unknown caliber, one field cannon and ten mortars.[115] To the North, CCA, 5th Armd Div started its attack in the direction of Kufferath at 07:30. CCA started the attack with two companies (CO A, 34th Tk Bn and Co A, 46th Armd Inf Bn), encountered little resistance, and the village was taken by 09:00. At the same time, a second combined group (Co B, 46th Armd Inf Bn and Co B, 34th Tk Bn) moved to the final objective of CCA, the heights southeast of Kufferath, which were also referred to as 'double slope 209/211'.

German opposition in this area was light and primarily provided by three or four assault guns east and southeast of the target. The Americans reported the destruction of several of these self-propelled guns. Elements of the Combat Command were now only a few hundred meters away from the Roer. The Germans had pulled back their infantry during the night. On the heights, the Americans were subjected to fire from artillery, mortar, anti-tank and self-propelled guns but with much less intensity than the day before. At 12:00, four German tanks were observed in the area. After one was destroyed, the rest of the tanks retreated around 14:00. The 3rd Bn, 331st Inf Rgt, which had been in reserve in Gey, relieved elements of CCA in Kufferath. Co I now occupied the heights near Kufferath, from which they could see the Roer river near Kreuzau. On the same heights were also elements of Cos A and B, 46th Armd Inf Bn. After relief by the 3rd Bn, 331st Inf Rgt, the 34th Tk Bn moved back to the Gey area. Only Co A remained behind to support the infantry. In the meantime, 2nd Bn, 331st Inf Rgt, together with a platoon of Co

B, 774th Tk Bn secured the heights southwest of Berzbuir by 10:50. Patrols were sent out to Berzbuir. The 2nd Bn ran into heavy German opposition, but were able to take the village with the support of tanks by nightfall. Co C, 331st Inf Rgt, advanced along the road from Gey - Rölsdorf until Height 500 south of Birgel, while the rest of the 1st Bn was taken back to Gey. The 83rd Inf Div reported 73 German prisoners.[116] A prisoner from the 344.Inf.Div. stated that out of the remnants of Gren.Rgt.1057, Gren.Rgt.1058, Feld.Ers.Btl.344 and Füsilier-Kompanie 344, a new *Kampfgruppe Komek* had been created. They were to cooperate with assault guns from an independent Sturmgeschütz unit. The G-2 of the V Corps thought that this could have been Sturmpanzer-Abteilung 217.[117]

During the night of 15/**16 December,** German units near Bogheim and Winden tried to retreat to the east bank of the Roer river. The Americans recognized this and tried to suppress them with artillery, while heavy caliber German artillery fire fell on the Kufferath area. While the Ardennes Offensive had started further south, CCB, 5th Armd Div continued its attack from Bergheim in a southeastern direction. Together with Troop A and B, 85th Cav Rcn Sqd, reinforced by a platoon of the 81st Tk Bn they tried to occupy the slope above the village. By 08:30 the Americans had reached their objective and secured the position. Then they searched the area for scattered Germans. Many German soldiers were captured. In the afternoon, the 15th Armd Inf Bn went south from Bergheim and shortly after 17:00 they reached the town of Bilstein. The remainder of CCB, with the 2nd Bn, 330th Inf Rgt still subordinated, had in the meantime consolidated its positions achieved the day before. A 2nd Bn company was still securing Bergheim, while the rest of the battalion was in a sheltered position near the town of Langenbroich. The rest of the 330th Inf Rgt spent the day in the rearward area, replenishing personnel, equipment, food and ammunition.

North of CCB, CCA, 5th Armd Div, consolidated its positions achieved the previous day. The 5th Armd Div reported 41 enemy killed, 50 prisoners, four self-propelled guns left behind by the Germans, three abandoned Pak guns, and much destroyed equipment, including, but not limited to twelve guns, two Pak guns, seven mortars and two vehicles. The 331th Inf Rgt had also been tasked to consolidate its positions along the heights from which Lendersdorf and Kreuzau could be surveyed. However, the regiment was to prepare for an attack to capture Lendersdorf. During the day, the 1st Bn, 331st Inf Rgt, was used along with CT 329 to clean up Birgel, while the 3rd Bn, 331st Inf Rgt, was replaced by CCA in the evening for an attack on Lendersdorf the next morning. During the night of 16/17 December German paratroopers jumped over the area of the 5th Armd Div, the misguided Operation Stösser had started a day late.[118]

The 16 December was probably the last combat day for Sturmpanzer-Abteilung 217 in the Hürtgenwald. On **17 December**, Heeresgruppe B reported that the advance personnel of Sturmpanzer-Abteilung 217 had arrived in the area of the 6. Panzer-Armee. Contrary to the original plans, the battalion could not be transferred to the assembly area in time to be able to participate in the offensive from the beginning.[119] Between 15-17 December Gefreiter Anton Skriba had deserted to the American lines in civilian clothes. Skriba was a *Volksdeutscher* from Poland, who had arrived as a replacement with Sturmpanzer-Abteilung 217 in Kufferath on 6 December. He was interrogated by the VII Corps and the 1st Army on 19 and 22 December respectively. Skriba made the following remarks: After the battle for Aachen, the battalion received new equipment in December to return it to full strength; that is three companies each with fourteen Sturmpanzer[120] and 70 soldiers. Each Sturmpanzer had a 150mm Haubitze (gun) and two light MGs as armament. Skriba was part of a group of 34 men, which had picked up seven Sturmpanzer at the Heereszeugamt in Bielefeld destined for the 1./ and 2./ Sturmpanzer-Abteilung 217. He further stated that the 3. Kompanie, which had been reconstituted by Pz.Ers.u.Ausb.18 in Kamenz, had arrived in Kufferath one day before his own transport train. Skriba named the following officers in the battalion: CO Hptm. Gauglitz, CO 1./217 OLt. Detzner (OLt. Johannes Tetzner), CO 3./217 Lt. Berringer.[121] Skriba's statements are of interest insofar as they clearly state the arrival of the six assault tanks which had been assigned to the battalion on 16 November, around 6 December. That Skriba indicated seven tanks can be very likely attributed to the transfer of the last remaining Sturmpanzer of 2./Stu.Pz.Abt.218 z.b.V., which according to a statement of a member of the battalion, would have handed over this tank at the end of November/beginning of December. On the other hand, it is unlikely that the 3./ Sturmpanzer-Abteilung 217 would have arrived one day before his transport train, because the first eight assault tanks for the company were assigned only on 8 December.

If his statement was correct, then only the advance personnel for the reestablished 3./ Sturmpanzer-Abteilung 217 arrived in Kufferath on 5 December. The total of fourteen Sturmpanzer IV for the 3. Kompanie were only supplied on 8 December (8 tanks), 16 December (3 tanks) and 22 December (3 tanks). It is difficult to be precise about the use of Sturmpanzer-Abteilung 217 in the Hürtgenwald, since the German reports are preserved only in part and American statements are too imprecise in relation to German tanks. In many cases, the American numbers seem to be too high, primarily due to multiple reports. Taking into account that all assault tanks assigned during the deployment in the Hürtgenwald only served to bring the battalion to the authorized strength of 45 assault tanks and only the tanks assigned at the end of December 1944 were to compensate the losses in the Hürtgenwald, then the battalion lost seven Sturmpanzer IV between 16 November and 16 December.

The battalion was visited at least three times by men of a propaganda company during the engagement in the Hürtgen Forest.

A film sequence showing Sturmpanzers moving in a snow shower was shown in the German newsreel from 30 November 1944.[122] Alongside the camera crew, a photographer must also have been present, because a number of still photographs were taken at the same time. The photos must have been taken between 11 and 29 November. Thanks to weather reports for November 1944, American G-2 reports and diaries of soldiers who fought in the Hürtgen Forest, it has been possible to narrow the event down to two possible dates: 15 or 17 November. The commentator makes one believe that the film was taken in the Vosges Mountains, but without doubt, the film shows Sturmpanzer-Abteilung 217 during an engagement in the Hürtgen Forest, and shows Oberleutnant Josef Gauglitz several times. Gauglitz, the commander of the 1. Kompanie, acted as the battalion Commanding Officer in November and December 1944, while Major Lemor was absent for unknown reasons. Gauglitz had a broken leg, and the images clearly show his left leg was stiff and he needed a stick to walk. The action starts with two Sturmpanzers moving along a trail through a forest break. The leading Sturmpanzer is of special interest. Although the images are a little blurred, one can recognize that the tank has a three-tone camouflage paint scheme, better known as the ambush-camouflage pattern and no *Zimmerit* is visible. A *Balkenkreuz* is visible on the right side of the superstructure, as well as the tactical number '3' or '8'. The next sequence shows Gauglitz and three other tank crew reconnoitering in snow-covered terrain. The men beckoned a Sturmpanzer forward and directed it to a firing position. Oberleutnant Gauglitz briefed the crew and the tank started to fire. A second Sturmpanzer arrives and moves forward, passing through a gap in a fence. Both Sturmpanzers had *Zimmerit*, a two-tone camouflage pattern, and *Balkenkreuze* painted on both sides of the superstructure. The camouflage was completed with branches attached to the front and back of the tank. The Sturmpanzer that fired at least one round also had a *Balkenkreuz* painted below the driver's vision port. All the Sturmpanzers in the film were model IVs.

As of 21 December[123], the battalion was again in the cinemas as part of the weekly newsreel. This film shows a Sturmpanzer tank crew in front of their tank. The Sturmpanzer is a model IV version, heavily camouflaged with branches. Despite the camouflage, a *Balkenkreuz* is clearly visible below the driver's vision port. The crew wear a variety of different tank uniforms. Of special interest is the fifth crew member, as he was a Russian volunteer. The Germans called these volunteers '*Hiwis*'. The next sequence shows Oberleutnant Gauglitz with a second officer awarding two crewmen with Iron Crosses, one of them Feldwebel Willy Schlicker, a commander in 2./ Sturmpanzer-Abteilung 217. Oberleutnant Gauglitz is still using a walking stick, seen in the earlier film.[124] The newsreel narrator said:

"These soldiers drove fearlessly with their heavy assault tank against the enemy and destroyed seven machine gun nests and two companies of infantry. The company commander, Knights Cross Holder Hauptmann Gauglitz, is awarding assault tank men."

There are two remarkable aspects. The statement that Gauglitz was a company commander could be a hint that Major Lemor had returned to his unit. The other interesting point is that Gauglitz was a Hauptmann. When he received the Knights Cross on 16 November 1944, his rank was Oberleutnant. He was awarded the German Cross in Gold on 30 December, and according to the documents, he was still an Oberleutnant and Company Commander in Sturmpanzer-Abteilung 217. In fact, Gauglitz was promoted to the rank of a Hauptmann on 15 January 1945, but this promotion was backdated to 1 November 1944.[125] As before, a propaganda photographer was present because two photographs are known; one showing the two crewmen in front of their Sturmpanzer. The name '*Jumbo 3*' is visible on the gun barrel. The other image shows Gauglitz and the crew enjoying a mouthful of Schnapps. According to the caption in the Bundesarchiv, the images were taken on 4 December 1944 by propaganda photographer Scheck. He took a third image the same day at a different location, showing Gauglitz with his injured leg boarding a Kübelwagen. The caption for this photo gives the location as Winden, a small village near Kufferath. Elements of the battalion were billeted at Kufferath in early December, which makes the author believe that these images and the film of the award ceremony were taken at Kufferath.

The well-known propaganda photographer Heinrich Hoffmann also visited Sturmpanzer-Abteilung 217 in late 1944. His photograph shows a Sturmpanzer IV in the foreground and two others in the background next to the edge of a forest. The Sturmpanzer in the foreground is a model IV with a three-color ambush camouflage and no *Zimmerit*. The name '*Dicker*' was painted onto the gun barrel and a *Balkenkreuz* is visible below the driver's vision port, both features typical of Sturmpanzer-Abteilung 217. Standing next to the tank is Oberleutnant Gauglitz, while several Grenadiers passing between the Sturmpanzers in the direction of the photographer. The caption is *"War events 12 January 1945"*. On that day, Sturmpanzer-Abteilung 217 was attached to 3. Fallschirmjäger-Division in the Ardennes. The ground was covered with a thick layer of snow and had been for more than two weeks, so it is obvious that the photograph must have been taken earlier. Considering that Gauglitz was evacuated to hospital on 14 December 1944, it is clear that the image was taken in the Hürtgen Forest as well.[126]

It is not completely clear where these two photos were taken, but they show a tank collection point with several German assault guns; most of which have the insignia of Sturm-Artillerie-Brigade 667. The insignia was a white unicorn on a red shield. *Timm Haasler*

This is the Sturmhaubitze 42 in the left of the photo on page 127 photographed on 28 November 1944, in Belgium, before it was moved to the dump. Note the unit insignia of Heeres-Sturmartillerie-Brigade 667 and prevalent *Balkenkreuz* on the bow armor.
The Tank Museum

The vehicle was a total loss after an internal explosion blew of the roof off the fighting compartment. Note the angle-iron used to keep the concrete in place on the sloping front of the fighting compartment. Although not directly hit, the concrete had split in half. This was a field modification.
The Tank Museum

The Sturmhaubitze was one of the first captured by the Allies without a muzzle brake. *The Tank Museum*

The rear view shows some closely grouped penetrations in the rear of the fighting compartment. Note the unique placement of the spare roadwheels on the sides of the engine compartment and the roof blown to one side.
The Tank Museum

5.2. Off-topic: 2./Stu.Pz.Abt.218 z.b.V.

A short departure at this point should help to clarify the relationship between Sturmpanzer-Abteilung 217 and 2./ Sturmpanzer-Abteilung z.b.V. 218, the only other Sturmpanzer unit engaged in the West in 1944.

Sturmpanzer-Kompanie z.b.V. 218 was raised at Bielefeld by order of OKH on 12 August 1944, its personnel coming from Panzer-Ersatz- und Ausbildungs-Abteilung 11 in Bielefeld and Panzer-Ersatz- und Ausbildungs-Abteilung 18 in Kamenz. The next day, ten Sturmpanzer IVs were allocated to the unit which came directly from the Army depot in Bielefeld. The company boarded a train heading for the Eastern Front the same day.

On 16 August another OKH order arrived stating that a second Sturmpanzer company should be raised at Bielefeld by 18:00 on 19 August. This company was named Sturmpanzer-Kompanie z.b.V. 2./ 218; later documents also show 2./ Sturmpanzer-Abteilung z.b.V. 218 and 2./ Sturmpanzer-Abteilung 218 z.b.V. as the unit name. This company too would receive ten Sturmpanzer IV from the Army Bielefeld depot. Other soft skin vehicles would have come from Army District VI but most of the vehicles were provided by Panzer-Ersatz- und Ausbildungs-Abteilung 11. Again it was intended to use personnel from both Panzer-Ersatz- und Ausbildungs-Abteilung 11 and 18 in order to form the company, but in the end all personnel came from Panzer-Ersatz- und Ausbildungs-Abteilung 11 who also provided the company commander, Oberleutnant Friedemann. Panzer-Ersatz- und Ausbildungs-Abteilung 18 was designated to become the replacement unit.

The ten Sturmpanzer IVs were allocated to the unit on 16 August and left the depot that day. Before the company started to board the train on 19 August it was bid farewell by the local Kreisleiter. The next day, the train left Bielefeld for France, where the company was to join another tank unit in the Versailles area. On 26 August, the train was finally unloaded at Chalons-sur-Marne. On 28 August, an ad-hoc force was created at Verneuil, comprising Panzer-Kompanie Meyer, Bau-Pionier-Bataillon 529, and 2./ Sturmpanzer-Abteilung 218 z.b.V. It appears that the company still had all ten tanks on hand that day. The force received the name *Kampfgruppe Oehmichen*, based on the name of the commander Oberst Oehmichen. The battle group was engaged by enemy tanks the next day at Chaumuzy, southwest of Reims. On 30 August, *Kampfgruppe Oehmichen* tried to defend Warmeriville on the road between Reims and Rethel. Some enemy tanks were knocked out by the battlegroup, but by 08:00 it had to abandon the village and continued to withdraw in a northeasterly direction. Late in the afternoon, orders arrived from A.O.K. 1 that *Kampfgruppe Oehmichen* was assigned to Panzer-Lehr-Division with immediate effect.

On 9 or 10 September, a member of the company was captured by the 4th Inf Div near Libramont, Belgium. The prisoner reported that his unit was newly raised and attached to *Kampfgruppe Hauser* of Panzer-Lehr-Division, acting as a rear guard with I./ Grenadier-Regiment 901 and five Panzer IV's from II./ Panzer-Lehr-Regiment. Only two of the Sturmpanzers remained when the company was ordered to withdraw to Ochamps on 8 September. On 9 September, the 'Ia' of Panzer-Lehr-Division reported that the division was forced to blow up a Sturmpanzer IV[127] the previous night due to a lack of fuel. At 18:30, the division reported that it had to blow up another Sturmpanzer for the same reason. On 10 September, Heeresgruppe B send out a message to A.O.K. 7 and 15 requesting information about the fate of the company.

The remnants of 2./ Sturmpanzer-Abteilung 218 z.b.V. arrived at Kaiserslautern on 17 September after having been ordered by A.O.K. 1 to return to Germany for rest and refitting. Only three officers, 16 enlisted men and one passenger car returned to Panzerstützpunkt Mitte. The next day, A.O.K. 1 ordered what was left of the company to move to Kamenz.

On 30 September, the 17. SS-Panzer-Grenadier-Division asked Panzerstützpunkt Mitte for support in the recovery of a Sturmpanzer IV at Marzellingen (Marsilly) 6 kilometers east of Metz. The division claimed that the tank was one of their vehicles. Werkstatt-Kompanie 924 intended to recover the vehicle but learnt on 4 October that this particular Sturmpanzer had already arrived at Siegelbach near Kaiserslautern, where Werkstatt-Kompanie 924 was located. The tank was still at Siegelbach a week later when the General der Panzertruppen West proposed to hand it over to Sturmpanzer-Abteilung 217. The tank, however, was still in need of repair, and Werkstatt-Kompanie 924 reported that it needed another seven days to have it in running order again. It is not known exactly when this tank was handed over to Sturmpanzer-Abteilung 217, but a member of the battalion later claimed that they took over a Sturmpanzer IV from Sturmpanzer-Abteilung 218 in November 1944.[128]

After the remaining 3. Kompanie personnel had moved to Kamenz in October 1944, it was rebuilt with Panzer-Ersatz- und Ausbildungs-Abteilung 18 at the end of November.[129] There are a couple of eyewitness reports available for this period.

Gefreiter Oskar Klein received his basic training in Kamenz between 11 July and 25 August 1944, and was assigned to 2./ Panzer-Ersatz- und Ausbildungs-Abteilung 18. After this he was relocated to 6./ Panzer-Ersatz- und Ausbildungs-Abteilung 18 for specialized training, which lasted until 15 November. He was trained as a Sturmpanzer IV gunner and loader. He remembered that the training included bailing out of a tank through the hatch, and to keep calm when a tank is rolling over a foxhole. There was also basic infantry training as well as getting used to firing the *Panzerfaust* After this training, he was assigned to 3./ Sturmpanzer-Abteilung 217 on 16 November. The same day, the company boarded a train and moved westwards. He believes that some Sturmpanzers were carried on this transport as well. Unloading took place at Nörvenich a couple of days later, where a pickup team was formed and sent to Bergisch-Gladbach to take over six new Sturmpanzers. He volunteered for the job and drove to Bergisch-Gladbach with some of his comrades. Much to their surprise, the tanks were actually there and ready for delivery. It is likely that these Sturmpanzers were replacement vehicles for the 1. and 2. Kompanie, because it was said that the 3. Kompanie only arrived with a full complement of new Sturmpanzer from the Army Depot in Bielefeld in mid-December.

His best friend, Hans Dusi, confirmed some of Oskar Klein's statement. Both men trained together in Kamenz and initially belonged to the same tank crew. A Stabsgefreiter in the 1. Kompanie, Kurt Kuhs, was interrogated by the Americans after his capture on 28 January 1945. He stated that the 3. Kompanie was rebuilt in Kamenz in early December 1944. He continued, stating that the Kompanie was made up of 45 men of the former 3. Kompanie, 15 men of 6./ Panzer-Ersatz- und Ausbildungs-Abteilung 18, and 20 men of an unspecified Marsch-Kompanie. This company left Kamenz on 3 December and moved to the Western Front. After arrival in the Grevenbroich area, it was supposed to take over eight new Sturmpanzers.

It is hard to say which of these conflicting statements is true. Eight Sturmpanzers were officially assigned to the battalion on 7 December 1944 and shipped the next day. There is no information available regarding the arrival date, but considering the average transfer time in December 1944/January 1945 of four to six days, the tanks should have arrived prior to the Ardennes Offensive, most likely between 12 and 14 December. Considering that another six Sturmpanzer were assigned to the battalion - three departed from Bielefeld on 16 December, and three on 22 December - it is clear that these fourteen Sturmpanzers were the full complement

of tanks needed to bring 3./Stu.Pz.Abt.217 back to its authorized strength. Kuhs' statements were pretty vague in terms of dates, and it is highly unlikely that the 3. Kompanie arrived in the Losheim area in time for the Ardennes offensive.[130]

The temporary battalion commander of Sturmpanzer-Abteilung 217, Oberleutnant Gauglitz, coordinates an artillery barrage in the Hürtgen Forest. When looking closely at the stills, it is clear that Gauglitz, was using a walking stick due to a wounded leg.
AMC S2583, Timm Haasler, AMC S7213

Oberleutnant Gauglitz and two members of the staff reconnoitering a firing position. While the others take cover, Gauglitz waves a Sturmpanzer forwards. Gauglitz commanded the battalion in November - December 1944. *AMC S7215*

This and next page: In addition to the PK photographer, a PK cameraman also captured the scene. At least three shells were fired by the Sturmpanzer IV and the cameraman films their effect when they land. As with the photographer's pictures, we see Oberleutnant Gauglitz several times in the film. *Timm Haasler*

After firing at least one round, the Sturmpanzer started to move again. Given the typical Allied artillery superiority, the crew was probably trying to avoid counter battery fire. The Sturmpanzer is coated with *Zimmerit*, and has its Fla.MG mount folded down. *AMC S7346*

Note the large wooden box wedged between the side armor and *Schürzen* rail, in front of the metal toolbox. Its purpose is not known, but it was clearly a field modification. *AMC S7347*

After the tank turned around, we can see other details on the right of the vehicle. It has a three-tone camouflage pattern and a *Balkenkreuz* painted on the superstructure side. All of the *Schürzen* are missing and some tools and the towing cable are visible by the engine compartment. *AMC S2584*

The photographer photographed a second Sturmpanzer in the same area. Although the front is heavily camouflaged, we can see spare tracks are fixed to the driver's position and a tow cable attached to one of the tow points. *ECPA*

This is the same Sturmpanzer with two parallel gouges in the *Zimmerit* on the side of the superstructure. Note the commander's SF14Z persicope and missing *Schürzen* rail. *ECPA*

After the Sturmpanzer left the firing position, an armored personnel carrier (Sd.Kfz.251) arrived and an officer joined Oberleutnant Gauglitz. Officially, the battalion only had two armored personnel carriers, both ambulance variants (Sd.Kfz.251/8). The vehicle here has two MG42s behind specifically shaped shields, indicating that this not an ambulance. *AMC S7216*

Oberleutnant Gauglitz gives instructions to officers and soldiers of the battalion from the Sd.Kfz.251 seen in the previous image. Note the tactical number '7' painted in white on the side. *AMC S2017*

Opposite: The film about Sturmpanzer-Abteilung 217's engagement in the Hürtgen Forest ends with a scene that showed the 15cm shell exploding. Then the cameraman filmed a German machine gun position in a destroyed farm with an American M10 tank destroyer in the background. Further scenes show that there are two M10s next to the ruins of the farm. German grenadiers inspect the wrecks as an Sd.Kfz.251 passes in the background. The PK photographer was also present and photographed the APC. The close-up identifies it as a heavily camouflaged Sd.Kfz.251/3 of 116.Panzer-Division. *Timm Haasler, Lee Archer*

The original caption says that this photo was taken by war photographer Heinrich Hoffmann on the Western Front on 12 January 1945. It is the authors' firm belief that this is incorrect, and that it was taken in late November/early December 1944 in the Hürtgen Forest. The northern Ardennes were covered in snow on 12 January 1945 and none of the soldiers are wearing winter clothing. The image shows an assembly position of at least three Sturmpanzers of Sturmpanzer-Abteilung 217 and Grenadiers from an unidentified infantry unit walking by. The Sturmpanzer IV Ausf.IV in the foreground has a three-tone disc camouflage pattern. Note the *Balkenkreuz* on the front of the driver's area and the name '*Dicker*' painted on the gun barrel jacket. Watching from behind the Sturmpanzer is Oberleutnant Gauglitz.
Bildarchiv Preußischer Kulturbesitz, No. 50077297

This photo was taken by an unknown German war photographer from Southern Germany. Heinrich Hoffmann was from Southern Germany so it is likely that this image was also taken by him at the same time as the photo on the previous page. Once again, we see Grenadiers walking past a camouflaged Sturmpanzer IV Ausf.IV.
William Auerbach Collection

Two crew members being awarded for destroying seven machine gun nests and dispersing two infantry companies. Behind them we can also see the gun barrel jacket barrel tube with the name 'Jumbo 3' name painted onto it, indicating that there were previously two other tanks with the same name.
Bundesarchiv 146-2009-0001, 183-2009-0108-500

Here we see the highly decorated Olt. Gauglitz, with wounded leg, being helped into the passenger seat of a Kübelwagen. *Bundesarchiv 183-2014-1013-500*

CHAPTER 06

THE ARDENNES OFFENSIVE

6.1 Preparation for the Ardennes Offensive

On 22 November 1944, the battalion was first mentioned in connection with the planning for the upcoming Ardennes Offensive.[1] Surprisingly, there are inconsistencies in the battalion's assignment before the offensive. A report from the Oberbefehlshaber West about combat-ready tanks and assault guns on the Western Front on 5 December, stated that Sturmpanzer-Abteilung 217 was assigned to Panzer-Armee-Oberkommando 6 with 21 Sturmpanzers.[2] In contrast, the war diary of the Oberkommando der Wehrmacht (OKW) stated on 15 December:

"Field Marshall Model has forwarded the Führer's order to the Commanding General of the Panzer-Armee-Oberkommando 6. In accordance with this, three assault gun brigades and one assault tank battalion (Sturmpanzer-Abteilung 217, sic.) of Armee-Oberkommando 15 were directed to reinforce the northern flank of Panzer-Armee-Oberkommando 6.

The units are due to arrive as of 16 December 1944."[3]

This clearly shows that the planned assignment was not finalized in time to have the battalion available for the start of the offensive. As we already know, the battalion was still engaged in the Hürtgen Forest when the Ardennes Offensive started.

Several reports reflect the strength and order of battle of the battalion prior to the offensive, but as so often they are conflicting. On 14 December, the battalion reported the following personnel strength with a reporting date of 8 December:

- 16 Officers (21)
- 2 Civil servants (2)
- 114 NCOs (219)
- 433 Enlisted men (354)
- 565 Total (596)

The figures in brackets show the authorized strength. For the first time the new K.St.N. (wartime table of organization) issued on 1 September is the basis for this report.[4]

Although the battalion was only 5% short of its authorized personnel strength, 24% of the officers and 48% of the NCOs were missing, while there was a surplus of 22% in terms of enlisted men.

The material strength on 8 December was reported as follows:

- 31 Sturmpanzer IVs (45)
- 2 Medium SPWs (2)
- 13 Medium motorcycles (19)
- 27 Passenger cars - cross country (23): 21 light and 6 heavy
- 8 Passenger cars - commercial (7): 6 light and 2 medium
- 7 *Maultiere* - halftrack trucks (15)
- 39 Trucks - cross country (51): 5 light, 21 medium, and 13 heavy
- 34 Trucks - commercial (6): 22 medium, and 12 heavy
- 2 Halftracks - towing trucks (5): 1 18-ton Sd.Kfz.9/1, and 1 18-ton
- 84 Machine guns (111): 20 light and 64 light - on board the Sturmpanzers
- 1 Omnibus
- 1 Trailer

- 288 Rifles
- 172 Pistols
- 12 Machine pistols
- 33 Machine pistols – on board the Sturmpanzers
- 1 Maintenance section
- 1 Medium maintenance platoon[5]
  (Authorized strength in brackets.)

Of interest is the shortfall of fourteen Sturmpanzers (equal to the strength of one company) and trucks. In general, this shortage of trucks was compensated for by allocating a higher number of civilian vehicles.

Information as to the number of Sturmpanzers needs further consideration:

- The actual reported strength on 8 December was thirty-one Sturmpanzers[6]
- Another report from the General der Panzertruppen showed an actual strength of twenty-eight Sturmpanzers on 10 December. Twenty-one Sturmpanzers were combat-ready and seven were under repair.[7]
- A further report from General der Panzertruppen showed an actual strength of thirty-two Sturmpanzers on 25 December, of which twelve were combat-ready and twenty undergoing maintenance.[8]
- The monthly report of the battalion for January 1945 showed an actual strength of thirty-six Sturmpanzers on 1 January, of which six were combat-ready and thirty under repair.[9]

On the basis of official records it becomes clear that the battalion received its batch of new Sturmpanzers before and during the offensive in an attempt to bring it back to authorized strength. The monthly tank allocation reports of the General der Panzertruppen show a number of allocations during this period, but only in a few cases were the actual arrival dates recorded:

- As previously mentioned, six Sturmpanzers were allocated on 16 November, five of which left the Bielefeld depot by rail the next day. The sixth Sturmpanzer was shipped two days later and arrived with battalion on 3 December, indicating that the other five tanks had already arrived. These six tanks were part of the battalion's monthly report for December, dated 14 December.
- On 29 November, another three Sturmpanzers were allocated from the Bielefeld depot, but did not depart until 16 December. Considering a transit time of 4-6 days, these tanks should have arrived at the battalion between 20 December and the year's end. It is the authors' assumption that these tanks were part of a batch of fourteen Sturmpanzers that were assigned to rebuild 3./ Sturmpanzer-Abteilung 217.[10]

- Another batch of eight Sturmpanzers were allocated on 7 December. Obviously, these tanks were the second batch of tanks needed to rebuild the 3. Kompanie. Although there is no information available as to when these tanks arrived, it is the authors' assumption that the tanks showed up before the end of the year. This would explain the increase in strength between 10 and 25 December (28 against 32 tanks)
- On 20 December, another batch of three Sturmpanzers were allocated, the final tanks needed to rebuild the 3. Kompanie. Surprisingly these tanks had already been loaded two days before. If these figures are correct, one has to assume that even these tanks had arrived before the end of the year.
- On 28 December another batch of six Sturmpanzers were allocated. As these were not entrained until 20 January 1945, these tanks are irrelevant for present purposes.[11]
- A report by the Generalinspekteur der Panzertruppen claimed that eleven Sturmpanzers were allocated to the West between 1-28 December 1944.[12]
- Another German report claimed that Sturmpanzer-Abteilung 217 received nine Sturmpanzers between 15 December 1944 and 5 January 1945. This number contradicts the data found in the allocation lists of the General der Panzertruppen.[13]

The available information can be summarized as follows:

- 8 December 1944: thirty-one Sturmpanzers, excluding the three Sturmpanzers still at the Bielefeld depot. It is the authors' belief that the battalion had thirty-one Sturmpanzers available on 16 December.
- 25 December 1944: thirty-two Sturmpanzers, including eight Sturmpanzers allocated on 7 December, thus indicating the loss of seven Sturmpanzers between 16 and 25 December in the Hürtgen Forest and the Ardennes.
- 1 January 1945: thirty-six Sturmpanzers, including six Sturmpanzers allocated on 29 November and 20 December, indicating the loss of a further two Sturmpanzers between 26 and 31 December in the Ardennes.

While this summary takes into account the battalion's engagements during the Ardennes Offensive, it is necessary to get an idea of the actual strength before the first engagements at Dom. Bütgenbach. One interesting aspect is the number of combat-ready Sturmpanzer IVs. The General der Panzertruppen reported twenty-one combat ready vehicles on 10 December, while this figure has been reduced to eight by 16 December.[14] The latter number is only based on secondary sources, but appears to be reliable considering the battalion's previous engagements in the Schafberg - Straß - Gey area (see chapter 5.1.) and the fact that the march to the assembly area near Losheim took place under difficult road and terrain conditions.

After his capture, Stabsgefreiter Kurt Kuhs of 1./ Sturmpanzer-Abteilung 217, told his interrogators that his battalion had been reorganized once more shortly before the offensive. According to him, the newly activated 3. Kompanie had been disbanded immediately after its arrival in the West. He continued that the men and material of the 3./ Sturmpanzer-Abteilung 217 were used to compensate for the high losses suffered by the other companies during the engagements in the Hürtgen Forest. All combat-ready elements of the battalion were merged into one combat group, while the remaining personnel of the 3. Kompanie became part of the staff company (Stabskompanie).[15] However, Kuhs' statement should be treated with caution. The monthly report of the battalion for January 1945 still shows one staff company, three assault tank companies, a supply company and a maintenance platoon.[16] The high number of tanks on hand does not indicate that there was a necessity to disband the 3rd Company. Two replacements that arrived with the 3. Kompanie in December later claimed that they stayed with their company and took part in several engagements in the Ardennes with their tanks. The 3./ Sturmpanzer-Abteilung 217 also reported two members as missing in action during December 1944.[17] It seems highly unlikely that the company was really disbanded. What could have happened is that the few combat-ready tanks were used to form two combat companies.[18]

There is also conflicting information regarding the final arrival of the battalion in the Losheim area. However, it is clear that the battalion was not present when the Ardennes offensive was launched on 16 December.[19] The OKW war diary mentioned on 15 December that one assault tank battalion had been ordered to move from Armee-Oberkommando 15 to the Ardennes, and was expected to arrive on or after 16 December. Other sources stated that the battalion was transferring to Panzer-Armee-Oberkommando 6 on 16 December[20], while the war diary of Heeresgruppe B noted that the advance personnel had arrived in the area of Panzer-Armee-Kommando 6 on 17 December.[21]

Contrary to the above, Feldwebel Vincenz Kuhlbach, a member of 1./Fs.Jg.Rgt.9, made the following observation early on the morning of 16 December at Stadtkyll:

"A very large German tank with an extremely short gun barrel has run into a house. The tank is blocking the road and the paratroopers are forced to make a detour in order to continue their march to the west".

Kuhlbach later saw the same tank, passing in the direction of the front.[22] Kuhlbach's statement is confirmed by Gefreiter Oskar Klein, who remembered that the 3. Kompanie was on the march from Mönchengladbach to the Hürtgen Forest via Kall. During this march, the company was redirected into a new assembly area near Ormont where they stayed for 2-3 days for resupply and maintenance. The company was then engaged a couple of times north of Lanzerath. Klein was convinced that the company must have arrived before the offensive started as he clearly remembered the opening German artillery barrage on 16 December.[23] On the other hand, Stabsgefreiter Kuhs was sure that the battalion arrived in the Ardennes on or about 20 December with twelve combat-ready Sturmpanzers. It seems that the 1. and 2. Kompanie had moved into the Ardennes separately from the 3. Kompanie.[24]

The 3. Kompanie most likely arrived in the Ardennes on the evening of 15 December, while the rest of the battalion started to move from the Zweifall area on 16 December. The first elements arrived in the new assembly area on 17 December. The short period of rest and refitting ended on 21 December when the combat-ready tanks were engaged for the first time at Dom. Bütgenbach.

6.2. Engagements at Dom. Bütgenbach

The planned breakthrough of Panzer-Armee-Oberkommando 6 did not develop as the German High Command had hoped. All three infantry divisions of the I.SS-Panzer-Korps failed to breach the American lines on **16 December**. On the corps' right, the 277.V.G.Div. was even pushed back to its start line, while the 12. VG.Div. attack in the central sector bogged down in front of Losheimergraben and Buchholz station. Only the 3.Fs.Jg.Div. on the left managed to penetrate the American lines near Lanzerath. However, the paratroopers halted their advance in the evening due to high losses suffered during the first day of the offensive. The corps ordered the armored elements of the 1. and 12.SS-Pz.Div. forward to get the attack moving again. According to the initial plan, these elements were only to be released after the infantry had successfully broken the first American line of resistance. Although the armored group of the 1.SS-Pz.Div. managed to break free in the early morning of **17 December**, the 12.SS-Pz.Div. did not perform much better than the infantry divisions the previous day, and its armored group was halted at Krinkelt-Rocherath. For three days the 12.SS-Pz.Div. tried to break through the American lines, but without success. The division lost almost half of its tanks in the twin villages. In a final, desperate attempt to get the attack moving again and in order to close the open gap between the two SS-Panzerdivisions, the 12.SS-Pz.Div. began to assemble an armored force in the area of Büllingen starting **19 December**. The remaining tanks of SS-Panzer-Regiment 12 finally arrived in the Büllingen area during the evening of **20 December** and the division intended to bypass the American stronghold in front of Elsenborn the next day by attacking Malmedy via Bütgenbach.

The II. SS-Panzer-Korps[25] launched the attack on Bütgenbach on the morning of **21 December** with the 12.SS-Pz.Div. on its left and the 12.V.G.Div. on the right flank. Although Sturmpanzer-Abteilung 217 was officially assigned to the 12.V.G.Div. that day, the battalion took part in the attack with the armored elements of SS-Panzer-Regiment 12.[26] The battalion had twelve Sturmpanzer IVs available according to the German situation map for 21 December.[27]

Several secondary sources claimed that the battalion was attached to the 12.V.G.Div. with two of its companies that day,[28] but other reports confirm the attachment to SS-Pz.Rgt.12. The chronicle of the 3./SS-Pz.Rgt.12, stated:

"The plan was designed to attack from the south and seize Domaine Bütgenbach, a farm complex beside the Büllingen to Bütgenbach road. The operation was ill-fated in so far as another attack from the east the day before had already failed. So there was no reason for an exaggerated optimism, in particular as the terrain offered great advantages for the defenders for an all-around defense. Nevertheless, there was some confidence in the ability of our own forces. Besides our own armored forces there was a heavy Army antitank battalion (s. Panzerjäger-Abteilung 560, sic.) and a heavy self-propelled infantry assault gun company (Sturmpanzer-Abteilung 217, sic.) on hand, which formed a considerable striking force."[29]

The tank commander in Panther 335, Untersturmführer Willi Engel, picked up the story:

"The order of march had not yet changed. The commander of the leading tank was Untersturmführer Schittenhelm, followed by Hauptmann Hils, Untersturmführer Engel and an Unterscharführer from the staff company. Behind it came the Panzer IVs of the 5th and 6th Company, then the tank destroyers and self-propelled infantry assault guns."[30]

Another eyewitness was Oberscharführer Willy Kretzschmar, a tank commander of a Panzer IV in 5. Kompanie:

"The attack had just started when we were welcomed by heavy enemy artillery and mortar fire. The right drive sprocket of our tank was hit and the track broke. We were now immobilized. A row of trees and hedges at a distance of about 150 meters was still occupied by the American infantry. We kept the infantry at a distance by firing with our two machine guns in this direction. Till that moment we still felt somehow secure as there were three Panzer IVs and one Sturmpanzer standing in the field around our tank. For the next two hours we played 'dead man' as every reaction or movement was answered by heavy enemy artillery fire. The snow covered landscape around us had turned into black mud. During a fire break I ran to a Panzer IV next to my tank, as the crew had to pull my tank back onto its track. Unfortunately, the tank was destroyed. The other two Panzer IVs and the Sturmpanzer had suffered the same fate,

most of them had been hit by the heavy artillery and mortar fire."[31]

While Oberscharführer Kretzschmar also refers to a '*Hummel*' or rather a "*heavy infantry assault gun - type Wespe*", another member of the 5. Kompanie is more precise. Sturmmann Heinz Müller was the tank driver in Otto Knoof's Panzer IV that day:

"We, the 5. Kompanie, were leading the attack on the left side of the road and reached the first buildings of the domain. Due to the heavy enemy artillery fire the Grenadiers could not keep pace with us. To the left of us, we were accompanied by an Army unit, in my opinion they were equipped with Sturmpanzer IVs - 'Brummbär' - with 15cm guns. During the attack the tank of my comrade Kretzschmar lost a track. One of the Sturmpanzers was also hit next to us and we picked up one crew member of this tank. That is why we continued the attack with a crew of six men. Our tank was then destroyed at the level of the first buildings of the village. We tried to reach our lines along the road, but failed."[32]

The memories of Gefreiter Oskar Klein, a member of 3./ Sturmpanzer-Abteilung 217, are pretty vague in this respect:

"Today I can only remember certain villages where we were engaged during the Ardennes Offensive. These were Hünningen, Büllingen, Dom. Bütgenbach and Möderscheid. We were primarily engaged together with Panzer IVs of the 'Hitlerjugend' Division. When we were engaged for the first time the entire area was snow covered and the ground was frozen."[33]

It is unclear if Oskar Klein took part in the attack on Dom. Bütgenbach on 21 December, but the Panzer IVs of SS-Pz.Rgt.12 were only engaged in this area on 21 and 23 December. If we consider the statement of Stabsgefreiter Kuhs as reliable, it seems clear that only the 3. Kompanie was engaged in the Ardennes in late December, while the other companies of Sturmpanzer-Abteilung 217 would see their first engagements in January 1945 in support of 3.Fs.Jg.Div.[34]

On the American side of the front, Captain Donald E. Rivette, the commanding officer of the anti-tank company of the 26th Inf Rgt, 1st Inf Div, experienced the German attack on Dom. Bütgenbach. He picks up the story:

"To the left of Kolar, Sergeant Joseph Harris secured the front of the other two guns with flanking fire from the right. The artillery and mortar fire had left only two men to handle the gun. Just when the shelling stopped, Sergeant Harris saw a tank rolling towards the main line of resistance, half way between his gun and Kolar's gun. When he ordered his gun to load, a shell was fired by the tank

The crew of a Sturmpanzer IV Ausf. IV pose in front of their tank during the winter of 1944/45. The Sturmpanzer has a fresh coat of whitewash and blends in well with the snowy landscape. A damaged farm building is visible behind the tank as well as two German soldiers and one civilian to the left of the tank. The civilian is probably the farmer, who showed an interest in the large tank. *Timm Haasler*

in the direction of the command post of the 2nd Bn. Through the dust Sergeant Harris could recognize that the tank was a self-propelled 15cm howitzer. He fired four rounds which disabled the tank and set it on fire."[35]

Other sources claim that the attack on Dom. Bütgenbach was continued at 10:00 on **22 December**. It is said that 12.V.G.Div. was in charge of the attack. Sturmpanzer-Abteilung 217, III./SS-Panzer-Grenadier-Regiment 26, and SS-Panzerjäger-Abteilung 12 were attached to the division for this attack.[36]

To date no other reports have been found that confirm further engagements involving the battalion until the end of December. We can conclude that the battalion remained in the area, as it was later assigned to the 89.Inf.Div. on 1 January 1945. The 89.Inf.Div. relieved the positions of the 12.V.G.Div. between Büllingen and Wirtzfeld during the night of 28-29 December, its command post being located in a bunker west of Ormont.[37]

On 25 December, a soldier of the battalion was captured by the Americans. He stated that the battalion's fuel dump was still located at Kelz. Further stores were kept in huts in the area.[38]

6.3 Condition of the Battalion at the end of 1944

Sturmpanzer-Abteilung 217 presented its monthly strength report on 1 January with reference date 1 January 1945. Surprisingly, the battalion issued a second report a fortnight later, this time with the reference date of 8 January. The December and two January reports are interesting because their figures are inconsistent. Due to a lack of further information, it is impossible to evaluate the discrepancies between these reports:

Status Report		
8 December 1944	1 January 1945	8 January 1945
16 Officers (21)	17 Officers	15 Officers
2 Civil Servants (2)	2 Civil Servants	2 Civil Servants
114 NCOs (219)	217 NCOs	149 NCOs
433 Privates (354)	354 Privates	395 Privates
565 Total (596)	590 Total	561 Total
Figures in brackets show the authorized strength		

The figures are even more inconsistent when one takes a closer look at the personnel losses and replacements for December. The battalion reported the loss of 37 men (KIA, WIA, MIA or ill). During the same period 2 Officers, 7 NCOs, and 54 privates joined the battalion.[39] The battalion commander described the training status, the state of health, and the morale of his soldiers on 1 January 1945 as follows:

"[…] Despite the new replacements, who are not as good as before, in general still satisfactory. Although continuously engaged since November, losses caused by illness are very low; the general state of health is satisfactory. A decrease in terms of morale and fighting spirit was not apparent at all."[40]

The order of battle was reported as follows:

- Staff and Staff Company
- 3 Sturmpanzer Companies
- 1 Supply Company
- 1 Maintenance Platoon[41]

The condition of the battalion in terms of vehicles and weapons was quite good, although the number of combat-ready Sturmpanzers was extremely poor.[42]

Major Lemor, the battalion commander, could not hide his worries when he assessed the material in the strength report:

"Status of the material organization:

Due to the delivery of a number of Sturmpanzers, the situation of the battalion in terms of tanks is looking pretty good, although the number of breakdowns had been consistently high caused by excessive stress on the tanks during the long-running engagements in the Eifel (Hürtgen Forest) and lengthy route distances.

The inventory of vehicles had been reduced significantly, which will lead to problems in terms of resupply as soon as the number of combat-ready fighting elements rises again."[43]

The Commanding General of the LXVII Armee-Korps, General of the Infantry Hitzfeld, added a short statement to the battalion's monthly report. He also mentioned the poor material status but saw the reason for it as lying elsewhere:

"The high number of damaged vehicles is caused by the condition of the terrain."[44]

Two more interesting details formed part of the second monthly report for January 1945. First, it contained a complete breakdown of light weapons:

- 327 rifles
- 221 pistols
- 21 machine pistols
- 14 light machine guns
- 36 machine pistols - on board the Sturmpanzers
- 74 light machine guns - on board the Sturmpanzers

Secondly, it included a detailed overview of the various vehicles that were part of the maintenance platoon:

- 1x 18-ton halftrack, Sd.Kfz.9/1
- 1x Rotary crane halftrack, Sd.Kfz.9/1
- 1x *Sammler* motor vehicle, Kfz.42
- 1x Medium motor vehicle maintenance platoon, Kfz.41
- 3x Maintenance motor vehicle, Kfz.2/40
- 1x Radio motor vehicle, Kfz.17
- 5x 2-ton trucks open, Sd.Kfz.3
- 1x Electric arc welding device
- 1x Trailer Sd.Anh.23
- 1x Trailer Sd.Anh.24 with machine set 'A'[45]

Another report, issued by the General der Panzertruppen, showed the number of armored vehicles in the West on 30 December. This report shows two armored personnel carriers, model Sd.Kfz.251/9 ('mittlerer Kanonenpanzerwagen'), as part of the battalion's inventory. One of the vehicles was reported as combat-ready while the other one was in need of maintenance.[46] Without question, the reported model number must have been a typographic error. The wartime table of organization (KStN 1107 d - *freie Gliederung*) only authorized the battalion to have two Sd.Kfz.251/8s ('mittlerer Krankenpanzerwagen') in its inventory.[47]

The final year of the war started with a change in command. On 2 January, Hauptmann Claus von Trotha arrived and was instructed to take over the battalion. On 10 January, Major Lemor handed over command to Hauptmann von Trotha. The new commander would lead the battalion until the end of the war.[48]

6.4 Assignment with the 3.Fs.Jg.Div.

By the end of December 1944, the center of gravity shifted to the left wing of LXVII A.K., where the 3.Fs.Jg.Div. defended a twelve kilometer wide front between Ligneuville - Faymonville - Morscheck. The first elements of Sturmpanzer-Abteilung 217 were assigned to the 3.Fs.Jg.Div. on New Year's morning according to Stabsgefreiter Kuhs.[49] However, the chronicle of the 3.Fs.Jg.Div. mentioned a number of soldiers from 1./ Sturmpanzer-Abteilung 217 having been killed prior to 31 December.[50] Nevertheless, the situation remained relatively calm for the first

Status Report 1 January 1945					
Materiel	Authorized strength	Actual Strength	Combat-ready	Actual Strength 08/01/45	Difference
Sturmpanzer IV	45	36	6	36	-
Medium SPW	2	2	2	2	-
Motorcycle & sidecars	15	0	0	0	-
Motorcycles	4	11	8	11	-
CC passenger cars	23	26	19	26	-
CO passenger cars	7	7	4	8	+1
Maultiere	15	7	5	5	-
CC trucks	51	31	29	30	-1
CO trucks	6	33	31	32	-1
Halftracks	5	5	2	5	-
Machine guns	111	87	27	88	+1

The Commanding General of the LXVII Armee-Korps, General of the Infantry Otto Maximilian Hitzfeld. *Timm Haasler*

two weeks of January 1945, but it was only a matter of time until the Americans would start their counterattack in order to push the Germans back. All the 3.Fs. Jg.Div. could do was to prepare for defense by mining roads and building strong points. The long expected American attack finally started on the morning of 13 January on the division's left flank.

During the morning of **13 January** the 2nd Bn, 120th Inf Rgt, 30th Inf Div, attacked Thirimont and Co G managed to recapture part of the village. The village of Thirimont and the high ground due south (Hauts-Sarts) was fiercely defended by the I./Fs.Jg.Rgt.9. Hauts-Sarts was held by the 1. Kompanie, the center of Thirimont by the 3. and 4. Kompanie, while the 2. Kompanie held the northern outskirts of the village. Companies E and F, 120th Inf Rgt, were pinned down by combined German small arms, mortar and artillery fire and were unable to relieve Co G. Therefore, Co G was ordered to withdraw at dusk. At 06:30, when Co G intended to disengage, they were attacked from the direction of Ondenval by a company of paratroopers[51] supported by two tanks. The Germans did everything to gain the upper hand and reinforced the attacking force with five additional tanks, soon followed by another five tanks. Co G was cut off and the Germans captured approximately 100 men. The German attacking force was composed of 1./Pz. Jg.Abt.348,[52] 1./ Sturmpanzer-Abteilung 217 and 15.(Pi.)/Fs.Jg.Rgt.9.[53]

The 120th Inf Rgt renewed its attack on Thirimont on **14 January**. The 3rd Bn received orders to attack the high ground south of the village from the West, while the 1st Bn, which had been in reserve, was ordered to execute a night attack from the area of Baugnez.[54] What was left of the 2nd Bn also tried to attack the village from the area of Waimes. Before these attacks started, 4 officers and 15 enlisted men of Co G managed to escape Thirimont under the cover of darkness.

At 03:30, German tanks were heard moving into Thirimont. Around 04:00, Co E secured Point 68, the crossroads 1 kilometer north of Thirimont, on the road to Waimes. The company continued to advance south and reached the outskirts of the village before dawn, where it ran into a German strongpoint. The German resistance was strong and forced Co E to fall back to Point 68. The 1st Bn did not perform any better. Reaching Thirimont before noon, the battalion only made very slow progress against German paratroopers fighting without any thought for their own preservation. The Germans had turned each house into a strongpoint and the Americans had to clear all floors before they could attack the next house. Two dug-in German tanks also supported the defenders. In order to keep the 1st Bn attack moving, the Americans intended to bring forward two platoons of tanks and tank destroyers.[55]

Around 13:00, the Germans launched their first counterattack of the day, approximately thirty paratroopers and one tank attacked elements of the 1st

Bn in Thirimont. The Americans quickly repulsed the attack. In the afternoon, the Germans obviously started to move their armor; four tanks being identified in the Ondenval area moving east in the direction of Schoppen. The Americans identified an area 800 meters east of Ondenval as an assembly area for these tanks. At 16:45, the sound of moving tanks was noticed in the Steinbach - Remonval area. The Americans presumed that these were their own tanks, coming down from the Waimes area, but at 17:25 it became clear that the tanks were part of a German counterattack launched from the area of Remonval. The strength of the German force was about one battalion of infantry, supported by between five and fifteen armored vehicles.[56] American artillery stopped the German attack 100 meters in front of the American forward line. At 19:35, the Germans attacked once more with two companies of paratroopers and five tanks, but again this attack was repulsed within a matter of minutes. The Americans claimed to have destroyed two German tanks with another as probable. POWs[57] confirmed that I./Fs.Jg.Rgt.9 was still defending Hauts-Sarts, Thirimont and the high ground on the northern outskirts of Thirimont, while the counterattacks were launched by 15.(Pi.)/Fs.Jg.Rgt.9, approximately forty men from 10./Fs.Jg.Rgt.9 and approximately fifteen tanks in total. While the Americans at first presumed that these tanks belonged to the 12. SS-Pz.Div., POWs consistently state that the supporting armor did not belong to the Waffen-SS. The tanks must again have belonged to 1./Pz.Jg.Abt.348 and 1./Sturmpanzer-Abteilung 217. Both tanks destroyed in Thirimont were assault guns on a Mark IV chassis and therefore obviously belonged to 1./Pz.Jg.Abt.348. POWs from 10./Fs.Jg.Rgt.9 later stated that the company lost eight men during this counterattack.[58]

Meanwhile, 3rd Bn, 120th Inf Rgt, also had a frustrating day. German opposition southwest of the Hauts-Sarts was very strong and progress painfully slow. By the end of the day, the 3rd Bn was still 500 meters short of its objective.[59]

While the attack of the 120th Inf Rgt was still stuck at Thirimont, other elements of the 30th Inf Div were more successful, capturing Ligneuville the same day, which was defended by elements of Grenadier-Regiment 293, 18.V.G.Div., and formed a bridgehead over the Amblève river. At 19:30, the Germans counterattacked with a battalion of infantry (III./Fs.Jg.Rgt.5 and 14.(Pz.Jg.)/Fs.Jg.Rgt.5), supported by six tanks (probably elements of Heeres-Sturmartillerie-Brigade 905).[60] The German counterattack was stopped before it reached the bridge over the Amblève.[61]

Late in the evening of 14 January, the Germans prepared for a new attack on Thirimont by moving eight to ten assault guns through Ondenval uphill in the direction of Thirimont. At 06:05 on **15 January**, the German counterattack was launched on the north of Thirimont. The Americans reported two companies of paratroopers and an unknown number of tanks, which belong to 1./Pz.Jg.Abt.348. The Germans tried to overrun the American outposts in the east of the village,

but were finally driven back again in less than an hour. Now it was time for the Americans to attack. The 1st Bn, 120th Inf Rgt, attacked the southeastern outskirts of the village at 08:00. German resistance was still very strong, with paratroopers and tanks refusing to give up ground easily, but at 13:30 the 1st Bn finally reported that it was in control of the entire village. Co B, 823rd TD Bn, claimed to have destroyed three German assault guns, while 743rd Tk Bn claimed to have destroyed another two assault guns. It is clear that these figures were exaggerated and most likely based on double counts. 1./Pz.Jg.Abt.348 lost up to five assault guns in Thirimont at most, and contrary to American reports German POWs claimed that two assault guns were destroyed by American artillery fire. Among the men captured by the 30th Inf Div on 15 January were three soldiers of the 1. Kompanie. They told the interrogation officer that their unit consisted of only one company, which was attached to the 3.Fs.Jg.Div. They also stated that their unit had already lost four or five assault guns since the start of their engagement in this area. According to the POWs there was a platoon of 75 men from 3.Fs.Jg.Div., which was attached to the company to provide infantry support. The 1st Bn spent the rest of day clearing the Germans from the northern bank of the Amblève. In the meantime, the 3rd Bn had also managed to capture Hauts-Sarts before dusk, completing the mission of the 120th Inf Rgt after three days of heavy fighting.[62]

Two days after the 30th Inf Div launched its attack, the neighboring division, the 1st Inf Div, launched its overall attack on the German lines between Waimes and Oberweywertz. The attached 23rd Inf Rgt attacked south from Waimes in the direction of Steinbach – Remonval. The 16th Inf Rgt had to take Faymonville from the North and West while the 18th Inf Rgt received orders to take the high ground between Tier and Klingesberg. All attacks were to commence between 06:00 and 10:00.[63]

The III./Fs.Jg.Rgt.9 was defending the area between Thirimont and Steinbach. The disposition of the companies is not entirely clear. The 10. Kompanie was defending the area east and north of Point 68 while the 11. Kompanie was in Remonval. It seems likely that the 9. Kompanie was also in Remonval. The three remaining mortars of the 12. Kompanie were in Ondenval while two of their platoons were supporting the 10. Kompanie near Point 68. At least one battery of II./Fs.Art.Rgt.3 was supporting the battalion with three or four 105mm howitzers that were in firing positions east of Am Kreuz. The 10./Fs.Jg.Rgt.9 had received thirty men as replacements after the engagement in Thirimont the day before. It now had a strength of sixty men.[64]

Defending Steinbach and Faymonville was the task of II./Fs.Jg.Rgt.9. Due to the attack on Thirimont, the battalion had taken over the defense of Steinbach the day before so as to free 11./Fs.Jg.Rgt.9, which had been defending the village. Therefore, when the 1st Inf Div started the attack in the morning, 7./Fs.Jg.Rgt.9

A Sturmgeschütz IV from 1./ Panzerjäger-Abteilung 348 knocked out in the fighting for Thirimont on 14 or 15 January 1945. The transmission access hatch has a hole in it and name painted has been painted in white by the side of the gun mount. *Stefan De Meyer*

Another 1./ Panzerjäger-Abteilung 348 Sturmgeschütz IV lost in January 1945. The caption states that it was photographed near the River Amblève.
NARA via Darren Neely

A veteran paratrooper of Fallschirmjäger-Regiment 5 tries to hide his face from the camera of an American war photographer. Oberweywertz, 15 January 1945. *NARA*

was defending Steinbach, while the 6. Kompanie was covering the open ground between Steinbach and Faymonville and the 5. and 10. Kompanie were defending Faymonville. The battalion command post was located in Faymonville church.[65]

The area east between Faymonville and Mon Antone was defended by II./FsJg. Rgt.5. The battalion was reinforced by 13.(I.G.)/ and 14.(Pz.Jg.)/Fs.Jg.Rgt.5, and 2./Fallschirm-Panzerjäger-Abteilung 3.[66] The 15.(Pi.)/Fs.Jg.Rgt.5 was held in reserve at Schoppen. The battalion command post was located in Schoppen as well as six 81mm mortars of the 8. Kompanie. At least one battery of III./Fs.Art. Rgt.3 supported the battalion with four 150mm howitzers, in firing positions at Eibertingen.[67]

The 2nd Bn, 23rd Inf Rgt, spent most of the day clearing Removal and the high ground east of Point 68. The battalion needed the support of tank destroyers before it finally captured the village in the late evening. The 1st Bn was slowed down by determined resistance from 7./Fs.Jg.Rgt.9 and mined roads. Two tank destroyers ran into mines (captured from the Americans) at the entrance to Steinbach; German anti-tank weapons destroyed another tank. After the capture of the village, more mines and enemy fire from the ridge east of the road slowed the advance to the South. The battalion stopped 400 meters south of Steinbach.[68]

The 1st Bn, 16th Inf Rgt, slowly approached Faymonville from the west and north. It was not until evening that they reached the center of the village. Further to the east, 3rd Bn, 16th Inf Rgt, first attacked the area around Mon Antone before attacking the wooded area south of the village, while other elements turned westwards, heading for Faymonville. Elements of II./Fs.Jg.Rgt.5 tried to disengage, falling back in the direction of Schoppen at dusk. In the evening, contact was made with elements of the I./Fs.Jg.Rgt.8 in the Faymonville area, indicating that the Germans had brought forward reserves in order to retake the forward line. At least two companies of II./Fs.Jg.Rgt.8 were engaged in the Faymonville area. The 6. Kompanie was engaged in Faymonville while the 5. Kompanie was held in reserve south of Faymonville. Later, the remnants of the 6. Kompanie were incorporated into the 5. Kompanie. The commander of II./Fs.Jg.Rgt.9, Hauptmann Harth, was killed in combat south of the village and Hauptmann Stark took command the next day. By the end of the day, 1st Bn, 16th Inf Rgt, had managed to penetrate the town in several places, three American tanks were lost to mines and two tanks bogged down in the snow.[69]

The 18th Inf Rgt advanced slowly in the direction of Klingesberg. Difficult terrain, the snow, and determined German opposition slowed the attack of the 3rd Bn. Co L was even forced to return to its original positions.[70]

Another strength report of the Generalinspekteur der Panzertruppen, issued on 1

February shows Sturmpanzer-Abteilung 217 with thirty-six Sturmpanzer IVs and two Flakpanzer IVs on 15 January. Fifteen Sturmpanzers were reported as combat-ready while the rest were in maintenance together with the two anti-aircraft tanks.[71]

After the capture and defense of Ligneuville the day before, the 119th Inf Rgt turned east on the morning of **16 January**. Elements of the regiment were heading for the Wolfsbusch height and captured the hill against little or no resistance, while the 3rd Bn advanced along the road to Montenau, which ran almost parallel to the east of Ligneuville. The battalion overran a German firing position east of the village and captured four 150mm field howitzers. To the right (west) of the regiment the 117th Inf Rgt of the same Division advanced along the Ligneuville - St.-Vith highway in the direction of the Kaiserbaracke crossroads. The forward elements of the regiment encountered elements of *Kampfgruppe Hoffmann* (approximately 60 soldiers) in this area, which were supported by five assault guns of Heeres-Sturmartillerie-Brigade 905.[72] During this advance one soldier of the brigade, most likely a member of 4.Batterie,[73] was captured south of Ligneuville. He told the Americans, that he believed that some of the brigade's assault guns were in the woods around the Kaiserbaracke crossroads.[74]

The 120th Inf Rgt, still in the Thirimont area, reported to have fired on two German tanks that were moving at the edge of the woods south of Thirimont at 04:00. The Germans were obviously falling back as no more tanks could be heard after. During the course of the day, the regiment continued to clear the area up to the banks of the Amblève. A group of 20 Germans was encountered at 08:35, 1 kilometer south of Thirimont, another group of 40 Germans was engaged at 09:55 in the same area.[75]

The 1st Inf Div also continued its attack. The 2nd Bn, 23rd Inf Rgt, attacked from Remonval at 06:45 and soon reached the outskirts of Ondenval without German resistance. The battalion noticed that the Germans in front of the 1st Bn were withdrawing to the east, in the direction of Am Stephanshof. Ondenval and the open ground to the east were captured by 12:00. Another group of Germans, made up of 50 soldiers and 4 armored vehicles, was discovered south of Croix des Sarts moving along the Montenau - Ligneuville road in the direction of Ligneuville. The Americans opened fire on the German group that had reached the bend in the road south of Croix des Sarts as well as on armored vehicles south of Ondenval near the bridge over the Amblève. The artillery fire dispersed the infantry and knocked out one of the armored vehicles. Co B continued to advance to the south and reached the railroad underpass, where a German halftrack was encountered and destroyed. The road south of the underpass was mined and held by Germans who opened fire with small arms and self-propelled guns. In the meantime, Co A had sent out patrols in the direction of Am Stephanshof but also encountered heavy

Hauptmann Elard Harth, Commanding Officer of II./Fs.Jg.Rgt. 9, killed in action on 15 January 1945 near Faymonville. *Timm Haasler*

German resistance. The company tried to bypass the German strongpoint but ran into opposition again. The Germans held positions at the edge of the Rohrbusch forest along the road from Am Kreuz - Am Stephanshof. The 23rd Inf Rgt was not able to overcome the German defenses in this area and halted its advance. The tank destroyers accompanying the 23rd Inf Rgt claimed to have destroyed a German Panzer V tank on the height south of Ondenval and presumed another German tank to be present in this area. Members of the reconnaissance company of 3.Fs.Jg.Div. later claimed to have seen two German assault guns in a field 200 meters west of the Am Kreuz crossroads in the evening. These guns were covering the draw and the road from Ondenval to Am Kreuz south of Croix des Sarts.[76]

At 07:00, the 1st Bn, 16th Inf Rgt, relaunched its attack as planned, and at 08:30 reported that it had finally captured Faymonville. Captured German soldiers confirmed that the I./Fs.Jg.Rgt.8 had been sent forward in support of the II./Fs.Jg.Rgt.9. Nevertheless, a large number of Germans had withdrawn during the night. The 1st Bn exploited its success, Co C pushed down to the road junction north of Am Stephanshof; Co A and B held their ground south of Faymonville and established contact with the 23rd Inf Rgt to the right.[77]

At 08:40, the 2nd Bn, 16th Inf Rgt, started to attack again from an assembly area southeast of Waimes. In the afternoon, the battalion reached the small patch of woods 1 kilometer northwest of Schoppen. As Co F approached the patch of woods, a platoon of Germans in the woods opened up with machine gun fire, supported by a self-propelled gun. A tank was brought up and drove off the self-propelled gun; most of the German infantry were killed and an officer candidate taken prisoner. He later stated that the patch of woods was defended by 15 men of 4./Fs.Jg.Rgt.8 and two 105mm assault howitzers, which had received orders in the morning to clear the woods of the enemy. Co F then moved on, only to draw lethal self-propelled and artillery fire from the northwestern edge of Schoppen and from the high ground north and south of the village. The Company was cut to pieces. The American tanks were unable to move forward over the uncleared road. The German self-propelled guns were firing from hull-down positions. Out of 6 officers and about 125 men of Co F, only 4 officers and 62 men managed to return the next morning. Co E, which tried to pass around to the south of Co F, found itself in nearly as bad a situation, and both companies were forced to withdraw to the eastern edge of the woods. Reconnaissance reported 40 soldiers and two German halftracks in the area of Derrière l'Ak and a couple of self-propelled guns in Schoppen. The 5./ and 6./Fs.Jg.Rgt.8 which had withdrawn to Schoppen after Faymonville had fallen, were now in charge of the defense of the village. At around 15:00, the Germans counterattacked; three self-propelled guns and 40 infantry launched an attack northwest from Schoppen. American artillery fired at the Germans and managed to disperse the infantry. The German attack force was composed of a platoon of 15.(Pi.)/Fs.Jg.Rgt.5 that had been attached to II./Fs.

Jg.Rgt.8 in order to recapture the patch of woods west of Schoppen. Nevertheless, the situation for the 2nd Bn, 16th Inf Rgt, remained critical. The German force at Derrière l'Ak and a single self-propelled gun west of Schoppen continued to fire at the Americans in the forest. The former tried to fall back in the afternoon by using the Tier - Schoppen road. They ran into the positions of Co K, 18th Inf Rgt, south of Tier. A firefight developed at dusk between the 50-60 German infantrymen supported by a single tank and the Americans.[78]

At dawn, elements of the 18th Inf Rgt reached the area west and southwest of Klingesberg, and ran into heavy German opposition. The Germans in this area belonged to 5./Fs.Jg.Rgt.5. This company had about 80 men left, eight light machine guns, one bazooka, and four to five *Panzerfäuste*. Support was provided by 81mm mortars of the 8. Kompanie in Schoppen. A German column of approximately 100 soldiers and a couple of armored vehicles approached along the road from Hepscheid to Möderscheid. In the afternoon, elements of 2nd Bn, 18th Inf Rgt, reached the Bütgenbacher Heck. Another German troop concentration was discovered along the road between Schoppen and Möderscheid at dusk. Another group was discovered in the Schleid forest.[79]

The German tanks in the area south of Ondenval belonged to 1./Pz.Jg.Abt.348 and 1./ Sturmpanzer-Abteilung 217. Those encountered around Schoppen also belonged to 1./ Sturmpanzer-Abteilung 217 according to a member of the 1. Kompanie.[80]

The 1st Inf Div spent most of **17 January** improving its positions and clearing isolated German pockets of resistance south of Faymonville and in the area of Tier - Klingesberg. No serious attempt was made to overcome the German strongpoints at Croix des Sarts and at Schoppen.

The situation in front of the 23rd Inf Rgt was quiet in the morning, there being no sign that the Germans were withdrawing. During the course of the day, 1st Bn, 18th Inf Rgt, arrived in the area four kilometers east of Ligneuville and started to replace elements of the 119th Inf Rgt around Point 553. In an effort to outflank the German positions south of the river, the battalion was attached to the 23rd Inf Rgt and sent out patrols to reconnoiter these. Patrols discovered a number of enemy positions including a motor park with eight vehicles. At 15:00 a coordinated attack was launched in which the 1st Bn, 18th Inf Rgt, attacked north and the 3rd Bn, 23rd Inf Rgt, attacked south into the Rohrbusch. By dark, both battalions had only penetrated a short distance into the woods against very determined enemy resistance. Facing 23rd Inf Rgt was *Kampfgruppe Schenk* which was defending the area between Am Kreuz and Iveldingen. Five Sturmpanzer IVs of Sturmpanzer-Abteilung 217 and three Sturmgeschütz IV of 1./Pz.Jg.Abt.348 were attached to this Kampfgruppe, but were obviously not engaged that day.[81]

Schoppen was considered the main center of resistance and despite bad weather with low visibility, a number of self-propelled guns were identified in this area. During the morning, 2nd Bn, 16th Inf Rgt, captured a soldier of 15.(Pi.)/Fs.Jg.Rgt.5 who stated that the small forest between Faymonville and Schoppen was occupied by an officer and 35 soldiers of his company. The entire company had arrived the night before and received orders to reoccupy the forests west and northwest of Schoppen. The POW continued that the company had a total strength of 2 officers and 120 enlisted men. American reports claimed that some Germans were still holding out between the 23rd and 16th Inf Rgt northwest of Am Stephanshof. Later reports confirm that these Germans belonged to Fs.Jg.Rgt.9, most of them stragglers. In the afternoon, a German tank was reported at the edge of the forest northwest of Schoppen. American tank destroyers opened fire at the tank which fell back.[82]

In the morning, the 18th Inf Rgt also reported German pockets of resistance. Smaller groups were obviously still holding out in the woods west of Tier and west of Klingesberg.[83] Later that day, 40-50 German infantry and two tanks attacked the positions of Co K southwest of Tier, but would be driven off. Co L attacked in the general direction of Schoppen and succeeded in getting to the southern extremity of Point 566 by dark after crossing the stream west of Klingesberg.[84]

While the 3.Fs.Jg.Div. avoided a breakthrough by the 1st Inf Div, the situation on the left flank looked alarming. The 18.V.G.Div. was falling back in the direction of St.-Vith and opened a wide gap between both divisions. The 3.Fs.Jg.Div. tried to close the gap by shifting what was left of Fs.Jg.Rgt.9 and one battalion of Fs. Jg.Rgt.8 into the gap.[85] Five soldiers of the Heeres-Sturmartillerie-Brigade 905 were captured by the 30th Inf Div, although no location was given in the American report. It is highly likely that they belonged to a gun crew from the 2nd Battery which was attached to the German forces defending the Kaiserbaracke crossroads. One platoon of 4./Heeres-Sturmartillerie-Brigade 905 was attached to the battery to protect the assault guns in close combat. Montenau was held by III./Fs.Jg.Rgt.8, neighbored by elements of III./Fs.Jg.Rgt.9, one kilometer east of Kaiserbaracke.[86]

On **18 January**, the situation for the 3. Fallschirmjäger-Division became critical. The 30th Inf Div exploited the successful advance south from Ligneuville and ordered 120th Inf Rgt to attack from the Wolfsbusch height in the direction of Point 552, south of Kaiserbaracke. The 1st Bn, 120th Inf Rgt, jumped off in the morning, bypassing Kaiserbaracke crossroads to the East and reaching Point 522 at 13:30. The battalion did not have to wait long for the expected German counterattack that came from the direction of Born. Approximately 100 soldiers, supported by five tanks, attacked the American position; the Americans destroying two of the attacking German tanks with bazookas. The German attack lost its momentum and the infantry started to fall back. Late in the afternoon the Germans

counterattacked once more, but the attack was again repulsed. Two tanks and one assault gun were hit, but managed to withdraw while 40 Germans were captured. At dusk the 3rd Bn, 120th Inf Rgt, arrived at Point 522 and reinforced the 1st Bn. The gap between Point 522 and the Wolfsbusch height was covered by the 30th Rcn Trp, while Wolfsbusch Height itself was defended by 2nd Bn, 120th Inf Rgt. To the north of the Wolfsbusch Height, contact was established with the 23rd Inf Rgt of the 1st Inf Div. No information has been found regarding the composition of the German forces that attacked from the East, but it is likely that they belonged to the 3.Fs.Jg.Div. and 1./Heeres-Sturmartillerie-Brigade 905. The same day 3./Heeres-Sturmartillerie-Brigade 905 was attached to II./Gren.Rgt.295.[87]

The arrival of 1st Bn, 18th Inf Rgt, the day before and the advance of the battalion during the course of the day, finally sealed the fate of the German forces still holding the line south of the Amblève between Croix des Sarts and Thirimont. The 1st Bn jumped off at 09:00 and advanced to the East. It soon reached the Amblève near Am Kloster. Here, various members of III./Fs.Jg.Rgt.8 were captured. The POWs stated that the III. Battalion was not at full strength. They claimed that the 12./Fs.Jg.Rgt.8 only had mortars and bazookas, while the II. Battalion was said to have been wiped out almost completely, and the whereabouts of the I. Battalion were unknown. The prisoners thought the line of withdrawal for the regiment was to the east through Eibertingen.

The 1st Bn then turned north and surprised the German force defending the southern bank of the Amblève. The Germans, who had previously offered bitter resistance, attempted to cross the river from the north, but failed when attacked from the south by the 1st Bn. At the end of the day 60 Germans had been taken prisoner and two 88mm guns plus a half-track were captured.[88] The rest of the day was spent reorganizing under constant artillery and mortar fire.

The German forces consisted of the remnants of I./Fs.Jg.Rgt.9, remnants of 7./Fs. Jg.Rgt.9, 15.(Pi.)/Fs.Jg.Rgt.8, and elements of the reserve companies of Fs.Jg.Rgt.8 and 9. The reserve companies were made up of clerks, butchers, signalmen and the like, and had been moved up from the supply trains to fill out the ranks. Artillery support was provided by 8./Fs.Art.Rgt.3. A forward observer of this battery was among the group of prisoners. He claimed that the battery, with three 105mm howitzers, had been in Iveldingen, but was believed to have moved to Eibertingen. The German forces were under the command of a major, the commander of I./Fs. Jg.Rgt.9. The major was 32 years of age and captured along with his adjutant. Before his arrival in this sector 14 days previously, he had been engaged on the Eastern front as an air observer. When he arrived in the area, he was initially attached to Fs. Jg.Rgt.8. Then, three days ago, the commander of the 1st Battalion was wounded by artillery and he had to take over.[89] The major stated that his battalion, before his last engagement, numbered 110 men and that contact with Fs.Jg.Rgt.8 on the

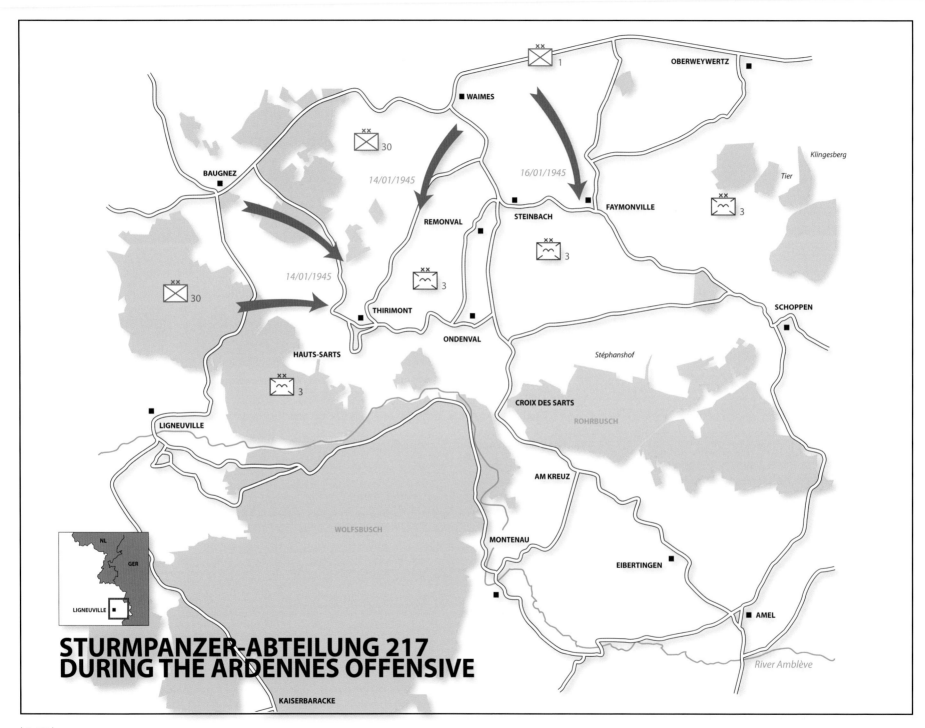

STURMPANZER-ABTEILUNG 217
DURING THE ARDENNES OFFENSIVE

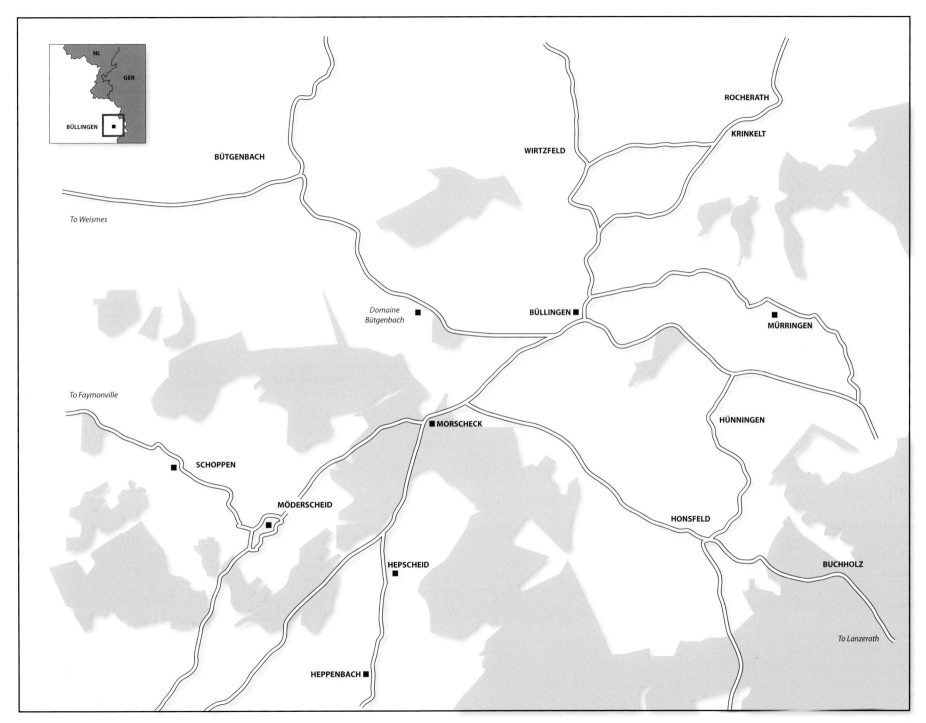

right had been broken the night before.[90]

During the night, in an attempt to close the gap between I./Fs.Jg.Rgt.9 west of the Amblève and the III./Fs.Jg.Rgt.9 east of the river, the Germans tried to insert the reconnaissance company of the 3.Fs.Jg.Div. 400 meters west of the bend in the road south of Croix des Sarts. The company had arrived from the Deidenberg area during the evening of 17 January and was said to have numbered 40 to 50 men. It appears that some of the company got lost in the darkness. Only a handful of men were captured by 1st Bn, 18th Inf Rgt west of the river, while others were engaged on the other side of the river. These elements had passed the Am Kreuz crossroads late in the night and moved northwest in the direction of Ondenval. Before the men passed the crossroads they had seen two assault guns in the field west of the village. These prisoners claimed that the company had been used as infantry since the last engagement in Düren in early December 1944.[91]

On the morning of 18 January the German forces east of the Amblève were as follows:

- Fs.Aufkl.Kp.3 and dispersed elements of the I./Fs.Jg.Rgt.9, defending both sides of the road from Ondenval to Am Kreuz on the height of the bend in the road south of Croix des Sarts
- Remnants of III./Fs.Jg.Rgt.9, Hauptmann Buchholz, defending the Rohrbusch forest northwest of Am Kreuz. The mortars of the 12./Fs.Jg.Rgt.9 were in position in Am Kreuz
- Remnants of II./Fs.Jg.Rgt.9, Hauptmann Stark, defending the Rohrbusch forest southeast of Am Stephanshof
- Reinforcing the II. and III. Battalion were the 13.(I.G.)/Fs.Jg.Rgt.9 and 14.(Pz. Jg.)/Fs.Jg.Rgt.9, acting as infantry

On the American side, the 23rd Inf Rgt had scheduled its jump-off at 09:00. However, the 3rd Bn, 23rd Inf Rgt, was harassed by self-propelled gun fire before 06:00. The battalion was unable to locate the source of the fire. During the next hour, about 25 more rounds fell on their positions. The Americans guessed that they were fired at from the direction of Deidenberg. According to a German prisoner, there was a German assault gun in this area. The battalion asked for artillery support to silence the German gun. At about the same time, the 2nd Bn, 23rd Inf Rgt, also reported to have received three concentrations of 10 rounds each during the previous hour. The battalion estimated that the fire was coming from 105mm howitzers.

At 08:00, unknown to the Americans, an attack by *Kampfgruppe Schenk* had started from the area of Am Kreuz. The main effort was along the road north through the Rohrbusch forest in the direction of Am Stephanshof with a secondary attack along the road to Ondenval. The primary target for the Germans was clearing the Americans from the Rohrbusch forest and the Croix des Sarts area.

The attacking force was composed of *Kampfgruppe Schenk* and a battalion of Fs. Jg.Rgt.8. *Kampfgruppe Schenk* was an ad-hoc unit under the command of the former commander of I./Fs.Jg.Rgt.9, Oberstleutnant Freiherr Schenk zu Schweinsberg. The combat group consisted of 1./ Sturmpanzer-Abteilung 217, 1./Pz.Jg.Abt.348, one platoon of engineers from Fs.Jg.Rgt.9 and three or four groups of paratroopers from Fs.Jg.Rgt.9. It is likely that the paratroopers and the engineers were providing infantry protection for the tanks during combat. According to German prisoners, only three Sturmpanzer IVs and two Sturmgeschütze IV were combat-ready on 18 January. The battalion of the Fs.Jg.Rgt.8 was also something of a melting pot. The strength of the battalion was 200-250 men, of which 160-200 had arrived at the front the previous morning. These newcomers had been with the Fs.Jg.Ers.Btl.3 in the Netherlands. The other men had been sifted out of other units within Fs. Jg.Rgt.8.

The Germans had planned to start the attack much earlier, but according to German prisoners, the three Sturmpanzer IVs did not arrive in time. When they finally did arrive at 08:00 they were assigned to the main attacking force and moved forward along the road from Am Kreuz to Am Stephanshof. Within the next hour, the 1st and 3rd Bn, 23rd Inf Rgt were attacked near Croix des Sarts and southwest of Am Stephanshof. The German infantry was supported by assault guns in both areas, which were firing directly on the American positions. At 10:30, the Germans secured the bend in the road at Croix des Sarts in the area defended by the 1st Bn, 23rd Inf Rgt. In the Rohrbusch forest, the Germans managed to infiltrate between Co L and I, 23rd Inf Rgt. A Sturmpanzer IV reached the northern edge of the Rohrbusch forest by noon and started to fire at the Americans lines. Another assault gun suddenly moved forward on the bend at Croix des Sarts and started to fire at the positions of 2nd Bn, 23rd Inf Rgt but pulled back after American tank destroyers fired two rounds in return. German infantry were identified moving eastwards in the Amblève valley. By 11:30, the ammunition situation started to become critical for the Americans. A furious battle raged in the dense woods until noon. After this the action moved east into the Rohrbusch forest. German infantry, supported by 2-3 tracked vehicles, infiltrated the American lines between Co I, 23rd Inf Rgt, and Co B, 16th Inf Rgt. The Americans ordered two tank destroyers forwards to challenge the German tanks. When they arrived, the German attack subsided, and at 14:00, remnants of the attacking force began to withdraw south. By 14:30, the counterattack was over and the Germans had been cleared out of the American positions in the woods. In the bitter fighting three company commanders became casualties. Soldiers of the 3.Fs.Jg.Div. later claimed that the assault guns inflicted heavy casualties on the American defenders. The 23rd Inf Rgt sent out patrols to the south. When they returned they brought back several German prisoners together with information that the ground was littered with enemy dead from previous fighting. There were no traces of the self-propelled guns which had supported the German counterattack. Prisoners stated that the three 150mm assault guns had either withdrawn towards Eibertingen or Iveldingen during the afternoon. At 15:20 the 1st Bn, 23rd Inf Rgt, reported that Co B had finally captured the road bend at Croix des Sarts. Around 18:00, 23rd Inf Rgt reported 150 Germans moving in the direction of Eibertingen, and from Eibertingen to Deidenberg. The Americans believed that the Germans would now move their remaining forces to the high ground between Eibertingen and Schoppen.[92]

After a day of consolidation and reorganization, the 1st Bn, 16th Inf Rgt moved out in the morning from the Am Stephanshof area. Co B was swinging around to the West through the positions of the 23rd Inf Rgt with the intention of taking its objective at the northern edge of the Rohrbusch from the East. However, as the Company struggled through the draw north of the woods it was caught by heavy artillery fire, and became involved in the powerful German counterattack directed at the 23rd Inf Rgt. With Co C striking due south from the road junction north of Stephanshof, Co B turned east and pushed through the woods although it had no contact on either side. As the company passed by, the Germans infiltrated from behind, but were finally driven out when the Americans brought up tank destroyers. By the end of the day the battalion had captured twenty-two Germans; twenty from 13./Fs.Jg.Rgt.9 and two from 5./Fs.Jg.Rgt.9. The rest of 16th Inf Rgt spent a quiet day in front of Schoppen.[93]

The 18th Inf Rgt attack continued on 18 January with 3rd Bn pushing south to the high ground north of Schoppen (Point 557) under very heavy enemy artillery and mortar fire. Elements of the 3rd Bn captured six members of the II./Fs.Jg.Rgt.5 in the woods north of Schoppen. These prisoners stated that the Sturmzug (Assault Platoon) was attached to the 5. Kompanie. The prisoner believed that the 5. Kompanie and Sturmzug had been wiped out, while the 6. Kompanie had approximately 70 men ten days ago. The 7. Kompanie had not been reformed after the engagement at Düren, and the 8. Kompanie had 80 men left. The morale of the soldiers was considered to be fair and health conditions were good except for lice. In one company, 10 out of 30 men suffered from trench foot.[94]

The capture of Point 522 on 18 January cut off the German troops and tanks defending the Kaiserbaracke crossroads. The Americans started to eliminate the encircled Germans on **19 January**. The 117th Inf Rgt attacked from the north while 3rd Bn, 120th Inf Rgt, attacked from the southeast in a pincer movement. The 3rd Bn first attacked a German road block north of Point 522 at the railroad crossing. A German tank and an assault gun are supposed to have been destroyed. Under pressure from the 117th Inf Rgt coming from the north, the Germans manning the roadblock north of Kaiserbaracke first fell back to crossroads, before they tried to break out along the road south in the direction of St.-Vith. They soon ran into

the positions of the 1st Bn, 120th Inf Rgt. The German group, mainly made up of assault guns, was ambushed and destroyed. While the outcome is clear, American sources are contradictory as to the number of vehicles destroyed during this encounter. The Americans first claimed to have destroyed four assault guns and one command car. Later the figures were changed to five Mark IVs (75mm), two assault guns (105mm) and one command car. An unknown number of POWs, belonging to the 2./ and 4./Heeres-Sturmartillerie-Brigade 905, were captured west of the crossroads. The prisoners again confirmed the order of battle provided by the other prisoners who had been captured before.[95] An order by Heeres-Sturmartillerie-Brigade 905 to the 1st Battery and the Headquarters Battery was captured the same day. The document was dated 9 January and contained information regarding the movement of the Brigade from Kyllburg to St.-Vith. Two days later, soldiers of the 264th FA Bn looked into one of the knocked out assault guns and discovered another document which showed an overview of the radio net used by Heeres-Sturmartillerie-Brigade 905.[96]

The 23rd Inf Rgt jumped off in the morning to seize Eibertingen, Iveldingen and Montenau, with the 1st Bn of the 18th Inf Rgt on the right, 3rd Bn, 23rd Inf Rgt in the center and 2nd Bn, 23rd Inf Rgt, on the left. In the advance towards Eibertingen significant numbers of wooden mines were encountered on the main Ondenval - Eibertingen road. An enemy strong point at the railroad crossing northeast of Montenau slowed down the attacks on Iveldingen and Montenau until Co L, supported by two tanks, eliminated it. At Iveldingen and Montenau approximately 22 prisoners were taken. Prisoners captured along the road to Eibertingen stated that their unit had received orders during the morning to withdraw to Amel. However, the Germans did not give up that easily and defended Eibertingen from dug-in positions on the northern perimeter with an estimated 300 soldiers supported by a tank and two self-propelled guns. The 2nd Bn, 23rd Inf Rgt, with approximately 100 riflemen left, and with strong artillery, tank and tank destroyer in support, launched the attack on the town. After divisional artillery fire had forced the Germans to desert their dug-in positions for the greater safety of the basements in the town, the 2nd Bn managed to occupy a number of houses on the northwestern edge. Then the Germans left their shelter and started to counterattack. Severe hand to hand fighting ensued but the Germans were outfought and started to withdraw towards Deidenberg at approximately 14:00. One hundred prisoners were taken in the town and more than 35 German dead were counted. The town was fully secured by 18:00. The three Germans tanks mentioned are one or two Sturmgeschütze IV of 1./Pz.Jg.Abt.348 and one or two Sturmpanzer IV of the 1./ Sturmpanzer-Abteilung 217. According to members of the 3.Fs.Jg.Div., the German tanks managed to destroy a couple of American tanks during their advance on Eibertingen near Am Kreuz, and claimed that a single German assault gun, which had lost it tracks, held out until the last round was fired, then the crew blew up the gun and withdrew. The Americans later identified

The road from Kaiserbaracke to St. Vith, north of Point 522. Three Sturmgeschütz IIIs and another overturned German vehicle. The assault guns belonged to Heeres-Sturmartillerie-Brigade 905 and were destroyed by 1st Bn, 120th Inf Rgt on 19 January 1945. *USAHEC via Lee Archer*

This might be the fourth assault gun mentioned in the American report on page 171. The original caption says St. Vith. Note the dead soldier on top of the fighting compartment, who was probably one of the crew. *NARA via Darren Neely*

Captured paratroopers from the 3. Fallschirmjäger-Division being checked by American MPs. *NARA*

this tank as a 75mm assault gun on a Mark IV chassis. Confirming the American report, German prisoners of the 3. Fallschirmjäger-Division stated that the assault gun belonged to Pz.Jg.Abt.348, which had arrived with a single company of ten assault guns from East Prussia in January 1945. The company would have lost four to five assault guns thus far.[97] The two other German tanks withdrew due to a lack of ammunition. Little is known about the defenders of Eibertingen, Montenau and Iveldingen, but soldiers of the II./ and III./Fs.Jg.Rgt.9 and of the 1./ and 4./Fs.Pi.Btl.3 were captured in the Eibertingen area. The commander of the III./Fs.Jg.Rgt.9, Hauptmann Buchholz, lost his life that day near Amel.[98]

The 16th Inf Rgt captured two prisoners from 5./Fs.Jg.Rgt.9 after midnight on the high ground northeast of Stephanshof. The prisoners stated that the 6. Kompanie was on their right and the 7. Kompanie on their left, while the command post of II./Fs.Jg.Rgt.9 was said to have been in Deidenberg. The 16th Inf Rgt attack on Schoppen started at 08:00 in weather so bad that the Germans did not expect it. Co K, 16th Inf Rgt, moved across the stream to the north of the village and into the woods. Co I followed the same course somewhat to the south and Co L pushed on towards the town just north of the Faymonville - Schoppen road. Tactical surprise was complete and more than 20 Germans were taken prisoner. The village had been defended by about 100 soldiers from various units of the 3.Fs.Jg.Div..The defenders belonged to I./Fs.Jg.Rgt.9, 2./ and 3./Fs.Pi.Btl.3, *Alarm-Kompanie Ostermann*, Fs.Gr.W.Btl.3, Fs.Art.Rgt.3 and Fs.Pz.Jg.Abt.3. Co K moved on through the village to the open hill directly to the south. A platoon was sent to the top of the hill; all but four men were wiped out. After dawn, the 2nd Bn was moving against the patch of woods west of Schoppen. Co F attacked against the northern perimeter of the woods and cleared them, whilst Co E attacked the south of the woods and Co G, the open ground to the south. The battalion took about 40 prisoners from 3./Fs.Pi.Btl.3, I./Fs.Jg.Rgt.8, and 13./Fs.Jg.Rgt.9. The German forces in the woods had a strength of about 100 men the night before and were under the command of Leutnant Wedding, who also had three self-propelled guns in support. The German prisoners reported that Leutnant Wedding and some of the men, together with the three assault guns had left in the direction of Schoppen before the American attack. The prisoners of 3./Fs.Pi.Btl.3 taken in Schoppen and the woods west of the village, claimed they were thrown into battle two days before. When they left Amel and moved to Schoppen on 17 January, the company had a strength of 70 men. In the meantime, the 1st Bn, 16th Inf Rgt in the Rohrbusch forest continued to the east and captured the Eibertingener Höhe before noon. In spite of this threat, however, the Germans counterattacked in an attempt to retake Schoppen with 100 infantry and three or four self-propelled guns. The attack failed after the tanks ran out of ammunition and the Germans fell back to the southeast. This counterattack was launched by *Kampfgruppe Schenk*, this time composed of the Headquarters Company of the Fs.Jg.Rgt.8, supported by three Sturmpanzer IVs of Sturmpanzer-Abteilung 217[99] and one other tank.[100]

Two soldiers of Sturmpanzer-Abteilung 217 who took part in the attack, stated after their capture on 28 January, that the battalion had only twelve combat-ready tanks left that day. In the afternoon the 1st Bn, 16th Inf Rgt made contact with 2nd Bn, 23rd Inf Rgt, north of Eibertingen and the entire regiment started to consolidate the front between Eibertingen – east of Eibertingener Höhe - edge of woods south and southeast of Schoppen.[101]

North of Schoppen, remnants of the Fs.Jg.Rgt.5, comprising 100-150 men, were still opposing the 18th Inf Rgt. The 3rd Bn, 18th Inf Rgt, continued its advance into the Schleid forest in order to cut the road from Bütgenbach into Schoppen. The 2nd Bn, 18th Inf Rgt, also moved east into the Klingesberg forest without making contact with the enemy. In the afternoon, 3rd Bn succeeded in cutting the road and also managed to reach the northern and southern edges of the Schleid forest east of the Bütgenbach - Schoppen road. Elements of Gren.Rgt.1055, 89.Inf.Div. were identified, which had relieved the eastern sector of the 3.Fs.Jg.Div. The Fs. Jg.Rgt.5 committed its last reserves and sent 6./ and 7./Fs.Jg.Rgt.5 forwards.[102]

For the next few days there are no sources of information that help to trace further engagements of Sturmpanzer-Abteilung 217 in the Ardennes.

On **28 January**, the 82nd Airborne Div attacked the defensive positions of 3.Fallschirmjäger-Division between Heppenbach and Meyerode. In support of the paratroopers, LXVII Armee-Korps ordered one regiment of 246.V.G.Div., one battalion of 89.Inf.Div., and elements of Sturmpanzer-Abteilung 217 to counterattack from Andler via Wereth in the direction of Heppenbach. Stabsgefreiter Kuhs was captured with two other members of 1./ Sturmpanzer-Abteilung 217 near Heppenbach. During his interrogation, he stated that his Company had lost three Sturmpanzers due to technical problems.[103]

At Heeresbach, the Americans captured four enlisted men of the battalion, guarding a Sturmpanzer IV that had been immobilized on 20 January with engine trouble. They had been waiting for the repair and maintenance platoon when American tanks surprised them. Having had a good rest for more than a week in a reasonably comfortable billet, these prisoners showed no sign of battle fatigue, but nevertheless they did not regret becoming prisoners. They were willing to talk, happy to be out of the war, but provided only limited information. Up to the time they were separated from their company, ammunition, gasoline and food were adequate. During their eight day stay in Heeresbach they were forced to 'improvise' as food supplies no longer reached them.[104]

On **29 January**, the Americans exploited their breakthrough in the direction of Manderfeld. Near Wereth they knocked out a Sturmpanzer IV which probably belonged to 1./ Sturmpanzer-Abteilung 217, as the Americans also captured five members of this Company in the same area. The elements of the battalion in this area were obviously attached to the 246.V.G.Div.[105] The American advance alarmed both LXVII A.K. and Panzer-Armee-Oberkommando 5 and caused them to react immediately. They sent in further reserves to the stop the advance on Manderfeld. The LXVII Armee-Korps also sent in other elements of Sturmpanzer-Abteilung 217 from the north[106] to the Honsfeld - Buchholz area.[107]

The next day, **30 January**, the battalion was under attack in the Buchholz area after the 30th Inf Div broke through the lines of the 89.Inf.Div. between Büllingen and Honsfeld.[108] These elements most likely belonged to the 3./ Sturmpanzer-Abteilung 217, which was also identified in the 82nd AB Div sector about two kilometers southwest of Honsfeld in support of Fs.Jg.Rgt.9.[109]

On **31 January**, Grenadier-Regiment 991, 277.V.G.Div., counterattacked the forward elements of the 1st Inf Div half way between Rocherath and Miescheid with infantry and self-propelled guns in an attempt to break out to the east. The Americans repulsed the attack and an unknown number of self-propelled guns were cut off west of a crossroads due east of Rocherath. The next day the XVIII AB Corps reported destroying six 150mm self-propelled guns in these battles, which must be the same tanks reported by the 1st Inf Div as being cut off east of Rocherath. These self-propelled guns were probably Sturmpanzers from Sturmpanzer-Abteilung 217.[110] A German prisoner of war, captured by the 26th Inf Rgt, 1st Inf Div, on 3 February, confirmed that elements of Sturmpanzer-Abteilung 217 were in the area. He had seen six to eight 150mm self-propelled guns along the road between Oberreiferscheid and Hellenthal on 1 February. These tanks had run out fuel.[111]

Gefreiter Oskar Klein, 3./ Sturmpanzer-Abteilung 217, remembered his experiences in the Ardennes. Unfortunately, he was no longer able to clearly remember places and dates:

"For our engagement in the Ardennes, we had not received winter clothes. Only blankets were issued to protect us from the cold. In contrast to this, we had received sufficient ammunition and fuel. Movements took place at night only, or when bad weather prevented Allied fighter-bombers from taking off from their airfields. For most of the time, our Company was engaged as an individual fighting unit. We shared our rest area near Lanzerath with some Panzer IVs of the 12.SS-Pz.Div., but I cannot remember if we had further joint engagements after our initial attack. The relationship with the SS-soldiers was not good, although some of their officers were former Army officers. One of these officers was still wearing his 'Großdeutschland' cuff title. We had parked our tanks and vehicles in the woods and used snow to camouflage the tanks as there was no whitewash available. When the snow started to melt, we used

branches to camouflage the vehicles, but for most of the time in January the ground was snow covered. My tank commander was wounded during one of our engagements by three artillery fragments that hit his back while he was standing in his commander's cupola. We immediately drove back and discovered an ambulance next to a house at a crossroads behind the front. The ambulance was out of fuel, therefore we gave them some of our fuel and in turn, they took care of our sergeant. I never heard of him again. The biggest threat to our lives was the ever present American artillery. In January 1945, the withdrawal from the Ardennes began. We had to abandon our rest area near Lanzerath and moved to the customs station at Losheimergraben. It was there, where we received MG 42s in exchange for our MG 34s. In January, we experienced fuel shortages for the first time."[112]

Initially Oskar Klein and his comrade Hans Dusi were together in the same tank, Klein serving as the loader while Dusi acted as the gunner. The driver was an Austrian by the name of Zerwar, who was later killed in the Ardennes. He also remembered that in one case, they had to abandon their tank through the belly hatch but he could not remember why.[113]

Roland Dusi, the son of Hans Dusi, picks up the story:

"My father did not talk much about the war and his experiences in the Ardennes. He mentioned that he had to abandon his knocked out Sturmpanzer a couple of times through the belly hatch. In one case the entire crew was able to get out of the tank unharmed, in another he was the only one who was able to get out of the burning tank. But most of the personnel losses were caused by tree bursts. He also mentioned the American practice of firing into the woods first before they started to approach. As a crew member in a Sturmpanzer he was used to perform different functions like being the loader, gunner or radio operator. He said that he was finally wounded during the Ardennes offensive by a shell fragment and evacuated in an ambulance. Inside the ambulance, a Sd.Kfz.251/8, there was a noncommissioned officer already laying on the top stretcher. He asked my father to change places. Due to his injury, the NCO was afraid that he could not leave the ambulance on his own in case of an emergency, when laying on the top stretcher. So my father agreed and after the NCO was placed on the bottom stretcher, while my father was placed on the top stretcher, the ambulance took off to the rear. On the road to the next clearing station the ambulance was attacked by an Allied fighter-bomber. While my father managed to get out of the open top of the burning ambulance, the NCO died inside. Although my father had suffered further injuries in the leg and in the stomach[114], he was finally evacuated to a field hospital. Despite these injuries, he had recovered by the end of the war."[115]

6.5 A Summary

What was the situation of the battalion at the end of January 1945, how high were the losses in terms of personnel and material?

The actual personnel strength report for January 1945 is dated 4 February, and shows 21 officers, 2 civil servants, 219 NCOs, 354 privates and 1 Russian volunteer - 'Hiwi'. This reported strength seems to be unreliable as the figure exactly matches the authorized strength. Of interest are the charts regarding the losses for December 1944/January 1945. The battalion had lost a total of 79 men in two months of fighting. These figures correspond approximately with another section of the report, which shows 3 officers, 6 NCOs and 33 privates as having been lost due to illness and injuries.

Measured by the authorized strength, the battalion had lost 6% of its personnel KIA or MIA. Another 7.2 % of the personnel had been temporarily lost to injuries, illness and other causes. These figures also included the losses suffered during the engagement in the Hürtgen Forest as part of LXXIV Armee-Korps before the Ardennes Offensive. During the same period the battalion received 6 officers, 12 NCOs and 77 privates as replacements, and one private returned as a convalescent. The 79 men reported as lost had been compensated by 96 replacements, i.e. the battalion was in a better personnel condition after the Ardennes Offensive than it had been at the start.[116] But this is only one side of the story, as we will see from the statement of the battalion commander:

- **Training status:**
  Good - the recently arrived replacements have been incorporated well

- **Material status:**
  Clothes very bad (only one shirt, large proportion of men only one pair of socks or foot rag, footwear ripped, no substitution)

- **Health status and morale:**
  Full of lice, caused by long engagements in the cold and wet. Cases of diarrhea and common colds at 35%, in some cases mange. Morale and fighting spirit of the men is good.[117]

It is difficult to analyze these figures, as the total number of Sturmpanzers on hand appear inconsistent. The figures vary between eleven and thirty-six tanks. Certainly, there had been losses and replacements, but the main reason for these discrepancies was most likely the different way of reporting. Often, only combat-ready tanks and tanks in short-term maintenance were reported, while tanks in long-term maintenance and those in depot-maintenance were excluded.

In summary, the number of combat-ready tanks is the most reliable piece of information that can be drawn from the various reports.

The report dated 5 February also contains the information that five Sturmpanzers were considered total losses since the last report.[118] Adding together all the information, the battalion had lost 17 Sturmpanzers between 16 December 1944 and 9 February 1945. A report issued by the General der Panzertruppen West on 12 February actually confirms these losses when stating:

Reporting date: 9 February 1945:[119]

Sturmpanzer-Abteilung 217:

- **Stu.Pz. 15cm**
  - Authorized strength: 45
  - Actual strength: 31
  - Combat-ready: 10
  - In maintenance up to 14 days: 9
  - In maintenance more than 14 days: 6
  - Broken down due to fuel shortage: 6
  - Total losses: 12
  - Blown up due to fuel shortage: 5
- **Fla.Pz. IV**
  - Authorized strength: 0
  - Actual strength: 1
  - Combat-ready: 1
- **SPW**
  - Authorized strength: 0
  - Actual strength: 2
  - In maintenance up to 14 days: 2

On 9 February, the tank support bases (Panzerstützpunkte) North, Center and J reported that they had one Sturmpanzer IV on hand, which required maintenance of up to seven days and three Sturmpanzer IVs that required maintenance of up to 14 days.[120] It is not clear if these four Sturmpanzers were part of the battalion's report or should be viewed separately.

The two Flakpanzer IVs, first reported by the General der Panzertruppen on 15 January, must be considered as an anomaly, as they were not traceable in any wartime table of organization. While both tanks were reported in maintenance on 15 January, another report stated that the tanks were only allocated to the battalion on 26 January.[121] Surprisingly, both tanks were not part of the report dated 4 February, while the report dated 12 February only mentioned one Flakpanzer.[122]

If this assumption is correct, then the six Sturmpanzer IVs and two Flakpanzer IVs, that arrived on 26 January, were not part of the report dated 4 February. It is highly likely that the missing Flakpanzer IV had already been lost in early February during the defense of Buchholz railroad station. The Americans captured this tank, which is today on display in the collection of the Anti-Aircraft-School of the Federal Armed Forces in Rendsburg. Gefreiter Oskar Klein remembers that he had seen a quad anti-aircraft gun on a Panzer IV chassis after the Ardennes Offensive next to a dam, covering the sky. He had been told that this tank belonged to the battalion.[123]

The available information on the two Sd.Kfz.251/8 ambulances showed the following figures (see table on page 180). By the end of the engagement in the Ardennes both halftracks were in long-term maintenance. As the battalion did not receive substitutes during this period, it is clear that no vehicles were lost, despite the contradictory information in the report dated 4 February.

For all other vehicles and weapons the situation looked like this (see tables on pages 180 - 181).

These figures again prove that the total losses suffered during the Ardennes Offensive had not been that high, but that the combat readiness of the unit had diminished significantly. This also becomes clear when reading the assessments of both the battalion commander and the commanding general:

> *"**Materiel status:**
> Armored and wheeled vehicles are combat-ready in such numbers that the vehicles engaged can be supplied at all times. Weapons and material fine.*
>
> *Note regarding the technical situation of the vehicles:*
> *Caused by the permanent excessive stress, all wheeled vehicles are in an unsatisfactory condition.*
> *Engine performance: approx. 50%*
> *Tires: partially below 30%, otherwise approx. 45%*
>
> *The number of available vehicles is not sufficient to ensure provision at all time.*
> *Signed: von Trotha, date 8 February 1945[124]*
>
> *To reach full combat readiness, the battalion is primarily missing final drives. The fuel shortage is also preventing the full exploitation of performance. Otherwise agreed*
> *Signed: Hitzfeld, Commanding General"[125]*

In a published speech of the General der Panzertruppen West regarding the condition of the tank units in the West, dated 8 February, the General states with respect to Sturmpanzer-Abteilung 217:

> *"Once the training of the replacements has been completed, the state of training can be designated as good. Armored and wheeled vehicles are combat-ready in such numbers that vehicles for engagements can be supplied at all times. The condition of the clothes is bad, in particular in terms of shoes. The morale and fighting spirit of the unit is good. Due to the long engagement in cold and wet weather conditions, the unit is suffering from colds and lice."[126]*

This notice reflects the statement of Hauptmann von Trotha, but as some of sentences have been deleted from his report, the notice has lost a lot of the initial explosiveness.

This Flakpanzer *Wirbelwind* was captured by the Americans at Buchholz station in 1945 and could have been one of the two anti-aircraft tanks allocated to Sturmpanzer-Abteilung 217. The battalion fought in this area on 29/30 January 1945 and reported one missing tank in early February. *NARA via Lee Archer*

Sturmpanzer IV Strength Overview							
Date	Inventory	Combat-ready	Maintenance	Date	Inventory	Combat-ready	Maintenance
15/12/1944	27	?	? a	05/01/1945	12	7	5 a
22/12/1944	20	12	8 a	06/01/1945	12	7	5 a
24/12/1944	21	12	9 a	07/01/1945	12	7	5 a
25/12/1944	21	12	9 a	08/01/1945	36	?	? [129]
25/12/1944	32	12	20 [127]	09/01/1945	23	10	13 a
26/12/1944	21	12	9 a	10/01/1945	23	10	13 a
27/12/1944	20	12	8 a	10/01/1945	36	13	23 [130]
28/12/1944	36	32	4 a	14/01/1945	26	12	14 a
29/12/1944	36	32	4 a	15/01/1945	36	15	21 [131]
30/12/1944	36	32	4 a	16/01/1945	26	12	14 a
31/12/1944	36	32	4 a	17/01/1945	26	12	14 a
01/01/1945	36	6	30 [128]	25/01/1945	36b	14	22 [132]
02/01/1945	11	6	5 a	04/02/1945	25	12	13 [133]
03/01/1945	11	6	5 a	05/02/1945	32	17	15 [134]
04/01/1945	11	6	5 a	09/02/1945	31	10	21 [135]

a. Situation map OB West – Lage Frankreich

b. Around 26 January, six Sturmpanzers arrived which had been allocated on 28 December 1944. These tanks were dispatched from the depot on 20 January, on train number 1944 together with two Flakpanzer IVs.[136] It remains unclear why these tanks were transferred so late. A message intercepted by ULTRA in late December 1944 had already provided information from the General der Panzertruppen West that six Sturmpanzer IVs and one Flakpanzer IV (3.7 cm) were available for dispatch to Sturmpanzer-Abteilung 217 in Duisburg.[137]

Sd.Kfz. 251/8 mittlerer Krankenpanzerwagen Strength Overview					
Date	Authorized Strength	Actual Strength	Combat-ready	Short-term Maintenance	Long-term Maintenance
08/12/1944	?	2	?	?	? [138]
01/01/1945	2	2	2	0	0 [139]
08/01/1945	?	2	?	?	? [140]
04/02/1945	2	1	0	1	? [141]
05/02/1945	0	2	0	0	2 [142]

Strength Report 4 February 1945[143]			
Materiel	Authorized Strength	Actual Strength	Combat-ready
Motorcycle & sidecars	15	3 (+3)	1 (+1)
Motorcycles	4	14 (-3)	6 (-2)
CC passenger cars	23	21 (-5)	10 (-9)
CO passenger cars	1	8 (+1)	5 (+2)
Maultiere	15	6 (-1)	3 (-2)
CC trucks	51	28 (-3)	14 (-15)
CO trucks	6	31 (-2)	21 (-10)
Halftracks	5	1 (-4)	0 (-2)
Machine guns	111	63 (-24)	36 (+9)

Losses Sustained December 1944 - January 1945						
Date	Rank	KIA	WIA	MIA.	III	Others
01/12/1944 - 31/12/1944	Officers	1	1	0	1	0
01/01/1945 - 31/01/1945	Officers	0	1	0	0	0
01/12/1944 - 31/12/1944	NCOs	4	4	0	0	0
01/01/1945 - 31/01/1945	NCOs	2	2	0	0	0
01/12/1944 - 31/12/1944	Privates	6	9	1	6	4
01/01/1945 - 31/01/1945	Privates	7	9	15	4	2
01/12/1944 - 31/01/1945	Total	20	26	16	11	6

A farmer's son stands amazed in front of an overturned Sturmpanzer IV Ausf.IV from Sturmpanzer-Abteilung 217 near Ollheim, east of Euskirchen. *Lee Archer*

CHAPTER 07

LAST TRACES OF STURMPANZER-ABTEILUNG 217

Only limited information can be found regarding further engagements following the end of the Ardennes Offensive. If mentioned at all, most of the reports dealt with its combat strength or armored vehicle allocation.

7.1 February 1945 – Defending the River Roer

The only recorded engagement in February 1945 took place east of Udenbreth on **5 February**.[1] The battalion was assigned to LXVII Armee-Korps for most of the month. Only between 10 and 13 February did the battalion come under the command of LXXIV Armee-Korps before being reattached to LXVII Armee-Korps until the end of the month. The reason for the short assignment to LXXIV Armee-Korps is unclear. The G-2 situation map of the 82nd AB Div for 11 February shows the battalion engaged on the left (southern) wing of the 353.Inf.Div. on the eastern bank of the River Roer. This engagement might have explained the assignment to LXXIV Armee-Korps, but the 353.Inf.Div. was attached to LVIII Panzer-Korps, although the left neighbor, 85.Inf.Div., belonged to LXXIV Armee-Korps. It is also strange that the American G-2 report only showed Sturmpanzer-Abteilung 217 on the map. According to a captured German document, six Sturmpanzers were attached to II./Art.Rgt.277 (277.V.G.Div.) in late February.[2]

On **12 February**, the battalion reported a strength of 31 Sturmpanzers. This report was probably missing another four Sturmpanzers that had already been assigned on 14 January. These tanks were only dispatched a month later, on train 2036.[3] Looking at the situation maps of the OB West one will find two additional strength reports mentioning the battalion. According to these maps, there were twenty-two combat-ready Sturmpanzers on hand on 21 and 25 February.[4]

The Americans launched 'Operation Grenade' on 23 February; the crossing of the River Roer between Roermond and Düren. On the first day the Americans managed to establish bridgeheads on the eastern bank of the river. They soon broke out from these bridgeheads and advanced in an easterly direction. The German defenders, most of whom had been engaged in the Ardennes and not received replacements, could no longer stop the Americans and were forced to fight a delaying action towards the Rhine. At the same time LXVII A.K. was still holding the line along the Westwall in the Eifel region and was in danger of being outflanked on the right (northern) wing. It is not clear when the order was issued to withdraw Sturmpanzer-Abteilung 217 from LXVII A.K. between Reiferscheid and Kronenburg and to reassign them to LXXIV A.K. in the Zülpich – Euskirchen area. A captured German document, dated 3 March, still showed the battalion attached to LXVII Armee-Korps along with Beobachtungs-Abteilung 14, s.Heeres-Artillerie-Abteilung 843, I./Werfer-Regiment 54, Mörser-Batterie 1120, Pionier-Bataillon 108, Pionier-Bataillon 600, and Bau-Pionier-Bataillon 798.[5]

7.2 March 1945

7.2.1 Fighting withdrawal to the Rhine

In early March, the 746th Tk Bn reported that it was in contact with Sturmpanzer-Abteilung 217. The American tank battalion was attached to the 9th Inf Div at that time and advancing west of Zülpich towards Cologne. On the German side, 3.Fs.Jg.Div. desperately tried to slow the Americans during the first three days of March. The division was supported by elements of Sturmpanzer-Abteilung 217 and Sturmgeschütz-Brigade 902. Unfortunately, the American S-2 reports are vague, only reporting German self-propelled guns at various locations, so it remains unclear if these armored vehicles belonged to Sturmpanzer-Abteilung 217 or to 2./ and 3./ Sturmgeschütz-Brigade 902.[6]

The 9th Armd Div entered Müddersheim, Disternich and Sievernich on the morning of **1 March**, but withdrew from Sievernich temporarily due to heavy small arms and machine gun fire from the southwest. Müddersheim was defended by 353.Inf.Div., while the area to the southwest, as far as Berg, was defended by 3.Fs. Jg.Div. Elements of the division received direct anti-tank fire in the Müddersheim - Sievernich area, and several heavy artillery concentrations fell in the vicinity of Sievernich. Müddersheim, Disternich and Sievernich were finally cleared of enemy forces and the outskirts of Weiler were reached during this period. In the center, the 9th Inf Div encountered stiff resistance in the Froitzheim - Ginnick area, where enemy infantry was supported by heavy fire from self-propelled guns and tanks as well as mortar fire. House to house fighting developed in Froitzheim but both towns were cleared before noon. After the enemy was pushed out of Froitzheim, mortar and the fire from the self-propelled guns and tanks continued to be heavy. Two self-propelled guns were destroyed in Ginnick. Other elements of the 9th Armd Div met determined opposition from enemy pillboxes and prepared field fortifications east of Berg. Self-propelled gun fire supported these positions from the vicinity of Wöllersheim. To the south, the progress of the 78th Inf Div was hindered by difficult terrain and stubborn enemy resistance at Hausen, where heavy automatic weapon, mortar and artillery fire was received. The fighting developed into a house to house battle against elements of the 272.V.G.Div., but was cleared by the end of the day. The wooded area to the northeast of Hausen was another enemy strong point, which offered considerable trouble.[7]

The Americans reported to have captured Weiler in the early hours of **2 March** after the 9th Armd Div had reached the village the day before. To the east, Borr, Friesheim and Rövenich were also cleared by the 9th Armd Div after heavy fighting against elements of the 353.Inf.Div. Feld-Ersatz-Bataillon 162 of the 62.V.G.Div. was encountered in the vicinity of Rövenich by the 9th Armd Div, indicating that at least elements of this division had been moved in between 353.Inf.Div. and 3.Fs. Jg.Div. The villages of Embken, Juntersdorf and Füssenich were not defended by the Germans and therefore quickly cleared in the morning. The 9th Inf Div pushed on to capture Geich and Bessenich where resistance was moderate with infantry offering some resistance from dug-in positions. Grenadier-Regiment 183 of the 62.V.G.Div. was identified in the fighting at Geich.[8] The only German offensive action came at 14:30, when an estimated 40 enemy counterattacked from Rövenich; the attack was repulsed and the Germans withdrew. Shortly after, a column of eight German tanks, seven halftracks and 200 infantry withdrew from Rövenich to Oberelvenich. During this period, heavy anti-tank fire was received from the vicinity of Zülpich, which was reported as being hastily prepared as a strong point by Fs.Jg.Rgt.8. In the 9th Armd Div zone, Wöllersheim was continuously

and stubbornly defended by elements of Fs.Jg.Rgt.5 and 6 from well-entrenched positions. The paratroopers were supported by self-propelled guns but forced from the town late in the afternoon. In the 78th Inf Div zone, Vlatten, Heimbach and Eppenich were cleared against moderate to heavy resistance by elements of the 272.V.G.Div., with house to house fighting developing in Heimbach. Shelling continued to be concentrated on forward elements and was primarily from self-propelled guns.[9]

The 9th Inf Div cleared Niederberg and Mühlheim on the morning of **3 March** against relatively light opposition and captured the bridge over the River Roth intact. At Lommersum, a strong counterattack by Grenadier-Regiment 183 with an estimated 250 Grenadiers supported by six to eight tanks and four or five self-propelled guns[10] was launched from the vicinity of Derkum and Hausweiler at 09:00. Bitter fighting developed between the Germans and elements of the 9th Inf Div and 9th Armd Div. Fire from self-propelled and anti-tank guns was particularly heavy along the Erft Canal, and the Germans used smoke to prevent American observation. The firefight in the town continued during the afternoon even after the German counterattack had been rebuffed at 13:30. Meanwhile, CCB of 9th Armd Div took Wichterich against light German opposition, before the combat command moved north in the direction of Weilerswist. Other elements of the 9th Inf Div cleared Oberelvenich and Oberwichterich, reporting stiff resistance from 200 enemy infantry in Oberwichterich. The 9th Inf Div had already captured Zülpich in the morning against light enemy resistance. A combat command of the 9th Armd Div captured Langendorf and Merzenich early in the morning, which had been defended by Fs.Jg.Rgt.5, and then moved on and cleared out Floren and Sinzenich, encountering moderate resistance. The 78th Inf Div cleared Bürvenich after house to house fighting against fairly stiff opposition by II./Fs.Jg.Rgt.5, 9./Fs. Jg.Rgt.6 and 3./ Sturmgeschütz-Brigade 902. Other elements of the division later captured Lövenich and Linzenich in conjunction with the 9th Armd Div.[11]

On **4 March**, the 9th Armd Div and 9th Inf Div advanced via Lommersum and Bodenheim in the direction of Euskirchen. The Germans tried to prevent the exploitation of the American bridgehead over the Erft River. Self-propelled guns fired into Derkum. Small arms fire from Hausweiler made any crossing of the Erft difficult. German mortar and artillery fire was considerable. At Wüschheim I./Fs.Jg.Rgt.6 was encountered. This battalion could not stop the American drive on Euskirchen. The city was captured by the end of that day, and almost 400 German soldiers were taken prisoner. Other elements of the division captured the villages of Elsig and Frauenberg to the northwest of Euskirchen. Another combat command of 9th Armd Div cleared Irresheim - Frauenberg in the early afternoon and captured 100 Germans; among them was a soldier from Sturmpanzer-Abteilung 217. This prisoner stated that the battalion had only six combat-ready tanks left, which were split into two combat groups of three Sturmpanzers each.

These groups were operating together with elements of 3.Fs.Jg.Div. in the vicinity of Enzen. Another soldier of 1./ Sturmpanzer-Abteilung 217 died the same day in combat at Frauenberg, clearly proving that the battalion had been engaged in this area.[12] Alongside Sturmpanzer-Abteilung 217 elements of 5./Artillerie-Regiment 185 and 1./Pionier-Bataillon 600 were engaged in the Frauenberg area. The area between Frauenberg and Durscheven was defended by various units of 3.Fs. Jg.Div. The prisoners taken belonged to 1./Fs.Jg.Rgt.8, St./ and 1./Fs.Füs.Btl.3, Fs. Jg.Ers.Btl.3, 1./Fs.Gr.W.Btl.3 plus elements of several alarm companies.

In the meantime, the 78th Inf Div had advanced from the Bürvenich area and captured Ülpenich and Enzen against light German resistance; Enzen being defended by III./Fs.Jg.Rgt.5. Another soldier from Sturmpanzer-Abteilung 217 was captured in Enzen. He was a mechanic and stated that the battalion had used Sturmpanzers in France the year before and received the same type of tank in Kall in December. He went on to say that the only thing wrong with the Sturmpanzer was the superstructure which was too heavy, and the engine was too powerful for the final drive. This was the cause of most repairs. They were told not to leave their engine idling and save gas as much as possible; but in their mission of infantry support, they could always deal with the gas situation, and never had trouble obtaining gas for their tanks. The unit is actually divided into Combat Commands Hinsken and Lehmann, named after their respective company commanders. Each group has three 150mm Sturmpanzers. The battalion's repair shop was located in Enzen.

German opposition grew by the end of the day, when the 78th Inf Div continued its attack towards Dürscheven. The village was eventually cleared and a bridge over the River Blei captured intact. Although the division reported the road between Zülpich and Ülpenich as mined, it had not encountered enemy armor.[13]

The 9th Armd Div started to clear enemy pockets of resistance north of Euskirchen on **5 March**, before continuing its advance in the direction of Ludendorf via Roitzheim - Kuchenheim - Weidesheim - Essig. Scattered forces from Fs.Jg.Rgt.8 and several alarm units of the 272.V.G.Div. tried to stop the American attack at Roitzheim but were quickly overrun. To the left, the 9th Inf Div also advanced east in the direction of Heimerzheim against 62.V.G.Div. At around 10:00, the forward elements captured Schwarzmaar. Facing southeast in the direction of Müggenhausen, the Americans discovered a German force of at least eight tanks and self-propelled guns and 200 infantry moving in their direction. Minutes later, it became clear that this German force had started a counterattack to recapture Schwarzmaar. The tanks reached the edge of the village before they were stopped by the Americans, while the infantry, probably elements of I./ Grenadier-Regiment 183, were stopped 500 meters from the village. American artillery hit the attackers very hard and by 11:15 the tanks, except one, started to fall back. The 9th Inf Div

reported that some of the attacking tanks might have been Sturmpanzer IVs from Sturmpanzer-Abteilung 217, which they had encountered before. The G-2 of the 1st Inf Div finally confirmed that the 9th Inf Div had been attacked by elements of Sturmpanzer-Abteilung 217 when he sent the following message to the 16th Inf Rgt (on the left flank): *"German infantry only got half way. We fired a lot of artillery at them. Armored vehicles, reported as tanks. 217 assault gun battalion – 12x 150mm guns. Captured 2, knocked out 2."*[14] At 15:00, the Germans attacked again from the Müggenhausen area with two companies of infantry and five tanks. The second attack was less severe, and repulsed easily. No tanks were seen to be damaged, but one prisoner later claimed to have seen one tank burning as it withdrew. To the south, the 78th Inf Div started a two pronged attack to bypass the Billiger Wald southwest of Euskirchen. The northern task force advanced via Obergartzem - Wisskirchen - Euenheim in the direction of Billig. As at Roitzheim, several scattered parts of 3.Fs.Jg.Div. and 272.V.G.Div. had built a hasty defense for Billig. The Americans pushed the defenders aside and the task force finished the day capturing Stotzheim and Rehder. A soldier of 2./ Sturmpanzer-Abteilung 217[15] and a Sturmpanzer IV[16] were captured south of Stotzheim.

The southern task force attacked via Firmenich to Satzvey. The village was defended by Grenadier-Regiment 980 and 981, which used roadblocks and self-propelled guns to slow down the Americans. House to house fighting developed and it took some time before the village was finally cleared. Antweiler was captured by the end of the day.[17]

On **6 March**, the 78th Inf Div advanced via Flamersheim to Schweinheim and captured a member of 3./ Sturmpanzer-Abteilung 217 captured near Flamersheim. At Schweinheim, the 78th Inf Div was slowed down by fire from self-propelled artillery and assault guns. By the end of the day, the division had cleared the Rheinbacher Wald south of Rheinbach. Meanwhile at Lessenich, two soldiers of the Headquarters Company of Sturmpanzer-Abteilung 217 were captured by men of the 26th Inf Rgt, 1st Inf Div, together with a damaged Sturmpanzer IV. They confirmed that the six remaining combat-ready Sturmpanzers had been divided into two combat groups, called Hinsken and Lehmann. Oberleutnant Theodor Bernhard Hinsken was the company commander of 1./ Sturmpanzer-Abteilung 217 and Leutnant Reinhold Clemens Lehmann was the platoon leader of the battalion's repair and maintenance platoon. One of the soldiers stated that only two combat-ready Sturmpanzers were actually left, while their unit had moved from Lessenich to the Queckenburg area (referred to as Loch in other reports), on 5 March with seven damaged Sturmpanzers. They stayed behind at the point of capture to take care of the damaged Sturmpanzers.[18]

On **8 March**, the 26th Inf Rgt reported to have captured two members of the Headquarters Company of Sturmpanzer-Abteilung 217, but the report did not say

Another view of the Ollheim Sturmpanzer after being attacked by an Allied fighter-bomber. Ollheim is on a secondary road between Euskirchen and Heimerzheim. Although the IX US Tactical Airforce claimed to have destroyed this tank on 3 March 1945, it is more likely that the tank was knocked out two or three days later during an engagement at Müggenhausen, two kilometers north of Ollheim. *Lee Archer*

RODNA

Wartime photos showing the roof of a Sturmpanzer are very rare indeed. The new commander's cupola is visible in this image as well as the extractor fan above the machine gun and sliding armored cover for the gunsight. A second fan above the gun is covered by a tarpaulin. Note the white cross on the left front track cover and name painted in white on the gun barrel jacket. *Lee Archer*

where. It is likely that both men were stragglers as the 26th Inf Rgt was in reserve that day.[19]

In the following days, the battalion disengaged from the enemy and crossed the Rhine at Andernach[20] and Remagen. The situation map of the OB West showed the battalion with only three combat-ready Sturmpanzers left as part of LXXIV Armee-Korps on 10 March. Gefreiter Oskar Klein picks up the story again:

"We were ordered to blow up our Sturmpanzer near Kronenburg as there was no fuel available. We then withdrew together with the I-Staffel. In early March, we belonged to one of the last units that crossed the Rhine via the intact bridge at Remagen."[21]

According to a report from the General der Panzertruppen dated 8 March, the Battalion had the following order of battle, and twenty-four Sturmpanzers plus two Flakpanzers in its inventory:

- Stab und Stabs-Kompanie
  - 2 Flakpanzer IV
- 1. Sturmpanzer-Kompanie
  - 8 Sturmpanzer IV
- 2. Sturmpanzer-Kompanie
  - 9 Sturmpanzer IV
- 3. Sturmpanzer-Kompanie
  - 7 Sturmpanzer IV
- Instandsetzungs-Zug
- Versorgungs-Kompanie[22]

The report is missing the date, but it is likely that the strength figures provided were from late February or early March, before the battalion had crossed the Rhine. Another report from the General der Panzertruppen, dated 14 March, showed twenty-eight Sturmpanzers on hand on 8 March, i.e. an increase of four Sturmpanzers from the report of 8 March. The reason for this increase could have been the arrival of the four previously mentioned Sturmpanzers allocated in January and sent to the Battalion mid-February. Considering the strength of thirty-one Sturmpanzers on 12 February and the arrival of the four Sturmpanzers, it becomes clear that the battalion had lost seven tanks between 12 February and 8 March. The report also shows the personnel strength on 8 March: 19 Officers, 3 Civil Servants, 145 NCOs, and 503 Privates. The high number of privates is probably a typographical error and could have been equal to the total strength of the battalion.[23]

7.2.2 Rest and Refitting at Bergisch-Gladbach

The assignment to LXXIV Armee-Korps ended on **14 March**, when the battalion was withdrawn from the front. It was attached to OB West and moved to the Bergisch-Gladbach area for rest and refitting.[24] The next day, the tank situation report 'West' contained the following information:

"Stu.Pz.Abt.217 in action with Army Group B, actual strength: 12 Sturmpanzers, combat-ready: 0, in short-term maintenance: 0, in long-term maintenance: 12."[25]

In less than a week, the battalion had obviously lost sixteen Sturmpanzers and was no longer a fighting unit as there were no combat ready tanks left. There is no information available as to whether the battalion was engaged during that week, but it is more likely that these losses were related to the Rhine crossing. Once more Gefreiter Oskar Klein picks up the story:

"When we crossed the Rhine the tank-less remnants of the 3. Kompanie were withdrawing together with the I-Staffel. The I-Staffel still had one tank engine on hand, but there was no tank left to install it in. Immediately after, the 3. Kompanie and the I-Staffel were disbanded in a quarry."[26]

It has proved problematic to find out the exact number of tanks allocated to the battalion during the short period of rest and refitting. The last recorded tank strength report dated 5 April, showed an actual strength of fifteen Sturmpanzers, clearly indicating that the battalion received replacement tanks in March. The previously mentioned report from the General der Panzertruppen dated 8 March, showed a handwritten note mentioning thirteen Sturmpanzers in Bensberg.[27] The tank allocation list of the General der Panzertruppen shows fourteen Sturmpanzers that had been allocated to the battalion the same day. This document is surprising as it states that these tanks were dispatched four days earlier, on 4 March.[28] Another interesting aspect is the production output of the Deutsche Eisenwerke in Duisburg. In January 1945 only one Sturmpanzer IV was manufactured with a further thirteen in February. These fourteen Sturmpanzers were accepted in February. The reported thirteen Sturmpanzers in Bensberg were equivalent to the February production lot of the Deutsche Eisenwerke, while the fourteen Sturmpanzers mentioned in the allocation list were equivalent to both the January and February production total. However, two other reports from the General der Panzertruppen clearly show that only half of these fourteen tanks were actually allocated to Sturmpanzer-Abteilung 217.

The first report, dated 26 March, claimed that seven Sturmpanzers from the February production were allocated to OB West on 1 March and were dispatched

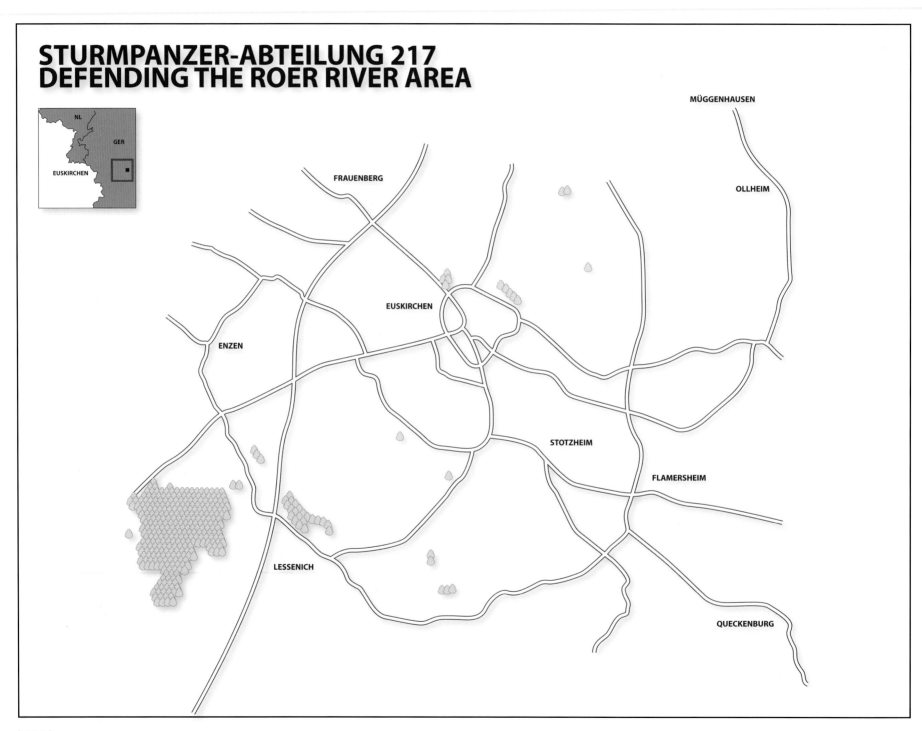

STURMPANZER-ABTEILUNG 217
DEFENDING THE ROER RIVER AREA

NL

GER

EUSKIRCHEN

MÜGGENHAUSEN

FRAUENBERG

OLLHEIM

EUSKIRCHEN

ENZEN

STOTZHEIM

FLAMERSHEIM

LESSENICH

QUECKENBURG

on 4 March.[29] The second report dated 1 April, stated that only three Sturmpanzers were manufactured in March.[30] The report continued that fourteen Sturmpanzers were dispatched during March,[31] of which seven were sent to the West and seven to the East.[32] An annex to the tank situation of the OB West in March mentioned that the seven Sturmpanzers allocated to OB West had finally arrived on 25 March.[33] Based on these sources it is highly likely that the battalion did not receive any replacements during the period of rest and refitting, and that everything was done to raise the number of combat-ready tanks by means of preferential maintenance. It remains unclear if the seven allocated Sturmpanzers really did not arrive until the end of March, and what happened to the last three Sturmpanzers manufactured by the Deutsche Eisenwerke in March.

According to the OB West situation maps, the battalion was attached to LXXXI Armee-Korps as Corps reserve between 18 and 24 March[34] but division order No. 24 of 353.Inf.Div., dated 23 March, stated that the battalion was the Corps reserve of LVIII Panzer-Korps billeted in the Happerschoss - Heisterschoss area, east of Siegburg. The division ordered Panzer-Jäger-Kompanie 1353 to assemble south of Happerschoss and establish contact with the battalion that day.[35]

7.2.3 Engagements south of the River Sieg

By the end of March, the situation required an immediate engagement of the battalion against the Americans, who had broken out of the Remagen bridgehead and were advancing in the direction of Siegen. The battalion's advance party, made up of one passenger car with two officers, one driver and one runner, arrived at the LIII A.K. command post in Obenroth on **24 March**. There, the two officers received the order to engage the Americans immediately using every available tank between Hennef and Uckerath. The advance party tried to reconnoiter the area of operations and drove in the direction of Uckerath. Unaware of the position of the front line, the advance party soon drove into the enemy lines. Taken under fire, the driver was killed and the runner wounded, while the two officers managed to escape. The runner was later reported missing in action.

On **25 March**, the first combat elements of the battalion had arrived and started to attack the Americans who were attacking north and northeast. A Sturmpanzer, named 'Eva' was destroyed by enemy artillery fire in Niederscheid west of Eitorf. In order to guide the indirect fire of the Sturmpanzers an officer was acting as a forward observer. For this task, he used one of the Flakpanzers to reach the main line of resistance. An ammunition dump for the battalion was set up in a wood southwest of Eitorf. On **26 March**, 1st Bn, 18th Inf Rgt found a 150 mm self-propelled during the evening in the battalion's area southeast of Eitorf. The Germans could not hold their positions for long and therefore they had to fall back behind the Sieg River. By 27 March, all elements of the battalion had been withdrawn to the northern bank of the Sieg.[36]

7.3 The final engagements in the Siegen - Freudenberg Area

The withdrawal towards Siegen[37] continued over the next few days. A reconnaissance party from the 2. Kompanie was ordered to move from the trains in Bergisch-Gladbach to the area of Siegen on **30 March**, to find out if the village of Eisern was still in German hands. One soldier from the party was captured and interrogated. This soldier was Heinz Radziszewski, who stated, that the battalion had three companies equipped with Jagdpanthers and Sturmpanzers. He had rejoined the 2. Kompanie from hospital on 29 March and was therefore not aware how many Jagdpanthers and Sturmpanzers were available. He knew that his battalion had just received a number of new tanks after having lost most of its armored vehicles west of the Rhine. He continued to report that all Flying Personnel had been withdrawn from his battalion during the last week to rejoin the German Air Force. He was told by comrades that these men were needed in connection with an intended large-scale use of pilot-less planes.[38]

The bulk of the battalion was gathered in the Siegen area on **31 March**, when orders came in for 2 and 3. Kompanies to counterattack, most likely east of Siegen. The 1. Kompanie was ordered to hold the ground outside the city. As the company strength was only 30 men by this time, it was allowed to retreat to the Fischbacher Barracks if it could not hold its ground. The 2 and 3. Kompanies left the area on the night 31 March.[39]

An intercepted Enigma message reported Sturmpanzer-Abteilung 217 with six combat-ready tanks north of Gosenbach, southwest of Siegen on **4 April**. Also in the area was Sturmgeschütz-Brigade 244 south of Freudenberg with three serviceable assault guns and awaiting a further eight.[40]

The previously mentioned final strength report was dated 5 April and showed fifteen Sturmpanzers of which ten were combat-ready and five in short-term maintenance. Surprisingly, the report also showed one combat-ready Jagdpanzer 38(t) - *Hetzer* in the battalion's inventory.[41] (Note, POW Heinz Radziszewski, 2./ Sturmpanzer-Abteilung 217, stated after his capture on 31 March - that his battalion had an unknown number of Jagdpanthers in its inventory. Therefore, it is likely that these tanks were in fact *Hetzers*.)

On **8 April**, the advance of the 310th Inf Rgt, 78th Inf Div, was held up by anti-tank and anti-personnel mines in the Niederfischbach and Oberfischbach area. Along the roads north of Niederfischbach towards Freudenberg, elements of Grenadier-Regiment 1035, 59.Inf.Div., and Volks-Artillerie-Korps 407 committed as infantry, supported by heavy self-propelled fire, delayed the American advance from successive positions. In the same area the 1. and 2. Kompanies of Sturmpanzer-Abteilung 217 were engaged. Prisoners of war later claimed that the 1. Kompanie had six to eight Sturmpanzers available and the 2. Kompanie was acting as infantry because it had no tanks left. The 3. Kompanie was not in the area.[42]

Grenadier-Regiment 48 effectively employed two self-propelled guns on the road north of Oberfischbach, which withdrew only after an engagement with the enemy. The 310th Inf Rgt claimed to have destroyed two self-propelled guns on Mark IV chassis that day.

Grenadier-Regiment 48 had suffered heavy losses in March. It was withdrawn for rest and refitting in the Bröhl and Waldbröhl area on 2 and 3 April, followed by another rest period near Schönau - Osthalden. On 7 April, the regiment was sent to south of Freudenberg to stop the advancing Americans. The 1st Battalion moved to Seelbach, while the 2nd Battalion went into position at Oberfischbach. Two assault guns, most likely two Sturmpanzers, were attached to the regiment for heavy weapons support. Elements of Grenadier-Regiment 1034, 59.Inf.Div., offered only light resistance as Freudenberg was cleared by the Americans.[43]

On **9 April** 1945, the 78th Inf Div again reported that it was in contact with Sturmpanzer-Abteilung 217, this time north of Freudenberg, in an area where II./ Grenadier-Regiment 48, 12.V.G.Div., I./ Grenadier-Regiment 330 and Füsilier-Bataillon 183, both 183.V.G.Div., were also engaged. It is likely that the identified elements of Sturmpanzer-Abteilung 217 were attached to II./ Grenadier-Regiment 48.[44]

The next day, **10 April**, a member of Sturmpanzer-Abteilung 217 was captured near Auchel, about 15 kilometers northwest of Freudenberg. The 62.V.G.Div. and several Kampfgruppen of 363.V.G.Div. were defending the area between Steimel and Erdingen against the 78th Inf Div, which was advancing in the direction of Wiehl. A soldier, most likely a straggler trying to reach his battalion in the Siegen area, told the Americans that his unit was made of three companies with three Sturmpanzers and 60 men each. According to him, only two companies were in the area, while the third company never made it across the Rhine. He continued to say that both companies were on the way to Siegen when his tank broke down with engine trouble in Osberghausen, five kilometers east of Engelskirchen. He obviously continued on foot, as he stated that his tank was still there. It is highly likely that these tanks came from the Bergisch-Gladbach area, where rest and refitting took place in March at what looked like the battalion's base. Osberghausen and Auchel are located on the road from Bergisch-Gladbach via Engelskirchen - Wiehl - Freudenberg to Siegen.[45]

Other soldiers of the battalion went into American captivity during the same period in the area of Siegen - Achenbach.[46] One of them was Leutnant Heinrich Otto Schilinsky, captured in Bechner north of Olpe on 10 April. Schilinsky was an original battalion member from when it was raised in 1944. After the withdrawal from Normandy, he was temporarily in command of the 2. Kompanie until he fell ill and was sent to Kamenz in early November. In early February 1945, he returned from the replacement unit and became a platoon leader in the 2. Kompanie. After his capture, he claimed that he had recently been a member of the battalion staff. The American interrogation officers called him a 'Booty German'; a 'tougher Nazi' than the average German officer. Schilinsky told the Americans that his former battalion had about twelve Sturmpanzer IVs on 10 April, out of which seven or eight were still combat-ready. He continued that the lack of spare parts was extremely serious, but there still was sufficient ammunition and gas available. The battalion still had a personnel strength of 500-600 men, but due to the lack of tanks, most of these men were employed as infantry. Hauptmann von Trotha was still the Commanding Officer of the battalion, which was attached to LXXXI Armee-Korps.[47] It is not clear if Schilinsky belonged to a group of 19 of the battalion's soldiers who were captured by the 28th Inf Rgt, 8th Inf Div, in the same area on 10/11 April. These prisoners stated that the battalion was down to three to five Sturmpanzer IVs, while it previously had three companies with twelve Sturmpanzer IVs each.[48] Among these captured soldiers were Oberleutnant Alfred Leonhardt, the commander of the Supply Company and Hermann Lothar Prager, the technical inspector of the Repair Platoon.[49]

On **11 April**, a total of 50 men of Sturmpanzer-Abteilung 217 were captured in the area of Eckenhagen, southeast of Bergneustadt. They reported that the battalion originally had a staff company, three tank companies, an engineer platoon and a repair company. Each of the three tank companies was supposed to have had twelve Sturmpanzer IVs, but only twelve Sturmpanzers were left. Three of these twelve tanks were under repair, while six tanks were sent to Buchen, south of Eckenhagen, the night before. Former tank crews that had lost their tanks, together with personnel from the repair company and any others available were used as infantry to support the remaining Sturmpanzers. The prisoners had noticed a general withdrawal of German forces in the direction of Eckenhagen the day before, during the afternoon. In particular horse-drawn artillery, as well as tanks and assault guns were observed.

One of the prisoners had a very interesting story to tell. Due to his technical background and knowledge, he was sent to a higher echelon for interrogation. Because of lack of gas, the unit had tested 'potato gas' for their tanks, but this synthetic gas had proven unsatisfactory for armored vehicles. As a result, the battalion was supposed to be changed to use 'Benzol' instead of 'potato gas'.[50]

The 78th Inf Div reported another nine soldiers from Sturmpanzer-Abteilung 217

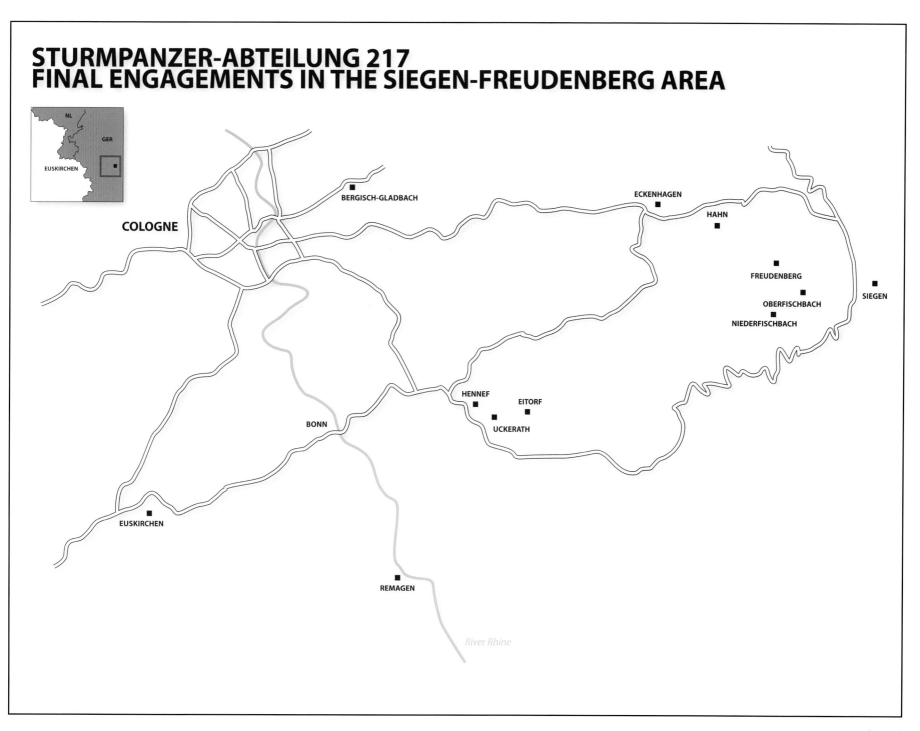

STURMPANZER-ABTEILUNG 217
FINAL ENGAGEMENTS IN THE SIEGEN-FREUDENBERG AREA

NL

GER

EUSKIRCHEN

COLOGNE

BERGISCH-GLADBACH

ECKENHAGEN

HAHN

FREUDENBERG

SIEGEN

OBERFISCHBACH

NIEDERFISCHBACH

HENNEF

EITORF

UCKERATH

BONN

EUSKIRCHEN

REMAGEN

River Rhine

captured on **12 April**. No further information was provided in the G-2 Report.[51]

The 99th Inf Div captured twelve soldiers from the workshop company on **13 April** with no location provided.[52] The 1st Army mentioned in their 13 April IPW report that all four companies of Sturmpanzer-Abteilung 217 had been combined into one *Kampfgruppe*, which had been committed in the vicinity of Hahn (north of Wiehl) with six Sturmpanzer IVs. According to POWs, each company originally had fourteen assault tanks. The battalion commander was Hauptmann von Trotha, who was said to be ruthless because he pushed his men into battle, no matter the odds. The report continued that 35 soldiers of the battalion were captured on 12/13 April.[53]

On **14 April**, the G-2 of 78th Inf Div reported that it had captured 27 men of Sturmpanzer-Abteilung 217 in the Wermelskirchen - Lennep area between 13/14 April, while the 1st Army reported capturing 30 of the battalion's soldiers on 13/14 April.[54/55]

Another five soldiers of the battalion were captured by the 78th Inf Div in the area of Burg - Wermelskirchen - Remscheid - Ronsdorf - Lüttringhausen - Lennep on **15 April**. The 99th Inf Div also reported prisoners from Sturmpanzer-Abteilung 217 on 15 April. The division was engaged in the area northeast of Lüdenscheid and reported to have captured eight men from Sturmpanzer-Abteilung 217.[56/57] The 1st Army reported a total of 22 prisoners captured on 14/15 April.

The 9th Army reported 4 prisoners of war on **16 April**.[58] The 1st Army reported capturing 49 men from the battalion on 15/16 April, and another 57 soldiers on 16/17 April.[59]

This brings to an end the history of the battalion that was raised in Grafenwöhr in May 1944 and fought in Normandy, Eastern Belgium, Aachen, Hürtgen Forest, the Ardennes, the Eifel, the Bergisches Land and the Sauerland in less than a year. For the very last time, Gefreiter Oskar Klein picks up the story:

> "We received the order to break through in the direction of Bautzen. En route, we organized civilian clothes and managed to escape from the Americans. We walked to Chemnitz and took the train to Dresden from there. Between Pirna and Königstein, we learned about the German surrender. Due to developments in the East, I turned around and walked back to the West."[60]

Right: The last official report of Sturmpanzer-Abteilung 217 dated 8 March 1945 which shows the structure and strength of the battalion at the beginning of March. *BAMA*

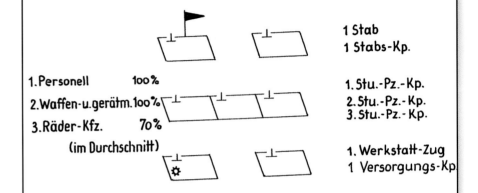

7.4.1 Hauptmann Josef Gauglitz

Hauptmann Josef Gauglitz entered service with 7./ Art.L.Rgt. in Jüterbog in 1935. In 1937 he changed the branch of service and became a non-commissioned officer in Pz.Rgt.5. He first saw action in the Polish campaign in 1939 and was wounded the first time in late autumn on the Western front. Until he was wounded once more in July 1941, he was a Zugführer (platoon leader) in Pz.Jg.Abt.123. He became an officer candidate in September 1940 and promoted to the rank of a Lieutenant on 1 January 1941. He served as a company and battalion commander on the Eastern Front and in the staff of Chef der Ersatzarmee (Chief of the Replacement Army) and OKH. In August 1944, he was assigned to Pz.Ers.u.Ausb.Abt. 18 before being assigned to Sturmpanzer-Abteilung 217 as an Oberleutnant on 20 September.

By this time, he was already a highly decorated veteran, who had earned the *Eiserne Kreuz I.* and *II. Klasse*, the *Verwundeten-Abzeichen in Schwarz*, and *Panzerkampf-Abzeichen in Silber* in 1940. In 1941 he received the *Verwundeten-Abzeichen in Silber*, and in 1942, the *Verwundeten-Abzeichen in Gold*. In February 1944 he received the *Nahkampfspange in Bronze*, before being awarded the *Ritterkreuz* on 16 November. The same month he was promoted to the rank of Hauptmann. On 30 December 1944, he was awarded the *Deutsche Kreuz in Gold*. Gauglitz was wounded again in December 1944, and after his recovery, he was assigned to Pz.Ers.u.Ausb.Abt.18 once again. *(Information taken from the personnel records of Josef Gauglitz).*

Znaimer Tagesblatt 15/12/44

Berlin: On the southern sector of the Aachen front, Knight's Cross bearer Captain Gauglitz, who despite his broken leg and his 17th wound, led all attacks himself. With his Sturmpanzer battalion, he fired over 24,000 shells in 20 days of fighting. He smashed numerous infantry and tank concentrations, stopped attacks by the enemy, and thus brought tangible relief to our hard-fighting grenadiers.

Berlin: Two reinforced American companies attacked an important height in the area of Aachen recently, which was defended by Sergeant Schlicker with his assault tank. In less than 20 minutes, the sergeant smashed the enemy battle group with the shell of his assault tank, destroying seven machine-gun positions and crews.

Znaimer Tagesblatt 19/12/44

You cannot break him! Despite his broken and plastered leg, First Lieutenant G., from Silesia, directs the attacks and counter-attacks of his Sturmpanzers on the Aachen front. This brave officer has been wounded 17 times, but he still insists on leading his tanks over and over again.

7.4.2 Unteroffizier Heinz Siegel

Heinz Siegel was drafted into the Wehrmacht on 1 October 1941 and received his basic training with Pz.Ers.Abt.100 in Schwetzingen. Later he was assigned to Pz.Rgt.201 until he was seriously wounded in 1942. On 25 May 1944 he was sent from Pz.Ers.u.Ausb.Abt.18 to 3./Stu.Pz.Abt.217. On 1 September 1944, he was promoted to the rank of Unteroffizier and also awarded the *Kriegsverdienstkreuz* 2nd class. When the 3. Kompanie was temporarily disbanded in autumn 1944, he was assigned to the supply company of Stu.Pz.Abt.217 until the end of the war.
Document courtesy of James Haley

7.4.3 Unteroffizier Franz Gantenbrink

Franz Gantenbrink joined Pz.Ers.Abt.11 in Paderborn as a volunteer in January 1941. He was assigned to 7./Pz.Rgt.18 on 4 August, and fought on the Eastern Front until 19 May 1942, when he was assigned to 3./Pz.Abt.18. After probably being wounded in autumn 1943, he stayed with Pz.Ers.u.Ausb.Abt.18 for a year until he was assigned to 1./Stu.Pz.Abt.217 on 2 October 1944. He was awarded several awards during his service with Pz.Abt.18 in the East: The *Panzerkampfabzeichen in Silber* on 1 June 1942, the *Ostmedaille* on 2 August 1942, and the Iron Cross 2nd class on 7 September 1942. On 1 December 1944 he was promoted to the rank of an Unteroffizier. As a tank commander in 1./Stu.Pz.Abt.217 he was awarded the *Panzerkampfabzeichen in Silber* for 25 days on 10 January 1945, the day Major Lemor handed over the command to Hauptmann von Trotha. Gantenbrink received two more awards before the end of the war, the *Panzerkampfabzeichen in Silber* for 50 days on 10 March 1945, and the Iron Cross 1st class on 26 March 1945.
Documents courtesy of Jeroen Appel

1. Franz Gantenbrink, Wehrpass pages 2-3. **2.** Panzerkampfabzeichen in Silber for 25 days in combat. **3.** Panzerkampfabzeichen in Silber for 50 days in combat. **4.** Iron Cross 1st Class. **5.** Wehrpass, page 1 and dog-tag. **6.** Wehrpass, pages 12-13.

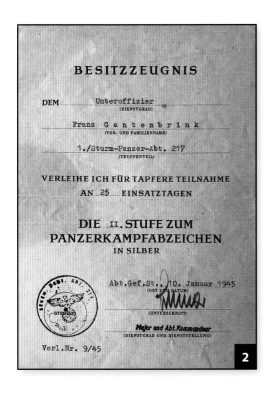

BESITZZEUGNIS

DEM   Unteroffizier
           (DIENSTGRAD)

Franz Gantenbrink
(VOR- UND FAMILIENNAME)

1./Sturm-Panzer-Abt. 217
(TRUPPENTEIL)

VERLEIHE ICH FÜR TAPFERE TEILNAHME

AN 25 EINSATZTAGEN

**DIE II. STUFE ZUM
PANZERKAMPFABZEICHEN**
IN SILBER

Abt.Gef.St., 10. Januar 1945
(ORT UND DATUM)

(UNTERSCHRIFT)

Major und Abt.Kommandeur
(DIENSTGRAD UND DIENSTSTELLUNG)

Verl.Nr. 9/45

2

BESITZZEUGNIS

DEM   Unteroffizier
           (DIENSTGRAD)

Franz Gantenbrink
(VOR- UND FAMILIENNAME)

1./Sturm-Panzer-Abteilung 217
(TRUPPENTEIL)

VERLEIHE ICH FÜR TAPFERE TEILNAHME

AN 50 EINSATZTAGEN

**DIE III. STUFE ZUM
PANZERKAMPFABZEICHEN**
IN SILBER

Abt.Gef.Std., den 10.3.1945
(ORT UND DATUM)

(UNTERSCHRIFT)

Hauptmann u. Abt.-Kommandeur
(DIENSTGRAD UND DIENSTSTELLUNG)

Verl.Nr. 4/45

3

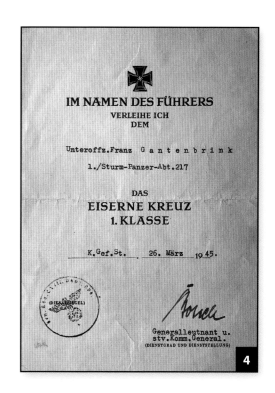

IM NAMEN DES FÜHRERS

VERLEIHE ICH
DEM

Unteroffz.Franz Gantenbrink

1./Sturm-Panzer-Abt.217

DAS

**EISERNE KREUZ
1. KLASSE**

K.Gef.St., 26. März 1945.

(DIE[?]EGEL)

Generalleutnant u.
stv.Komm.General.
(DIENSTGRAD UND DIENSTSTELLUNG)

4

5

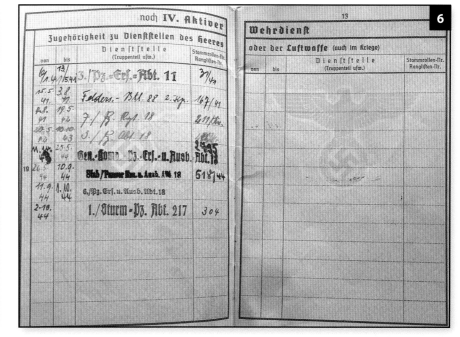

6

The first Sturmpanzers were assembled at the Heeres-Kraftfahrzeug-Werkstatt Wien. *AMC*

CHAPTER 08
THE STURMPANZER IV

8.1 Models

The idea to introduce an assault tank with a heavy infantry gun mounted on a Panzer IV chassis dates back to 2 October 1942, when 'Altmärkische Kettenwerk GmbH' (Alkett) in Berlin presented a conceptual design study. A wooden model of this tank was completed by February 1943 and presented to the Führer. In April 1943 it was agreed to build sixty 15cm Sturmhaubitzen (assault howitzers) in a special production run. The tanks were to be assembled on rebuilt Panzer IV chassis, the superstructure was provided by two Austrian companies, and the main gun, called 'Sturmhaubitze 43', came from a Czech company.

It is said that out of the sixty tank chassis, fifty-two came from Panzer IV production at 'Nibelungenwerke' in St. Valentin, making them Ausf.Gs. Twenty chassis were delivered in April 1943, the other thirty-two chassis in May. The remaining eight chassis were taken from the maintenance pool and comprised Ausf.E and Fs. The superstructures were delivered by 'Eisenwerke Oberdonau' in Linz (42 units) and 'Böhlerwerke' in Kapfenberg (10 units), but it is not known who delivered the remaining eight superstructures. Czech armament manufacturer 'Skoda-Werke' manufactured six Sturmhaubitzen 43 L/12 in March, followed by forty in April and finished the production run with the delivery of fourteen howitzers in May 1943.

Assembly took place at the Heeres-Kraftfahrzeug-Werkstatt Wien (Army vehicle repair depot in Vienna) and was supported by various Austrian arms manufacturers. Weapon inspectors accepted the first twenty assault tanks in April 1943 and the remaining forty tanks were accepted in May. The majority had been handed over to the Army depot in Vienna by June 1943.

On 4 May 1943 the '15-cm Sturmhaubitze' was officially renamed 'Sturmpanzer'. Although Adolf Hitler released fifty Sturmpanzers for immediate commitment, intending to keep ten tanks back for special assignment, all sixty Sturmpanzers were actually assigned to Sturmpanzer-Abteilung 216 between June and August 1943.[1] The first lot of Sturmpanzers was classified as Ausführung (model) I, with the following features:

- Panzer IV chassis, model G or older
- *Fahrersehklappe 80* (driver's visor)
- 3 two-piece hatches
- Short jacket tube
- No *Zimmerit*

The new tank type stood the test of time, but serious technical damage to the chassis continued to reoccur. The assault howitzer was simply too heavy for the chassis. The running gear could not absorb the resulting high stresses when the howitzer was fired, causing the running gear to crack or wearing out the roadwheels. The 'Skoda-Werke' was asked to modify the Sturmhaubitze 43 and at the same time, reduce the weight of the howitzer considerably. To eliminate wear, steel roadwheels would be substituted for the rubber-tyred roadwheels. These modifications were said to have been implemented on the second batch of sixty Sturmpanzers, production of which started in December 1943 but this statement must be challenged. The 'Skoda-Werke' did not receive the order for modification until the end of January 1944 and by that time the weapon inspectors had already accepted thirty Sturmpanzers of the second batch. The longer tube jacket identifies the modified Sturmhaubitze 43 L/12 externally, which was now designated '15cm Sturmhaubitze 43/1'. The real weight reduction was achieved by reducing the thickness of the armored cover of the assault howitzer. No images have yet been found showing steel roadwheels on Ausf.I-III. It appears that this modification was introduced as of May 1944, when production of the model IV started in Duisburg. The Sturmpanzer IV, Ausführung IV, was manufactured with different combinations of steel- tyred roadwheels; either the first pair were steel-tyred, the first two pairs, or all roadwheels.

Sixty Panzer IV Ausf.H chassis formed the basis for the second batch of Sturmpanzers that became the Ausf.II. In general terms, the modified drive sprocket assists in identifying this model, but as a number of former Ausf.Is were also converted into Ausf.IIs, one can also find Ausf.IIs based on Panzer IV chassis, Ausf.E, F and G. The 'Nibelungenwerke' delivered the first ten chassis to Vienna in October 1943, followed by the remaining fifty chassis in January 1944.[2] The most typical features of the Ausf.II were:

- Panzer IV chassis, Ausf.H, respectively older models – upgraded Ausf.I
- *Fahrersehklappe 80* (driver's visor) with armored plate fixed over the lower section
- Long jacket tube, respectively with short jacket tube when upgraded Ausf.I
- *Zimmerit* applied

It is unclear how many Sturmpanzer IV Ausführung II were built, as the number of upgraded Ausf.Is is unknown. As of May 1944, the Ausf.III was introduced,[3] which can be identified by the following features:

- Panzer IV chassis, Ausf.H or J
- Modified driver's visor port
- Long jacket tube
- *Zimmerit* applied

The next change took place in June 1944 with the introduction of the Ausf. IV, which was also called the production vehicle. At the same time, production was moved from Vienna to 'Deutsche Eisenwerke' in Duisburg to assemble the final version of the Sturmpanzer IV. The Panzer IV Ausf.J chassis still came from the 'Nibelungenwerke' in St. Valentin, the superstructure now came from the 'Bismarckhütte' in Königshütte / Upper Silesia, while the Sturmhaubitze 43/1 still came from 'Skoda-Werke'. A production order of 450 assault howitzers was placed.[4] Its characteristic features were:

- Rectangular superstructure instead of the hexagonal form of the Ausf.I-III
- Machine Gun MG 34 in a *Kugelblende* above the driver's seat
- Modified driver's visor port
- Steel-tyred roadwheels (to some extent mixed with rubber-tyred roadwheels)

- Redesigned rear hatch
- New commander's cupola with vision blocks (identical to the Sturmgeschütz III)

Except for the different number of steel-tyred road wheels and the discontinuation of *Zimmerit* as of September 1944, no other modifications for the model IV are known. Tanks that were returned to Germany for maintenance, were of course overhauled and modified. Inevitably some earlier models of the Sturmpanzer IV could still be found in Italy and Normandy.

8.2 Special features of Sturmpanzer-Abteilung 217

The battalion's assault tanks displayed some special features on the Western Front, and varied between campaigns.

The battalion received its first batch of forty-five Sturmpanzers between May and July 1944, which meant that it received a mixture of Ausf.III and IV, and at least one Ausf.II was assigned to the battalion. All known images of Sturmpanzers in Normandy show tanks with *Zimmerit*, but no *Balkenkreuze* were painted on the superstructure sides. It is likely that *Balkenkreuze* were painted onto the right side forward fender but there is only one image that shows it in this position. The battalion's tanks had brackets fixed to the sides of the superstructure to hold spare track links. Ausf.IV vehicles also had brackets attached to the front of the superstructure. The standard bracket could hold seven track links. Shorter brackets were also fitted to the Ausf.IV that could hold three spare tracks. As far as we can see, all tanks were painted in a two-tone camouflage pattern, with sand yellow as the base color. One image from Normandy also shows another feature that is unique to Sturmpanzer-Abteilung 217; a name painted in white onto the jacket of the howitzer. The names are visible on many tanks, but not on all, which leads to the possibility that they were a particular feature of only one of the three companies.[5] Tactical numbers are only visible on one tank each in Normandy, Belgium and the Hürtgen Forest.

All forty-five Sturmpanzers were either lost in Normandy or during the retreat through Northern France and Belgium. By the end of August/early in September, the battalion received a total of twenty-four new Sturmpanzer IV Ausführung IVs. The first twenty Sturmpanzers came from the Army depot in Bielefeld and still had *Zimmerit*. These tanks were painted only in sand yellow. The characteristic brackets for the spare tracks were no longer in place and were not reintroduced after Normandy. No *Balkenkreuze* were visible on any of the Sturmpanzers during this period but it is interesting to note that two, lost on 11 September, had names painted onto the howitzer jacket, only four days after the tanks had

Characteristic Features of the Sturmpanzer IV				
	Ausf.I	Ausf.II	Ausf.III	Ausf.IV
Chassis	Panzer IV Ausf.E, F and G	Panzer IV Ausf.E, F, G and H	Panzer IV Ausf.H and J	Panzer IV Ausf.J
Roadwheels	Rubber-tyred	Rubber-tyred	Rubber-tyred	All steel-tyred, 4 steel-tyred + 4 rubber, 2 steel and 6 rubber-tyred
Spare Wheels	2	4	4	2
Return rollers	4 rubber-tyred	4 rubber-tyred	4 steel-tyred	4 steel-tyred
Headlight	1-2 in front	1-2 in front	1-2 in front	1 in front
Toolbox	Rear right side	Rear left side	Rear left side	Rear left side
Driver's visor	Fahrersehklappe 80	Fahrersehklappe 80 with additional armour	Periscope	Periscope with sun shield
Gun Armoured Jacket	Short	Short and Long	Long	Long
Side skirts	Screwed on*	Hinged	Hinged	Hinged
Superstructure	Hexagonal	Hexagonal	Hexagonal	Rectangular
MP Port	2 (front side)	2-4 (2 on the front side and 2 on the side)	4 (2 on the front side and 2 on the side)	4 (on the side)
Close-combat MG	No	No	No	Ball mount above the driver
Ventilator	Two at the rear of the superstructure	Two at the rear and one on top of the superstructure	One on top of the superstructure	Two on top of the superstructure
Rear Hatch	Two-piece hatch centered to the right	Two-piece hatch centered to the right	Two-piece hatch centered to the right	Two-piece hatch centered to the left
Commander's Cupola	Two-piece circular	Two-piece circular	Two-piece circular	One-piece with optical squares
Gunner's Hatch	Two-piece rectangular	Discontinued		
Loader's Hatch	Two-piece rectangular	Two-piece rectangular	Two-piece rectangular	Discontinued
Antenna Mount	2	1	1	1
Zimmerit	No	Yes	Yes	Yes/No**

* Up to the time of delivery the Sturmpanzers had no *Schürzen* mounts.

** *Zimmerit* was no longer applied to Sturmpanzer IVs assembled after 9 September 1944.

Geheim

Sturmpanzer 15,5

The prototype of the Sturmpanzer IV was completed in February 1943 with a wooden superstructure and 100mm thick armor on the front. *Timm Haasler*

Adolf Hitler and other Third Reich dignitaries including Albert Speer, Karl-Otto Saur and Dr. Ferdinand Porsche at a weapons exhibition in Rastenburg on 14 May 1943. The visit included a demonstration of the 15cm Sturmhaubitze 43 auf Panzer IV. *Thomas Anderson*

One of the first production Sturmpanzer IV Ausf.Is. Note the license plate WH 015151 and opened roof hatch. *Timm Haasler*

been taken over by the battalion. The other four Sturmpanzer came directly from 'Deutsche Eisenwerke' in Duisburg. These vehicles no longer had *Zimmerit* but had *Balkenkreuze* on both sides of the superstructure. It is also likely that a third was painted on the driver's armored cover. These tanks have a three-tone camouflage paint pattern.

When the preferred maintenance and refitting period was over in early November, all tanks had:

- A three-tone camouflage pattern - in some cases special patterns (ambush & disc)
- *Balkenkreuze* on both sides of the superstructure
- A *Balkenkreuz* on the armored cover of the driver's visor,
- Some Sturmpanzers still had *Zimmerit* applied, while others continued to have names on the gun barrel jacket.

8.3 Battle Reports from Stu.Pz.Abt.217

How did the soldiers of Sturmpanzer-Abteilung 217 judge the technical and tactical reliability of the Sturmpanzer IV?

Stabsgefreiter Kurt Kuhs, Richtschütze, 1./ Sturmpanzer-Abteilung 217:

"My unit was equipped with the last model Sturmpanzer, with a commander's cupola to the left rear, and an MG42 on a flak mount, fired by the commander. An MG34 is fitted in the front left, its barrel protruding through the front plate of the superstructure. It is operated by the gunner. The Sturmpanzer has a crew of five including a radio-man operating a FuG 5 (transmitter and receiver). Their high silhouette determines their tactical employment, and are usually committed in company strength and always in combination with tanks or assault guns. In the attack they concentrate on enemy anti-tank guns, MG positions, and infantry concentrations (in this order). For flank protection they rely on tanks or assault guns and on infantry for protection against bazookas. They retreat as soon as they encounter enemy tanks or draw artillery fire because they offer too good a target and the heavy weight of the superstructure impedes their mobility. Sturmpanzers are never committed at night. Rate of ammo issue was 38 shells (HE and hollow charge). Maximum range is 8,000 meters, effective range 4,500 meters, effective range against armor 800 meters. We would attempt to knock out a Sherman tank at a range of 2,000 meters. Most technical breakdowns were due to final drive damage." [6]

The same tank from a low angle showing off the armor interlocks. *Timm Haasler*

A Sturmpanzer IV Ausf.I from Sturmpanzer-Abteilung 216 in the Pawlograd area in 1943. The tank carried the tactical number '28' and has a toolbox on the right side of the engine compartment, a feature of the first model. *Timm Haasler*

A Sturmpanzer IV Ausf.II from Sturmpanzer-Abteilung 216 at St. Pölten, Austria, in April 1944. The tank was probably an upgraded Ausführung I. *Timm Haasler*

A tank of Sturmpanzer-Abteilung 216 in Italy, early 1944. The Sturmpanzer IV is an Ausf.III. *Timm Haasler*

The most noticeable difference between the first three versions and the final version, was the now rectangular construction of the superstructure and *Kugelblende* for the machine gun. This is a Sturmpanzer IV Ausf. IV of Sturmpanzer-Abteilung 217 at Houyoux, Belgium as seen on pages 44-48. ***NARA via Darren Neely***

The Sturmpanzer IV was a technically vulnerable vehicle. Even experienced repair crews seldom managed to keep more than 50% of the existing tanks operational. The crews therefore took every opportunity to technically care for their vehicles. The picture shows again a vehicle of Sturmpanzer-Abteilung 216 on the Eastern Front in the summer of 1943. *Timm Haasler*

An artillery strike probably wrecked this Sturmpanzer IV Ausf.I. A repair team from Sturmpanzer-Abteilung 216 assesses the damage.
Timm Haasler

The same tank. The damage was so severe that it could not be repaired. The tank may have been used for spare parts or transported back to the Reich for rebuilding. Note the sun shade over the driver's visor. *James Haley via Lee Archer*

Schütze Rudolf Strache, 2./ Sturmpanzer-Abteilung 217:

"The assault tank is a 15cm heavy howitzer installed in a Panzer IV chassis with enclosed fighting compartment. Details of performance: 30° traverse, maximum range of 4300 meters, ammunition capacity is 44 rounds (high explosive and hollow charge), 5-man crew, speed 50 km/h on good roads, rate of fire 2-3 rounds per minute."[7]

Gefreiter Oskar Klein, Gunner and Loader, 3./ Sturmpanzer-Abteilung 217:

"The 'Brummbär' had a 15cm howitzer in an armored ball mount, based on a Panzer IV chassis. The sighting mechanism allowed 180° coverage, 9 o'clock to 3 o'clock. The firing mechanism worked electrically. The fuse of the shell allowed switching between 'delay' and 'no delay'. Each of the crew had an MP40 and for close defense, and there was a MG34.[8] The assault tank had a three-tone camouflage pattern, the colors were brown, gray and green. The tank was coated with Zimmerit and had armored side skirts, but no tactical number, even during engagements. His Sturmpanzer was a technically very reliable vehicle that only once broke down when it lost a track. Primary targets were enemy anti-tank guns, barricades and buildings. These targets were generally fired at directly."[9]

Gefreiter Anton Skriba, Sturmpanzer-Abteilung 217:

"Employment of the Sturmpanzer: According to the training, the Sturmpanzer, which has a 150mm howitzer on Mark IV chassis, is to be employed in the attack like a normal assault gun and in defense and delaying actions, like any other artillery piece. In the attack, the Sturmpanzers move forward in a wedge formation, dependent on the terrain, with 50 to 300 meters between each gun. In the defense they are preferably emplaced at the forward edges of the woods."[10]

Ammunition used by the Sturmpanzer: High-explosive and armor-piercing with six charges. Experience has shown that best results are achieved with five charges. Instructions to use five charges are now printed on each shell. The initial issue per gun is forty-eight rounds of which forty-two are high-explosive and six are armor-piercing.

Four enlisted men, captured on 28 January 1945 at Heeresbach, pointed out the following weak spots of the Sturmpanzer: Breakdowns were frequently caused by defects in the suspension and also by the electrical system of the engine. The Panzer IV chassis was not durable enough to carry the heavy 150mm howitzer. The gun is exceedingly top-heavy, thus reducing its maneuverability.[11]

The final statement regarding the operational principles of the Sturmpanzer is from a captured non-commissioned officer who commanded a Sturmpanzer IV in Sturmpanzer-Abteilung 216 in Italy. He considered it essential that assault tanks should, whenever possible, be supported by tanks or assault guns capable of dealing with enemy armor. In general, targets most commonly engaged were machine gun nests, pillboxes, gun positions and infantry or motorized concentrations. Tanks were not supposed to be engaged, but were on occasion with good results. The maximum range allowed was 4,700 yards, but in reality, engagements over 2,750 yards were rare. Hollow-charge ammunition was permitted against armor up to 1,650 yards, although in Italy the prisoner had successfully used high explosive rounds against armor at greater ranges. In general, assault tanks engaged at the closest range at which they could fire without exposing themselves to undue danger. In defense the normal role is immediate counter-attack; the assault tanks will try to remain undetected until the enemy infantry attack has been launched, when they will emerge to disperse enemy infantry before they reach the forward edge of the main defense belt. Rarely are assault tanks dug in as pillboxes; the prisoner considered such a method would throw away the advantage of the guns' mobility, but confessed that he had dug in his own tank when used in a purely anti-tank role.[12]

8.4 Battle Reports from Stu.Pz.Abt.219

Proposal for the reorganization of the intended Stu.Pz.Abt.219 (20 September 1944)

Based on experience on the Eastern Front, a mixed composition is proposed for the battalion:

- *Kompanietrupp: 2 Jagdpanzer IV*
- *I. Zug: 2 Jagdpanzer IV and 2 Sturmpanzer IV*
- *II. and III. Zug: see I. Zug*

A purely Sturmpanzer equipped battalion limits its own use in combat to infantry targets. The indirect fire and speed of fire of the Sturmpanzer is no match for enemy tanks. Therefore the Sturmpanzer can only be used in cooperation with anti-tank weapons. A Sturmpanzer battalion with mixed companies and platoons enables the commander to attack both infantry and tank targets. With the aid of the guns, an indirect fire weapon can be brought closer to the enemy and therefore indirect targets can be attacked. The presence of the Sturmhaubitzen [author: Sturmpanzer IV] can replace the use of artillery pieces.

Battle Report Stu.Pz.Abt.219. 9 - 27 December 1944

1. Tactical commitment

- *During combat, both in defense and attack, the Sturmhaubitzen [author: Sturmpanzer IV] were used on a broad front in the role of a Sturmgeschütz unit, without any additional support from armored vehicles.*
- *The unit was placed close behind the main line of resistance, not only to reinforce the infantry but also to avoid unnecessary technical breakdowns.*
- *During counterattacks, the Sturmpanzers were used as Sturmgeschütze, i.e. they moved in front of the infantry. In most cases, the Sturmpanzers took the objective. The infantry linked up very slowly and only when they were sure that there were no more enemy. They gave up the captured ground during the next Russian counterattack. In a few cases, mot Z-Pak were ordered to protect the Sturmpanzers. However, these are vulnerable and can not move with the Sturmpanzers while offering anti-tank protection.*
- *Combat against infantry, due to their role as Sturmgeschütze, took place at short-range, from at least 30 meters. The effect against infantry is devastating when hit by the first shot and affects morale when using combined fire.*
- *Due to the lower rate of fire and the curved trajectory of its shells, action against anti-tank guns is inferior. Despite these shortcomings, a few satisfactory encounters have been recorded. However, these could have been dealt with by Sturmgeschützen in a quicker and more efficient way.*
- *Action against armor is similar to anti-tank guns. Due to technical breakdowns, combined fire against armor was not possible. Therefore, single Sturmpanzers had to engage.*
- *On one occasion the battalion was used in its designated role. The Sturmpanzers gave combined supporting fire across the front and flanks against anti-tank weapons. They were committed in the third wave (1st wave armor, 2nd wave halftrack units)*

2. Technical aspect of the commitments

- *Technical breakdowns were far more common than anticipated. The smallest dislocation, even on tracks with frozen earth and at low speed caused problems for the Sturmpanzers' drive train. This forced the commander to position his companies directly behind the main line of resistance. Between 9 and 27 December 1944, the battalion made 91 technical repairs on twenty-eight Sturmpanzers. Most of these involved the drive sprockets (16 cases), the planetary gear (4 cases), brake bands ripping off (12 cases), bolts of the brake housing shearing off (3 cases), top bolts of the brake housing plate shearing off (10 cases), tie rods of the braking slides of the steering brake shearing off (4 cases), ripping of the cardan discs (6 cases), engine damage (3 cases), gearbox*

damage (2 cases), the drive levers breaking off (20 cases), damage to the fan's drive shaft and Hardy disc (6 cases), belt pulley ripping off (2 cases), ruptured fuel tank (1 case). These numbers do not include the repairs made by the repair groups (I-Gruppen).

- *The cause of these breakdowns is the heavy superstructure on the Panzer IV's chassis, especially the top-heaviness. In general the drive is too weak and the motor not powerful enough for the heavy weight. The original Panzer IV was designed for a load of 17 to 19 tons; the Sturmpanzer has a weight of 29 tons (with full ammunition load, crew and baggage).*
- *The off road capabilities of the Sturmpanzer are unsatisfactory. During the 'mud-period' west of Budapest, it was impossible to leave the roads. Even during periods of frost, off road movement was very slow.*
- *The tracks of the Sturmpanzer wear out quickly, due to the top-heaviness of the vehicle and the steel-tyred return rollers. A set of tracks lasts 500 kilometers.*

Experience report from Stu.Pz.Abt.219 on proposals and changes for the Sturmpanzer IV. 9 - 27 December 1944

- *General reinforcement of the Sturmpanzer's drive. The drive sprocket teeth and the bolts which fix the drive sprocket to the hub have a tendency to break*
- *Reinforcement of the braking bands*
- *Reinforcement of the tie rods of the braking slides of the steering brake, and the braking slides (Bremsschlitten) themselves*
- *Reinforcement of the retaining bolts of the brake housing*
- *Reinforcement of the cardan discs (Seilgelenkscheibe) or modification of the cardan joints*
- *Re-engineering of the mount for the fan heater belt pulleys*
- *Installation of a more powerful engine to increase mobility and to avoid over-stressing in ordinary terrain*
- *The steel-tyred return rollers have proven to be reliable, however, they stress and increase wear on the tracks*
- *The drive levers are too weak, twenty have broken. Damage mainly occurred on the forward and rear roller carriages, as these are most stressed during maneuvering. Reinforcement seems necessary.*
- *The seat for the driver is too high. Driver hits his head against the hatch. A field modification has been made, resulting in a seat that is 3cm lower.*
- *Optics for the driver have a tendency to steam up due to the difference between interior and exterior temperatures. Solution: better sealing of the mirror.*
- *The ceiling-mounted headrest for the driver is too far away from the optic. In order to see something, the driver has to get very close to the optic. A field modification has been made.*
- *A sheet metal rain cover for the optic (10x30cm with an angle of 45°) has been very successful in bad weather conditions.*

- *The towing eyes are very weak, they get ripped off when pulling with a rope. Solution: attach the rope with S-hooks to the open brake access hatches.*

8.5 Surviving tanks of Sturmpanzer-Abteilung 217

Four Sturmpanzer IV have survived World War II and are on display today. A model I is on exhibition in the Russian tank museum at Kubinka. An Ausf.III had been on display at Aberdeen Proving Ground in the United States for decades. Today this tank is in the US Army Artillery Museum collection at Fort Sill. The French Musée des Blindés in Saumur and the German Panzermuseum in Munster each have a Ausf.IV in their inventory. Both Ausf.IVs were lost by Sturmpanzer-Abteilung 217 in Normandy in August 1944.

Left: A view of the gunsight and breech of the 15cm Sturmhaubitze 43. The gun has the Rohr Nr.26 and the letter code 'BXB', indicating it was manufactured by Skoda. *AMC*

Above: The interior of a new Sturmpanzer IV Ausf.I. The driver's and gunner's positions to the left of the main gun. Note the four gas mask canisters and two machine pistols attached to the front. The square section ducting on the roof was attached to the ventilator on the rear wall to extract fumes from the gun after firing. Like all German armored vehicles of the period, the interior is painted in RAL 1001 'Elfenbein'. *AMC*

Looking at the left side gives a more complete view of the ammunition stowage and the bracket for the SF14Z scissors periscope. The ducting attached to the roof draws fumes to the left side extractor fan. *AMC*

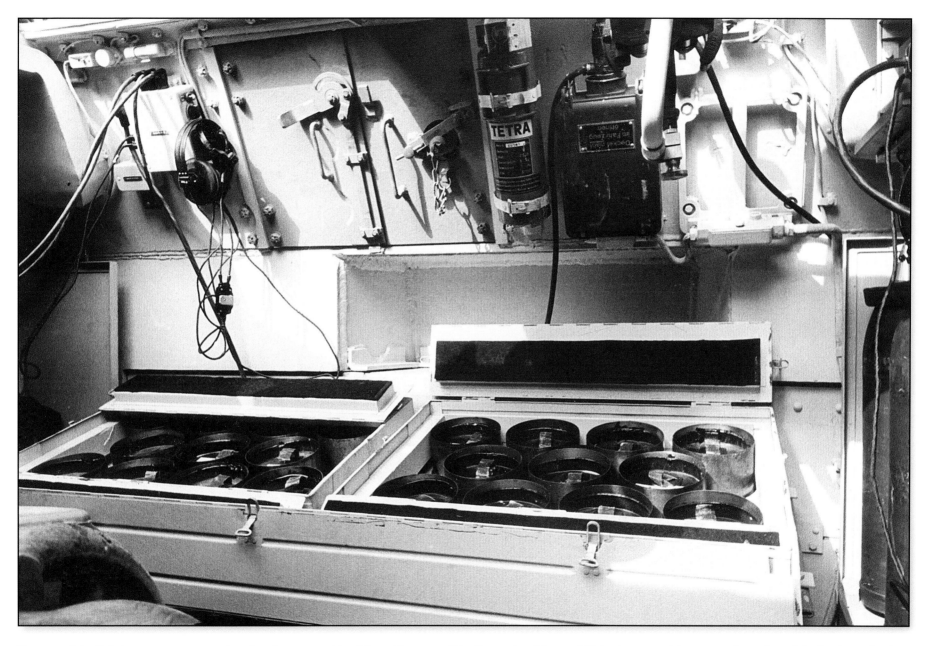

The rear of the fighting compartment, showing the ammunition bins with some of the *Kartuschen* (charges). This photo provides an excellent view of the latch mechanism of the rear hatch and the closed pistol port. *AMC*

Seven *Aufbauten* (superstructures) at the Heeres-Kraftfahrzeug-Werkstatt Wien. From left to right, *Aufbauten* 36, 32 and 42. Note how the pistol ports have not yet been painted in primer and appear shiny. *AMC*

Aufbauten 45 and 47 are being prepared as *Befehlswagen* (command vehicle) with an extra antenna mount on the rear wall of the superstructure. Five 15cm Sturmhaubitze 43 in cradles are waiting to be fitted to vehicles. *AMC*

In May 1944, assembly of the Sturmpanzer IV was transferred from Vienna to Deutsche Eisenwerke in Duisburg. The vehicle to the left is yet to receive its MG *Kugelblende* above the driver's position. **Collection Hilary Louis Doyle**

Sturmpanzer IV with the serial number '13' shows that *Zimmerit* was even applied to the front fenders, while areas covered by spare tracks such as the bow and the transmission access hatch had none. Note the light colour of the *Zimmerit* compared to the dark colour of the primer on the bow and MG *Kugelblende*.
Collection Hilary Louis Doyle

The Sturmpanzer in the foreground has the serial number '15'. *Collection Hilary Louis Doyle*

The Sturmpanzers are moved outside for painting and final preparation. The vehicle in the foreground has been painted, but the one in the background still in its primer colour with light patches of *Zimmerit*. **Collection Hilary Louis Doyle**

The first 12 Sturmpanzer IV Ausf.IV were completed by Deutsche Eisenwerke in May 1944 but not accepted until June. Here Sturmpanzer IV Fgst. Nr. 90069 is ready for acceptance, and now has its *Schürzen* attached. Note the mount for the anti-aircraft machine gun on top of the superstructure to the right of the howitzer. The small tie-downs around the gun mount were for a canvas cover. *Collection Hilary Louis Doyle*

A three-quarter view of the same Sturmpanzer shows its eight steel-tyred wheels, a feature of the first batch of Sturmpanzer IVs assembled in Duisburg. By the end of 1943, steel-tyred wheels were demanded due to stresses on the running gear caused by the howitzer firing. *Collection Hilary Louis Doyle*

Vehicles manufactured later in Duisburg replaced some of the steel-tyred roadwheels with rubber-tyred examples. Note the mount for the anti-aircraft machine gun and unusual position of the *Balkenkreuz* on the *Schürzen*. **Collection Hilary Louis Doyle**

A rear three-quarter view, showing the modified brackets for the spare roadwheels; the number of these was reduced from four to two for the Ausf.IV.
Collection Hilary Louis Doyle

A rear view of the same Sturmpanzer. The two spare roadwheels are fitted an uneven distance away from the edge of the engine deck. *Collection Hilary Louis Doyle*

Saumur's Sturmpanzer IV lost the spare track bracket on the superstructure side but still has one on the front next to the gun. The vehicle has the usual *Zimmerit* seen on Sturmpanzers in Normandy. ***Collection Nuts & Bolts***

The Sturmpanzer at the Panzer Museum in Munster was also captured in Normandy, but was in poor condition and had to be completely rebuilt. During the restoration in Germany, the characteristic features of Sturmpanzer-Abteilung 217 were omitted. *Timm Haasler*

Both the Munster and Saumur vehicles are missing the distinctive toolbox beside the engine deck, and the brackets for spare tracks on the sides of the fighting compartment. The lack of *Zimmerit* makes the two pistol port plugs obvious. ***Timm Haasler***

The rear of the Saumur Sturmpanzer showing the plate above the exhaust muffler and spare wheel brackets. Note the offset rear doors and their locking mechanism. *Collection Nuts & Bolts*

An interesting view from the roof down onto the ball mount for the howitzer, MG *Kugelblende* and driver's position. The larger of the two brackets on the right trackguard held the wooden track block. *Collection Nuts & Bolts*

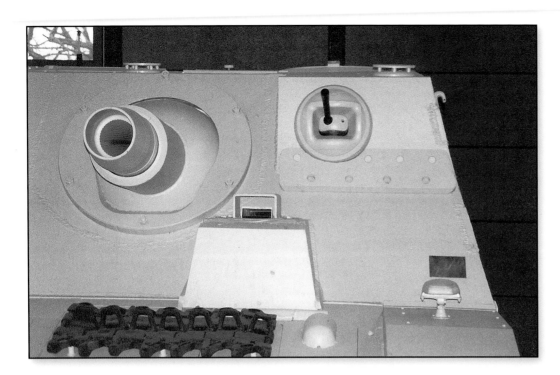

The same on the front of the Munster Sturmpanzer. Note the small additional extractor fan above the MG *Kugelblende*. The photo was taken after the tank was handed over to the Panzermusuem, and the camouflage pattern added several years later. *Timm Haasler*

A good view of the armored 'fillet' below the MG *Kugelblende*. *Timm Haasler*

Period photographs of the top of the Sturmpanzer IV Ausf.IV are rare. The circular commander's hatch, armored cover above the gunsight and fan above the machine gun are clearly visible. *Collection Nuts & Bolts*

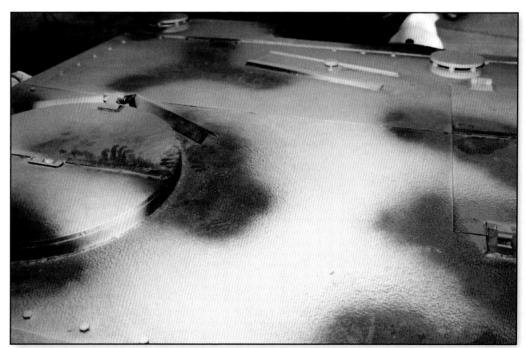

Surprisingly, the reconstruction of the missing roof of the Munster Sturmpanzer IV was not based on the Saumur example. Instead of the Sturmgeschütz cupola, a flat two-piece hatch much like the Ausf.III was created. Also, the armored slide over the gunsight is incorrect. *Collection Nuts & Bolts*

Taken from looking forward to the gunner's and driver's positions. Under the elevation handwheel for the howitzer, the driver's seat and steering levers can be seen. The bolts protruding through the front armor under the MG mounts held the fillet of armor in place over what might have been a weak point. *Collection Nuts & Bolts*

The howitzer in the Saumur vehicle is almost perfectly preserved, complete with an intact recoil guard, that prevented the gun's recoil from injuring the crew. The Munster vehicle, on the right, is missing this. *Collection Nuts & Bolts*

A good view of the left of the fighting compartment. Ammunition stowage was in the left sponson with the shells held upright. The MG mount, complete with headpad and sprung counterbalance is in remarkably good condition although the ventilator directly above it is missing. The gunner's seat is missing, and just its mount remains, attached to the gun mount. *Collection Nuts & Bolts*

In the right sponson was a second ammunition rack. The ventilator for extracting fumes from the gun after firing is still in position on the roof. Note the closed but not locked pistol port and the multitude of fixings on the front wall. *Collection Nuts & Bolts*

A view of the Sturmhaubitze 43/1 and how it was fixed to the chassis. The photo also shows two brackets used to bolt the superstructure to the chassis.
Collection Nuts & Bolts

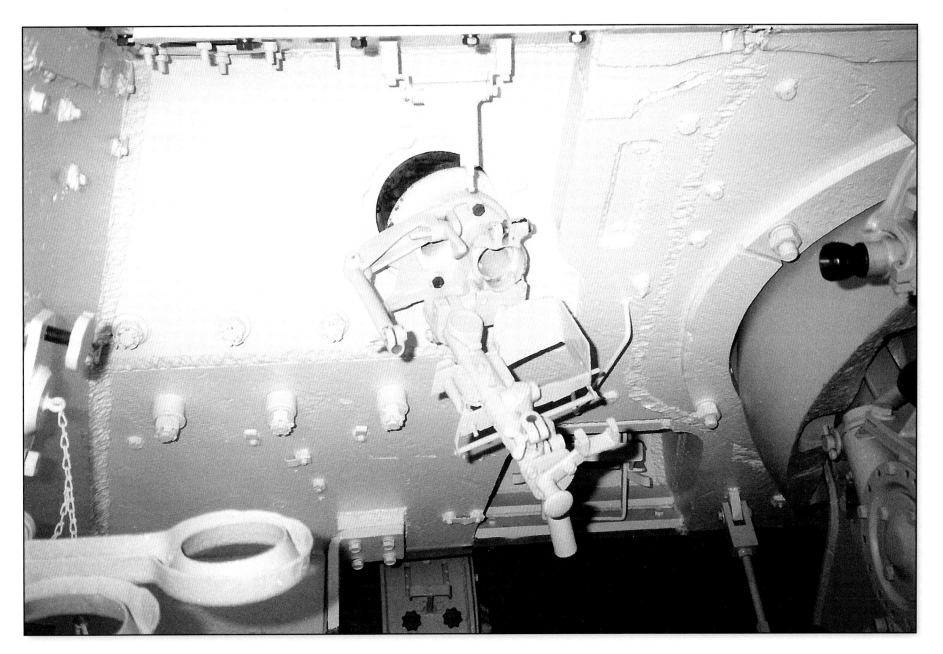

The Munster vehicle's MG mount which is missing the headpad and spring counterbalance, but does show the travel lock hanging from the roof. Between this and the howitzer is the aperture for the driver's periscope. With the periscope in place, he would have rested his forehead on a pad to see out. *Collection Nuts & Bolts*

This is how the Munster Sturmpanzer looked after discovery in a Normandy scrapyard. The tank was restored in Großenhain, Germany. The vehicle was missing not only the roof but also the Sturmhaubitze 43. Note the hole in the rear wall. *Collection Nuts & Bolts*

The Sturmpanzer's chassis consisted of a few parts, which meant a lengthy and complex restoration. The section of front armor missing in the previous photo sits on a pallet under the chassis. *Collection Nuts & Bolts*

The Sturmpanzer received its 15cm Sturmhaubitze 43/1 in Großenhain, shown here at the Wehrtechnische Sammlung in Koblenz. *Timm Haasler*

The chassis, superstructure and howitzer were assembled in Großenhain. This photograph shows the gun being installed. *Collection Nuts & Bolts*

A Sturmpanzer IV Ausf.IV of Sturmpanzer-Abteilung 219 captured by the Russians in Hungary in 1945. The tank had the tactical number '222', while a second vehicle in the background had the tactical number '110'.
Lee Archer

CHAPTER 09

APPENDIX

9.1 Readiness Reports

Date					
24/05/44	Allocation:	19	Inventory:	19	Assigned from Sankt-Pölten arsenal
June 1944	Arrival:	17	Inventory:	36	Assigned from Sankt-Pölten arsenal
21/06/44	Allocation:	2	Inventory:	38	Departure 25/06/44 from Sankt-Pölten arsenal
22/06/44	Allocation:	7	Inventory:	45	Departure 10/07/44 from Sankt-Pölten arsenal
21/07 - 04/09/44	Loss:	45	Inventory:	0	Losses in Normandy and during the retreat
-08/08/44	Loss:	4			Cintheaux area
-08/08/44	Loss:	1			Roucamps, blown up by the crew
-09/08/44	Loss:	1			Cintheaux-Bretteville
-20/08/44	Loss:	1			Saint-Lambert-sur-Dives
-August 1944	Loss:	1			Ondefontaine
-August 1944	Loss:	1			Falaise
-August 1944	Loss:	1			Elbeuf
05/09/44	Arrival:	10	Inventory:	10	Allocation 08/08/44, departure from arsenal 24/08/44
09 - 18/09/44	Loss:	1	Inventory:	9	Lost while assigned to Panzer-Brigade 105
11/09/44	Loss:	4	Inventory:	5	Lost during engagement in the Limbourg area
17/09/44	Arrival:	10	Inventory:	15	Departure 16/09/44 from Bielefeld arsenal
28/09/44	Arrival:	4	Inventory:	19	Assigned from Deutsche Eisenwerke, Duisburg

Date					
04/10/44	Loss:	3	Inventory:	16	Lost in action in the Übach - Palenberg area
14/10/44	Loss:	3	Inventory:	13	Blown up in Aachen due to damaged drive sprockets
18/10/44	Loss	1	Inventory:	12	Lost in Aachen - Hindenburgstraße
20/10/44	Loss:	2	Inventory:	10	Lost in action in Aachen
20/10/44	Arrival:	4	Inventory:	14	Assigned from Deutsche Eisenwerke-Duisburg
21/10/44	Arrival:	5	Inventory:	19	Assigned from Deutsche Eisenwerke-Duisburg
25/10/44	Arrival:	3	Inventory:	22	Assigned from Deutsche Eisenwerke-Duisburg
09/11/44	Arrival:	3	Inventory:	25	Allocation 08/11/44, departure 08/11/44
10 - 25/11/44	Loss:	1	Inventory:	24	Lost in action in the Hürtgen Forest
06/12/44	Arrival:	6	Inventory:	30	Allocation 27 - 29/11/44, picked up in Bergisch-Gladbach
06/12/44	Arrival:	1	Inventory:	31	Presumably from 2./Stu.Pz.Abt.218 z.b.V.
08 - 16/12/44	Loss:	6	Inventory	25	Lost in action in the Hürtgen Forest
12 - 14/12/44	Arrival:	8	Inventory:	33	Allocation 07/12/44, departure 08/12/44
21/12/44	Loss:	1	Inventory:	32	Lost in action in the Domaine Bütgenbach area
26 - 31/12/44	Arrival:	3	Inventory:	35	Allocation 29/11/44, departure 16/12/44
26 - 31/12/44	Arrival:	3	Inventory:	38	Allocation 20/12/44, departure 18/12/44
26/12/44 - 01/01/45	Loss:	2	Inventory:	36	Lost in action in the Büllingen area
26/01/45	Arrival:	6	Inventory:	42	Allocation 28/12/44, departure 20/01/45
02/01 - 09/02/45	Loss:	6	Inventory:	36	Lost in action in the Möderscheid - Schoppen area
02/01 - 09.02.45	Loss:	5	Inventory:	31	Blown up due to fuel shortages
10/02 - 07/03/45	Loss:	7	Inventory:	24	Losses in the Eifel and west of the Rhine
-early March	Loss	1			Blown up at Kronenburg
-05/03/45	Loss	4			2 destroyed and 2 captured at Schwarzmaar
-06/03/45	Loss	1			Lost at Lessenich
08/03/45	Arrival:	4	Inventory:	28	Allocation 14/01/45, departure 13/02/45
09 - 15/03/45	Loss:	16	Inventory:	12	Lost in the Ruhr Pocket
Ca. 30/03/45	Arrival:	7	Inventory:	19	Partly allocated on 08/03/45
16/03 - 05/04/45	Loss:	4	Inventory:	15	1 tank lost on 25/03/45 at Niederscheid and 1 tank lost on 26/03/45 near Eitorf

9.2 Assignments

Date	Assigned Unit	Corps	Army/Army Group
21/07 - 28/07/44[b]	21.Pz.Div.	LXXXVI A.K.	Panzergruppe West
29/07 - 05/08/44[b]	1.SS-Pz.Div.	I. SS-Pz.K.	Panzergruppe West
05/08 - 09/08.44[b]	89.Inf.Div.	I. SS-Pz.K.	Pz.G. West/Pz.AOK 5
09/08 - ??/08.44[b]	12.SS-Pz.Div.	I. SS-Pz.K.	Pz.AOK 5
??/07 - 29/07/44[c]		II. SS-Pz.K.	Panzergruppe West
30/07 - ??/08/44[c]		LXXIV A.K.	Pz.G. West/Pz.AOK 5
06/08/44[a]		II. SS-Pz.K.	Panzergruppe West
07/08 - ??/08/44[a]	271., 276., 277. Inf.Div.	LXXIV A.K.	Pz.AOK 5
05/09 - 06/09/44		II. SS-Pz.K	H.Gr. B
07/09/44			AOK 7
08/09 - 07/11/44		LXXXI A.K.	AOK 7
08/09/44	Kpf.Kdt. Lüttich	LXXXI A.K.	AOK 7
09/09 - 19/09/44[d]	Pz.Brig.105	LXXXI A.K.	AOK 7
17/09 - 18/09/44[d]	116.Pz.Div.	LXXXI A.K.	AOK 7
18/09 - 26/09/44	49.Inf.Div.	LXXXI A.K.	AOK 7
27/09 - 28/09/44	Corps Reserve	LXXXI A.K.	AOK 7
29/09/44	49.Inf.Div.	LXXXI A.K.	AOK 7
30/09/44	183.VG.D.	LXXXI A.K.	AOK 7
01/10 - 02/10/44	Corps Reserve	LXXXI A.K.	AOK 7
02/10 - 07/10/44	183.VG.D.	LXXXI A.K.	AOK 7
08/10/44	49.Inf.Div.	LXXXI A.K.	AOK 7
09/10 - 12/10/44	12.VG.D.	LXXXI A.K.	AOK 7
13/10 - 06/11/44	246.VG.D.	LXXXI A.K.	AOK 7
08/11 - 10/11/44			H.Gr. B-Reserve
11/11 - 15/12/44		LXXIV A.K.	15. Armee
16/12 - 17/12/44		I. SS-Pz.K.	6. Panzerarmee
18/12 - 22/12/44[b]		II. SS-Pz.K.	6. Panzerarmee

Date	Assigned Unit	Corps	Army/Army Group
22/12/44 - 21/01/45		LXVII A.K.	6. Panzerarmee
22/01 - 09/02/45		LXVII A.K.	5. Panzerarmee
10/02 - 13/02/45		LXXIV A.K.	5. Panzerarmee
14/02 - 24/02/45		LXXIV A.K.	5. Panzerarmee
End of Feb - Mar 45			7. Armee
March 45			15. Armee
May 45		LXVII A.K.	?

a: 1./Stu.Pz.Abt.217
b: 2./Stu.Pz.Abt.217
c: 3./Stu.Pz.Abt.217
d: Combat Company Stu.Pz.Abt.217

9.3 Personnel

Commander

10/05/44 - October 44	Major Eberhard Lemor *(Bn Commander)*[1]
October 44	OLt. Johannes Tetzner *(CO)*
November - 14/12/44	OLt. Josef Gauglitz *(CO)*
14/12/44 - 09/01/45	Major Eberhard Lemor *(Bn Commander)*[2]
10/01/45 - 10/04/45**	Hptm. Claus von Trotha *(Bn Commander)*[3]

Adjutant

May 44 - 15/02/45*	Lt. Werner Pöttgen

Orderly

19/01/45 - 15/02/45*	Lt. Günter Schick

Doctor

? - 15/02/45*	Stabsarzt Dr. Werner Zill

Motor Pool Officer

? - 15/02/45*	Lt. Erwin Böse

CO Staff Company

20/09/44 - 15/02/45*	Lt. Gottfried Leuthold

CO 1./Stu.Pz.Abt.217

May 44 - 07/08/44	OLt. Hans Lucas *(MIA 07/08/44)*
07/08/44 - 15/08/44	Lt. Björn-Dieter Olowson *(KIA 15/08/44)*[4]
15/08/44 - 21/09/44	Lt. Wolfgang Kiefer
21/09/44 - End of October 44	OLt. Josef Gauglitz *(evacuated 14/12/44)*[5]
End of October 44 - 14/12/44	OLt. Johannes Tetzner *(WIA 14/12/44)*
19/01/45 - 15/02/45*	OLt. Theodor Hinsken
Field post number	39961 B

CO 2./Stu.Pz.Abt.217

May 44 - August 44	Lt. Gerhard Beduwé
August 44	OLt. Karl Ulrich von Manteuffel
September 44 - 16/11/44	Lt. Heinrich Schilinsky
December 44	Lt. Günther Schmidt
19/01/45 - 15/02/45*	Lt. Heinz Höhn
Field post number	39961 C

CO 3./Stu.Pz.Abt.217

01/05/44 - August 44	OLt. Hans-Jürgen Heigl
August 44 - 14/12/44	Lt. Gerhard Beduwé *(KIA 14/12/44)*
December 44	Lt. Berringer
December 44 - 15/02/45*	Lt. Kurt Becker
Field post number	39961 D

CO Combat Company Stu.Pz.Abt.217

September 44 - October 44	OLt. Hans-Jürgen Heigl

CO Workshop Company Stu.Pz.Abt.217

May 44 - ?	Lt. Hans Bruno Schulte

CO Repair and Maintenance Platoon Stu.Pz.Abt.217

December 1944	OLt. Schulz
19/01/45 - 15/02/45*	Lt. Clemens Lehmann

CO Supply Company Stu.Pz.Abt.217

27/09/44 - 15/02/45*	OLt. Alfred Leonhardt[6]

* The last official report was issued on 15 February 1945.
** Mentioned by a prisoner of war.

---

[1] BA-MA RH 10/219, p. 113 and 122 ; BA-MA, Master Card Eberhard Lemor, born 16/05/05
[2] BA-MA, Master Card Johannes Tetzner, born 11/11/21
[3] BA-MA, Master Card Claus von Trotha, born 27/01/13
[4] www.volksbund.de, Lt. Björn-Dieter Olowson, born 27/05/19 in Pleß, KIA 15/08/44
[5] BA-MA, Master Card Josef Gauglitz, born 13/09/18
[6] NARA, T-314, Roll 1594 65166-1, Frame 512, KTB LXXXI A.K. 06/11/44 ; NARA, 1st Army, PWI Report No. 2, 13/12/44 ; NARA, 1st Army, PWI Report No. 1, 20/10/44; VII Corps, G-2 Periodic Report No. 190, 12/12/44 ; VII Corps, G-2 Periodic Report No. 197, 19/12/44 ; Data File Stu.Pz.Abt.217 ; Interrogation of St.Gefr. Kurt Kuhs, 1./Sturmpanzer-Abteilung 217, PW IB No 1/40, 12/03/45 ; Panzer Marsch, Nr. 2, April 1997, Sturmpanzer Abteilung 217, p. 9 f

9.4 Bibliography

Bundesarchiv-Miltärarchiv Freiburg

BA-MA H16/129, Overview of GHQ, Army and Corps tank units

BA-MA RH 2 W, Lage Frankreich (West) 1944/45

BA-MA RH 2 W/854 Lage West 1945

BA-MA RH 7/2459 II. SS-Panzer-Korps, awards 1944

BA-MA RH 10/16, General der Panzertruppen, Various reports, Aug 43 - Aug 44

BA-MA RH 10/26, Gen.d.Pz.Tr., Organization reports

BA-MA RH 10/70, Gen.Insp.d.Pz.Tr., Org.Abt.

BA-MA RH 10/90, Gen.Insp.d.Pz.Tr., Reports to the Führer

BA-MA RH 10/107, General der Panzertruppen, Overview armored units, 1944/45

BA-MA RH 10/115, General der Panzertruppen, Strength reports 1945

BA-MA RH 10/219, General der Panzertruppen, Status reports Stu.Pz.Abtn.

BA-MA RH 10/324, General der Panzertruppen, Strength and OOB reports 1945

BA-MA RH 10/349, General der Panzertruppen, Allocation of armored vehicles, Vol. starting May 1943

BA-MA RH 10/350, General der Panzertruppen, Allocation of armored vehicles, Vol. starting October 1944

BA-MA RH 10/352, General der Panzertruppen, Strength reports 31/12/44

BA-MA RH 10/354, General der Panzertruppen, Strength reports 15/03 - 10/04/45

BA-MA RH 19 IV/55, Annexes to KTB OB West v. 01 - 10/09/44

BA-MA RH 19 IV/56, Annexes to KTB OB West v. 11 - 20/09/44

BA-MA RH 19 IV/79, Annex 402, KTB OB West

BA-MA RH 19 IV-85, Annexes to KTB OB West

BA-MA RH 19 IX/10, Daily reports Heeresgruppe B 01/09 - 15/10/44

BA-MA RH 19 IX/12, Morning, noon, evening reports H.Grp. B 11/08 - 30/09/44

BA-MA RH 19 IX/13, Morning, noon, evening reports H.Grp. B 01/10 - 16/10/44

BA-MA RH 19 IX/89, KTB Heeresgruppe B 01 - 15/09/44

BA-MA RH 21-5/50, Panzergruppe West

BA-MA RH 24-80/68 KTB LXXX A.K.

BA-MA RH 24-81/97, KTB LXXXI A.K.

BA-MA RH 24-81/98, Annexes to KTB Ia LXXXI A.K.

BA-MA RH 24-81/99, KTB LXXXI A.K.

BA-MA RH 24-81/101, Annexes to KTB LXXXI A.K.

BA-MA RH 24-81/103, Annexes to Ia KTB LXXXI A.K.

BA-MA RH 24-81/105, KTB LXXXI A.K., 28/07 - 21/10/44

BA-MA RH 24-81/108, Situation maps LXXXI A.K.

BA-MA RH 24-81/109, Situation maps LXXXI A.K.

BA-MA RH 24-81/111, KTB LXXXI A.K., Battle for Aachen

BA-MA RH 26-353/4, 353.Inf.Div.

BA-MA RH 53-17/148, WBK XVII (Wien)

BA-MA RW 4 v. 636, Panzerlage West 1944/45

BA-MA WF03/4692, Activity report Gen.d.Pz.Trp. West

BA-MA WF03/4693, Activity report Gen.d.Pz.Trp. West

BA-MA MS# B-345, Generalmajor Müller: 9.Pz.Div.,11 - 16/09/44

BA-MA MS# B-563, Generalleutnant von Trierenberg: 347.Inf.Div., 15/09 -15/11/44

BA-MA MS# B-753, Generalleutnant Lange: 183.V.G.Div.

BA-MA MS# B-792, General Machholz: 49.Inf.Div.

BA-MA MS# C-016, Gen. der Inf. Erich Straube: LXXIV Korps Sept. - Dec. 1944

BA-MA MS# P-174, Oberst Wilck: 246. Volksgrenadier-Division

US National Archives

NARA, T78, R136, H53-15, Heeresgruppe D, Situation maps, 26/12/44 - 18/01/45

NARA, T78, R407, Stammtafeln, January 1944 - April 1945

NARA, T78, R418, OKH, Gen.St.d.H./Org.Abt., KTB June - November 1944

NARA, T78, R720, Generalinspekteur der Panzertruppen

NARA, T311, R3, Operational reports Heeresgruppe B

NARA, T311, R4, Heeresgruppe B, Reports

NARA, T311, R18, Activity reports General der Panzertruppen West.

NARA, T311, R25, OB West Ia

NARA, T311, R30, Heeresgruppe D, Transportation reports

NARA, T312, R1571, Transportation Reports Bv.T.O. to AOK 7

NARA, T313, R420, Panzergruppe West, Abt.Ia.

NARA, T314, R1591-61659-1, Kriegstagebuch LXXXI A.K.

NARA, T314, R1591-61659-1-3, Annexes to KTB LXXXI A.K.

NARA, T314, R1591-61659-2-3, Annexes to KTB LXXXI A.K.

NARA, T314, R1592-61659-4, Annexes to KTB LXXXI A.K.

NARA, T314, R1593-61659-7, Annexes to KTB LXXXI A.K.

NARA, T314, R1593-61659-8, Annexes to KTB LXXXI A.K.

NARA, T314, R1594-61659-12, LXXXI A.K. Battle for Aachen

NARA, T314, R1594-61661, Annexes to KTB IIa/b - 01/08 - 20/10/44

NARA, T314, R1594-65166-1, KTB LXXXI A.K., Combat Reports 22/10 - 31/12/44

NARA, T314, R1595-65166-7, Radio messages LXXXI A.K.

NARA, T314, R1596-65166-11, Experience Reports LXXXI A.K.

NARA, T713, R421-63181-6, Kriegsgliederung Pz.AOK 5

NARA, PWI Reports 1st Army, October, December 1944

NARA, G-2 Reports 9th Army, December 1944, March 1945

NARA, G-2 Reports V Corps, November 1944

NARA, G-2 Reports VII Corps, September - November 1944

NARA, G-2 Reports XIX Corps, October 1944

NARA, G-2 Reports 4th Inf Div, August - December 1944.

NARA, G-2 Reports 5th Armd Div, November - December 1944
NARA, G-2 Reports 30th Inf Div, October 1944
NARA, G-2 Journal 30th Inf Div, October - November 1944
NARA, G-2 Reports 83rd Inf Div, December 1944

Military Archive Prague

War Diary I./SS-Pz.Rgt.12
War Diary II./SS-Pz.Rgt.12

Unpublished sources

After Action Report 4th Inf Div, November - December 1944
After Action Report 33rd Armored Regiment
After Action Report 3/117th Inf Rgt, Breaching the Siegfried Line
After Action Report 330th Inf Rgt, December 1944
After Action Report 331st Inf Rgt, December 1944
After Action Report, 629th TD Bn, December 1944
After Action Report, 774th Tk Bn, December 1944
Journal & log 32nd Armored Regiment
Journal 3rd Bn, 26th Inf Rgt, 1st Inf Div.
Log Book of 2nd Battalion, 33rd Armored Regiment
S-2 Periodic Report, 120th Inf Rgt, October 1944
S-2 Periodic Report 746th Tk Bn for March 1945
S-3 Journal, 22nd Inf Rgt, 4th Inf Div, September 1944
1st Inf Div: Selected Intelligence Reports, Volume 1, June 1944 - November 1944
V Corps: Intelligence Summary, December 1944
Fort Leavenworth, Doc.No. N-2253.17, LtC Daniel: Capture of Aachen
Canadian IPW Report, C.S.D.I.C. (U.K.), SI.R. 788, 16/08/44
Aachen, Military Operations in Urban Terrain
Landesarchiv Nordrhein-Westfalen, Bestand RW37-11, Einsatzberichte Polizeiverbände 1944/45, S. 185-191
Ultra-Meldung BT 970, Ref: CX/MSS/R407, 413, 415 dated 02/01/45
Ultra-Meldung BT 9722, Ref: CX/MSS/T512/31 dated 07/04/45
War Diary Gren.Rgt.981
Data File Sturmpanzer-Abteilung 217: a compilation of personnel data created from: identification tag list Sturmpanzer-Abteilung 217, loss reports, pay books, German Red Cross, missing in action picture list, German War Graves Commission, G-2 Interrogation Reports, Personal Accounts, Master Cards
Register of the War Cemetery in Hürtgenwald

Books

Kompanie Kameradschaft: Die 3. Kompanie - SS-Panzer-Regiment 12
Eupener Geschichts- und Museumsverein, Geschichtliches Eupen, Vol. 36, 2002
Panzer Marsch, Vol. 2, April 1997, Sturmpanzer Abteilung 217
Amberg: Es kamen die schlimmsten Tage unseres Lebens
Archer/Auerbach: Panzerwrecks 1
Christoffel: Krieg am Westwall 1944/45
Dieckhoff: 3.Pz.Gren.Div.
Doyle, Friedli, Jentz: Panzer Tracts No. 8-1, Sturmpanzer
Dupuy: Hitlers Last Gamble
Erkens, W: Wie ich die Befreiung von Membach erlebte
Esser: 'Aus dunkelsten Tagen'
Frühbeißer, Rudi: 3.Fs.Jg.Div.
Guderian, Heinz: 116.Pz.Div.
Haasler, Timm: Hold the Westwall
Haasler, Timm: Panzer-Brigade 105
Hahn: Waffen und Geheimwaffen des deutschen Heeres
Haslob, Gevert: 89.Inf.Div.
Heeren, Bernhard: Kettenis, 11/09/1944 - Zeitzeugen berichten
Hewitt: 30th US Inf Div.
Jansen: 'Aus dunkelsten Tagen'
Jaugitz, Markus: Der Sturmpanzer IV - 'Brummbär', WA Vol. 160
Jentz, Thomas: Die deutsche Panzertruppe, Vol. 2
McKaughan, Jeffrey D., Tech Intel - World War II U.S. Army Technical Intelligence Reports and Summaries, Volume 1
Keldenich, H. und Willems, M.: Welkenraedt dans la tourmente
Kuhl: 'Aus dunkelsten Tagen'
Kortenhaus: 21. Panzer-Division
Massenaux, G: Baelen-sur-Vesdre
Mehner, Kurt: Die geheimen Tagesberichte der deutschen Wehrmachtsführung im II. Weltkrieg 39-45, Vol. 11
Meyer, Hubert: Geschichte der 12.SS-Pz.Div.
Münch, Karlheinz: Combat History of s.Pz.Jg.Abt.654
Pallud, J.P: Battle Of The Bulge
Parker, Danny S: Battle of the Bulge
Poll, Bernhard: Das Schicksal Aachens im Herbst 1944, in ZAGV, Vol. 66/67
ZAGV, Kapitel 2. II. 2. Kämpfe um Aachen 8. bis 15. Oktober 1944
Quarrie, Bruce: The Ardennes Offensive, VI Panzer Armee
Roppelt, Fritz: 3.Fs.Jg.Div.
Schadewitz, M: Geschichte der Panzer-Ersatz- und Ausbildungs-Abteilung 11
Schneider, Wolfgang: Tigers in Combat, Vol. I
Schramm, Percy S: KTB des OKW, Vol. 7

Spielberger: Der Panzerkampfwagen IV und seine Abarten, Vol. 5

Tessin: Verbände und Truppen, Vol. 6, 8 and 9

Tiemann: Die Leibstandarte, Vol. IV/I

Trees/Hohenstein: Hölle im Hürtgenwald

Wegmann, Günter: Ritterkreuzträger der Panzerwaffe

Whiting/Trees: Die Amis sind da!

Wijers, Hans: Ardennenoffensive, Vol. 3

Wildemeersch, Henri: 'Si Bilstain m'etait conté …' - L'entre-deux-guerres. Du 10 1940 à la libération

Eye witness reports

Sturmpanzer-Abteilung 217

Statements Richard Gottwald via Ralf-Anton Schäfer

Statements Roland Dusi from 12 - 17/11/2007

Statement Oskar Klein dated 24/09/2005

Interrogation Report St.Gefr. Kurt Kuhs, 1./Sturmpanzer-Abteilung 217, PW IB No 1/40, 12/03/45

Interrogation Report Gefr. Anton Skiba, Stu.Pz.Abt.217, 1st Army, PIR No 12, 22/12/45

Interrogation Report Lt. Heinrich Schilinsky, St./ Stu.Pz.Abt.217, 1st Army, IPW-Report No 4, 13 - 14/04/45

BA-MA MSG 2/4755: In question Panzer-Regiment 18 by Wolfgang Kiefer

Panzer-Brigade 105

Statement H. Arloth dated 08/10/2002

Statement W. K. dated 22/11/85

Statement E. Lies dated 18/04/86 and 06 & 20/12/2003

Statement E. Philipp dated 08/09/86

Statement E. Treutler dated 07/11/82

Statements H. Wolf to R. Hülsheger, no date

Statement H. Wrobel dated 02/04/86, 08/09/86, 02/12/2003, 02/01/2004 & 28/03/2004

Statements E. Zettier dated 20 & 25/01/2004

1.SS-Pz.Div.

Experience report Günther Zaag: In question Kampfgruppe Rink in Aachen, no date.

SS-Panzer-Regiment 12

BA-MA RS 7/ 86, Letter Willy Kretzschmar to Hubert Meyer dated 27/10/80

BA-MA RS 7/ 86, Letter Heinz Müller to Hubert Meyer dated 17/06/80

3.Fs.Jg.Div.

Statements Vincent Kuhlbach 29 - 30/09/2002

Stug.Brig.341

Statement G. Buntrock dated 21/09 & 02/11/2003

Heeres-Pionier-Bataillon 73

Diary Eugen Welti, via Doug Nash

Correspondence

H. Bebronne dated 19/06/2004

H. Keldenich dated 18/12/2003

F. Deprun dated 29/03/2001 & 28/03/2014

Statements Roger Props, January/February 2013, via Wolfgang Grote

Public authorities

WASt: Identification tag index Sturmpanzer-Abteilung 217

DRK: Missing in Action picture index Sturmpanzer-Abteilung 217

Homepage Volksbund Deutsche Kriegsgräberfürsorge: www.volksbund.de

Newspapers and journals

Journal 9.Pz.Div. No 30 and 94

Grenz-Echo, Volume No 209 dated 10/09/49

Grenz-Echo, Volume No 210 dated 11/09/54

Grenz-Echo, Volume No 211 dated 12/09/ 69

Grenz-Echo dated 11/09/1979

Grenz-Echo dated 06/12/94

Waffen-Revue No 86

Engel: Alte Kameraden, Vol 6/76.

Rink in Tiemann: Kampf um Aachen, Der Freiwillige No 11/1984.

Internet

www.wetterzentrale.de

www.militaerhistorie.de

www.oldhickory30th.com

www.historical-media.com

wwii.germandocsinrussia.org (GDIR)

9.6 Endnotes

Chapter 01

1. On 12 January 1944, a meeting took place at III./Panzerjäger-Regiment 656 with a representative from Panzer-Ersatz-und-Ausbildungs-Abteilung 18. Sturmpanzer-Abteilung 216 had to hand over three of its officers for the creation of Sturmpanzer-Abteilung 217. However, during formation of the battalion, only one of these officers, Oberleutnant Carl Freiherr von Manteuffel, was actually transferred to Sturmpanzer-Abteilung 217. BA-MA, RH 53-17/148, WBK XVII (Wien), Aktennotiz dd. 12/01/44.
2. BA-MA, RH 10/16, Gen.d.Pz.Tr., p.213.
3. BA-MA, RH 10/26, Gen.d.Pz.Tr., p.176 ; NARA PWI Report First Army, No. 3, dd. 22/10/44.
4. BA-MA, RH 10/26, Gen.d.Pz.Tr., p.176, KStN 1107 dd. 01/11/43, 1156 dd. 01/11/43, 1160 dd. 01/11/43 and 1185 dd. 01/06/42 ; Jaugitz: Der Sturmpanzer IV - 'Brummbär', WA Vol. 160, p.38 ; Jentz: Die deutsche Panzertruppe, Vol. 2, p.261.
5. NARA, T-78 Roll 418, Frame 6387799 f ; BA-MA, H16/129, Übersicht der Heeres-, Armee- und Korps-Panzertruppen, p.7.
6. Data File Stu.Pz.Abt.217.
7. BA-MA, RH 10/26, Gen.d.Pz.Tr., p. 177.
8. Ibid.
9. Data File Stu.Pz.Abt.217 ; Panzer Marsch, Vol. 2, April 1997, Sturmpanzer Abteilung 217, p.9 f.
10. BA-MA, RH 10/219, p.103 f.
11. BA-MA, RH 10/26, Gen.d.Pz.Tr., p.178.
12. BA-MA, RH 10/349, Verteilung der Panzerfahrzeuge, Bd. ab Mai 43, p.236.
13. BA-MA, RH 10/349, Verteilung der Panzerfahrzeuge, Bd. ab Mai 43, p.235.
14. Ibid.
15. GDIR, Findbuch 12451, Akte 481, OKH/Gen.d.Pz.Tr., p.16.
16. BA-MA, RH 10/349, Verteilung der Panzerfahrzeuge, Bd. ab Mai 43, p.235.
17. BA-MA, RH 10/349, Verteilung der Panzerfahrzeuge, Bd. ab Mai 43, p.140.
18. BA-MA, RH 10/219, p.102 f.
19. NARA, T-78 Roll 418, Frame 6386849, OKH, Gen.St.d.H. / Org.Abt.vom 01/06/44.
20. NARA, T-78 Roll 418, Frame 6386849, OKH, Gen.St.d.H. / Org.Abt.vom 10/06/44.
21. NARA, T-78 Roll 418, Frame 63866929, Org.Abt.Nr. I/6284/44 geh. vom 18/06/44.
22. NARA, T-78 Roll 418, Frame 6386849, OKH, Gen.St.d.H. / Org.Abt.vom 20/06/44.
23. NARA, T-311, Roll 25, Frame 7029822, OB West Ia Nr. 4297/44 geh. Kdos. vom 24/06/44 ; Tessin: Verbände und Truppen, Vol. 8, p.84.
24. GDIR, Findbuch 12451, Akte 475, OKH/Gen.d.Pz.Tr., p.2
25. BA-MA, RH 10/70, Gen.Insp.d.Pz.Tr. Org.Abt.(III) Nr. 7557/44 geh. vom 28/06/44.
26. Data File Stu.Pz.Abt.217.

Chapter 02

1. BA-MA, RH 10/219, p.103.
2. Doyle, Friedli, Jentz state that the transfer from Grafenwöhr started on 1/2 July, Panzer Tracts No. 8-1: Sturmpanzer, p.65.
3. NARA, T-313 Roll 420, Frame 8713847, Panzergruppe West, Abt.Ia 210/44 g. Kdos., dated 07/07/44.
4. NARA, T-312 Roll 1571, Frame 1286, Transportation reports Bv.T.O. to AOK 7, dated 09/07/44.
5. NARA, T-313 Roll 420, Frame 8713939, Panzergruppe West, Abt.Ia 423/44 g. Kdos., order of battle dated 17/07/44.
6. BA-MA, RH 21-5/50, Order of battle Panzergruppe West, dated 18/07/44.
7. BA-MA, RH 10/219, p.103.
8. BA-MA, RH 10/219, General der Panzertruppen, p.103 f.
9. BA-MA, RH 21-5/50, Panzergruppe West Ia Nr. 517/44 g.Kdos., dated 21/07/44 ; NARA, T-313 Roll 420, Frame 8713983, Panzergruppe West, supplement to daily report dated 21/07/44 ; BA-MA, RH 21-5/50, Panzergruppe West Ia Nr. 557/44 geh. dated 25/07/44, supplement to daily report dated 24/07/44 ; Jaugitz: Der Sturmpanzer IV - 'Brummbär', Waffen-Arsenal, Vol. 160, p.38 ; Interrogation report St.Gefr. Kurt Kuhs, 1./Sturmpanzer-Abteilung 217, PW IB No 1/40, dated 12/03/45.
10. Kortenhaus: 21. Panzer-Division, p.272.
11. NARA, T-313 Roll 420, Frame 8714006, Panzergruppe West, supplement to daily report dated 24/07/44 ; BA-MA, RH 21-5/50, Panzergruppe West Ia Nr. 557/44 geh., dated 25/07/44, supplement to daily report dated 24/07/44.
12. Kortenhaus: 21. Panzer-Division, p.272.
13. Data File Stu.Pz.Abt.217.
14. NARA, T-313 Roll 420, Frame 8714049, Panzergruppe West, supplement to daily report dated 30/07/44.
15. Data File Stu.Pz.Abt.217.
16. NARA T-313, Roll 420, F8714049, Panzergruppe West Ia Nr. 665/44 g. Kdos., dated 31/7/44, supplement to daily report dated 30/07/44 ; BA-MA, RH 21-5/50, Panzergruppe West Ia Nr. 678/44 g. Kdos., dated 01/08/44.
17. NARA, T-313 Roll 420, Frame 8714068, Panzergruppe West, supplement to daily report dated 01/08/44; NARA, T-313 Roll 420, Frame 8714090, Panzergruppe West, supplement to daily report dated 03/08/44 ; BA-MA, RH 21-5/50, Panzergruppe West Ia Nr. 734/44 geh., dated 04/08/44, supplement to daily report dated 03/08/44 ; NARA, T-313 Roll 420, Frame 8714096, Panzergruppe West, supplement to daily report dated 04/08/44.
18. Tiemann: Die Leibstandarte, Vol. IV/I, p.201 f. ; Meyer: History of 12.SS-Pz.Div., p.295 ; Haslob: 89.Inf.Div., page 22.
19. NARA, T-313 Roll 420, Frame 8714118, Panzergruppe West, supplement to daily report dated 06/08/44; NARA, T-313 Roll 420, Frame 8714129, Panzergruppe West, supplement to daily report dated 07/08/44.

20. Haslob: 89.Inf.Div., p.22 f. ; Meyer: History of 12.SS-Pz.Div., Vol. 1, pp. 299 - 306 ; Map Cintheaux.

21. Ibid.

22. Data File Stu.Pz.Abt.217. Oberleutnant Heinz Adolf-Wilhelm Höhn, 2./ 217-WIA, Günther Neumann, 2./ 217-MIA, Schütze Erhart Rönitz, 2./ 217-KIA, Obersoldat Heinz Seidel, St./ 217-KIA.

23. Ibid.: Oberfeldwebel Oskar Rau, 2./ 217-MIA, Herbert Größer, 2./ 217-MIA, Schütze Rudolf Strache, 2./ 217-MIA, Emil Hahr, 2./217-MIA.

24. This is the first time that von Manteuffel is mentioned in relation to 2./ Sturmpanzer-Abteilung 217. If true, he must have relieved Oberleutnant Beduwé, who was said to have taken over command of the 3. Kompanie in September 1944. The only other information available in respect to von Manteuffel is that he was a member of the staff of the battalion and had been sent to a hospital in Evreux after an accident.

25. Canadian IPW-report, C.S.D.I.C. (U.K.) – S.I.R 788, 16/08/44.

26. NARA T-313, Roll 420, Frame 87141177, Panzergruppe West Ia Nr. 853/44 g. Kdos. dated 10/08/44, supplement to daily report from 09/08/44.

27. Meyer: History of 12. SS Panzer-Division, Vol. 1, p.318.

28. NARA T-313, Roll 420, 63181, Frame 87141181, Panzergruppe West Ia Nr. 890/44 g. Kdos. vom 11/08/44, supplement to daily report dated 10/08/44.

29. Archive Prague: War diary I./SS-Pz.Rgt.12, p.15.

30. Archive Prague: War diary II./SS-Pz.Rgt.12, p.41.

31. Ibid., p.42 f.

32. Meyer: History of 12.SS-Pz.Div., p.287.

33. Archive Prague: War diary II./SS-Pz.Rgt.12, p.45 ; Data File Stu.Pz.Abt.217 Information about Gefreiter Heinz Kühn.

34. Archive Prague: War diary II./SS-Pz.Rgt.12, p.46 ; Meyer: History of 12.SS-Pz.Div., p.287.

35. Ibid., p.47.

36. Meyer: History of 12.SS-Pz.Div., p.295.

37. Archive Prague: War diary II./SS-Pz.Rgt.12, p.47.

38. Platoon leader Ustuf. Alban was still leading 3. Kompanie, replacing the wounded commander. His platoon was taken over by Oscha. Mende.

39. Archive Prague: War diary I./SS-Pz.Rgt.12, p.17 f.

40. Ibid., p.17 f. and 39 ff. ; Truppenkameradschaft: Die Dritte, p.50 ff.

41. Meyer: History of 12.SS-Pz.Div., p.298.

42. Archive Prague: War diary I./SS-Pz.Rgt.12, p.17 f. and 39 ff.; Truppenkameradschaft: Die Dritte, p.50 ff.

43. Data File Stu.Pz.Abt.217: Heinz Beck, Karl Ehringer, Karl Melzer, Erhard Zeiler.

44. Ibid.

45. Leutnant Felix Haslinger was born on 01/10/15 and had been a member of Panzer-Kompanie 40 before being assigned to Sturmpanzer-Abteilung 217. He died on 14/08/44 from wounds suffered a week before. He is buried in the German war cemetery at Champigny-Saint-André ; Data File Stu.Pz.Abt.217.

46. Oberschütze Siegfried Schreiber is buried in the German war cemetery at Champigny-St. Andre; Data File Stu.Pz.Abt. 217.

47. Data File Stu.Pz.Abt.217.

48. NARA T-313, Roll 420, Frame 87141177, Pz.Gruppe West Ia Nr. 853/44 g. Kdos. dated 10/08/44, supplement to daily report dated 09/08/44.

49. NARA T-313, Roll 420, Frame 87141181, Pz.Gruppe West Ia Nr. 890/44 g. Kdos. dated 11/08/44, supplement to daily report dated 10/08/44 ; NARA T-313, Roll 420, Frame 87141187, Pz.Gruppe West Ia Nr. 899/44 g. Kdos. dated 12/08/44, supplement to daily report dated 11/08/44.

50. NARA, T-313, Roll 420, Frame 8714187, Pz.AOK 5 Ia Nr. 899/44 g. Kdos. dated 12/08/44.

51. War diary No. 9 s.Pz.Jg.Abt.654 in Münch: Combat History 654, p.280.

52. War diary No. 9 s.Pz.Jg.Abt.654 in Münch: Combat History 654, p.281.

53. Leutnant Björn-Dieter Olowson and Obergefreiter Wilhelm Biermann are buried in the German war cemetery at Saint-Desir-de-Lisieux ; homepage Volksbund Deutsche Kriegsgräberfürsorge.

54. Data File Stu.Pz.Abt.217. Information about Leutnant Björn-Dieter Olowson and Obergefreiter Wilhelm Biermann.

55. Data File Stu.Pz.Abt.217.

56. Gefreiter Alfred Bluhm is buried in the German war cemetery at La Cambe ; Data File Stu.Pz.Abt.217.

57. BAMA RH 7/2459, II. SS-Panzer-Korps, List of awards 1944.

58. NARA T-313 Roll 420, Frame 8714049, Panzergruppe West, supplement to daily report dated 30/07/44, NARA, T-313, Roll 420, Frame 8713566, KTB Pz.AOK.5-Ia: 30/07/44, 17.00 Uhr ; NARA, T-313 Roll 420, Frame 8714045, supplement 229 to KTB Panzergruppe West, Evening report of 30/07/44.

59. Oberschütze Heinrich Kaiser, Obergefreiter Heinz Schreyer, Gefreiter Georg Sowka and Panzerschütze Willi Wachtel are all buried in the German war cemetery at La Cambe (Data File Stu.Pz.Abt.217).

60. NARA, T-313 Roll 420, Frame 8714119, Panzergruppe West, supplement to daily report dated 06/08/44; NARA, T-313, Roll 420, Frame 8714118, Pz.Gruppe West Ia Nr. 801/44 g. Kdos. dated 07/08/44, supplement to daily report dated 06/08/44.

61. NARA T-313, Roll 420, Frame 8713594, KTB Pz.AOK.5-Ia: 06/08/44, 23:15.

62. NARA T-313, Roll 420, Frame 8713594, KTB Pz.AOK.5-Ia: 06/08/44, 23:20.

63. NARA, T-313 Roll 420, Frame 8714129, Panzergruppe West, supplement to daily report dated 07/08/44.

64. Obergefreiter Friedrich Christianus (06/08/44) is buried in the German war cemetery Champigny-St. Andre, while Feldwebel Hans Ziegenhorn (08/08/44) is buried in the German war cemetery at La Cambe.

65. These soldiers were Obergefreiter Friedrich Baumeister (MIA Bosrobert), Panzerschütze Horst Gröbe (MIA Rouen), Oberleutnant Max Mentzel (MIA Montdidier) German Red Cross: Photo index.

66. BA-MA RH 10/219, p 102 f

Chapter 03

1. McKaughan: Tech Intell, Vol. 1, pages 16 ff.
2. Information provided by Frédéric Deprun on 28/03/2014.
3. NARA T-314, Roll 1591, Frame 339, KTB LXXXI A.K.
4. BA-MA, RH 10/219, General der Panzertruppen, page 109.
5. Unlike Mentzel, Wallerstorfer was a member of 1./ Sturmpanzer-Abteilung 217.
6. Data File Stu.Pz.Abt.217 ; Letter of OLt. Gauglitz to the family of Obergefreiter Wallerstorfer, dated 16/10/44 ; BA-MA, RH 10/219, p.103.
7. Data File Stu.Pz.Abt.217 ; 22nd Inf Rgt, S-3 Jnl, 05/09/44.
8. Jaugitz: Der Sturmpanzer IV - 'Brummbär', Waffen-Arsenal, Vol. 160, p.38.
9. BA-MA, WF03/4692, Activity report General der Panzertruppen West, Annexes 3, 9 and 11.
10. BA-MA, RH 19 IV/55, Annexes to KTB OB West dated 01/09 - 10/09/44., p.124 ; BA-MA, WF03/4692, Activity report General der Panzertruppen West, Annex 13, frame 019810.
11. BA-MA, RH 10/349, Tank allocation lists General der Panzertruppen, p.233.
12. BA-MA, WF03/4692, Activity report General der Panzertruppen West, Annex 14, frame 019811 f.
13. NARA, T-313, Roll 420, 63181, frame 8714266: Heeresgruppe B Ia No. 6973/44 g. Kdos. dated 05/09/44.
14. BA-MA, WF03/4692, Activity report General der Panzertruppen West, Annex 17a, frame 019819.
15. BA-MA, RH 19 IV/55, Annexes to KTB OB West dated 01 - 10/09/44, p.232 ff ; BA-MA, RH 19 IX/12, Morning, noon, evening reports Heeresgruppe B dated 11/08 - 30/09/44, p.165 ; BA-MA, RH 19 IX/89, KTB Heeresgruppe B, p.105 ; BA-MA, RH 24-81/103, Annexes to Ia KTB LXXXI A.K., p.183 ff.
16. Data File Stu.Pz.Abt.217 ; BA-MA, WF03/4692, Activity report General der Panzertruppen West, Annex 58, frame 019908 f.
17. BA-MA, RH 19 IV/55, Annexes to KTB OB West dated 01 - 10/09/44, p.218 ff.
18. BA-MA, RH 24-81/101, Annexes to KTB LXXXI A.K., Telex at 10:10 on 08/09/44 ; BA-MA, RH 19 IX/89, KTB Heeresgruppe B, p.116 ; BA-MA, RH 24-81/97, KTB LXXXI A.K., p.180.
19. BA-MA, RH 19 IV/55, Annexes to KTB OB West dated 01 - 10/09/44, p.243 ; BA-MA, RH 24-81/97, KTB LXXXI A.K., pages 184 ff; BA-MA, RH 19 IX/12, Morning, noon, evening reports Heeresgruppe B dated 11/08 - 30/09/44., p.171 ; BA-MA, RH 24-81/103, Annexes to KTB LXXXI A.K., Telex 4123 dated 08/09/44.
20. BA-MA, RH 19 IX/89, KTB Heeresgruppe B, p.121.
21. BA-MA, RH 10/349, Tank allocations lists General der Panzertruppen West, p.72 and 232.
22. BA-MA, RH 24-81/101, Annexes to KTB LXXXI A.K., Telex at 09:15 on 09/09/44; BA-MA, RH 19 IX/89, KTB Heeresgruppe B, page 142; BA-MA, RH 24-81/97, KTB LXXXI A.K., p.185 f.
23. Haasler: Panzer-Brigade 105, p.70 ff.
24. Statements Roger Props dated 24/01/2013 and 05/02/2013 via Wolfgang Grote.
25. BA-MA, RH 24-81/103, Annexes to Ia KTB LXXXI A.K., Telex 2304, 2311 & 6102 dated 10/09/44 ; BA-MA, RH 19 IV/55, Annexes to KTB OB West dated 01 - 10/09/44, p.313 and 318 ; BA-MA, RH 19 IX/89, KTB Heeresgruppe B, p.148 f ; BA-MA, RH 24-81/97, KTB LXXXI A.K., p.191 ff ; 9th Inf Div, G-2 Reports.
26. BA-MA, WF03-4692, Activity reports General der Panzertruppen West, Annex 58 ; After Action Report 33rd Armd Rgt, pages 19 f; Journal and log, 32nd Armd Rgt, pages 3 f.
27. BA-MA, WF03-4692, Activity report General der Panzertruppen West, Annex 58 and 63 ; BA-MA, B- 345, Gen.Maj. Müller: Activity report 9.Pz.Div. for period 11 - 16/09/44, p.3 ; Wildemeersch: Bilstain, p.187 ; Newsletter 9.Pz.Div. No. 94, p.22 ; Newsletter 9.Pz.Div. No. 30, p.6 ; Grenz-Echo, Issue No. 210, dated 11/09/54 ; Statement H. Wolf to R. Hülsheger, without date, p.2 ; Statement E. Lies dated 18/04/86 ; Statement H. Arloth dated 08/10/2002 ; Statement W.K. dated 22/11/85 ; Statement E. Zettier dated 20 & 25.01.2004 ; Statement H. Wrobel dated 08/09/86 & 28/03/2004.
28. BA-MA, RH 24-81/97, KTB LXXXI A.K., p.194 ; BA-MA, RH 19 IX/12, Morning, noon, evening reports H.Gr. B dated 11/08 - 30/09/44, p.184 and 186 ; BA-MA, RH 24-81/103, Annexes to Ia KTB LXXXI A.K., Telex 6097 & 6105 dated 11/09/44 ; Newsletter 9.Pz.Div. No. 30, p.6 ; Newsletter 9.Pz.Div. No. 94, p.22 ; Journal & Log 32nd Armd Rgt, p.3 f; 33rd Armd Rgt, AAR, p.20; Bernhard Poll: Das Schicksal Aachens im Herbst 1944, ZAGV, Vol. 66/67, page 208; Grenz-Echo, Issue No. 209 dated 10/09/1949.
29. Statements E. Lies, dated 06. and 20.12.2003.
30. Newsletter 9.Pz.Div. No. 94, p.23; Newsletter 9.Pz.Div. No. 30, p.6 ; 32nd Armd Rgt, Journal and Log, p.4 ; Statement W.K. dated 22/11/85; Statement H. Keldenich dated 18/12/2003 ; Grenz-Echo, Issue No. 210 dated 11/09/54 ; Keldenich-Willems: Welkenraedt dans la tourmente, p.259 f.
31. BA-MA, RH 24-81/97, KTB LXXXI A.K., p.194 ; Wildemeersch: Bilstain, p.187 ; Statements Roger Props dated 24/01/2013 and 05/02/2013 via Wolfgang Grote ; Newsletter 9.Pz.Div. No. 94, p.23; Newsletter 9.Pz.Div. No. 30, p.6.
32. BA-MA, RH 24-81/97, KTB LXXXI A.K., p.194 ; BA-MA, B-345 ; Generalmajor Müller: Activity report 9.Pz.Div. for period 11 - 16/09/44, p.3; 33rd Armd Rgt, AAR, p.20 ; 33rd Armd Rgt, Log Book 2nd Battalion, p.10 ; Grenz-Echo, Issue No. 210 dated 11/09/54 ; Grenz-Echo, Issue No. 211 dated 12/09/69, Grenz-Echo Issue 11/09/79; Newsletter 9.Pz.Div. No. 30, p.6.
33. The two crew members were tank commander Sgt. Bradford S. Conley and his driver/radio operator Tec.5 Harry F. Kested. Both men belonged to Co B, 83rd Armd Rec Bn. A small monument was erected in Membach after the war in memory of both soldiers.

34. *Newsletter 9.Pz.Div. No. 94, p.23; Newsletter 9.Pz.Div. No. 30, p.6 ; W. Erkens: Wie ich die Befreiung von Membach erlebte ; Grenz-Echo Issue 06/12/94, p.12; Statement H. Keldenich dated 18/12/2003.*

35. *Newsletter 9.Pz.Div. No. 94, p.23 ; Newsletter 9.Pz.Div. No. 30, p.6 ; 9th Inf Div, G-2 Report dated 12/09/44 ; 33rd Armd Rgt, AAR, p.20 ; Keldenich -Willems: Welkenraedt dans la tourmente, p.260; Massenaux: Baelen-sur-Vesdre, p.91; Statement H. Wolf to R. Hülsheger, without date, p.3 ; Statement E. Philipp dated 08/09/86 ; Statement E. Lies dated 18/04/86.*

36. *Massenaux: Baelen-sur-Vesdre, page 91.*

37. *Statement H. Wolf to R. Hülsheger, without date, p.3 f.*

38. *Statement H. Bebronne to Timm Haasler on 19/06/2004.*

39. *Statements E. Lies to Timm Haasler on 18/04/86, 06 & 20/12/2003 ; Statement E. Zettier on 20 & 25/01/2004.*

40. *Statements H. Wrobel to Timm Haasler on 02/04/86, 02/12/2003 & 02/01/2004; Statement E. Treutler on 07/11/82.*

41. *33rd Armd Rgt, AAR, p.20 ; 32nd Armd Rgt, Journal and Log, p.4 ; 33rd Armd Rgt, Logbook 2nd Battalion, p.10 ; Keldenich-Willems: Welkenraedt dans la tourmente, p.260 and 266 ; Statement H. Keldenich dated 18/12/2003 ; Grenz-Echo, Volume No. 210, dated 11/09/54.*

42. *It is possible that these armored reconnaissance vehicles were armored personnel carriers (SPW).*

43. *Geschichtliches Eupen Volume 36-2002, Eupener Geschichts- und Museumsverein ; Heeren: Kettenis, 11/09/44 – Eye-witness report, pages 5 ff ; Casualty report Panzer-Grenadier-Bataillon 2105 ; 33rd Armd Rgt, AAR, p.20 ; 32nd Armd Rgt, Journal and Log, p.4 ; 33rd Armd Rgt, Log book 2nd Battalion, p.10 ; Newsletter 9.Pz.Div. No. 30, p.6, Grenz-Echo, Issue No. 209 dated 10/09/49 ; Grenz-Echo, Issue No. 210 dated 11/09/54.*

44. *BA-MA, B-345, Gen.Maj. Müller: Activity report 9.Pz.Div. for period 11 - 16/09/44, p.4 ; Newsletter 9.Pz.Div. No. 30, p.6 f ; Newsletter 9.Pz.Div. No. 94, p.23 ; BA-MA, WF03/4692, Activity report General der Panzertruppen West, Annex 63.*

45. *BA-MA, WF03/4692, Activity report General der Panzertruppen West, Annex 63 ; BA-MA, RH 19 IX/10, Daily reports Heeresgruppe B, page 48; BA-MA, RH 24-81/103, KTB LXXXI A.K., Combat report 9.Pz.Div. dated 23/09/44 ; BA-MA, RH 19 IX/89, KTB H.Gr. B, p.162 & 184 ; BA-MA, RH 24-81/97, KTB LXXXI A.K., p.194 ; Casualty report Pz.Gren.Btl. 2105 ; Data File Stu.Pz.Abt.217 ; Newsletter 9 Pz.Div. No. 94, p.23.*

46. *BA-MA, RH 19 IV/56, Annexes to KTB OB West v. 11/09 - 20/09/44, p.12 ff; BA-MA, RH 10/349, General der Panzertruppen, Allocation of tanks, Vol. 1, p.232; BA-MA, WF03/4692, Activity report General der Panzertruppen West, Annex 34, Frame 019859, and Annex 53, Frame 019900; BA-MA, WF03/4693, Activity report General der Panzertruppen West, Annex 104, frame 019996.*

47. *BA-MA, WF03/4692, Activity report General der Panzertruppen West, Annex 35, frame 019858.*

48. *Ibid., Annex 58, frame 019908 f.*

49. *The named soldier was most likely Unteroffizier Herbert Langer, 3./ Stu.Pz.Abt.217.*

50. *BA-MA, RH 24-81/101, Annexes to Ia KTB LXXXI A.K., Permit for Stu.Pz.Abt.217.*

51. *BA-MA, WF03/4692, Activity report General der Panzertruppen West, Annex 41, frame 019871 ff.*

52. *Ibid., Annex 58, frame 019908 f.*

53. *BA-MA, RH 24-81/101, KTB LXXXI AK dated 15/09/44.*

54. *BA-MA, RH 24-81/101, KTB LXXXI AK dated 16/09/44 ; BA-MA, RH 24-81/103, KTB LXXXI A.K., Order of battle 9.Pz.Div. dated 16/09/44 ; BA-MA, RH 24-81/99, KTB LXXXI A.K., Report AOK 7 to H.Gr. B dated 16/09/44; BA-MA, RH 24-81/101, KTB LXXXI A.K., Telex LXXXI A.K. to AOK 7 dated 16/09/44 ; Haasler: Hold the Westwall, p.288 ff.*

55. *BA-MA, RH 24-81/97, KTB LXXXI A.K., p.226.*

56. *Ibid., p.232 ff ; BA-MA, RH 24-81/98, KTB LXXXI A.K., Daily report 16/09/44.*

57. *BA-MA, RH 24-81/97, KTB LXXXI A.K., p.239.*

58. *Ibid., p.239.*

59. *Ibid., p.240.*

60. *Ibid., p.242 ff.*

61. *Ibid., p.245 f.*

62. *Ibid., p.246.*

63. *BA-MA, WF03/4692, Activity report General der Panzertruppen West, Annex 17a, frame 019836.*

64. *Ibid., Annex 34, frame 019859.*

65. *BA-MA, RH 24-81/97, KTB LXXXI A.K., p.241 and 248.*

66. *Ibid., p.248.*

67. *Ibid., p.245 f.*

68. *Ibid., p.249.*

69. *Ibid., p.250.*

70. *Ibid., p.252 ; BA-MA, RH 24-81/108, Situation map LXXXI A.K. dated 17/09/44.*

71. *BA-MA, RH 24-81/97, KTB LXXXI A.K., p.243.*

72. *Ibid., p.241.*

73. *BA-MA, RH 24-81/98, KTB LXXXI A.K., Tank and anti-tank situation report dated 17/09/44.*

74. *BA-MA, WF03/4692, Activity report General der Panzertruppen West, Annex 58, frame 019908 f.*

75. *BA-MA, WF03/4692, Activity report General der Panzertruppen West, Annex 68, p.1.*

76. *It was not possible to assign the document to a register number. The author holds a copy of the document.*

77. *BA-MA, RH 24-81/97, KTB LXXXI A.K., p.252 f; BA-MA, RH 24-81/98, KTB LXXXI A.K. dated 18/09/44.*

78. *BA-MA, RH 24-81/97, KTB LXXXI A.K., page 254.*

79. *Ibid., p.255.*

80. *Ibid., p.255.*

81. Ibid., p.256.

82. Ibid., 258 ; BA-MA, MS # B-792, 49.Inf.Div., p.15 ff.

83. The situation map of LXXXI A.K. for 18/09/44 at 21:00 shows two Sturmpanzers attached to Panzer-Brigade 105, while the tank and anti-tank situation report of the corps only mentioned one Sturmpanzer allocated to Panzer-Brigade 105 at 22:00.

84. BA-MA, RH 24-81/98, Annexes to KTB LXXXI A.K., Tank and anti-tank situation report dated 18/09/44 ; BA-MA, RH 24-81/108, KTB LXXXI A.K., Situation map at 21:00 on 18/09/44.

85. BA-MA, WF03/4692, Activity report General der Panzertruppen West, Annex 59, frame 019911.

86. BA-MA, RH 24-81/98, KTB LXXXI A.K., Daily report 19/09/44 ; BA-MA, RH 24-81/97, KTB LXXXI A.K., p.262.

87. BA-MA, RH 24-81/97, KTB LXXXI A.K., p.264.

88. BA-MA, MS # B-792, 49.Inf.Div., p.18

89. BA-MA, RH 24-81/105, KTB LXXXI A.K., p.34, BA-MA, RH 24-81/98, Enclosures to KTB LXXXI A.K., Tank and anti-tank situation report 19/09/44.

90. BA-MA, RH 24-81/97, KTB LXXXI A.K., p.269.

91. BA-MA, RH 24-81/98, KTB LXXXI A.K., Daily report LXXXI A.K. dated 20/09/44.

92. BA-MA, RH 24-81/101, KTB LXXXI A.K., Tank and anti-tank situation report 20/09/44.

93. Ibid., Telex LXXXI A.K. dated 20/09/44.

94. BA-MA, RH 24-81/105, KTB LXXXI A.K., p. 40 ; BA-MA, RH 24-81/98, Annexes to KTB LXXXI A.K., Tank and anti-tank situation report dated 21/09/44.

95. BA-MA, RH 24-81/97, KTB LXXXI A.K., p.274 ; BA-MA, RH 24-81/98, KTB LXXXI A.K., Daily report dated 22/09/44.

96. BA-MA, RH 24-81/97, KTB LXXXI A.K., p.277 f ; BA-MA, RH 24-81/98, Annexes to KTB LXXXI A.K., Tank and anti-tank situation report dated 22/09/44.

97. BA-MA, RH 24-81/98 and 101, KTB LXXXI A.K., Tank and anti-tank situation report 23/09/44 ; Data file Sturmpanzer-Abteilung 217.

98. BA-MA, RH 24-81/97, KTB LXXXI A.K., p.281.

99. Ibid., p.282.

100. BA-MA, RH 24-81/98, Annexes to Ia KTB LXXXI A.K., p.205.

101. BA-MA, RH 24-81/105, KTB LXXXI A.K. dated 24/09/44.

102. Guderian: 116.Panzer-Division, p.570.

103. BA-MA, RH 24-81/97, KTB LXXXI A.K., p.291.

104. BA-MA, RH 24-81/105, KTB LXXXI A.K., p.45.

105. BA-MA, RH 24-81/97, KTB LXXXI A.K., p.291.

106. BA-MA, RH 24-81/97, KTB LXXXI A.K., page 293 ; BA-MA, RH 24-81/101, Annexes to KTB LXXXI A.K., p. 433 f.

107. BA-MA, RH 24-81/97, KTB LXXXI A.K., p.296.

108. BA-MA, RH 24-81/101, KTB LXXXI A.K. dated 26/09/44 ; BA-MA, RH 10/349, Allocation of armored vehicles, General der Panzertruppen, p.232.

109. BA-MA, RH 24-81/97, KTB LXXXI A.K., p.303 f.

110. Ibid., p.304 ; BA-MA, RH 24-81/105, KTB LXXXI A.K., Table of organization Arko 117 dated 29/09/44.

111. BA-MA, MS # B-792, 49.Inf.Div., p.21 ; BA-MA, RH 24-81/105, KTB LXXXI A.K. dated 30/09/44 ; BA-MA, RH 24-81/109, KTB LXXXI A.K., Situation map dated 01/10/44.

112. BA-MA, RH 10/219, General der Panzertruppen, p.106 f. There is another report with the same date and slightly different numbers, but these are illegible. The major difference relates to the superior military organization. One document states AOK 7 while the other states LXXXI A.K.

113. BA-MA, MS # B-563, Generalleutnant von Trierenberg: 347.Inf.Div., 15/09 - 15/11/44, p. 1 ; 33rd Armd Rgt, AAR, p.9 ; 33rd Armd Rgt, Logbook 2nd Battalion, p.10.

114. BA-MA, RH 10/219, General der Panzertruppen, p.106 ff.

115. OKH/General Staff of the Army/ Department of Organization Nr. I/10792/44 geh. dated 22/09/44.

116. NARA, T-311, Roll 4, Reports Heeresgruppe B dated 02/10/44, frame 7003369 and 7003373

117. NARA, T-314, Roll 1591 – 61659-2-3, Annexes to KTB LXXXI A.K., frame 872 f. ; NARA, T-314, Roll 1593-61659-7, Annexes to KTB LXXXI A.K., frame 749 ff. and 817.

118. BA-MA, RH 24-81/97, KTB LXXXI A.K., pp.318-324 ; BA-MA, RH 24-81/101, KTB LXXXI A.K. dated 03/10/44 ; BA-MA, MS # B753, Generalleutnant Lange: 183.V.G.Div., p.5 f. ; NARA, T-314, Roll 1591 – 61659-2-3, Annexes to KTB LXXXI A.K., frame 877 f, 880, 882 f and 884 ff ; NARA, T314, R1592 – 61659-4, Annexes to KTB LXXXI A.K., frame 950 ; NARA, T-314, Roll 1593 - 61659-7, Annexes to KTB LXXXI A.K., frame 818 ; VII Corps, G-2 Report, 07/10/44; 30th Inf Div, G-2 Reports dated 02 & 03/10/44 ; Hewitt: 30th Inf Div, p.114 ff.

119. BA-MA, RH 24-81/97, KTB LXXXI A.K., pp.318-330 ; BA-MA, RH 24-81/101, KTB LXXXI A.K. dated 03/10/44 ; BA-MA, MS # B753, Generalleutnant Lange: 183.V.G.Div., p.5 f. ; NARA, T-314, Roll 1591–61659-2-3, Annexes to KTB LXXXI A.K., frame 884-893 ; NARA, T-314, Roll 1592–61659-4, Enclosures to KTB LXXXI A.K., frame 955 ; NARA, T314, Roll 1593–61659-7, Annexes to KTB LXXXI A.K., frame 818 ff ; NARA, T-314, Roll 1594–61661, Annexes to KTB LXXXI A.K., frame 256; 30th Inf Div, G-2 Reports dated 02 - 04/10/44; Kuhl in: aus dunkelsten Tagen, p.11 f. ; Jansen in: aus dunkelsten Tagen, p.46; Hewitt: 30th Inf Div, pp.114 ff. and 118 ff.

120. Stu.Pz.Abt.217 and II./Gren.Rgt.148 are not shown as part of the southern attack group on the situation map of LXXXI A.K. for 04/10/44.

121. BA-MA, RH 24-81/97, KTB LXXXI A.K., pp.330 - 333 ; BA-MA, RH 24-81/111, KTB LXXXI A.K. dated 04/10/44 ; NARA, T-314, Roll 1591–61659-2-3, Annexes to KTB LXXXI A.K., frame 893-897, 899-903 and 910 ; NARA, T-314, Roll 1592–61659-4, Annexes to KTB LXXXI A.K., frame 959 ff ; NARA, T-314, Roll 1593–61659-7, Annexes to KTB LXXXI A.K., frame 819 f ; BA-MA, RH 24-81/98, Annexes to KTB LXXXI, Tank and anti-tank situation report LXXXI A.K. dated 04/10/44 ; 30th Inf Div, G-2 Report No. 109, dated 04/10/44 and G-2-Report No. 110, dated 05/10/44 ; 30th Inf Div,

Ferris Report, 04/10/44 ; 30th Inf Div, G-2-Journal, 04/10/44, Report 2nd Armd Div ; website Old Hickory 30th: Capture of McDowell ; Kuhl in: aus dunkelsten Tagen, p. 11 f and 16 f ; Jansen in: aus dunkelsten Tagen, page 45; Guderian: 116. Panzer-Division, p.240.

122. NARA, T314, R1592–61659-4, Annexes to KTB LXXXI A.K., frame 962.

123. NARA, T314, R1592–61659-4, Annexes to KTB LXXXI A.K., frame 964.

124. BA-MA, RH 24-81/97, KTB LXXXI A.K., pp.334 - 338; NARA, T-314, Roll 1591–61659-2-3, Annexes to KTB LXXXI A.K., frame 903, 906-910 and 915 f; NARA, T-314, Roll 1593–61659-7, Annexes to KTB LXXXI A.K., frame 821 f; BA-MA, RH 24-81/98, Annexes to KTB LXXXI, Tank and anti-tank situation report 05/10/44; 30th Inf Div, G-2 Report No. 110, dated 05/10/44; 30th Inf Div, G-2 Report IPW-Team 117, 05/10/44.

125. NARA, T-314, Roll 1591–61659-2-3, Annexes to KTB LXXXI A.K., frame 909.

126. BA-MA, RH 24-81/97, KTB LXXXI A.K., pp.339-345 ; NARA, T-314, Roll 1591–61659-2-3, Annexes to KTB LXXXI A.K., Frame 915-917, 919-923 and 926; NARA, T-314, Roll 1592–61659-4, Annexes to KTB LXXXI A.K., frame 973 and 975 ; NARA, T-314, Roll 1593–61659-7, Annexes to KTB LXXXI A.K., frame 800 and 822 f ; NARA, T-314, Roll 1594–61661, Annexes to KTB LXXXI A.K., Strength and loss reports; 30th Inf Div, G-2 Reports dated 03-06/10/44 ; 120th Inf Rgt, S-2 Interrogation Report, 07/10/44 ; Hewitt: 30th Inf Div, p. 122 f ; ZAGV, Chapter 2. II. 2. Kämpfe um Aachen 8. bis 15. Oktober 1944 ; Jansen in: aus dunkelsten Tagen, p.43 and 45 ff ; Esser in: aus dunkelsten Tagen, p.52 f.

127. BA-MA, RH 24-81/97, KTB LXXXI A.K., pp.346-350 ; NARA, T-314, Roll 1591–61659-2-3, Annexes to KTB LXXXI A.K., frame 930 f, 933 ff and 938 f ; NARA, T-314, Roll 1592–61659-4, Annexes to KTB LXXXI A.K., frame 978 ; NARA, T-314, Roll 1593-61659-7, Annexes to KTB LXXXI A.K., frame 775, 800 and 828 f ; NARA, T-314, Roll 1594–61659-12, LXXXI A.K. Battle for Aachen, frame 61 f ; Guderian: 116. Panzer-Division, p.240 ; Christoffel: Krieg am Westwall 1944/45, p.124; 3./117th Inf Rgt, AAR Breaching the Siegfried Line, p.4 ; Hewitt: 30th Inf Div, p.119 ff.

128. BA-MA, RH 19 IX/13, Morning, noon, evening reports H.Gr. B dated 08/10/44 ; BA-MA, RH 24-81/97, KTB LXXXI A.K., pp.350-354 ; BA-MA, RH 24-81/101, Annexes to KTB LXXXI A.K., Tank and anti-tank situation report 08 - 09/10/44 ; NARA, T-314, Roll 1591–61659-2-3, Annexes to KTB LXXXI A.K., frame 938- 950 ; NARA, T-314, Roll 1592-61659-4, Annexes to KTB LXXXI A.K., frame 995-997 ; NARA, T-314, Roll 1593-61659-7, frame 786-802 ff ; NARA, T-314, Roll 1594–61659-12, LXXXI A.K., Battle for Aachen, frame 62 f.

129. BA-MA, RH 24-81/97, KTB LXXXI A.K., pp.348, 351 and 356 ; NARA, T-314, Roll 1591–61659-2-3, Annexes to KTB LXXXI A.K., frame 949-958 ; NARA, T-314, Roll 1591-61659-4, Annexes to KTB LXXXI A.K., frame 1005, 1008, 1013 f and 1017 ; NARA, T314, R1593-61659-7, Annexes to KTB LXXXI A.K., frame 772-793 and 800-806 ; NARA, T-314, Roll 1594–61659-12, LXXXI A.K. Battle for Aachen, frame 63 f ; Erkennungsmarkverzeichnis Sturmpanzer-Abteilung 217 ; Amberg: Die schlimmsten Tage unseres Lebens, p.66 ff ; Hewitt: 30th Inf Div, p. 129 ff.

130. BA-MA, RH 24-81/97, KTB LXXXI A.K., pp. 356 and 358 ff ; NARA, T-314, Roll 1591–61659-1-3, Annexes to KTB LXXXI A.K., frame 574 f ; NARA, T-314, Roll 1591–61659-2-3, Annexes to KTB LXXXI A.K., frame 958-964 and 967 f ; NARA, T-314, Roll 1592-61659-4, Annexes to KTB LXXXI A.K., frame 1033 ; NARA, T-314, Roll 1591 – 61661, Annexes to KTB LXXXI A.K., frame 249 ; NARA, MS # P-174, Wilck: 246.V.G.Div., p. 14 f.

131. NARA, T-314, Roll 1593– 61659-7, Annexes to KTB LXXXI A.K., frame 840.

132. BA-MA, RH 24-81/97, KTB LXXXI A.K., pp. 356, 358 ff and 386 ; NARA, T-314, Roll 1591-61659-2-3, Annexes to KTB LXXXI A.K., frame 958-962, 964, 967-973 and 975 ff ; NARA, T-314, Roll 1592-61659-4, Annexes to KTB LXXXI A.K., frame 1035, 1038, 1042, 1062 and 1070 ; NARA, T-314, Roll 1593-1659-7, Annexes to KTB LXXXI A.K., frame 844 ; NARA, T-314, Roll 1594-61659-12, LXXXI A.K., Battle for Aachen, frame 64 f ; NARA, T-314, Roll 1594-61661, Annexes to KTB LXXXI A.K., frame 249 ; NARA, T-314, Roll 1596-65166-11, Experience reports LXXXI A.K. dated 23/10 - 30/12/1944, frame 799 ff ; NARA, MS # P-174, Wilck: 246.V.G.Div., p.14 f ; Guderian: 116. Panzer-Division, p.242 ff.

133. BA-MA, RH 24-81/97, KTB LXXXI A.K., pp.361–364 ; NARA, T-314, Roll 1591-61659-2-3, Annexes to KTB LXXXI A.K., frame 980 ff and 986 ff ; NARA, T-314, Roll 1592-61659-4, Annexes to KTB LXXXI A.K., frame 1047 and 1062 f ; NARA, T-314, Roll 1593–61659-8, Annexes to KTB LXXXI A.K., frame 1041 ff ; NARA, T-314, Roll1594-61659-12, LXXXI A.K. Battle for Aachen, frame 66 f; NARA, MS # P-174, Wilck: 246.V.G.Div., p.15 f and 18 ff ; Aachen, Military Operations in Urban Terrain, p.18 ; Whiting/Trees: Die Amis sind da!, p.123.

134. Surprisingly the daily report of the OB West for 13/10/44 states: "LXXXI A.K.: Single enemy tanks about 150 m from the Quellenhof (west of the railroad station Aachen-Nord) at 13:30. Countermeasures with Sturmpanzer-Abteilung 217 in progress" (Morning, noon, evening report OB West, dated 13/10/44). At this time the battalion was still in the Würselen area.

135. BA-MA, RH 24-81/97, KTB LXXXI A.K., pp.363 - 370 ; BA-MA, RH 19 IV/79, Annex 402, KTB OB West dated 26/10/44, Report KG Rink ; NARA, T-314, Roll 1591–61659-2-3, Annexes to KTB LXXXI A.K., frame 989-1000 ; NARA, T-314, Roll 592-61659-4, Report LXXXI A.K. dated 14/10/44, frame 1053, 1055, 1063 f and 1070 ; NARA, T-314, Roll 1593–61659-7, Annexes to KTB LXXXI A.K., frame 858 ; NARA, T-314, Roll 1594–61659-12, LXXXI A.K., Battle for Aachen, frame 67 f und 96 f ; NARA, T-314, Roll 1596-65166-11, Experience reports LXXXI A.K. dated 23/10 - 30/12/1944, frame 774 ff ; Fort Leavenworth, Doc. No. N-2253.17, LtC Daniel: Capture of Aachen, p.10 ; 26th Inf Rgt, Journal 3rd Bn, p.2 ; Guderian: 116. Panzer-Division, p.248 ff ; Hewitt: 30th Inf Div, p.138; Amberg: Es kamen die schlimmsten Tage unseres Lebens, p.76 ; Whiting/Trees: Die Amis sind da!, p.130.

136. BA-MA, MSG 2/4755: Concerning Panzer-Regiment 18 by Wolfgang Kiefer.

137. BA-MA, RH 24-81/97, KTB LXXXI A.K., p.374.

138. BA-MA, RH 24-81/97, KTB LXXXI A.K., pp.368-376 ; BA-MA, RH 19 IX/13, Combat report KG Rink 09-22/10/1944 ; NARA, T-314, Roll 1591–61659-2-3, Annexes to KTB

LXXXI A.K., frame 1000-1014 ; NARA, T-314, Roll 1592-61659-4, Reports LXXXI A.K. dated 14/10/44, frame 1061-1079 ; NARA, T-314, Roll 1593–61659-7, Annexes to KTB LXXXI A.K., frame 860 ; NARA, T-314, Roll 1594–61659-12, LXXXI A.K., Battle for Aachen, frame 68 and 97; NARA, T-314, Roll 1596-65166-11, Experience reports LXXXI A.K., frame 788 ff and 799 ff; NARA, FUSA IPW-Report, 21/10/44, No 1; 26th Inf Rgt, Journal 3rd Bn, p.2; Fort Leavenworth, Doc. No. N-2253.17, LtC Daniel: Capture of Aachen, p.11; Guderian: 116. Panzer-Division, p.250 f ; Hewitt: 30th Inf Div, p.138 ; Dieckhoff: 3. Panzergrenadier-Division, p.351 f.

139. BA-MA, RH 24-81/97, KTB LXXXI A.K., p.375 ff ; BA-MA, RH 19 IX/13, Combat report KG Rink dated 09 - 22/10/44 ; NARA, T-314, Roll 1591–61659-2-3, Annexes to KTB LXXXI A.K., frame 1012-1019 and 1023 f ; NARA, T-314, Roll 1592-61659-4, Annexes to KTB LXXXI A.K., frame 1071-1076 ; NARA, T-314, Roll 1594–61659-12, LXXXI A.K., Battle for Aachen, frame 68 f and 99 ; NARA, MS # P-174, Wilck: 246.V.G.Div., p.23 ; BA-MA, RH 24-81/98, Annexes to KTB LXXXI, Tank and anti-tank situation report 15/10/44; Fort Leavenworth, Doc. No. N-2253.17, LtC Daniel: Capture of Aachen, p.12; 26th Inf Rgt, Journal 3rd Bn, p.3 ; Landesarchiv Nordrhein-Westfalen, Asset RW37-11, Combat reports police units 1944/45, pages 185-191 ; Aachen, Military Operations in Urban Terrain, p.22 f ; Guderian: 116. Panzer-Division, p.250 ; Amberg: Die schlimmsten Tage unseres Lebens, p.122 ; Hewitt: 30th Inf Div, p.139 ; Rink in Tiemann: Battle for Aachen, Der Freiwillige No. 11/1984, p.14 ; Whiting/ Trees: Die Amis sind da!, p.148 f.

140. NARA, T-314, Roll 1594–61659-12, LXXXI A.K., Battle for Aachen, frame 82.

141. BA-MA, RH 24-81/97, KTB LXXXI A.K., pp.379-383 f ; NARA, T-314, Roll 1591–61659-2-3, Annexes to KTB LXXXI A.K., frame 1025- 1039 ; NARA, T-314, R1592-61659-4, Annexes to KTB LXXXI A.K., frame 1080 ; NARA, T-314, Roll 1596-65166-11, Experience report LXXXI A.K. dated 23/10 - 30/12/44, frame 774-781 ; NARA, T-314, Roll 1594–61659-12, LXXXI A.K., Battle for Aachen, frame 70 and 100 ; NARA, MS # P-174, Wilck: 246.V.G.Div., p.23 f ; BA-MA, RH 24-81/98, Annexes to KTB LXXXI, Tank and anti-tank situation report 16/10/44 ; Fort Leavenworth, Doc. No. N-2253.17, LtC Daniel: Capture of Aachen, p.14 ; Journal 3rd Bn, 26th Inf Rgt, 1st Inf Div, p.3 ; Aachen, Military Operations in Urban Terrain, p.23 f ; Guderian: 116. Panzer-Division, p.253 ff ; Hewitt: 30th Inf Div, p.139 ff ; Whiting/Trees: Die Amis sind da!, p.153 f and 158 f ; Dieckhoff: 3. Panzergrenadier-Division, p.352 ; Schneider: Tigers in Combat, Volume I, p.320.

142. The American report does not specify if the tank was an assault tank or an assault howitzer.

143. BA-MA, RH 24-81/97, KTB LXXXI A.K., pp.383-388 ; NARA, T-314, Roll 1591–61659-2-3, Annexes to KTB LXXXI A.K., frame 1040-1048 ; NARA, T-314, Roll 1593–61659-7, Annexes to KTB LXXXI A.K., frame 907, 928 and 964 ; NARA, T-314, Roll 1596-65166-11, Experience report LXXXI A.K. dated 23/10 - 30/12/44, frame 799 ff ; NARA, T-314, Roll 1594–61659-12, LXXXI A.K., Battle for Aachen, frame 70 f and 101 ; BA-MA, RH 24-81/98, Annexes to KTB LXXXI, Tank and anti-tank situation report, 17/10/44 ; NARA, FUSA IPW-Report, 21/10/1944, No 1 ; NARA, MS # P-174,

Wilck: 246.V.G.Div., page 24 ; Journal 3rd Bn, 26th Inf Rgt, 1st Inf Div, p.3 ; Guderian: 116. Panzer-Division, p.255 f ; Hewitt: 30th Inf Div, page 142.

144. It should be mentioned that Leutnant Wolfgang Kiefer was captured wounded by the Americans that day (BA-MA, MSG 2/4755: Concerning Pz.Rgt.18 by Wolfgang Kiefer).

145. NARA, T-314, Roll 1591–61659-2-3, Annexes to KTB LXXXI A.K., frame 1052.

146. BA-MA, RH 24-81/97, KTB LXXXI A.K., p.388 ff ; BA-MA, RH 19 IX/13, Combat report KG Rink, 09 - 22/10/44 ; NARA, T-314, Roll 1591–61659-2-3, Annexes to KTB LXXXI A.K., frame 1050-1054 and 1080 ; NARA, T-314, Roll 1592-61659-4, Report LXXXI A.K. dated 18/10/44, frame 1092 ; NARA, T-314, Roll 1593–61659-7, Annexes to KTB LXXXI A.K., frame 906, 928 and 964 ; NARA, T-314, Roll 1596-65166-11, Experience reports LXXXI A.K. dated 23/10 - 30/12/44, frame 785 ff ; NARA, T-314, Roll 1594–61659-12, LXXXI A.K,. Battle for Aachen, frame 71 and 102 ; NARA, 1st Inf Div, Consolidated Interrogation Report, 18/10/44 ; NARA, 1st Inf Div, G-2 Jnl, 18/10/44 ; BA-MA, RH 24-81/98, Annexes to KTB LXXXI A.K., Tank and anti-tank situation report 18/10/44 ; NARA, MS # P-174, Wilck: 246.V.G.Div., p.24 f ; G-2 Report XIX Corps, 18/10/44 ; Fort Leavenworth, Doc. No. N-2253.17, LtC Daniel: Capture of Aachen, p.14 ; 26th Inf Rgt, Journal 3rd Bn, p.3 ; 30th Inf Div, G-2 Report, 18/10/44 ; Günther Zaag: Experience report concerning the engagement of Battle group Rink in Aachen, undated ; Aachen, Military Operations in Urban Terrain, p.28 ; Dieckhoff: 3. Panzergrenadier-Division, p.354 f ; Hewitt: 30th Inf Div, page 142 ; Guderian: 116. Panzer-Division, page 258 ; Whiting/Trees: Die Amis sind da, p.168 ff.

147. BA-MA, RH 19 IX/13, Morning, noon, evening reports H.Gr. B, dated 19/10/44 ; BA-MA, RH 19 IX/13, Combat report KG Rink dated 09 - 22/10/44 ; BA-MA, RH 24-81/97, KTB LXXXI A.K., pp.391-395 ; NARA, T-314, Roll 1591–61659-2-3, Annexes to KTB LXXXI A.K., frame 1059-1067 ; NARA, T-314, Roll 1592-61659-4, Annexes to KTB LXXXI A.K., frame 1103 and 1122 ; NARA, T-314, Roll 1593–61659-7, Annexes to KTB LXXXI A.K., frame 909-918, 927-933 and 944 ; NARA, T-314, Roll 1594–61659-12, LXXXI A.K. Battle for Aachen, frame 71 and 103 ; NARA, T-314, Roll 1596-65166-11, Experience reports LXXXI A.K., frame 761, 785 ff and 799ff ; NARA, MS # P-174, Wilck: 246.V.G.Div., p.25 f ; BA-MA, RH 24-81/98, Annexes to KTB LXXXI, Tank and anti-tank situation report 19/10/44 ; Fort Leavenworth, Doc. No. N-2253.17, LtC Daniel: Capture of Aachen, p.15 ; 26th Inf Rgt, Journal 3rd Bn, p.3 ; Aachen, Military Operations in Urban Terrain, p.28 ; Whiting/Trees: Die Amis sind da, pages 201 f ; Guderian: 116. Panzer-Division, page 257 ; Dieckhoff: 3. Panzergrenadier-Division, p.355 ff.

148. BA-MA, RH 24-81/97, KTB LXXXI A.K., pp.396-402 ; BA-MA, RH 19 IX/13, Morning, noon, evening reports H.Gr. B, dated 20/10/44 ; BA-MA, RH 19 IX/13, Combat report KG Rink dated 09 - 22/10/44 ; NARA, T-314, Roll 1591–61659-2-3, Annexes to KTB LXXXI A.K., frame 1067-1082 ; NARA, T-314, Roll 1592-61659-4, Annexes to KTB LXXXI A.K., frame 1122 ff ; NARA, T-314, Roll 1593–61659-7, Annexes to KTB LXXXI A.K., frame 942 f ; NARA, T-314, Roll 1594–61659-12, LXXXI A.K., Battle

for Aachen, frame 106 ; BA-MA, RH 24-81/98, Annexes to KTB LXXXI, Tank and anti-tank situation report, 20/10/44 ; Journal 3rd Bn, 26th Inf Rgt, 1st Inf Div, p.3 ; Fort Leavenworth, Doc. No. N-2253.17, LtC Daniel: Capture of Aachen, p.15 ; Aachen, Military Operations in Urban Terrain, p.28 ; Guderian: 116. Panzer-Division, pages 259 f ; Whiting/Trees: Die Amis sind da!, p.203 ff.

149. BA-MA, RH 24-81/97, KTB LXXXI. A.K., pp.384, 403-406 ; NARA, T-314, Roll 1591–61659-2-3, Annexes to KTB LXXXI A.K., frame 1082-1094 ; NARA, T-314, R1593–61659-7, Annexes to KTB LXXXI A.K., frame 849 ff, 956 f, 961 f and 964 ; NARA, T-314, Roll 1594–61659-12, LXXXI A.K,. Battle for Aachen, frame 72 ; NARA, T-314, Roll 1594-65166-1, KTB LXXXI. A.K., Combat development, frame 452 ; NARA, T-314, Roll 1596-65166-11, Experience reports LXXXI. A.K. 23/10 - 30/12/44, frame 738-745 and 761 ; MS# P-174: Oberst Wilck: 246.V.G.Div., pages 22 ff ; 26th Inf Rgt, Journal 3rd Bn, pages 1-6 ; Fort Leavenworth, Doc.No. N-2253.17, LtC Daniel: Capture of Aachen, pages 15 f; 1st Inf Div: Selected Intelligence Reports, Volume 1, June 1944 – November 1944, pages 83 ff ; Aachen, Military Operations in Urban Terrain, page 29 ; Whiting/Trees: Die Amis sind da!, page 219 ff ; Guderian: 116. Panzer-Division, page 260 f ; Hewitt: 30th US Inf Div, pages 142 f ; Dieckhoff: 3. Panzer-Grenadier-Division, pages 357 f ; Amberg: Es kamen die schlimmsten Tage unseres Lebens, page 88.

150. BA-MA RH 10/219, pages 106 and 110 ; NARA, T-314, Roll 1594, KTB LXXXI A.K., frame 466 ; BA-MA, MSG 2/4755: Concerning Pz.Rgt. 18 by Wolfgang Kiefer ; NARA, T-314, Roll 1594-65166-1, KTB LXXXI A.K., Combat development, frame 466 ; NARA, T713, Roll 421 63181-6, Frame 8714557, Combat order of battle Pz.AOK 5 dated 23/10/44 ; BA-MA RH 24-81/98, Annexes to KTB LXXXI, Tank and anti-tank situation report LXXXI A.K., Reports dated 22, 23 & 27/10/44, and 06/11/44 ; XIX Corps, G-2 Report, 21/10/44, Annex 1.

Chapter 04

1. It is obvious that at the time of reporting, the information was not available that one Sturmpanzer had already been lost on 18 October 1944 on its way to Aachen.
2. Tank/Anti-tank reports LXXXI A.K. dated 19 & 20/10/44.
3. BA-MA, WF03/4693, Activity Report Gen.d.Pz.Trp., Annex 135, frame 020050 f.
4. BA-MA, WF03/4693, Activity Report Gen.d.Pz.Trp., Annex 135, frame 020051 ; BA-MA, WF03/4693, Activity Report Gen.d.Pz.Trp., Annex 136, frame 020053 ; War diary LXXXI A.K., frame 65166/5 and LXXXI A.K. dated 22/10/44.
5. BA-MA, WF03/4693, Activity Report Gen.d.Pz.Trp., Annex 136, frame 020053 f.
6. NARA, T-78 Roll 407, Frame 6376636, Stammtafel.
7. BA-MA, RH 10/219, pages 106 and 110.
8. BA-MA, RH 10/219, General der Panzertruppen, pages 113 ff ; Interrogation report St.Gefr. Kurt Kuhs, 1./Sturmpanzer-Abteilung 217, PW IB No 1/40 dated 12/03/45 ; Data File Stu.Pz.Abt.217.
9. BA-MA, RH 10/350, General der Panzertruppen, p.231.

10. BA-MA, RH 10/219, General der Panzertruppen, p.110 f.
11. BA-MA, RH 10/219, General der Panzertruppen, p.113.
12. 30th Inf Div, G-2 Report No. 137, 01/11/44.
13. NARA, T78 Roll 407, Frame 6376636, Stammtafel, I/13408g. dated 02/11/44.
14. BA-MA, RH 24/81, War diary LXXXI A.K., Entry 06/11/44, 10:30.
15. BA-MA, RH 24-81, Action report LXXXI A.K. dated 07/11/44.
16. Probably a typo in the war diary of LXXXI A.K. There was an Oberleutnant Johannes Tetzner with Sturmpanzer-Abteilung 217, who was reportedly the commander of the 1. Kompanie in December 1944.
17. NARA, Annexes to War diary LXXXI A.K., Tank/Anti-tank reports dated 30/10 - 06/11/44 ; NARA, T-314, Roll 1594 65166-1, frame 512, War diary LXXXI A.K. dated 06/11/44 ; NARA, T-314, Roll 1594 65166-2, la Combat report LXXXI A.K., page 2 ; NARA, T-314, Roll 1595 65166-7, frame 960, Telex LXXXI A.K. dated 06/11/44.
18. BA-MA, RH 10/219, General der Panzertruppen, p.114 ff.
19. BA-MA, RH 10/350, General der Panzertruppen, p.78.

Chapter 05

1. BAMA, MS C-016, Gen. der Inf. Erich Straube: LXXIV A.K., Sept. - Dec. 1944, 04/11/48 ; Haslob: 89. Infanteriedivision, pages 92, 120 and 173 ff ; Trees/Hohenstein: Hölle im Hürtgenwald, p.161 ff.
2. Guderian: 116.Pz.Div., p.293 ff.
3. Annex to war diary LXXXI A.K., dated 15/11/44
4. In particular, the number of 13 soldiers reported as missing in action seems to be relatively high. It is also possible that these figures contain further losses related to those occurred in Aachen during the siege. For instance, Leutnant Wolfgang Kiefer, who was captured wounded in Aachen was only reported as missing in action by his unit one month later, on 17/11/44.
5. Data File Stu.Pz.Abt.217: Loss report Oberleutnant Gero von der Schulenburg.
6. Data File Stu.Pz.Abt.217: BA-MA, RW59, Recommended list for the Casualty Award in Black, Reserve-Lazarett Bad Rothenfelde, 30/11/44.
7. Data File Stu.Pz.Abt.217: Homepage German War Graves Commission.
8. BA-MA, RH 10/350, General der Panzertruppen, p.78.
9. Guderian: 116.Pz.Div., p.304.
10. V Corps, G-2 Report, 21/11/44 ; VII Corps, G-2 Report, 20/11/44 ; BA-MA, MS C-016, Gen. derInf. Erich Straube: LXXIV A.K., Sept. - Dec. 1944, 04/11/48 ; Haslob: 89. Infanteriedivision, p.92, 120 and 173 ff. ; Trees/Hohenstein: Hölle im Hürtgenwald, p.161 ff.
11. 4th Inf Div, G-2 Reports 22, 23 & 25/11/44 ; VII Corps, G-2 Report, 22/11/44.
12. 4th Inf Div, G-2 Reports 23 & 25/11/44 ; V Corps, G-2 Reports, 26 & 27/11/44 ; VII Corps, G-2 Reports, 23 & 29/11/44.
13. BA-MA RH 19 IX/13, Morning, noon, evening reports, H.Gr. B dated 24/11/44.
14. The division was officially renamed on 3 November 1944. However, soldiers stated

that the their division was renamed on 25 November. (Tessin: Verbände und Truppen, Bd. 6, p.118 and Bd. 9, p.344).

15. 4th Inf Div, G-2 Report, 25/11/44 ; 4th Inf Div, AAR, 16/11 - 07/12/44 ; VII Corps, G-2 Report, 25/11/44 ; 1st Army, G-2 IPW Report, 02/12/44.

16. 4th Inf Div, G-2 Reports, 25 & 26/11/44 ; 4th Inf Div, AAR, 16/11 - 07/12/44 ; VII Corps, G-2-Report, 25/11/44.

17. 4th Inf Div, G-2 Report, 25/11/44 ; V Corps, G-2 Report, 26/11/44.

18. BA-MA RH 10/107, General der Panzertruppen, p.5 ; BA-MA RH 10/350, General der Panzertruppen, p.78 ; BA-MA RH 10/219, General der Panzertruppen, p.118 ff ; VII Corps, G-2 Report, 19/12/44 ; 1st Army, G-2 Report, 23/12/44 ; Interrogation report of St.Gefr. Kurt Kuhs, 1./Sturmpanzer-Abteilung 217, PW IB No 1/40 dated 12/03/45.

19. 4th Inf Div, G-2 Report, 26/11/44.

20. 4th Inf Div, G-2 Report, 26/11/44 ; 4th Inf Div, AAR, 16/11 - 07/12/44 ; VII Corps, G-2 Report, 26/11/44 ; 1st Army, G-2 IPW Report, 01/12/44.

21. 4th Inf Div, G-2 Report, 26/11/44 ; 4th Inf Div, AAR, 16/11 - 07/12/44 ; V Corps, G-2 Report, 27 & 29/11/44 ; 1st Army, G-2 IPW Report, 01/12/44.

22. 4th Inf Div, G-2 Report, 02/12/44 ; 1st Army, G-2 IPW Report, 03 & 05/12/44 ; OB West: Tagesmeldung dated 28/11/44 in Hohenstein: Hölle im Hürtgenwald, p.190

23. 4th Inf Div, G-2 Report, 27/11/44 ; 4th Inf Div, AAR, 16/11 - 07/12/44 ; V Corps, G-2 Report, 28/11/44 ; VII Corps, G-2 Report, 27/11./44.

24. V Corps, G-2 Report, 28/11/44.

25. Panzerschütze Eustachius Tkaczyk must have joined the battalion in autumn 1944. He came from 2./ Panzer-Ersatz-Abteilung 18 in Kamenz and is buried today in the Hürtgenwald war cemetery (Register of the war cemetery in Hürtgenwald).

26. 4th Inf Div, AAR, 16/11 - 07/12/44 ; V Corps, G-2 Report, 29/11/44 ; VII Corps, G-2 Reports, 28/11 & 01/12/44 ; 1st Army, G-2 IPW Report, 05/12/44.

27. V Corps, G-2 Report, 29/11/44.

28. 4th Inf Div, G-2-Report, 29/11/44 ; Haslob: Ein Blick zurück in die Eifel, p.178.

29. Data File Stu.Pz.Abt.217: Leutnant Max Moritz Paul Pörschmann, reported wounded in action on 28/11/44. Awarded the Iron Cross 2nd Class on 12/12/44.

30. 4th Inf Div, G-2 Report, 30/11/44 ; V Corps, G-2 Report, 29/11/44 ; BA-MA RH 19 IX/13, Morning, noon, evening reports H.Gr. B dated 28/11/44.

31. Data File Stu.Pz.Abt.217: Unteroffizier Herbert Schimanski reported wounded in action on 29/11/44. The next day, he died from his wounds at the casualty station in Kelz.

32. 4th Inf Div, G-2 Report, 29/11/44 ; V Corps, G-2 Report, 30/11/44 ; VII Corps, G-2 Report, 29/11/44 ; 1st Army, G-2 IPW Report, 01/12/44; BA-MA RH 19 IX/13, Morning, noon, evening reports H.Gr. B dated 29/11/44.

33. 4th Inf Div, G-2 Report, 30/11/44 ; 4th Inf Div, AAR, 16/11 - 07/12/44 ; V Corps, G-2 Reports, 30/11, 01 - 03/12/44; VII Corps, G-2 Report, 29/11/44 ; 1st Army, G-2 IPW Reports, 01 & 02/12/44 ; BA-MA RH 19 IX/13, Morning, noon, evening reports H.Gr. B dated 29/11/44; Memo Telephone Conversations Gerhard Buntrock, StuG.Brig.

34. BA-MA RH 19 IX/13, Morning, noon, evening reports H.Gr. B dated 29/11/44; BA-MA RH 24-81, Combat report LXXXI A.K. dated 29/11/44.

35. 4th Inf Div, G-2 Report, 30/11/44 ; V Corps, G-2 Reports, 30/11, 01 & 02/12/44 ; VII Corps, G-2 Reports, 29/11/44 ; 1st Army, G-2 IPW Reports 01, 03 & 04/12/44.

36. According to another report, these were 8 tanks and 4 self-propelled guns. (VII Corps, G-2 Report, 30/11/44).

37. 4th Inf Div, G-2 Report, 30/11/44; 4th Inf Div, AAR, 16/11 - 07/12/44 ; V Corps, G-2 Report, 01/12/44 ; VII Corps, G-2 Reports, 30/11 & 01/12/44 ; 1st Army, G-2 IPW-Report, 10/12/44 ; BA-MA RH 19 IX/13, Morning, noon and evening reports H.Gr. B dated 29/11/44.

38. 4th Inf Div, G-2 Report, 01/12/44 ; V Corps, G-2 Report, 03/12/44.

39. V Corps, G-2 Report, 01/12/44.

40. 4th Inf Div, G-2 Report, 01/12/44 ; 5th Armd Div, G-2 Report, 01/12/44 ; V Corps, G-2 Report, 03/12/44; VII Corps, G-2 Report, 01 - 02/12/44 ; 1st Army, G-2 IPW Reports 02, 04 & 07/12/44.

41. Data File Stu.Pz.Abt.217: Register War Cemetary Hürtgen Forest.

42. Data File Stu.Pz.Abt.217: Register War Cemetary Hürtgen Forest ; 4th Inf Div, G-2 Report, 01/12/44; 1st Army, G-2 IPW Report 13/12/44 ; 1st Army, G-2 IPW Report, 04/12/44 ; V Corps, G-2 Report, 02/12/44 ; V Corps, G-2 Report, 03/12/44 ; V Corps, G-2 Report, 04/12/44 ; 5th Armd Div, G-2 Report, 01/12/44.

43. 4th Inf Div, G-2 Report, 02/12/44 ; 5th Armd Div, G-2 Report, 02/12/44 ; VII Corps, G-2 Report, 02 & 09/12/44.

44. 4th Inf Div, G-2 Report, 02/12/44 ; 1st Army, G-2 IPW Reports, 03 & 07/12/44.

45. 330th Inf Rgt, AAR, December 1944, p.2.

46. 1st Army, G-2 IPW Report, 03/12/44 ; BA-MA RH 19 IX/13, Morning, noon, evening reports H.Gr. B dated 02/12/44 ; KTB Gren.Rgt.981, 02/12/44; Hohenstein/Trees: Hölle in Hürtgenwald, p.202.

47. 4th Inf Div, G-2 Report, 02/12/44; 5th Armd Div, G-2 Report, 02/12/44 ; V Corps, G-2 Report, 04/12/44.

48. 5th Arm Div, G-2 Report, 02/12/44 ; V Corps, G-2 Report, 03/12/44 ; VII Corps, G-2 Report, 02/12/44 ; 1st Army, G-2 IPW Report, 03/12/44 & 06/12/44.

49. KTB Gren.Rgt.981, 03 & 04/12/1944.

50. 4th Inf Div, G-2 Reports, 03 & 04/12/44 ; VII Corps, G-2 Report, 03/12/44; 330th Inf Rgt, AAR, December 1944, p.1.

51. 4th Inf Div, G-2 Report, 03 & 04/12/44 ; V Corps, G-2 Report, 04 & 05/12/44 ; VII Corps, G-2 Report, 03/12/44; 1st Army G-2 IPW Report, 08/12/44.

52. KTB Gren.Rgt.981, 03/12/44.

53. 330th Inf Rgt, AAR, December 1944, p.1 ; 4th Inf Div, G-2 Report, 03/12/44; 1st Army, G-2 IPW Report, 04/12/44.

54. 4th Inf Div, G-2 Report, 04/12/44 ; 5th Armd Div, G-2 Report, 03/12/44 ; V Corps, G-2 Reports, 04 & 05/12/44 ; VII Corps, G-2 Report, 06/12/44 ; 1st Army, G-2 IPW Report, 04/12/44 ; Christoffel: Krieg am Westwall 1944/45, p.202.

55. KTB Gren.Rgt.981, 04/12/44.

56. Ibid.

57. VII Corps, G-2 Report, 04/12/44 ; KTB Gren.Rgt.981, 04/12/44.

58. 330th Inf Rgt, AAR, December 1944, p.1 f ; 4th Inf Div, G-2 Report, 04/12/44 ; 1st Army G-2 IPW Reports, 07 & 09/12/44.

59. The German sources mentioned Füs.Btl.363. This is most likely a typo as all other sources report Füs.Btl.353 in this sector. (KTB Gren.Rgt.981, 04/12/44).

60. VII Corps, G-2 Report, 04/12/44 ; KTB Gren.Rgt.981, 04/12/44.

61. KTB Gren.Rgt.981, 04/12/44.

62. 5th Armd Div, G-2 Report, 04/12/44; V Corps, G-2 Report, 05/12/44 ; 1st Army, G-2 IPW Report, 05/12/1944 ; Mehner: Die geheimen Tagesberichte der deutschen Wehrmachtsführung im II. Weltkrieg 1939-45, Vol. 11, Karte: Heeresgruppe B vom 04/12/44.

63. KTB Gren.Rgt.981, 05/12/44.

64. 330th Inf Rgt, AAR, December 1944, p.1f ; 4th Inf Div, G-2 Reports, 05 & 06/12/44 ; VII Corps, G-2 Reports, 05 & 06/12/44 ; 1st Army, G-2 IPW Reports, 06 & 09/12/44 ; KTB Gren.Rgt.981, 05/12/44.

65. Data File Stu.Pz.Abt.217: OLt. Johannes Tetzner, transferred on 27/09/44 from Pz. Ers.u.Ausb.Abt.18 to 1./ Stu.Pz.Abt.217, wounded on 14/12/44 (did not stay with the troops).

66. 4th Inf Div, G-2 Report, 06/12/44 ; 1st Army, G-2 IPW Report, 06/12/44 ; KTB Gren. Rgt.981, 05/12/44.

67. Data File Stu.Pz.Abt.217: Lt. Werner Böhme, was transferred on 27/09/1944 from Pz.Ers.u.Ausb.Abt.18 to 1./ Stu.Pz.Abt.217, later platoon leader in the 2./ Stu. Pz.Abt.217. Iron Cross 2nd Class on 12/12/44.

68. KTB Gren.Rgt.981, 05/12/44 ; Data File Stu.Pz.Abt.217.

69. 330th Inf Rgt, AAR, December 1944, p.1f ; 4th Inf Div, G-2 Report, 05/12/44. According to the 'Panzerlage West', the company had 14 combat ready Jagdpanzer 38(t) Hetzer. on 05/12/44. (RW 4 v 636, Panzerlage West 1944/45).

70. The interrogation of members of Pz.Jg.Abt.1277, who were captured on 10 December revealed some interesting details about Panzerjäger -Abteilungen 1272 and 1277. Pz.Jg.Abt.1277 was established in Czechoslovakia and was equipped with 14 Panzerjäger 'Hetzer'. The 277.V.G.Div. reinforced the battalion, which actually only had the strength of a company, with 6-8 2cm Flaks on trucks. For the protection of the tanks, all three Grenadier regiments of the division each had to deliver about 14-15 men, also the Pi.Btl.277 assigned 12 men for the Panzerbegleitzug. Four soldiers each were assigned to protect a tank hunter. The Pz.Jg.Abt.1277 had the following structure:

Kompanietrupp with 2 Jagdpanzers
I. Zug with 4 Jagdpanzers
II. Zug with 4 Jagdpanzers
III. Zug with 4 Jagdpanzers
Grenadier-Begleit-Zug with 55-60 men
Flak-Zug with 6-8 2cm Flak

Due to high losses in the identically structured Pz.Jg.Abt.1272, the battalion was relocated to the Bergstein area. Between 5 and 7 December, Pz.Jg.Abt.1277 lost 10 Jagdpanzers and Pz.Jg.Abt.1272 lost 6 Jagdpanzers (V Corps, G-2, 10/12/44 ; V Corps, G-2 Report, 11/12/44).

71. According to the 'Panzerlage West', the Brigade had 22 combat-ready Sturmgeschütze on 05/12/44 (RW 4 v 636, Panzerlage West 1944/45).

72. 4th Inf Div, G-2 Report, 06/12/44 ; 5th Armd Div, G-2 Report, 05/12/44 ; V Corps, G-2 Report, 06/12/44 ; 1st Army, G-2 IPW Report, 06/12/44 ; BA-MA RH 19 IX/13, Morning, noon, evening reports H.Gr. B dated 05/12/44; Haslob: 89.Inf.Div., p. 195 ; Hohenstein: Hölle im Hürtgenwald, p.202.

73. 629th TD Bn, AAR, December 1944, p. 3 ; 330th Inf Rgt, AAR, December 1944, p. 2 ; 4th Inf Div, G-2 Report, 06/12/44; 5th Armd Div, G-2 Report, 06/12/44 ; VII Corps, G-2-Report, 06/12/44 ; KTB Gren.Rgt.981, 06/12/44.

74. V Corps, G-2 Report, 07/12/44 ; BA-MA RH 19 IX/13, Morning, noon, evening reports H.Gr. B dated 06/12/44 ; BA-MA WF03-4694, KTB OB West, Vol. 2, p.131 ; Hohenstein: Hölle im Hürtgenwald, p.203.

75. VII Corps, G-2 Report, 08/12/44 ; KTB Gren.Rgt.981, 07/12/44.

76. 629th TD Bn, AAR, December 1944, p.3 ; 330th Inf Rgt, AAR, December 1944, p.2 ; 331st Inf Rgt, AAR, December 1944, p.5 ; 1st Army, G-2 IPW Reports, 08 & 09/12/44.

77. 83rd Inf Div, G-2 Report, December dated 01/01/45.

78. 5th Armd Div, G-2 Report, 07/12/44 ; 1st Army, G-2 IPW Report, 08 & 09/12/44 ; BA-MA RH 19 IX/13, Morning, noon, evening reports H.Gr. B dated 07/12/44 ; Christoffel: Krieg am Westwall 1944/45, p.202 ; Hohenstein: Hölle im Hürtgenwald, p.203.

79. According to another source, 1 officer and 22 enlisted men were captured (83rd Inf Div, G-2 Report December 1944 dated 01/01/45).

80. 330th Inf Rgt, AAR, December 1944, p.2 ; 331st Inf Rgt, AAR, December 1944, p.5 ; 83rd Inf Div, G-2 Report December 1944 dated 01/01/45.

81. 1st Army, G-2 IPW-Reports, 11 & 12/12/44.

82. BA-MA RH 10/219, p.118 ff.

83. Data File Stu.Pz.Abt.217: Obergefreiter Paul Wolff was transferred from St./ Stu. Pz.Abt.217 to 1./ Stu.Pz.Abt.217 on 13/09/44. His remains were buried in the Hürtgen Forest military cemetery.

84. 5th Armd Div, G-2 Report, 08/12/44 ; V Corps, G-2 Report, 09/12/44 ; BA-MA RH 19 IX/13, Morning, noon, evening reports H.Gr. B dated 08/12/44.

85. BA-MA WF03-4694, KTB OB West, Vol. 3, p.45.

86. 629th TD Bn, AAR, December 1944, p.5 ; 330th Inf Rgt, AAR, December 1944, p.3 ; 331st Inf Rgt, AAR, December 1944, p.5 ; 83rd Inf Div, G-2 Report December 1944 dated 01/01/45 ; VII Corps, G-2 Report, 09/12/44 ; 1st Army, G-2 IPW Reports 10 & 11/12/44.

87. 1st Army, G-2 IPW Reports, 10 & 11/12/44.

88. The Fs.Jg.Rgt.6 consisted of 3 battalions, a 13.Kp. (120mm grenade launcher) and a 14.Kp. (composition unknown, possibly Panzerjäger). The regimental command post under Colonel von der Heydte was in Untermaubach, while the command post of II./Fs.Jg.Rgt.6 was in Bogheim. The companies of the II. Bataillon had a strength of 60-100 men. For each company there were 2 platoons with 2 squads, per squad one light MG, some semi-automatic weapons, otherwise carbines. The heavy company had about five or six 81mm mortars and 5 heavy MGs. The few heavy MGs were mostly old 08/15 models. Members of the 7. Kompanie, who fell into American captivity on 10 December, said that the company had a strength of 96 men in the morning, but only 12 were former paratroopers. The rest of the company is said to have been made of young and inexperienced air-defence personnel; mostly Luftwaffe technicians without combat experience. In addition, 5-6 assault guns from an unknown SS unit had recently been assigned (G2-Report, V Corps, Nr. 186, 11/12/44 ; G2-Report, VII Corps, Nr. 190, 12/12/44 ; G2-Report, VII Corps, Nr. 191, 13/12/44).

89. 331st Inf Rgt, AAR, December 1944, p.6 ; 774th Tk Bn, AAR December 1944, p.7 ff ; 83rd Inf Div, G-2 Report December 1944 dated 01/01/45 ; VII Corps, G-2 Report, 10/12/44 ; 1st Army, G-2 IPW Reports, 13 & 15/12/44 ; BA-MA RH 19 IX/13, Morning, noon, evening reports H.Gr. B dated 10/12/44.

90. The American sources reported tanks or assault guns instead of assault tanks.

91. 330th Inf Rgt, AAR, December 1944, p.3 ; 774th Tk Bn, AAR, December 1944, p.7 f ; 83rd Inf Div, G-2 Report, December 1944 dated 01/01/45 ; 1st Army, G-2 IPW Report, 14/12/44.

92. VII Corps, G-2 Report, 10/12/44 ; 1st Army, G-2 IPW Report, 14/12/44.

93. Data File Stu.Pz.Abt.217: Major Eberhard Lemor was the battalion's commanding officer until October 1944. He returned on 14 December, but only temporarily remained in command. It is an educated guess that he was on sick leave in November/December 1944, and that OLt. Josef Gauglitz was his substitute. In January 1945, he officially handed over to Hauptmann von Trotha.

94. Data File Stu.Pz.Abt.217: OLt. Hans Bruno Schulte, commanding officer of the tank maintenance platoon.

95. 1st Army, G-2 IPW-Report, 13/12/44 ; 9th Army, G-2 Report, 14/12/44.

96. Data File Stu.Pz.Abt.217: OLt. Gero von der Schulenburg, 1./ Stu.Pz.Abt.217, reported wounded on 15/11/44 in Obermaubach.

97. Data File Stu.Pz.Abt.217: Lt. Günther Schmidt, 2./ Stu.Pz.Abt.217 ; V Corps, G-2 Report, 12/12/44.

98. Data File Stu.Pz.Abt.217: OLt. Josef Gauglitz, Kp.Fhr. commanding officer 1./ Stu. Pz.Abt.217, commanding officer of Stu.Pz.Abt.217 in November/December 1944,

despite injury in November he stayed with the battalion until he was finally sent to a hospital on 14 December.

99. 5th Armd Div, G-2 Report, 10/12/44 ; VII Corps, G-2 Report, 12/12/44 ; 1st Army, G-2 IPW Report, 13/12/44.

100. BA-MA RH 10/107, General der Panzertruppen, p.7.

101. 774th Tk Bn, AAR, December 1944, p.8 ; 331st Inf Rgt, AAR, December 1944, p.6 ; 83rd Inf Div, G-2 Report December 1944 dated 01/01/45 ; V Corps, G-2 Report, 13/12/44 ; VII Corps, G-2 Report, 11/12/44 ; 1st Army, G-2 IPW Report, 13/12/44.

102. 330th Inf Rgt, AAR, December 1944, p.4 ; 774th Tk Bn, AAR, December 1944, p.8 ; 83rd Inf Div, G-2 Report December 1944 dated 01/01/45 ; V Corps, G-2 Reports, 12 & 13/12/44 ; VII Corps, G-2 Report, 11/12/44 ; Intelligence Summary V Corps, 11/12/44 ; 1st Army, G-2 IPW Report, 14/12/44.

103. Data File Stu.Pz.Abt.217: Gefreiter Josef Horaczeck was reported killed in action in Kelz on 11/12/44.

104. Also named 'self-propelled' in the same source (VII Corps, G-2 Report, 12/12/44).

105. 774th Tk Bn, AAR, December 1944, p.8 ; 331st Inf Rgt, AAR, December 1944, p.6 ; V Corps, G-2 Report, 13/12/44 ; VII Corps, G-2 Report, 12/12/44.

106. 774th Tk Bn, AAR, December 1944, p.8 ; 629th TD Bn, AAR, December 1944, p.6 ; 330th Inf Rgt, AAR, December 1944, p.4 ; V Corps, G-2 Report, 14/12/1944 ; VII Corps, G-2 Report, 12/12/44 ; 1st Army, G-2 IPW Report, 13/12/44.

107. 331st Inf Rgt, AAR, December 1944, p.6 ; 774th Tk Bn, AAR, December 1944, p.9 ; 629th TD Bn, AAR, December 1944, p.3 ; V Corps, G-2 Reports, 13 & 14/12/44 ; VII Corps, G-2 Reports, 11 & 13/12/44 ; 1st Army, G-2 IPW Report, 13/12/44.

108. 330th Inf Rgt, AAR, December 1944, p.4 ; 331st Inf Rgt, AAR, December 1944, p.6 ; 629th TD Bn, AAR, December 1944, p.3 ; 774th Tk Bn, AAR, December 1944, p.9 ; VII Corps, G-2 Report, 13/12/44.

109. 331st Inf Rgt, AAR, December 1944, p.7 ; 774th Tk Bn, AAR, December 1944, p.9 f ; V Corps, G-2 Report, 15/12/44 ; VII Corps, G-2-Report, 14/12/44.

110. V Corps, G-2 Report, 13/12/44 ; VII Corps, G-2 Reports 11 & 14/12/44 ; 1st Army, G-2 IPW Reports, 13 & 15/12/44.

111. 330th Inf Rgt, AAR, December 1944, p.5 ; 774th TK Bn, AAR, December 1944 p.10 ; VII Corps, G-2 Report, 14/12/44.

112. Data File Stu.Pz.Abt.217: Hauptmann Josef Gauglitz had his left leg in a cast since the end of November. If the injury was related to his hospitalization on 14 December is not known.

113. Data File Stu.Pz.Abt.217: Oberleutnant Johannes Tetzner, reported WIA and evacuated on 14/12/44, but no place of injury mentioned.

114. Data File Stu.Pz.Abt.217: Leutnant Gerhard Jacob Michael Beduwé, reported KIA on 14/12/44, but no place of death mentioned. It remains unclear where Beduwé's remains are as he is not listed in any of the war cemeteries in the region.

115. 330th Inf Rgt, AAR, December 1944, p.5 ; 774th Tk Bn, AAR, December 1944, p.10 ; 5th Armd Div, AAR, December 1944 ; VII Corps, G-2-Report, 15/12/44.

116. 331st Inf Rgt, AAR, December 1944, p.7 ; 774th Tk Bn, AAR, December 1944, p.10 ;

5th Armd Div, AAR, December 1944 ; VII Corps, G-2 Report, 15/12/44.

117. V Corps, G-2 Report, 16/12/44.

118. 330th Inf Rgt, AAR, December 1944 ; 331st Inf Rgt, AAR, December 1944 ; 5th Armd Div, AAR, December 1944.

119. BA-MA RH 19 IX/13, Morning, noon, evening reports H.Gr. B dated 17/12/44.

120. Named in the report as '150mm assault gun on Panzer IV chassis'.

121. VII Corps, G-2 Report, 19/12/44 ; 1st Army, G-2 IPW Report, 23/12/44.

122. The 'Deutsche Wochenschau' No. 743.

123. The 'Deutsche Wochenschau' No. 746.

124. Newspaper 'Znaimer Tagesblatt' issue 19/12/44.

125. BA-MA, Master card of Josef Gauglitz ; Wegmann: Ritterkreuzträger der Panzerwaffe, pages 93 ff.

126. VII Corps, G-2 Periodic Report, 14/11/44; Diary of Eugen Welti, Heeres-Pionier-Bataillon 73 via Doug Nash; www.wetterzentrale.de

127. The German report mentioned 'Sturmhaubitzen' but Panzer-Lehr-Division did not have 'Sturmhaubitzen' in its inventory by that time. Considering that 2./Stu.Pz.Abt. 218 z.b.V. was assigned to Pz.L.Div., it is the authors' belief that these 'Sturmhaubitzen' were actually the two remaining Sturmpanzer IVs of 2./Stu.Pz.Abt.218 z.b.V.

128. BA-MA RH 10/26, General der Panzertruppen, Organizational reports ; BA-MA RH 10/90, Generalinspekteur der Panzertruppen, Reports to the Führer ; BA-MA RH 10/349, General der Panzertruppen, Tank allocation lists for 1944/45; BA-MA RH 24-80/68, KTB LXXX A.K. ; NARA T311, R018, Activity reports General der Panzertruppen West; NARA T311, R003, Operational reports Heeresgruppe B, September 1944; NARA, 4th Inf Div, G-2 Reports, August-September 1944; Interrogation report of St.Gefr. Kurt Kuhs, 1./Stu.Pz.Abt.217, PW IB No 1/40 dated 12/03/45 ; Schadewitz: Geschichte der Panzer-Ersatz- und Ausbildungs-Abteilung 11, Münster 1989.

129. BA-MA RH 10/219, General der Panzertruppen, Sturmpanzerabteilungen, page 113 ; Interrogation report of St.Gefr. Kurt Kuhs, 1./Stu.Pz.Abt.217, PW IB No 1/40 dated 12/03/45.

130. NARA RG 407, 101-2.2-2.3, G2 Records, Box 1497; First Army PWI Report No. 12, 22 & 23/12/44 ; Statement Oskar Klein, dated 24/09/2005 ; Statements Roland Dusi between 12 & 17/11/2007 ; Interrogation report of St.Gefr. Kurt Kuhs, 1./Stu.Pz.Abt.217, PW IB No 1/40 dated 12/03/45; BA-MA RH, 10/351, General der Panzertruppen, page 77 f.

Chapter 06

1. BA-MA, RW 4 v. 636, Summary of the independent tank, assault guns, and tank destroyer units in the area of the OB West, dated 22/11/44.

2. BA-MA, RW 4 v 636, Tank situation West 1944/45, report dated 05/12/44.

3. Schramm: War diary of the OKW, volume 7, pages 446 f.

4. Panzer Marsch, Vol. 2, April 1997, Sturmpanzer Abteilung 217, page 16.

5. BA-MA, RH 10/219, General der Panzertruppen, pages 118 ff.

6. BA-MA, RH 10/219, General der Panzertruppen, pages 118 ff.

7. BA-MA, RH 10/107, General der Panzertruppen, page 7.

8. BA-MA, RH 10/107, General der Panzertruppen, page 9.

9. BA-MA, RH 10/219, General der Panzertruppen, page 122.

10. BA-MA, RH 10/350, General der Panzertruppen, page 78.

11. BA-MA, RH 10/350, General der Panzertruppen, page 77.

12. GDIR, Findbuch 12451, OKH, Gen.d.Pz.Tr., Akte 493, p.4.

13. NARA, T-78, Roll 720, Frame 727.

14. Parker: Battle of the Bulge, S. 310 ; Quarrie: The Ardennes Offensive, VI Panzer Armee, page 39.

15. Interrogation report St.Gefr. Kurt Kuhs, 1./Sturmpanzer-Abteilung 217, PW IB No 1/40 dated 12/03/45.

16. BA-MA, RH 10/219, General der Panzertruppen, page 123.

17. Datafile: Sturmpanzer-Abteilung 217 ; Statement Oskar Klein, dated 24/09/2005 ; Statements Roland Dusi between 12 & 17/11/2007.

18. The author Bruce Quarrie (The Ardennes Offensive, VI Panzer Armee, page 39) mentioned in his book about the fighting in the area of 6. Panzer-Armee an order of battle with two combat companies, but did not provide a source for his statement.

19. Schramm: War diary of the OKW, volume 7, page 446 f.

20. Dupuy: Hitler's Last Gamble, page 442 ; Quarrie: The Ardennes Offensive, VI Panzer Armee, page 39.

21. BA-MA, RH 19 IX/13, Morning, noon, afternoon reports H.Gr. B, dated 17/12/44 ; NARA, T-311, Roll 31, Frame 7038648, Daily report OB West for 17/12/44, dated 18/12/44.

22. Statement Vincent Kuhlbach, dated 29 & 30/09/2002.

23. Statement Oskar Klein, dated 24/09/2005.

24. Interrogation report St.Gefr. Kurt Kuhs, 1./ Sturmpanzer-Abteilung 217, PW IB No 1/40 dated 12/03/45.

25. The war diary of Heeresgruppe B misleadingly recorded on 21/12/44 that I. SS-Panzer-Korps was in charge of the attack, but the war diary of the OB West corrected this error the next day. On 18 December, Panzer-Armee-Oberkommando 6 had assigned the infantry divisions of I. SS-Panzer-Korps to LXVII Armee-Korps in order to free the staff of I. SS-Panzer-Korps, which had to keep pace with the 1.SS-Pz. Div. after the successful breakthrough of Kampfgruppe Peiper on 17 December. This new assignment had to be canceled after it was realized that the staff of LXVII Armee-Korps had become inoperable for several days after an air attack on 17 December. Command of the German units in the area of Losheim-Büllingen-Krinkelt-Rocherath was therefore assigned to II. SS-Panzer-Korps, which remained in command until 18:00 on 22 December, when II. SS-Panzer-Korps was relieved and ordered to take over command of 2. and 9.SS-Pz.Div. again (BA-MA, RH 19

IX/13, Morning, noon, afternoon reports H.Gr. B dated 21 & 22/12/44 ; NARA, T311, Roll R031, Frame 7038809, Daily report OB West for 21/12/44, dated 22/12/44 ; Pallud: Battle of the Bulge, Then and Now, page 96).

26. BA-MA, RH 19 IX/13, Morning, noon, afternoon reports H.Gr. B dated 22/12/44 ; Engel: Alte Kameraden, volume 6/76, page 27 ; Pallud: Battle of the Bulge, Then and Now, page 96.

27. OB West, Situation map France, 21 - 22/12/44.

28. Dupuy: Hitler's Last Gamble, page 442 ; Quarrie: The Ardennes Offensive, VI Panzer Armee, page 39.

29. Kompanie Kameradschaft: Die 3. Kompanie, page 96.

30. Ibid., pages 96-100.

31. BA-MA, RS 7/86, Letter Willy Kretzschmar to Hubert Meyer, dated 27/10/80.

32. BA-MA, RS 7/86, Letter Heinz Müller to Hubert Meyer, dated 17/06/80.

33. Wijers: Ardennenoffensive, Vol. 3, page 154.

34. Interrogation report St.Gefr. Kurt Kuhs, 1./Stu.Pz.Abt.217, PW IB No 1/40 dated 12/03/45.

35. Wijers: Ardennenoffensive, Volume 3, page 153.

36. BA-MA, RH 19 IV-85, Attachments to the war diary of OB West, page 23 ; Quarrie: The Ardennes Offensive, VI Panzer Armee, page 49 ; Pallud: Battle of the Bulge, page 103.

37. Daily report OB West, dated 28/12/44 ; BA-MA, RH 10/219, General der Panzertruppen, page 122 ; Haslob: Ein Blick zurück in die Eifel, page 212.

38. 1st Inf Div, FUSA Report, 18/02/45.

39. BA-MA, RH 10/219, General der Panzertruppen, page 122.

40. BA-MA, RH 10/219, General der Panzertruppen, page 122.

41. BA-MA, RH 10/219, General der Panzertruppen, page 123.

42. BA-MA, RH 10/219, General der Panzertruppen, pages 122 ff.

43. BA-MA, RH 10/219, General der Panzertruppen, page 122.

44. BA-MA, RH 10/219, General der Panzertruppen, page 122.

45. BA-MA, RH 10/219, General der Panzertruppen, pages 124 ff.

46. BA-MA, RH 10/352, General der Panzertruppen, page 56

47. KStN 1107 d (f.G.) dated 01/09/44.

48. BA-MA, Master Card Claus von Trotha ; Magazine Panzer Marsch, No. 2, April 1997, Sturmpanzer Abteilung 217, page 10.

49. Interrogation report St.Gefr. Kurt Kuhs, 1./ Sturmpanzer-Abteilung 217, PW IB No 1/40 dated 12/03/45.

50. Roppelt: 3.Fs.Jg.Div., page 515.

51. First reports of 30th Inf Div, as well as of XVIII AB Corps, claimed a full battalion of infantry attacked Company G. The AAR of 120th Inf Rgt clearly mentioned that only about 100 paratroopers had attacked; the equivalent of a company (NARA XVIII. AB Corps, G-2 Report, dated 13/01/45).

52. The battalion officially arrived for rebuilding in Mielau, East Prussia, on 3 October. By this time, the battalion was only composed of the Staff, the Staff Company, and the 1st Company. The Commanding Officer was Major Schweiger, and in command of 1./Pz.Jg.Abt.348 was Lieutenant Schmidt. While in Mielau, 10 Sturmgeschütze IV were allocated on 4 November. These assault guns left the ordnance depot on 10 November and arrived four days later, bringing the Company up to full strength. It is unclear when the decision was taken to attach the battalion to 3.Fs. Jg.Div., but on 17 December it left Mielau by rail for transfer to the Western Front. According to an official report to the General der Panzertruppen, the battalion still had 10 assault guns on 15 January 1945: 8 combat-ready and 2 in maintenance. As this report officially showed the actual tank strength of all German units in the West on 1 January 1945, it is highly likely that the figures provided by 3.Fs. Jg.Div. showed the strength of the battalion before its first commitment in Thirimont on 13 January (BA-MA, RH 10/106, General der Panzertruppen, page 6 f ; BA-MA, RH 10/109, General der Panzertruppen, Page 49 ; 30th Inf Div, G-2 Report, 15/01/45 ; BA-MA, RH 10/106, General der Panzertruppen, page 6 f ; BA-MA, RH 10/350, General der Panzertruppen, page 36 ; BA-MA, RH 10/352, General der Panzertruppen, page 34).

53. 120th Inf Rgt, AAR, January 1945, page 100 f ; NARA, XVIII AB Corps, G-2 Report, dated 13/01/45, NARA, 1st Inf Div, G-2 Jnl, 14/01/45 ; Roppelt: 3.Fs.Jg.Div., page 491.

54. NARA, 120th Inf Rgt, AAR, January 1945, page 100 ff.

55. G-2 Journal, 1st Inf Div, 14/01/45.

56. The G-2 journal of the 1st Inf Div gives inconsistent figures. It is also likely that only 100 paratroopers and 5 tanks launched the German counterattack.

57. The Americans claimed to have captured 52 men from I./Fs.Jg.Rgt.9 and 4 men of 15.(Pi.)/Fs.Jg.Rgt.9 on 14 January 1945 (NARA, 30th Inf Div, G-2 Report, 14/01/45).

58. NARA, 1st Inf Div, G-2 Journal, 14/01/45 ; NARA, 30th Inf Div, G-2 Report, 14/01/45 ; NARA, XVIII AB Corps, G-2 Report, dated 14/01/45 ; NARA, 23rd Inf Rgt, IPW-Report, 17/01/45.

59. NARA, 1st Inf Div, G-2 Jnl, 14/01/45 ; NARA, 30th Inf Div, G-2 Report, 14/01/45 ; 120th Inf Rgt, AAR, January 1945, p.102 f.

60. The brigade was raised in Jüteborg (Army District III) on 15 December 1942 as Sturmgeschütz-Abteilung 905 with three batteries. The unit received field post number 48027. On 27 July 1943 the replacement unit, to which the brigade was assigned, changed to Sturmgeschütz-Ersatz- und Ausbildungs-Abteilung 400, located in Frederikshavn (Army District X) in Denmark. On 14 February 1944 the brigade was renamed Sturmgeschütz-Brigade 905. The unit was engaged in late August / early September in Romania, in the area of Jassy-Kishinev, where it was annihilated by Russian forces. In November, the decision was made to rebuild the brigade, and on 23 November it was officially renamed Heeres-Sturmartillerie-Brigade 905. The brigade was reconstructed at Neisse (Army District VIII) in Silesia with four Batteries and an overall strength of 750 men. Twenty-two Sturmgeschütze III and nine Sturmhaubitzen III were allocated to the 1st, 2nd and 3rd Battery. The 4th Battery was a Grenadier Escort Company. The brigade

arrived in the West around 14 January 1945 and was immediately engaged north of Sankt-Vith (Tessin: Verbände und Truppen, Vol. 13, page 111 ; Information provided by Martin Block ; NARA, G-2 Report, 30th Inf Div, dated 16/01/45 ; NARA, G-2 Reports XVIII AB Corps, dated 19, 23, & 25/01/45).

61. NARA, 1st Inf Div, G-2 Jnl, 15/01/45 ; NARA, XVIII AB Corps, G-2 Report, dated 14/01/45.

62. NARA, 1st Inf Div, G-2 Jnl, 15 & 16/01/45 ; NARA, 30th Inf Div, G-2 Report, 15/01/45 ; NARA, XVIII AB Corps, G-2 Report, 15/01/45 ; 120th Inf Rgt, AAR, January 1945 page 103 f ; Information provided by B. Mackenzie on 18/04/99.

63. NARA, 1st Inf Div, G-2 Jnl, 15/01/45 ; NARA, 1st Inf Div, G-2 Report, 20/01/45.

64. NARA, 1st Inf Div, G-2 Jnl, 15 & 16/01/45 ; 23rd Inf Rgt, IPW Report, 17/01/45.

65. NARA, 1st Inf Div, G-2 Jnl, 15/01/45.

66. The company was without anti-tank guns and used in this area as infantry (NARA, G-2 Journal, 1st Inf Div, 16/01/45).

67. NARA, 1st Inf Div, G-2 Journal, 15 & 16/01/45.

68. NARA, 1st Inf Div, G-2 Journal, 15 & 16/01/45, ; NARA, 1st Inf Div, G-2 Report, 20/01/45.

69. NARA, 1st Inf Div, G-2 Journal, 15 & 16/01/45 ; NARA, 1st Inf Div, G-2 Report, 20/01/45, Roppelt: 3.Fs.Jg.Div., page 619.

70. NARA, 1st Inf Div, G-2 Journal, 15 & 16/01/45 ; NARA, 1st Inf Div, G-2 Report, 20/01/45.

71. GDIR, Findbuch 12451, OKH/Gen.Insp.d.Pz.Tr., Akte 501

72. NARA, 30th Inf Div, G-2 Report, 16/01/45 ; 120th Inf Rgt, AAR, page 105.

73. The PW provided the name of the commander of the 4. Batterie as well as the information that this battery was composed of three platoons. He went on to say that one platoon was attached to each assault gun battery in combat, to protect the guns against enemy infantry. Other information on the order of battle of the three other batteries was imprecise.

74. NARA, 30th Inf Div, G-2 Report, 16/01/45.

75. NARA, 1st Inf Div, G-2 Jnl, 16/01/45.

76. NARA, 1st Inf Div, G-2 Jnl, 16 & 17/01/45, ; NARA, 1st Inf Div, G-2 Reports, 17, 18 & 20/01/45.

77. NARA, 1st Inf Div, G-2 Jnl, 16/01/45 ; NARA, 1st Inf Div, G-2 Report, 20/01/45.

78. NARA, 1st Inf Div, G-2 Jnl, 16/01/45 ; NARA, 1st Inf Div, G-2 Report, 20/01/45 ; NARA, IPW Report 16th Inf Rgt, 17/01/45.

79. NARA, 1st Inf Div, G-2 Jnl, 16/01/45 ; NARA, 1st Inf Div, G-2 Report, 20/01/45.

80. Interrogation report St.Gefr. Kurt Kuhs, 1./Sturmpanzer-Abteilung 217, PW IB No 1/40 dated 12/03/45.

81. NARA, 1st Inf Div, G-2 Report, 21/01/45 ; NARA, 1st Inf Div, G-2 Jnl, 17/01/45 ; NARA, 30th Inf Div, G-2 Report, 17/01/45, Roppelt: 3.Fs.Jg.Div., page 498.

82. NARA, G-2 Journal, 1st Inf Div, 17/01/45.

83. NARA, G-2 Journal, 1st Inf Div, 17/01/45.

84. NARA, G-2 Report No. 216, 1st Inf Div, 21/01/45.

85. NARA, G-2 Report No. 212, 1st Inf Div, 17/01/45.

86. NARA, 1st Inf Div, G-2 Reports, 17 & 18/01/45 ; NARA, 30th Inf Div, G-2 Report, 17/01/45 ; NARA, XVIII AB Corps, G-2 Report, 19/01/45.

87. NARA, XVIII AB Corps, G-2 Report, 23/01/45, 120th Inf Rgt, AAR, January 1945, page 106.

88. The figures varied a lot, the final report of the 1st Bn, 18th Inf Rgt, mentioned a total of three towed 88mm guns, four 105mm howitzers, one half-track, one Sherman tank and an ammunition dump. The initial report mentioned two assault guns, but these were obviously the 88mm guns, mentioned in all other reports (NARA, 1st Inf Div, G-2 Report, 21/01/45).

89. The name of the Major is not mentioned in the American reports. The former commander of I./Fs.Jg.Rgt.9 was Hauptmann Fritz Schiffke who was killed on 15/01/45 (Roppelt: 3.Fs.Jg.Div., page 617).

90. NARA, 1st Inf Div, G-2 Report, 18/01/45 ; NARA, 1st Inf Div, G-2 Jnl, 18/01/45.

91. NARA, 1st Inf Div, G-2 Report, 18/01/45 ; NARA, 1st Inf Div, G-2 Jnl, 18/01/45.

92. NARA, V Corps, G-2 Report, 19/01/45 ; NARA, 1st Inf Div, G-2 Reports, 18, 19 & 21/01/45 ; NARA, 1st Inf Div, G-2 Jnl 18/01/45 ; 23rd Inf Rgt, S-2 Report, 18/01/45 ; Roppelt: 3.Fs.Jg.Div., pp.500 and 502 ; 1st Inf Div, G-2 Jnl, January-May 1945, 18/01/45.

93. NARA, 1st Inf Div, G-2 Jnl 18/01/45 ; NARA, 1st Inf Div, G-2 Jnl, 21/01/45.

94. NARA, 1st Inf Div, G-2 Jnl, 18/01/45 ; NARA, 1st Inf Div, G-2 Report, 21/01/45.

95. Some prisoners claimed that the assault guns were mounted on Mark IV chassis but German allocation lists clearly show that these statements were wrong. Other prisoners provided false information when they claimed that the 3rd Battery had self-propelled 'Werfers' attached. Other captured German soldiers finally corrected this wrong statement on 25 January (NARA, XVIII AB Corps, G-2 Reports, 19 & 25/01/45 ; NARA, 7th Armd Div, G-2 Report, 20/01/45).

96. 120th Inf Rgt, AAR, January 1945, p.106f ; 7th Armd Div, G-2 Report, 20/01/45 ; NARA, XVIII AB Corps, G-2 Reports, 19, 21 & 22/01/45.

97. After having lost 6 out of 10 assault guns by 23 January 1945, the remnants of 1./Panzerjäger-Abteilung 348 were gathered at Amel (Amblève) and ordered to return the last two combat-ready guns to Germany while the two damaged guns were in need of maintenance (NARA, 7th Armd Div, G-2 Report, 23/01/45).

98. NARA, 1st Inf Div, G-2 Reports, 19 & 21/01/45 ; NARA, 7th Armd Div, G-2 Report, 20/01/45 ; NARA, XVIII AB Corps, G-2 Report, 20/01/45 ; Roppelt: 3.Fs.Jg.Div., pp.503 f and 619 ; 1st Inf Div, G-2 Jnl, 19/01/45.

99. The self-propelled guns that had been operating at Schoppen and Am Kreuz were said to have been manned by soldiers wearing tanker's uniforms (NARA,1st Inf Div, G-2 Report, 19/01/45).

100. NARA, 1st Inf Div, G-2 Reports, 19, 20 & 21/01/45 ; Roppelt: 3.Fs.Jg.Div., pp.498 and 505ff.

101. NARA, 1st Army, G-2 Report, 01/02/45 ; British XXX Corps, Intelligence Summary No. 610, 26/02/45 ; NARA, 1st Inf Div, G2-Journal, 19/01/45.

102. NARA, 1st Inf Div, 19/01/45 ; 1st Inf Div, G-2 Jnl, 19/01/45.

103. Interrogation report St.Gefr. Kurt Kuhs, 1./Stu.Pz.Abt.217, PW IB No 1/40 dated 12/03/45 ; situation map OB West, 28/01/45.

104. G2-Report 1st Army, 01/02/45.

105. NARA, XVIII AB Corps, G-2 Report, 29/01/45 ; NARA, V Corps, G-2 Report, 30/01/45.

106. These elements probably came from the Ramscheid area, south of Hollerath. On 29/01/45, Leutnant Werner Mothes, a member of the staff of Sturmpanzer-Abteilung 217, was seriously wounded near Ramscheider ridge (Officers list Sturmpanzer-Abteilung 217, dated 13/02/45).

107. Situation map OB West, 29/01/45.

108. Situation map OB West, 30/01/45.

109. NARA, 106th Inf Div, G-2 Report, 30/01/45.

110. NARA, XVIII AB Corps, G-2 Report, 31/01/45 - 01/02/45 ; NARA, 1st Inf Div, G-2-Report, 31/01/45 - 01/02/45.

111. NARA, 26th Inf Rgt, S-2 Report, 03/02/45.

112. Statement Oskar Klein, dated 24/09/2005.

113. Ibid.

114. The shrapnel remained in Hans Dusi's body until he died. His children were sometimes allowed to touch the fragments (Statements of Roland Dusi between 12 & 17/11/2007).

115. Statements Roland Dusi between 12 & 17/11/2007.

116. BA-MA, RH 10/219, General der Panzertruppen, pages 122 and 128 ; BA-MA, RH 10/115, Gen.d.Pz.Tr. West, report dated 10/02/45, pages 138 ff.

117. BA-MA, RH 10/219, General der Panzertruppen, page 128.

118. BA-MA, RW 4 v. 636, Tank situation West 1944/45, report dated 05/02/45.

119. BA-MA, RH 10/219, General der Panzertruppen, page 122.

120. BA-MA, RH 10/115, Gen.d.Pz.Tr. West report dated 12/02/45, page 158.

121. BA-MA, RH 10/352, General der Panzertruppen, page 22 and BA-MA, RH 10/350, General der Panzertruppen, page 84.

122. BA-MA, RH 10/115, Gen.d.Pz.Tr. West, report dated 12/02/45, page 158.

123. Statement Oskar Klein, dated 24/09/2005.

124. BA-MA, RH 10/219, General der Panzertruppen, page 128.

125. BA-MA, RH 10/219, General der Panzertruppen, page 128.

126. BA-MA, RH 10/115, Gen.d.Pz.Tr. West, report dated 10/02/45, page 136.

127. BA-MA, RH 10/107, General der Panzertruppen, page 9.

128. BA-MA, RH 10/219, General der Panzertruppen, page 122.

129. BA-MA, RH 10/219, General der Panzertruppen, pages 124 ff.

130. BA-MA, RH 10/107, General der Panzertruppen, page 11.

131. BA-MA, RH 10/352, General der Panzertruppen, page 22.

132. BA-MA, RW 4 v. 636, Tank situation West 1944/45, report dated 05/02/45.

133. BA-MA, RH 10/219, General der Panzertruppen, page 128 ; BA-MA, RH 10/115, Gen.d.Pz.Tr. West, report dated 10/02/45, pages 138 ff.

134. BA-MA, RW 4 v. 636, Tank situation West 1944/45, report dated 05/02/45.

135. BA-MA, RH 10/115, Gen.d.Pz.Tr. West, report dated 12/02/45, page 158.

136. BA-MA, RH 10/350, General der Panzertruppen, pages 77 and 84.

137. ULTRA-Report BT 970, Ref: CX/MSS/R407, 413, 415 dated 02/01/45.

138. BA-MA, RH 10/219, General der Panzertruppen, pages 118 ff.

139. BA-MA, RH 10/219, General der Panzertruppen, page 122.

140. BA-MA, RH 10/219, General der Panzertruppen, pages 124 ff.

141. BA-MA, RH 10/219, General der Panzertruppen, page 128 ; BA-MA, RH 10/115, Gen.d.Pz.Tr. West, report dated 10/02/45, pages 138 ff.

142. BA-MA, RH 10/115, Gen.d.Pz.Tr. West, report dated 12/02/45, page 158.

143. BA-MA, RH 10/219, General der Panzertruppen, pages 122 und 128 ; BA-MA, RH 10/115, Gen.d.Pz.Tr. West, report dated 10/02/45, pages 138 ff.

Chapter 07

1. Leutnant Werner-Joachim Zabransky died in combat on 05/02/45 at Schnorrenberg, east of Udenbreth. Zabransky was born on 23/10/23 and assigned to the battalion on 14/01/45. He had been an officer of Sturmpanzer-Abteilung 216 and 218 before (NARA, T-78M, Roll 940-II, Frame 2132, reference to Lt. Werner Zabransky ; BA-MA, Master Card, Hans-Joachim Zabransky).

2. G-2 Report, 82nd AB Div, dated 11/02/45 ; G-2 Report V Corps, 06/03/45 ; BA-MA, RH 2 W/854, Situation maps OB West for February 1945.

3. BA-MA, RH 10/350, General der Panzertruppen, page 76.

4. BA-MA, RH 2 W/854, Situation maps OB West, dated 22 & 26/02/45.

5. NARA, VII Corps, G-2 Report, 26/03/45.

6. NARA, 746th Tk Bn, S-2 Report, March 1945.

7. NARA, III Corps, G-2 Report 01 & 02/03/45.

8. The 62.V.G.Div. suffered heavy losses during the Ardennes offensive and only the remnants of Grenadier-Regiment 164 stayed at the front in the Schleiden area, while Grenadier-Regiment 183 was refitting in the Euskirchen area. Grenadier-Regiment 190 was temporarily disbanded due to the lack of personnel (NARA, III Corps, G-2 Report, 02/03/45).

9. NARA, III Corps, G-2 Report, 02/03/45.

10. There are no hints regarding the German tank units engaged at Lommersum, but the only German tank units reported in this area were Sturmgeschütz-Brigade 902 and Sturmpanzer-Abteilung 217.

11. NARA, III Corps, G-2 Report, 03/03/45.

12. Obergefreiter Richard Marbach joined the battalion on 25/05/44, during the activation period. He was a former member of Panzer-Ersatz- und Ausbildungs-Abteilung 18 and was assigned to 3./ Sturmpanzer-Abteilung 217. He was seriously wounded during the withdrawal from Normandy and only returned to the battalion in November 1944. He became a member of 1. Kompanie and stayed with this company even after the 3. Kompanie was reassigned in December 1944 (Data File Stu.Pz.Abt.217).

13. NARA, III Corps, G-2 Report, 04/03/45; NARA, 9th Inf Div, G-2 Report, 04/03/45; XXX British Corps, Intelligence Summary No. 615, 06/03/45.

14. 16th Inf Rgt, Journal, January-May 1945, 05/03/45.

15. Coordinates provided by III Corps refer to Kirchheim as the place where this soldier was captured. (NARA, III Corps, G-2 Report, 05/03/45).

16. The 78th Inf Div G-2 Report did not provide a location (NARA, 78th Inf Div, G-2 Report No. 83, 05/03/45).

17. NARA, III Corps, G-2 Reports, 05 & 06/03/45; 1st Inf Div, G-2 Report, 05/03/45; 16th Inf Rgt, Journal, January - May 1945, 05/03/45; 9th Inf Div, G-2 Report No. 227, 05/03/45; 78th Inf Div, G-2 Report No. 83, 05/03/45.

18. NARA, III Corps, G-2 Report, 06/03/45; V Corps, G-2 Report, 06/03/45; 1st Inf Div, G-2 Report, 06./03/45; 78th Inf Div, G-2 Report, 06/03/45.

19. 1st Inf Div, G-2 Report, 08/03/45.

20. German Red Cross: Photo index for missing members of Sturmpanzer-Abteilung 217; Tessin: Verbände und Truppen, Vol. 8, page 84; Jaugitz: Der Sturmpanzer IV - 'Brummbär', Waffen-Arsenal, Vol. 160, page 38;

21. Statement by Oskar Klein, dated 24/09/2005.

22. BA-MA RH 10/219, General der Panzertruppen, page 129.

23. BA-MA RH 10/324, General der Panzertruppen, page 23.

24. BA-MA, RH 2 W/854, Situation maps OB West: Situation West dated 13 & 14/03/45.

25. BA-MA RW 4 v. 636, Tank situation report West 1944/45, Report dated 15/03/45.

26. Statement by Oskar Klein, dated 24/09/2005.

27. BA-MA RH 10/219, General der Panzertruppen, page 129.

28. BA-MA RH 10/350, General der Panzertruppen, page 74.

29. NARA, T-78, Roll 720, Frame 554, Attachment 1 to Gen.Insp.d.Pz.Tr. Nr. F390/45gK, dated 26/03/45.

30. This corresponds to the production volume manufactured by 'Deutsche Eisenwerke' in March 1945, production was stopped afterwards.

31. Production volumes January/February 1945.

32. NARA, T-78, Roll 720, Frame 533, Attachment 1 to Gen.Insp.d.Pz.Tr. Nr. F460/45gK, dated 01/04/45.

33. BA-MA RW 4 v. 636, Tank situation report West 1944/45, Attachments March 1945.

34. BA-MA, RH 2 W/854, Situation map OB West: Situation West for 18, 20, 22 & 24/03/45.

35. BA-MA, RH 26-353/4, 353.Inf.Div., Divisional order No. 20, 23/03/45.

36. 1st Inf Div, G-2 Journal, 26/03/45; Statements of Richard Gottwald, interviewed by Anton Schäfer, without date.

37. One member of the 3. Kompanie was also reported MIA in the area, according to the Deutsches Rotes Kreuz – Photo index for missing members of Sturmpanzer-Abteilung 217.

38. NARA, G2-Report 8th Inf Div,

39. NARA, G2-Report 8th Inf Div,

40. Tessin: Verbände und Truppen, Vol. 8, page 84.

41. Jaugitz: Der Sturmpanzer IV - 'Brummbär', Waffen-Arsenal, Vol. 160, page 38,

42. Ultra-Report BT 9722, Ref: CX/MSS/T512/31, dated 07/04/45.

43. BA-MA RW 4 v. 636, Tank situation report West 1944/45, dated 05/04/45.

44. NARA, 78th Inf Div, G-2 Report, 09/04/45.

45. NARA, 78th Inf Div, G-2 Report, 10/04/45; XVIII AB Corps, G-2 Report No. 9, 10/04/45.

46. Information by Richard Gottwald to Anton Schäfer, without date; Jaugitz: Der Sturmpanzer IV - 'Brummbär', Waffen-Arsenal, Volume 160, page 38.

47. NARA, 1st Army, IPW-Report No. 4, 12 - 13/04/45.

48. NARA, 8th Inf Div, G-2 Report, No. 272, 11/04/45.

49. NARA, 1st Army, IPW-Reports, 13/04/45.

50. The report is inaccurate in this aspect, stating that a total of 16 prisoners of war were taken from s. Panzerjäger-Abteilung 654, Sturmpanzer-Abteilung 217 and Panzerjäger-Abteilung 1219.

51. NARA, 78th Inf Div, G-2 Report, 11/04/45.

52. NARA, 78th Inf Div, G-2 Report, 12/04/45.

53. NARA, 99th Inf Div, G-2 Report, 13/04/45.

54. NARA, 1st Army, IPW-Report, 13/04/45.

55. NARA, 78th Inf Div, G-2 Report, 14/04/45.

56. NARA, 1st Army, IPW-Report, 14/04/45.

57. NARA, 78th Inf Div, G-2 Report, 15/04/45; 99th Inf Div, G-2 Report, 15/04/45.

58. NARA, 1st Army, IPW-Report, 15/04/45.

59. NARA, 9th Army, IPW-Report, No. 225, 17/04/45.

60. NARA, 1st Army, IPW-Report, 16 & 17/04/45.

61. Information by Oskar Klein, dated 24/09/2005.

Chapter 08

1. Spielberger: Der Panzerkampfwagen IV und seine Abarten, Vol. 5, pages 101 f; Doyle, Friedli, Jentz: Panzer Tracts No. 8-1, Sturmpanzer IV, page 13; Hahn: Waffen und Geheimwaffen des deutschen Heeres, page 317; Waffen-Revue Vol. 86, page 28; Jaugitz: Der Sturmpanzer IV 'Brummbär', pages 8 and 12.

2. Doyle, Friedli, Jentz: Panzer Tracts No. 8-1, Sturmpanzer IV, page 40; Jaugitz: Der Sturmpanzer IV 'Brummbär', page 12; Waffen-Revue, Vol. 86, pages 28 and 32 ff.

3. Spielberger: Der Panzerkampfwagen IV und seine Abarten, Vol. 5, page 105; Jaugitz: Der Sturmpanzer IV 'Brummbär', page 12.

4. Spielberger: Der Panzerkampfwagen IV und seine Abarten, Vol. 5, page 105; Jaugitz: Der Sturmpanzer IV 'Brummbär', page 14.

5. The guess is that the names were typically for 2./Stu.Pz.Abt.217. Some tanks with names on the barrel jacket were identified during the period October - December 1944 when the 3. Kompanie had been disbanded, which rules out the 3. Kompanie. A soldier of the 2nd Company mentioned the loss of a Sturmpanzer with the name 'Eva' in March 1945. Tanks with names had been identified in

Normandy ('Gudrun'), Belgium (names unreadable on two tanks), Aachen (name unreadable), Hürtgen Forest ('Dicker', 'Jumbo III', names unreadable on two other tanks), and near Eitorf ('Eva').

6.   See Interrogation report St.Gefr. Kurt Kuhs, 1./Sturmpanzer-Abteilung 217, PW IB No 1/40 dated 12/03/45.
7.   Canadian IPW-report, C.S.D.I.C. (U.K.) - S.I.R 788, 16/08/44.
8.   Wijers: Ardennenoffensive, Vol. 3, page 154.
9.   Statement Oskar Klein, dated 24/09/2005.
10. 1st Army, PWI Report No. 12, 22 - 23/12/44.
11. 1st Army, G 2-Report, 01/02/45.
12. 9th Inf Div, G-2 Report, 06/03/45.
13. NARA, 9th Army, G2-Periodic Report No. 228, 06/03/45.
14. GDIR, Folder 406, War diary AOK 6, Folder E, Volume 5: Battle and experience reports 01/04/44 - 07/01/45, Experience report Sturmpanzer-Abteilung 219.

INDEX